DATE DUE

APR 0 2 2001	

DEMCO, INC. 38-2931

AMERICAN DIALECTS

AMERICAN DIALECTS

A Manual for
Actors, Directors and Writers

by
LEWIS HERMAN
and MARGUERITE SHALETT HERMAN

Theatre Arts Books

NEW YORK

Copyright as Manual of American Dialects for Radio, Stage, Screen and Television, 1947 by Lewis and Marguerite Shalett Herman.

Sixth Printing, 1978

Library of Congress Catalog Card Number: 59-13238
ISBN 0-87830-003-1

Published by THEATRE ARTS BOOKS
333 Sixth Avenue, New York 14

Printed in U.S.A. by
NOBLE OFFSET PRINTERS, INC.
NEW YORK, N.Y. 10003

To Our Children

STEPHANIE,

JUDITH,

and

HELMAR

FOREWORD

U NLIKE OTHER art professions, acting cannot be practiced well at home or in the studio-school, for it is an interpretive art that demands an audience. There is no instrument or method of exercise for it other than the human body and the activity of the brain. Therefore, there are few textbooks to which the actor may refer, the art of make-up being the possible exception, though even here no specific method or trick is applicable to every face.

Now, again, Mr. and Mrs. Lewis Herman have brought out of their experience as actors and writers a reference book for actors which can be used at home, in the studio, and in the schools, to prepare an actor for a specific part of his trade — the art of interpreting and projecting American dialects.

Their first book, *Manual of Foreign Dialects*, was published a few years ago and proved its value and necessity to the actor in radio, on the screen, and in the theater, by going into a second edition. It is a fascinating book for anyone, for the foreigner who wants to know and correct his speech peculiarity and for English-speaking people who wish to study the dialects of those of foreign birth or descent, who make up so great a part of our land.

But it seems to me that this book, *Manual of American Dialects*, for which it is my privilege to write this preface, is an even greater contribution. For here, we can listen to the intriguing voice of America, a voice which speaks with the different tongues of all times — a voice which makes for the song of our land, the speech of our land.

In this book, from which the actor can extract the true speech flavor of almost every section of America, are the explanations and ways to reproduce this multiple, polyglot tongue. The student, the actor — even the amateur adventurer — can wander from north to south, from east to west, from state to state. It is an exciting excursion, not only into places, but into the very music of America, the intangible rhythm everyone must feel when traveling across or up and down this land. It is as indispensible to the acute taster of this country as a cook book, for it places, directly on the tongue, the flavor of America.

A man's dialect is as much, if not more, of his personality than his education. It stamps his charm, his wit, his whole mode of expression. To know a man's sound is to know something of his soul. The understanding of regional dialects is a key to the appreciation of his make-up as a man, his capacity for joy and laughter, for drama and tears. The dialect comedian who cannot turn his command of dialect from comedy to pathos soon loses his public, for, behind comedy lies pathos, and behind the clown's tear there is always a smile.

I recall vividly a dialect experience of my own that proved, to myself at least, the importance of American regional dialects. In preparing for the screen role of a Southern gentleman — Francis Marion in *The Eve of St. Mark* — I decided to use a Southern dialect which I thought to be authentic. Actually, I was born in Missouri, but my superimposed dialect was an *olla podrida* of various Southern dialects I had heard — a vowel change from here and a consonant change from there — so much so that, after the picture had been released, I received a number of letters from admirers scattered all over the southern states each of whom was positive I hailed from his particular locality, to judge from the manner of my speech.

I feel very sincerely that there is a further purpose in this book — to let us in on the American secret. From all the world comes the American into this greatest experiment in the admixture of peoples civilization has ever known. Therefore, we must remind ourselves constantly that, in our understanding and toleration and acceptance, one peoples of another, each of us of another American, we must not forget that the boy with the Georgia drawl is no more American than the Negro with a similar drawl, or the girl in New York with a chewing-gum whine. If we know each other with this truth, we are well on our way toward knowing the world, especially this world of today which is so desperately in need of world-citizens.

And, again, despite the serious need of this book, and the factual need of the actor for it, for the average reader it should be enormous fun. Perhaps if only to be able to tell your favorite joke better; or to recount, with more color, some unusual experience away from home; or to appreciate better the masters of American literature — Mark Twain when he goes down the Mississippi with Huck Finn, or O. Henry when he digs into the excitement of one corner of America after another. To know what these men knew, to capture the flavor of the places they described — this is made possible with a more acute perception of the dialect arts they practiced.

All in all, I would say that *Manual of American Dialects* will take its place in that special section of every bookcase which houses the extraordinary tale of man's expression, from his first words to the most elucidating parables of his experiences in the one endowment inordinately and exclusively his — the power of speech.

VINCENT PRICE

PREFACE

*"Everybody says words different," said Ivy. "Arkansas
folks says 'em different, and Oklahomy folks says 'em
different. And we seen a lady from Massachusetts, an'
she said 'em differentest of all. Couldn't hardly make out
what she was sayin'."*

The Grapes of Wrath*
by John Steinbeck

THE MAIN PURPOSE of this book is to teach the regional American
dialects to actors. Until now there has been no single source
to which actors could refer for such dialect material. There
is a vast library of source material on American dialects, to be sure,
but most of it is of a pedantic nature. None of it has ever been sim-
plified and collated into groups. As a result, the average actor gives
a slipshod, often completely erroneous, portrayal of American dialect
speech.

This book is not a scientific study of the superfine shades of
pronunciation for the professional phonetician. It does not strive
to corral certain dialect variants to pinprick points on a map. However, the authors have tried to be as accurate as possible, within
limits determined by our purpose. That is to say, we have concentrated on simplicity. We have avoided scientific pedantry in favor
of practicality. For, as stated, this book proposes to be a practical
manual and guide for the actor who is called upon to reproduce
authentic American dialect speech on the stage, on the screen, on the
radio, and in television.

This does not mean that the dialect variants listed in this book
apply to all people who live in the areas designated. People living
in certain sections of the country may disagree with some of the
suggestions put forth. "I don't talk that-a-way!" they may snort
indignantly. But, this book does not claim to teach the individual
dialect variants of each person. That would be an impossibility. It
does try to represent the speech that is, or was, typical of the section
as a whole.

No two people speak exactly alike. There are as many dialects
in America as there are people. In one section of the country, for
example, the word "yes" was heard to be pronounced in thirty-seven
different ways. The word "aunt" was recorded with eight different

---

* Reprinted with permission of The Viking Press, Inc.

pronunciations in Richmond, Virginia. Coal miners in southern
Illinois were heard to refer to a "hOYstUHn" (hoisting) engineer
who "hIs:" (hoists) coal. Although both the authors speak with a
Middle-Western dialect, we found ourselves in frequent disagreement
about the typical pronunciation of certain vowel sounds.

Each person, for that matter, uses varying pronunciations for
the same vowel or consonant sound. Careless, lax pronunciation, of a
very informal nature, is commonly used in the confines of a friendly
or family circle. A more careful speech is affected in business rela-
tions. There is usually an attempt at concise enunciation in a public
address, whereas inebriation often results in the traditional hot-
potato-in-the-mouth garblings.

For a dialect, after all, is actually more than the reported speech
patterns of a certain group of people. As George P. Krapp has
stated in his book *The English Language in America,** "Dialects are
merely the convenient summaries of observers who bring together
certain homogeneities of the speech habits of a group and thus secure
for themselves an impression of unity. Other observers might secure
different impressions by assembling different habits of the same
group."

This book, then, is a "convenient summary" of American regional
dialects for the use of members of the acting professions. It will
offer the typical, generalized representation of dialect speech as
spoken by the average individual. We are well aware of the fact
that, in simplifying, we have been forced to omit certain odd variants,
rather than confuse the student with extra material that was not
absolutely necessary to the dialect speech. Obviously, it was impossible to treat all the minor dialects spoken in various isolated
speech islands, such as those that occur in New England, for example.
A few of these minor dialects have been dealt with, in the section
on the Southern dialect particularly, because they contain many
variants from the Southern dialect.

Nor has it been possible to discuss in full the degree of dialect
speech used by various types of characters since that depends largely
on the age, education, and awareness of the speaker. Younger people
are rapidly losing many of the dialect elements that were once typical
of the communities in which they live. The radio and motion pic-
tures have stimulated the spread of General-American pronunciation.
Communities such as those in isolated mountain fastnesses have
retained their dialects because they were speech islands separated
by geographical barriers from the influence of speech habits sur-

---

* Reprinted with permission of D. Appleton-Century Company.

rounding them. Social barriers have also been instrumental in the retention of older dialect speech by the poorly-educated inhabitants while many of the well-educated have discarded the older forms. Throughout this book we have concentrated, in the main, on full, rich dialect speech that embodies the typical elements of a region. In a lesser degree, we have discussed the variant pronunciations used by people who are gradually adopting General-American pronunciations. Although regional variations have been frequently noted, it must not be inferred that these variations are restricted solely to the specified regions.

It will be observed that, throughout, the basis of comparison has always been made with, what is commonly termed "General-American" as it is spoken in the Middle West. Such a comparison is necessary if an attempt at clarification is to be successful. There must be a basic norm—a standard—with which to judge the qualitative values of sounds. This standard, however, is not put forward as being the standard speech for Americans, for no regional pronunciation may be considered more correct than another.

General-American was chosen, as a working standard only, for two reasons. It happens to represent, to a great extent, the speech used by the authors. But the choice was actuated by more than personal motives. The General-American form of regional American speech is currently spoken by more Americans than any other form. Some ninety million people speak with a basic General-American dialect. What is more, many of its elements are being adopted, or readopted, by residents in other dialect regions. The use of "A," for example, in words like "ask" and "half" is reasserting itself. It was commonly used in the seventeenth and eighteenth centuries until it was replaced by the once disfavored "AH" sound.

The dropped "r" also, that was so typical of Eastern and Southern speech a century ago, is gradually being restored and pronounced again. The process began by using final "r" as a link to the next word if it began with a vowel sound, as in "jinjUHr AYl" (ginger ale). In addition, many speakers erroneously add an excrescent "r" to words ending in "UH" or "AW," particularly when the following word begins with a vowel, as in "sOHdUHr UHn pOp" (soda and pop) or "lAWr UHn AWdUH" (law and order). This habit of adding the excrescent "r" is typical only of those regions in which "r" is dropped in certain words, indicating a desire to sound "r" even in the wrong places. In the South, where "r" between vowels was once almost universally dropped, as in "vEHi" (very), the trend is now to a lightly sounded "r."

New England has been the mother source of many of the American regional dialects. Yet, Boston, once a Brahmin citadel

where residents spoke an extremely British dialect, is slowly leveling
off to General-American. Western New England already uses many
Middle Western pronunciations. Southeastern New England is
gradually dropping its dialect variants. In the main, northeastern
New England stands fast.

But it is not within the scope or purpose of this book to make
a case for the spread of General-American speech nor to detract from
the dialect speech of the various regions. The fact remains that the
trend of dialect speech is toward the General-American or Middle
Western variety. And, until the time when all Americans use the
same dialect speech, a manual such as this is an absolute necessity
for the actor.

The correct dialect speech is as important to a characterization
as the correct make-up, gestures, or physical habits. It is inept to
use a turn of phrase typical of one region and pronounce this phrase
in the dialect speech of another region. The competent actor should
be able to spot his character in the exact milieu necessary by the
simple expedient of using the correct dialect. In this way, his characterization will be more effective because it will be more authentic
and, therefore, more believable.

Using the correct regional dialect is particularly important when
the actor's work is being viewed in the region from which the dramatic
character is supposed to stem. Nothing is more ludicrous to a
Virginian, for example, than to hear an actor who is supposed to
be portraying a Virginian, speak in a dialect that is Negro in some
aspects, Middle Western in others, and pure corn in the balance.
For these listeners, at least, the actor's work would lack authenticity,
and the character he is trying to limn would be unbelievable.

The actor is confronted with another problem. Audiences
frequently identify certain dialects erroneously. That is to say, they
use the incorrect dialect portrayals of inept dialectitians as a gauge.
They assume the dialectitian knows his business, and they proceed
to judge other dialect interpretations by this incorrect one. The
supposed pronunciation of "OI" as "ER" is a case in point. Certain
New Yorkers are supposed to say "ERl" (oil), "bERl" (boil), and
so on. This change seems rather fanciful in view of the fact that
New Yorkers are reticent with the "r" sounds. Actually, the typical
substitute for "OI" is "uhEE" as in "nuhEEz" (noise); although
under certain conditions it should be pronounced as "AWi" as in
"EHnjAWi" (enjoy). Another variant, which is closer to the alleged
"ER" sound, is "ER-EE" as in "tchER-EEs" (choice) In this instance, the vowel sound of "ER" remains the same, but the "r" is
not sounded (ER). At the most, the vowel may have a slight "r"
coloring, but this does not indicate a full pronunciation of the "r"

sound. However, because "ER" has been heard so often as a substitute for "OI," in the dialect speech of unwitting actors, many New Yorkers have taken over the incorrect substitute—incorrect because it does not follow the true speech traditions of the region. Thus it is that, as Wilde had it, "Life apes art."

Most actors believe implicitly that anyone using an "UEE" variant for "ER" is strictly from Brooklyn or the Bronx in New York City. This "UEE" variant embodies the "U" of "Up" (up) and the "EE" of "bEE" (be) and is heard in such words as "UEEn" (earn), "pUEEsn" (person) and "kUEEb (curb). It is a very common sound in the deep South, and a modified form of it is found in older New England speech.

As far as the actor is concerned, the dialect to be used should be the one that is most typical of the character he is portraying. To adjust his interpretation to suit the erroneous whims of his audience is to betray his art. If the audience can be mustered into accepting the false as truth, then by the same token it can be brought around to accepting the truth.

The writer who uses dialect characters should also find this book helpful. By writing believable dialect dialogue, his script will be more alive and the actor can do a better job of interpretation. It is annoying to the actor and the producer if they find that Colonel Julep, the fine Southern gentleman, has been given the dialogue of a Georgia cracker. It is incumbent upon the writer to know the distinctions between the various regional dialects.

The writer should follow the same pattern of study as outlined for the actor in the chapter "How to Use the Manual." He should pay special attention to distinctive vowel and consonant changes, such as are frequently found in words like "ask," "sauce," "park," "egg," "out," "curb," "willow," "noise," and "idea." He must be aware of the influences that form an individual's speech. For example, some Middle Westerners who are ambitious for social prestige, feel they must pronounce "A:sk" (ask) as "AHsk" although this pronunciation is not typical of the General-American dialect. For the most part, women are inclined to be more careful with their speech. Travel and education can influence the character's pronunciation. A character's speech can be revealing, and the writer has the responsibility of making the correct revelations.

The sections on "Grammar Changes," "Typical Words and Phrases," and "Similes" should prove of special importance to the writer. Many of these variances from General-American speech will give the necessary flavor to the speech of a character from another region.

Monologs written in "eye-dialect" follow each major chapter.

These have not been transcribed phonetically because of the numerous variances that were possible.

At this time, the authors wish to express their gratitude to the many Americans who have patiently submitted to the barrage of questions which must have seemed inane to many of them. Scattered over most of the forty-eight states, these people have been the experimental guinea pigs from whom the authors derived much of their information. We also wish to acknowledge the unwitting help given us by the hundreds of casuals in streetcars, buses, and other gathering places; by the hundreds of regional speakers whose words we recorded over the radio from such interview programs as "Vox Pop," "Town Meeting," and the like. We were also extremely fortunate in being able to record the speeches made by delegates of the two political conventions at Chicago in 1944. As an eclipse of the sun, such an agglomeration of American dialects could have been culled from one source only once in a long period of time.

We also wish to acknowledge the help given us by the files of the magazines *American Speech*, published at Columbia University, and *Dialect Notes*, published by the American Dialect Society. Their magnificent work in recording the dialect speech of many American districts has been of considerable aid in checking our own findings in the field. Supplemental dialect information was obtained from them and from many other published sources whose number is too great for individual mention here but will be found listed in the Bibliography. Some furnished a point, others more. But all were highly instrumental in the fashioning of this book.

If there are errors, and we trust there will be few, the authors hasten to assume all responsibility. We have tried to make this book as authentic as possible. At the same time, however, we have kept the actor and his problems constantly in mind. Hence, if we have strayed occasionally, and then only slightly, from what some may believe to be the "proper interpretation of the facts," our defense will be that it was done solely for the purpose of simplification.

The success of our work will depend on the manner in which it is accepted by the members of the acting professions, by those who teach the techniques of acting, and by those who are striving to learn them. We are gratified with the continued response to our first book, *Manual of Foreign Dialects*. And we choose to believe that the improvement of foreign dialect interpretation which we have been hearing on the radio, stage, and screen is directly attributable to that book.

If this sequel receives the same ready acceptance, if it supplies the wherewithal for improving American dialect interpretations, if it stimulates greater understanding and tolerance for the dialect speech of others, if it encourages the desire to portray honest characterizations rather than slovenly caricatures, if it succeeds in furnishing the first comprehensive and authentic guide to the proper professional use of American regional dialects, then we will feel that our work has not been in vain.

LEWIS HERMAN

MARGUERITE SHALETT HERMAN

CONTENTS

HOW TO USE THE MANUAL

DIALECTS CANNOT BE learned overnight or in a few short lessons. A dialect is like another language if it is unfamiliar to the student. Months of work are required to learn a new language; the same diligence should be applied in learning a dialect. It may be paradoxical to state that it is more difficult to learn a regional American dialect than a foreign dialect. Because the regional dialect is so close to the native dialect of the actor, he has a tendency to slip more easily into his native pronunciation. On the other hand, he frequently attempts to exaggerate the sounds that are new to him. Throughout this book, the actor should be particularly observant of the suggestions given for the production of certain sounds. These sounds must be practiced until they can be produced naturally and with ease. This is particularly true of sound changes that seem odd to the student.

PHONETIC SYMBOLS

It is essential that the actor become thoroughly conversant with the system of phonetics used in this book before he attempts to learn a dialect. The student should know the phonetic symbols as well as he knows the alphabet. With the exception of a very few all the phonetic representations should be familiar to the average person. For example, the long "a" sound in "tAYk" (take) is written phonetically as "AY"; the long "o" sound in "bOHn (bone) is "OH"; the short "u" of "Up" (up) is "U" and so on. All vowel sounds are written in capital letters with the exception of the "i" of "it" (it), and the "oo" of "good" (good).

Symbols for the consonant sounds are written in lower-case letters, with the exception of the voiced "TH" (th) of "THAt" (that).

Unless otherwise indicated, the symbol (:) indicates that the preceding sound is to be elongated, as in "A:sk" (ask).

The symbol (/) indicates the glottal stop. This is discussed in those dialects of which it is an integral part. A preliminary discussion of it will be found on page 24 in the chapter on "The Common Speech."

The symbol (-) is used only as an aid in reading. It will be found particularly between the two elements of a diphthong, as in "dAW-OHg" (dog). It does not indicate a pause.

The symbol "UH" or "uh" indicates the General-American treatment of the mute or unstressed vowel sound, as in "UHbOWt"

1

(about) or "uhlOHn" (alone). The reason for the variance in type is simply in the interests of easier identification and reading. The capital "UH" is used when followed or preceded by a lower case consonant, except "l"; while the lower-case "uh" will be found next to "l" or a capital letter vowel or "TH."

Syllables printed in **bold-face** are to be accented, as in "**AW**lw**UH**z" (always).

Syllables or letters printed in *italics* merely indicate the letter or syllable affected by a change, as in "v**EH**d*i*" (ve*r*y).

The symbol "*n*" indicates that the "n" sound is dropped, and the preceding vowel sound is given a nasal treatment, as in "s**AY**n/p**AW**uhl" (Saint Paul).

The absence of diacritical markings, inverted letters, reversed signs, and foreign symbols endows this system with a simplicity that should make its application universally understood.

CHARACTERIZATION

Once the symbols have been mastered and the dialect to be learned chosen, the student should study the historical and emotional characteristics of the people who use the dialect. Certain speech habits result from the emotional nature of the people. The speech of the Southerner, for instance, is drawled because of the slow, easygoing temperament with which warm climates endow their inhabitants. The speech of the "businesslike" Yankee emerges as a sharp, dry, succinctly enunciated crackle.

In this book only a brief—and very generalized—resume of these regional characteristics was attempted—and only in the major dialects. But the student should go beyond these sketchy character suggestions. He should obtain books written about the people who speak the dialect he is studying. Reading lists of regional American novels and nonfiction are to be found in almost every public library. The average student will thus gain a greater insight into the character of the people and a better understanding of their habits and emotional make-up. As a result, he will be able to bring to his own characterization a richer and more complete interpretation.

In much of the regional literature you will find examples of what is known as "eye-dialect." This is an attempt at transcribing dialect speech with the ordinary alphabet. Too much credence should not be placed in these representations. Only a few of the true dialect variants are permitted to emerge, because "eye-dialect" is considerably watered for readability. The use of "o' " for "of" is typical. Obviously most dialect writers suggest with the apostrophe that the "f" is dropped. But there is no intimation given as to the pronunciation of the "o." Should it be "fool OH bEEnz" (full o' beans), "fool AW bEEnz," "fool U bEEnz," or "fool UH bEEnz"? The last pronunciation is actually the most common, yet many actors would interpret this example of "eye-dialect" as "OH."

Many books that feature "eye-dialect" do offer excellent examples of grammatical changes, colloquialisms, and various other dialect elements which could be of considerable aid to the student and particularly to the writer.

Most important of all, the regional literature has been written by authors who know the people of whom they write, and a three-dimensional background of the character of the people can be obtained from them.

LILT AND STRESS

In each major dialect there is a section on the general lilt or intonation, word stress, and syllabic stress. The points given should be studied thoroughly so that they can be applied to the material that follows in the rest of the chapter. For those who are unable to read music, a visual device of stepladdering the rise and fall of the individual syllables has been used. The student can determine from these illustrations the rise and fall of the syllables, the gradual rising and falling vowel or consonant glides, and the abrupt, glideless risings and fallings.

But for the student who can read music, there has been included, in addition to the stepladder device, a regular staff on which the notes of the lilt have been transcribed by an eminent musician — Professor Robert Dolejsi of Chicago.

In these tonal settings — which are only approximations of the human voice in the various speech dialects — one of the most striking revelations is the extraordinary scope or range that is evident in even a brief phrase of only two or three syllables — and that too during ordinary every day speech. When the stress of any emotion such as excitement, fear or anger is present, the pitch variation and range is naturally greatly accentuated. It will be observed that the examples emphasize also the rhythmic meter of each phonetic illustration. This will enable the student to determine not only the voice pitch and range, but also the actual rhythm of each example, which is of paramount importance.

Each notation has been purposely retained in one clef — although some unusually extended intervals occur which ordinarily would demand the use of two clefs — in order to give a more impressive visual portrait of tonal skips and glides. The fact must be explained, though, that there are at times certain inflections in the speaking voice that fall into a category that defies actual notation. They are an almost imperceptible degree above or below the note indicated, but do not demand the next full semi-tone above or below to serve as an illustration. It is, in fact, this characteristic of tonal variation that distinguishes speech from actual song. In addition, there will be present a degree of variance in different individuals. But the tonal illustrations, as given in the following chapters, under the "lilt" sections, are as near to actual tones spoken in the various phrases as the notation of musical science permits.

VOWEL CHANGES

The detailed explanation of each vowel change should be studied. Special attention should be paid to the production of the sound. The long "OH" sound in "coat" as it is pronounced in the New England dialect cannot be accurately represented by phonetics alone. Professional phoneticists, using the most exact of the phonetic systems (the method evolved by the International Phonetic Association) offer varying symbols for this sound. The explanatory matter concerning the production of many of the vowel sounds is therefore often of paramount importance.

Next, the example words should be spoken aloud slowly, clearly, and distinctly. Any note of falseness or over-exaggeration should be corrected, and the drill words repeated. The student should improvise very short sentences in which the vowel sound is repeated once or twice. During the drill practice, reference should be made to the section on **"Lilt and Stress"** to determine whether unusual stress is suggested for certain words. The words should then be practiced with an increasing tempo until the natural speed is reached.

Single vowel or diphthong changes should never be forced. When stressed, the diphthong usually receives emphasis on the first element, and the second element has the light quality of a glide. These sounds must be produced with ease, and they must be studied thoroughly in relation to the dialect speech as a whole. The actor who is portraying a character with a light dialect should not dip into the particular dialect chapter and extract certain sounds arbitrarily. The complete dialect treatment should be learned, and then the process of bringing the dialect variants closer to General-American should be practiced.

In regions where the General-American dialect has all but wiped out the regional dialect, certain of the older variants remain. These are usually the regional pronunciations of "ER" (girl), "AW" before "r" plus a vowel (forest), and final "r" (car). While studying the drill words, the student may encounter odd consonant changes. He should refer to the corresponding General-American sound in the section on **"Consonant Changes,"** particularly if the variants are foreign to his normal speech. This reference should be made only to acquaint the student with the reason for the consonant change suggested. The complete discussion of the consonant should not be studied until the student has learned the vowel changes and the usual treatment given to unstressed vowels and syllables.

CONSONANT CHANGES

By this time the student should be familiar with various consonant changes. Now the complete text under each consonant sound should be studied. This is important since one consonant may have several variant pronunciations.

The student should then turn back to the section on the vowels and practice the drill words with the complete dialect changes in vowels and consonants. Short, impromptu sentences should again be practiced.

GRAMMAR CHANGES

Although the grammar section is more vital to the writer than to the actor, the latter should study it for a better understanding of the dialect. Most dialogue is written more or less "straight" so that the actor may find it difficult to superimpose dialect changes on erroneous grammatical forms. The actor can learn from these sections what grammar changes are most characteristic of the dialect and, when necessary and feasible, can make the adjustment in his lines.

These sections can also be used by the actor as a source of practice material. All the example sentences are written out phonetically. References should be made to the section on **"Lilt and Stress."**

The typical phrase and interjections sections should be studied. Here, again, it should be within the province of the writer to insert them. But if certain ones suit the characterization, the actor should insert them occasionally to authenticate the dialect speech.

Most of the grammatical errors listed in **"The Common Speech"** can be applied to any regional character, providing the character is the kind who uses incorrect grammatical constructions.

PHONETIC SYMBOLS USED IN THIS BOOK

These symbols represent only the *sounds* of the vowels and consonants used in General-American speech (they do not represent the spelling). Symbols for sounds peculiar to each of the American regional dialects will be found in the chapter devoted to that particular dialect. For clarity, symbols are shown in **BOLD-FACE** type in this chart. However, in the actual text of the book, this heavier type is used only to denote emphasis. *Italic* letters will be used throughout the text to indicate the changes made from the General-American word to the regional-American dialect word.

VOWEL SYMBOLS

VOWEL	WORD	SYMBOLS	VOWEL	WORD	SYMBOLS
"a"	"take"	**"AY"**	"o"	"on"	**"O"**
"a"	"alone"	**"UH"**	"o"	"bone"	**"OH"**
"a"	"palm"	**"AH"**	"o"	"off"	**"AW"**
"a"	"ask"	**"A:"**	"oo"	"food"	**"OO"**
"a"	"bad"	**"A"**	"oo"	"good"	**"oo"**
"a"	"ball"	**"AW"**	"u"	"unit"	**"yOO"**
"e"	"he"	**"EE"**	"u"	"up"	**"U"**
"e"	"get"	**"EH"**	"u"	"curb"	**"ER"**
"i"	"ice"	**"I"**	"ou"	"out"	**"OW"**
"i"	"sit"	**"i"**	"oi"	"oil"	**"OI"**

CONSONANT SYMBOLS

CONSONANT	WORD	SYMBOLS	CONSONANT	WORD	SYMBOLS
"c"	"cat"	**"k"**	"ch"	"loch"	**"kh"**
"g"	"go"	**"g"**	"ch"	"church"	**"tch"**
"g"	"George"	**"j"**	"sh"	"she"	**"sh"**
"q"	"quick"	**"kw"**	"th"	"the"	**"TH"**
"x"	"tax"	**"ks"**	"th"	"thin"	**"th"**
	"exert"	**"gz"**	"z"	"azure"	**"zh"**
	"luxury"	**"ksh"**			
	"xenon"	**"z"**			

The symbols for the other consonant sounds are the same as the standard spelling.

(/) glottal stop

(:) vowel elongation except where otherwise noted

(-) a hyphen used between letters does not indicate a pause. It is inserted only for the sake of phonetic clarity.

CHAPTER I

THE COMMON SPEECH

UNDERLYING EVERY AMERICAN regional dialect is a stratum of bedrock that serves as the common foundation for all varieties of American speech. It accounts for the oft-spoken, erroneous statement that there are few distinguishable American dialects. This common foundation is composed of the grammatical errors made by the less educated groups who comprise the majority of the American public. It can be found in the totally illiterate speech of the Gullah Negroes and in the speech of many of the educated people of the South, the difference being only one of degree.

For example, the word "ain't" has been accepted in colloquial American speech although its use is still frowned upon by many. The phrase "it's me" rather than "it's I" has gained a recognition that endangers the grammatical rule. The words "shall" and "will" are interchangeably used not only by illiterates in all their talk, but by the educated in off-guard moments.

The degree or quantity of grammatical errors is important in distinguishing the speech of the majority from that of the group which has received and profited from better education. Yet, many people who phrase their sentences incorrectly do so out of habit rather than lack of knowledge.

Certain local peculiarities of grammatical construction have been observed in the various dialects and have been noted in the particular dialect chapter. But the following material will cover almost all of the common errors made by most of the common people. A judicious choice of these to fit the character to be portrayed should make for a more accurate dialect presentation.

The actor should be as interested in this subject as the writer. Much of the script writing of today is being done by writers who do not use, or do not know, the grammatical errors of the common people. It is therefore incumbent on the actor to rephrase his lines, if they are grammatically too correct for the character.

VERB MISUSE

Verbs seem to be the most common stumbling block in common speech. The use of "was" as a conditional, instead of "were," is very common, even among many educated people. There is a tendency to say, "if it was" instead of "if it were."

Another frequent error involves the use of "shall" and "will." The latter is generally favored in all cases, and by all classes. Thus, instead of saying the correct, "I shall be there tomorrow," indicating a simple future action with a first-person pronoun, the ordinary American would say "I will be there tomorrow." More often he will say, "I'll be there tomorrow," in which neither "shall" nor "will" is indicated.

Even in the inflection of these verbs, the same preference is observed. Only a rank Anglophile would say, "I shan't be there." Illiterate and educated alike say, "I won't be there." In the same way "should" has been avoided for the more common "ought to" as in "I ought to be early" rather than "I should be early." A more informal pronunciation would make it "oughta." A character who is sensitive about his poor grammar may try to improve it by saying, "I should oughta be early."

The adoption of "ain't" is rapidly becoming universal despite the fight against it. Even in England, where the awkward "amn't" is used, "ain't" is being fostered as a legitimate substitute for "am not," "is not," and "are not." Here in America the use of "ain't" is not regional; it may be used in the speech of all but the well-educated although there are of course exceptions caused by an individual's family or community background. Sentences like "I ain't afraid," "We ain't goin'," and "He ain't alone" are characteristic of the common speech.

Another common error is the failure to make the verb agree with its subject in person, number, or case, as in *"Was you* always afraid?" and "There's *five* of us."

The most frequent error in verb use in American speech comes with the confusion of past tense and past participle. The less educated are prone to say, "I seen," rather than "I saw," or "I knowed all along" rather than "I knew all along."

This misuse of the past tense is, perhaps, the most frequent of all errors and is to be found in the dialect speech of practically every mountain or rural district. Following is a list of the commonest present-tense verbs together with their frequently incorrect past tenses and past participles. In some instances, as indicated, the common use of the past tense or participle is correct. You will also find in this list common examples of the failure to make the verb agree with the subject.

AM
    PRES: I am right.
    PAST: I was right. (correct)
    PART: I been right all along.

BLOW
    PRES: We blow loud.
    PAST: We blew loud. (correct)
    PART: It was blowed loud.

BREAK
    PRES: Break it off.
    PAST: I broke it off. (correct)
    PART: It was broke off.

BRING
    PRES: Bring me another.
    PAST: I brang it to him.
    PART: It was brung home.

BURST
    PRES: Bust the balloon now.
    PAST: I bust it already.
    PART: It was busted yesterday.
            (Except in careful, educated speech, "bust" is almost always used for "burst.")

BUY
    PRES: Will you buy it?
    PAST: I bought it yesterday. (Correct)
    PART: It was boughten at a store."

CATCH
    PRES: Catch the ball.
    PAST: I catched it.
    PART: It was catched by a fielder.
            (The word "cotched" is used mainly by Southern Negroes and mountaineers and seldom by other Americans.)

CLIMB
    PRES: Climb the tree.
    PAST: I clumb down first.
    PART: The hill was clomb by him.
            ("Clomb" is used in mountain districts only and is ordinarily "clumb" in the past tense.)

COME
    PRES: Come here!
    PAST: I come late.
    PART: You've came late again.

DIVE
　　PRES:　Dive in deep!
　　PAST:　I dove deep.
　　PART:　I've dived many times.　(correct)

DO
　　PRES:　Do it now!
　　PAST:　I done it already.
　　PART:　It was did yesterday.

DRAG
　　PRES:　Drag it here!
　　PAST:　I drug it past the tree.
　　PART:　It was drug down along here.

DRAW
　　PRES:　Draw only one drink.
　　PAST:　He drawed me another.
　　PART:　He's drawed too many.

DREAM
　　PRES:　I always dream.
　　PAST:　I dremp lots last night.
　　PART:　He's dremp a lot of guff.

DRINK
　　PRES:　Drink 'er down.
　　PAST:　I drunk it down.
　　PART:　I've drank too much.

DRIVE
　　PRES:　Drive slow-like.
　　PAST:　I driv her easy.
　　PART:　It was druv too fas'.

DROWN
　　PRES:　Y' might drown.
　　PAST:　It drownded las' week.
　　PART:　Two was drownded here-bouts.

EAT
　　PRES:　Eat it all up.
　　PAST:　I et it all down.
　　PART:　I've et that before.

FETCH
　　PRES:　Fetch it here.
　　PAST:　I fetched it to him.
　　PART:　It was fotched by me.
　　　　　　("Fotch" is a Negroism and is also used by many un-
　　　　　　educated whites in the mountain regions.)

FIGHT
PRES: Can y' fight him?
PAST: I fought a good fight.
PART: He was fit fair.
> ("Fit" in the past tense or as a participle is often pronounced "fit" in many rural and mountain areas.)

FLING
PRES: Fling her down.
PAST: I flang her away.
PART: It was flung hereabouts. (correct)

GO
PRES: Can y' go now?
PAST: I went yesterday. (correct)
PART: He's went already.

GROW
PRES: I grow 'taters.
PAST: We growed corn here.
PART: It was growed up in these parts.

HEAR
PRES: I hear he's gone.
PAST: Have you heard from him? (correct)
PART: I've hearn the news.

KNOW
PRES: I know all about it.
PAST: I knowed it was gone.
PART: It was knowed before it happened.

LEARN
PRES: I learn fast.
PAST: He learnt a lesson. (correct)
PART: I was learnt readin'.

LET
PRES: Let him go.
PAST: I let him have it. (correct)
PART: We've left her go.
> (The infinitive "to let" is rapidly being supplanted by "to leave" so that a great many people use "left" in the past tense and as a participle.)

RING
PRES: Ring the bell.
PAST: I rang it already. (correct)
PART: It was rang twice.

SEE
  PRES: I see him.
  PAST: I seen it.
  PART: I've saw it twice.
         (Rural areas often use "seed" for the past, as in "I seed
         he was a-comin' " or "sawn" in the participle as in
         "I've sawn all there was t' see.")

SIT
  PRES: Set down a spell.
  PAST: I set there four hours.
  PART: I've sat by her many a time. (correct)
         (In the mountain areas "sot" is used in the past and
         past participle.)

SAY
  PRES: Wadda y'say?
  PAST: I sez is zat so?
  PART: It was said already. (correct)

SHAKE
  PRES: Shake a leg.
  PAST: I shuck the mop out already.
  PART: I've shuck many a hen's neck.

SNEAK
  PRES: Sneak under the tent.
  PAST: I snuck up real quiet.
  PART: We've snuck in many a circus.

SPRING
  PRES: Spring the trap.
  PAST: It sprang wide open. (correct)
  PART: It was sprang when we got there.

STING
  PRES: It stings awful.
  PAST: The bee stang me.
  PART: We was all stung plenty.

SWELL
  PRES: It's startin' to swell.
  PAST: It swole up big.
  PART: It was all swole up like a balloon.

SWIM
  PRES: Can y' swim?
  PAST: I swum it twice.
  PART: It was swum in Friday.

SWING
PRES: Swing the bat sharp.
PAST: I swang it fast.
PART: The gate was swung wide open. (correct)

TAKE
PRES: Take her down easy now.
PAST: I tuck her down.
PART: She was tuck down already.

THROW
PRES: Throw it away.
PAST: I throwed it away.
PART: He was throwed for a loss.
       (Also heard in the past and past participle is "thrun"
       with the "th" pronounced as "t" by some uneducated
       city folk who would say "He trun the game like I
       told ya.")

WIN
PRES: Win the game, now!
PAST: I won it myself. (correct)
PART: It was won already. (correct)
       ("Winned" is also heard, especially in rural areas, as
       in "We winned everything.")

WRITE
PRES: Write me a letter, huh?
PAST: I rit it myself.
PART: We've wrote twice this week.

PRONOUN MISUSE

The pronoun is generally misused by the average American.
"Who y' talkin' to?" is more typical than "To whom are you talking?"
A substitution for "that" or "who" is often "what," as in, "It's
the house what's painted red," or "He's the man what knows."
In rural sections especially, a "but" may precede "what" as in
"I don't know but what I'll go."
An objective pronoun is often used in the subject of a sentence,
as in, "Me and the boss is pals." The nominative case, however,
is always used when the pronoun is immediately followed by the
verb, as in, "I found him." It will be noticed that when the subject
contains two pronouns, they are often both in the objective case, as
in, "Me and him went there." This is also true if the first word is a
noun, as in, "Hank and her was married."

The nominative pronoun is often incorrectly used in prepositional phrases in the predicate of a sentence, as in, "He threw it to him and I," or "He used to bring apples to we kids."

One of the commonest pronoun errors comes with the failure to make possessive pronouns in the predicate agree with the subject in number, as in "Each man should do their duty," or "None of them had eaten their dinner."

Another popular error, particularly in rural speech, is the use of "hisself," and "theirselves," as in, "He wanted it for hisself," and, "They got theirselves to blame."

The speech of the South and Southwest, including the mountain areas, is particularly larded with the use of adverbial pronouns such as "that there," "this here," "them there," and so on. "Is this here man O.K.?" "Them there apples is ripe." "That there feller's the one."

Finally, in sub-standard American speech, "our" becomes "ourn," as in, "That ball's ourn"; "you" becomes "yourn," as in, "The money's yourn"; "you" becomes youse," as in, "Youse goin' now?"; "his" becomes "hisn," as in, "The fault's hisn"; "their" becomes "theirn," as in, "The pork is theirn"; and "her" becomes "hern," as in, "They told us it was hern."

NOUN MISUSE

The most characteristic error in the use of nouns in the speech of rural America is the omission of "s" from the plural of a noun when the noun is preceded by a numeral. Thus, "mile," "pound," "gallon," "bushel," "pair," and "peck" retain their singular form although used in the plural, as in, " 'bout two mile down," "four pound onions," "twenny peck t' the acre," "put five gallon in," "nets me 'bout a dozen bushel a corn," and "bought me three pair shoes." Also used in the singular is "foot," as in, "five foot tall."

Another common error is the pluralization of the incorrect word of a compound noun, as in, "My son-in-laws are coming soon." In the same way, the possessive "s" is not added to its noun but to the following preposition, as in, "It's the guy I work with's." It is never added, however, when "belongs to" or "owned by" is used, as in, "It belongs to the man I work for," or "That car is owned by the girl I work with."

ADJECTIVE MISUSE

The typical American vocabulary of adjectives is singularly limited, especially in colloquial speech. Anything unusual is termed "funny" even though the situation it applies to may be tragic, as in, "That's funny—he's dead!" Something difficult is usually described as "hard," as in, "Hard times are hard to live in." The word "nice" covers anything that is satisfactory, as in, "It's a nice bat," or "We had a nice time." The excellence of anything is usually expressed by "swell," as in, "What a swell pitcher!" or "We had swell cheeseburgers."

In the mountain and rural areas, particularly, comparisons are often made by adding "er" to comparative forms of adjectives, as in, "I was worser 'n last time"; or to adjectives that require "more," as "She was beautifuller than Jane." Also many Americans add a superflous "more," as in, "I like it more better'n the other one."

ADVERB MISUSE

The most common error in the use of adverbs is to be found in the supplanting of an adverb by an adjective. "Slow" for "slowly" is almost universal, as in, "Go slow," instead of, "Go slowly." Less frequently used are such locutions as "Take it serious"; "This kind sells quick"; "He was hit bad"; or "He done hisself proud."

Instead of "very," the words "sure," "real," or "mighty" are generally substituted, as in, "I'll write real soon" or "We like it mighty fine."

Rural people add "s" to certain adverbs as in, "Goin' some'eres?" and "Anyways, he's gone" and "Ain't goin' nowheres."

These same rural folk add the neutral "a" particle before many words, particularly verbs, as in, "I'm a-goin that-a-way," and "He's headin' for this-a-way."

DOUBLE NEGATIVES

The double negative is a characteristic of all regional dialects. It is common to all speakers, except to the educated. "I ain't never comin' back" is typical. Other examples are:

> "I don't see nobody around."
> "I ain't only got but one buck."
> "He was not no loafer."
> "I ain't never goin' no more nohow."
> "We couldn't hardly see nothin'."

LIAISON

The habit of liaison, or joining of words, is quite common to American speech. Complete phrases are often pronounced so that they sound like one word. Among the most common of these are:

"fAHrzUHnOH"	(as far as I know)
"zAtsOH?"	(is that so?)
"wI:ntchUH?"	(why don't you?)
"mI:zwEHl"	(might as well)
"wUjUHgUn:dOO?"	(what are you going to do?)
"wEHrjEEt?"	(where did you eat?)
"hOOjUHA:s'?"	(who did you ask?)
"wI:jUH?"	(why did you . . . ?)
"wEHnjUH?"	(when did you . . . ?)
"wEHryUH?"	(where are you . . . ?)

WEAK AND STRONG WORDS

Certain sounds may have two or more pronunciations. Most of these are in short words which change according to their emphasis in a sentence. The greeting, "How do you do?" is commonly "hOW *dUH* yUH **dOO**?" The first "do" is weak; the second "do" is strong. The unstressed vowel generally takes a weakened form and becomes "uh." This habit is not confined to the masses alone. It is an intrinsic part of informal speech for the professor as well as for the common man. Again, the difference is one of degree, and the less educated use more weak sounds, more contractions, and more syllabic elisions.

In this book, the example sentences will be written with the weak and strong treatment so that the true flavor of the dialect may be seen. This means that instead of giving the precise pronunciation of words in a sentence, they will be given as they are spoken informally. Thus, "I went to the store to buy an orange" would be written as "I wEHntuh THuh stAWr tUH bI uhn AWrnj."

Following is a list of the most common words together with their "strong" and "weak" variations: Words in **boldface** are to be emphasized while those in *italics* indicate the word affected by the variation.

AM

STRONG: "I **Am** gOHing."
             (I *am* going.)

WEAK: "I UHm **gOHing**."
             (I *am* going.)

WEAK: "Im **gOHing**."
             (I'*m* going.)

AND

> STRONG: "hEE **And** yOO."
> (He *and* you.)

> WEAK: "THis UHn **THAt'**
> (This *and* that.)

ARE

> STRONG: "**AHr** yOO uhlOHn"
> (*Are* you alone?)

> WEAK: "wI UHr yOO **uhlOHn**"
> (Why *are* you alone?)

> WEAK: "wir **AWl** frEE"
> (We'*re* all free.)

BE

> STRONG: "wEHr wil yUH **bEE**"
> (Where will you *be?*)

> WEAK: "wil yUH bi **lAYt**"
> (Will you *be* late?)

BY

> STRONG: "THAY rAn **bI**"
> (They ran *by*.)

> WEAK: "UH **tOO** bUH fAWr"
> (A two *by* four.)
> (Particularly frequent in rural speech.)

CAN

> STRONG: "I **kAn** dOO UHt"
> (I *can* do it.)

> WEAK: "I kUHn **dOO** UHt **nOW**"
> (I *can* do it now.)

COULD

> STRONG: "hEE **kood** sEE UHt **AWl** THuh tIm"
> (He *could* see it all the time.)

> WEAK: "hEE kUHd **sEE** UHt"
> (He *could* see it.)

DO
STRONG: "hOW dUH yUH **dOO**"
          (How do you *do?*)

STRONG: "wI dOO EHgz **sEHI**"
          (Why *do* eggs sell?)
(When final or before a vowel.)

WEAK: "hOW **dUH** yUH dOO"
          (How *do* you do?)
(When before a consonant.)

FOR
STRONG: "hOO UHz UHt **fAWr**"
          (Who is it *for?*)

WEAK: "iz UHt fUHr **yOO**"
          (Is it *for* you?)

HAD
STRONG: "I **hAd** UH bIt AWlrEHdEE
          (I *had* a bite already.)

WEAK: "if wEE hUHd **nOHn**"
          (If we *had* known.)

WEAK: "if wEEd **nOHn**"
          (If we*'d* known.)

HAS
STRONG: "shEE **hAz** UH kAHr"
          (She *has* a car.)

WEAK: "dik UHz **gAWn**"
          (Dick *has* gone.)

WEAK: "hEEz **nOH rIt**"
          (He*'s* no right.)

HAVE
STRONG: "bUHt **hAv** yUH dUn UHt"
          (But *have* you done it?)

WEAK: "wEE hUHv **nOt** sUfERd"
          (We *have* not suffered.)
(After a vowel sound.)

WEAK: "THAY **kAnt** UHv gAWn"
          (They can't *have* gone.)
(After a consonant sound.)

WEAK: "THAYv **AWl gAWn**"
          (They*'ve* all gone.)

HE
    STRONG: **"hEE** nOHz wI"
                    (*He* knows why!)

    WEAK: "I **nOH** EE iz"
                    (I know *he* is.)

HER
    STRONG: "tAYk **hER** nAYm tOO"
                    (Take *her* name too.)

    WEAK: "tAYk UHr **nAYm** dOWn"
                    (Take *her* name down.)

HIM
    STRONG: "shEE wAHnUHd **him**"
                    (She wanted *him*.)

    WEAK: "tAYk UHm **hOHm**"
                    (Take *him* home.)

HIS
    STRONG: "its **hiz** hAHrd lUk"
                    (It's *his* hard luck.)

    WEAK: "giv UHm UHz **dinER**"
                    (Give him *his* dinner.)

I
    STRONG: **"I** nOH wI"
                    (*I* know why.)

    WEAK: "UH **wil** trI hAHrd"
                    (*I* will try hard.)
     (Used mainly in rural speech.)

IS
    STRONG: "hEE **iz** rIt"
                    (He *is* right!)

    WEAK: "its **nOH yOOs**"
                    (It'*s* no use!)

    WEAK: **"AWlz lAWst"**
                    (All'*s* lost.)

IT
    STRONG: "THAts **it** AWlrIt"
                    (That's *it* all right!)

    WEAK: "giv UHt tUH **mEE**"
                    (Give *it* to me.)

    WEAK: "its **nOd** it"
                    (*It's* not *it!*)

MANY
   STRONG: "AHr THEHr **mEHnEE** mAWr"
                 (Are there *many* more?)

   WEAK: "hOW mUHnEE **mAWr**"
                 (How *many* more?)

MAY
   STRONG: "I **mAY** sEE UHm tUHmOrOH"
                 (I *may* see him tomorrow.)

   WEAK: "yEHs yUH mUH **gOH** nOW"
                 (Yes, you *may* go now.)

MY
   STRONG: "UHts **mI** biznUHs"
                 (It's *my* business!)

   WEAK: "tAYk mUH nAYm **nOW**"
                 (Take *my* name now.)

NO
   STRONG: "Iv **nOH** yOOs fUHr UHt"
                 (I've *no* use for it.)

   WEAK: "hEEz **gOt** nUH mAWr **lEHft**"
                 (He's got *no* more left.)

NOT
   STRONG: "Im **nOt** UH fOOl"
                 (I'm *not* a fool!)

   WEAK: "hEE iznt uh**lOHn**"
                 (He isn'*t* alone.)
(Before a vowel sound.)

   WEAK: "hEE **izn** lAYt"
                 (He isn'*t* late.)
(Before a consonant sound.)

OF
   STRONG: "wUt **Uv** UHt"
                 (What *of* it?)

   WEAK: "UHv **kAWrs**"
                 (*Of* course!)
   WEAK: "UH bOks UH **pEHuhrz**"
                 (A box *of* pears.)
(Seldom before a vowel sound except by rural speakers, as in the next example.)

   WEAK: "UH glAs UH **AWrUHnj** jOOs"
                 (A glass *of* orange juice.)

ONE
STRONG: **"wUn UH THuhm did UHt"**
(*One* of them did it.)

WEAK: **"witch wUHn"**
(Which *one?*)

OR
STRONG: "tAYk THis **AWr** THAt"
(Take this *or* that.)

WEAK: "tAYk **THis** UHr **THAt** UHn **gOH"**
(Take this *or* that and go.)

SHALL
STRONG: "wEE **shAl** bEE frEE"
(We *shall* be free.)

WEAK: "wEE shUHl bEE **frEE** sOOn"
(We *shall* be free soon.)

SHOULD
STRONG: "yOO **shood** gOH"
(You *should* go!)

WEAK: "I shUHd wUrEE"
(I *should* worry!)

SO
STRONG: "it wUHz **sOH** kOHld"
(It was *so* cold!)

WEAK: "wUHz UHt sUH **kOHld"**
(Was it *so* cold?)

SOME
STRONG: "OHnlEE **sUm** UH THuhm kAYm"
(Only *some* of them came.)

WEAK: "hAv sUHm **grAYps"**
(Have *some* grapes.)

THAN
(Seldom sounded as "THAn")
WEAK: "bEHtUHr THUHn **EHvUHr"**
(Better *than* ever.)

WEAK: "its lEHsUHn I **thAWt"**
(It's less *than* I thought.)

THAT
>   STRONG: **"THAts** nOt rIt"
>   (*That's* not right!)

>   WEAK: "hEE **nOHz** THUHt Im rIt"
>   (He knows *that* I'm right.)

THE
>   STRONG: "THEE **ingk** UHz **drI"**
>   (*The* ink is dry.)
>   (Before a vowel sound only.)

>   WEAK: THUH **tIm** UHz **rIp"**
>   (*The* time is ripe.)
>   (Before a consonant sound only.)

>   WEAK: "THUH **ink** UHz **drI"**
>   (*The* ink is dry.)
>   (Used by rural speakers all over the country.)

THERE
>   STRONG: "wER yUH **THEHr"**
>   (Were you *there?*)

>   WEAK: "iz THUHr UH **mAn** hiUHr"
>   (Is *there* a man here?)

THEM
>   STRONG: "kAWl **THEHm** nOt Us"
>   (Call *them*, not us!)

>   WEAK: "kAWl THUHm **nOW"**
>   (Call *them* now!)

TO
>   STRONG: **"tOO** UHn frOH"
>   (*To* and fro.)
>   (Always "tOO" before a vowel sound except by many rural speakers
>   who use the weak form) as in:

>   WEAK: "I **hAYt** tUH **A:sk"**
>   (I hate *to* ask.)

>   WEAK: "trI tUH bEE **ERlEE"**
>   (Try *to* be early.)
>   (Before a consonant sound.)

US
STRONG: "dUH yUH wAHnt **Us** tUH kUm"
(Do you want *us* to come?)

WEAK: "shOH UHs **hOW**"
(Show *us* how.)

WEAK: "lEHts gOH **hOHm**"
(Let's go home.)

WAS
STRONG: "I **WUz** uhlOHn"
(I *was* alone!)

WEAK: "I wUHz **uhlOHn**"
(I *was* alone.)

WERE
STRONG: **"wER** yUH sik"
(*Were* you sick?)

WEAK: "wEE wUHr **AWl** sik"
(We *were* all sick.)

WHAT
STRONG: **"WUt nOW"**
(*What* now?)

WEAK: hEE **nOHz** wUHts good"
(He knows *what's* good.)

WILL
STRONG: **"wil** THAY dOO UHt"
(*Will* they do it?)

WEAK: "THAYl nOH **sOOn**"
(They'*ll* know soon.)

WOULD
STRONG: "bUHt **wood** yOO THOH"
(But *would* you, though?)

WEAK: "it UHd bEE **nIs**"
(It *would* be nice.)
(After a consonant.)

WEAK: **"hEEd** nOH wI"
(He'*d* know why.)
(After a vowel.)

YOU
STRONG: **"yOO** nOH wI"
(*You* know why!)

WEAK: "dOO yUH **nOH** wI"
(Do *you* know why?)

YOUR
> STRONG: "THis iz **yoor** dOOing"
> (This is *your* doing!)
>
> WEAK: **"dOO yUHr dOOdEE"**
> (Do *your* duty!)

THE GLOTTAL STOP

The very name "glottal stop" has deterred many actors from studying the Scottish dialect in which it is widely used. Yet, they continue to learn the German dialect, even though many Germans use the glottal stop, which they call *Kehlkopfverschlusslaut*, before every stressed initial vowel. And many of these same actors who feel that the glottal stop is some strange and intricate process make use of the sound in their own speech.

The glottal stop will be represented as (/) in this book. It is produced in the larynx and results from the sudden closing and then opening of the glottis. It has been aptly compared with a slight cough or catch in the throat, but it must be very slight. It may also be heard if the student forcefully whispers "/I /Am /OWt" (I am out). This must be whispered so that stress is given to each initial vowel sound.

The admonishing "ah ah" which is commonly spoken to a child, is also preceded frequently by a glottal stop so that it becomes "/AH /AH." The affirmative "/mmhmm" and the negative "/mm/mm" are also examples. Not all Americans use the glottal stop, and the majority of those who do are unaware of its presence.

The glottal stop is frequently used before an initial vowel in emphatic speech, as in "hEE iz gOHing" (He is going!). In informal, rapid speech it is frequently used to replace final "t," as in, "THuh hA/ wUHz gAWn" (The hat was gone); and "hEEz /OW/ frU/" (He's out front). It is also commonly used to replace the first two letters of the verb "can" ("/ng") when this verb is unstressed, as in, "I /ng gOH" (I can go). It may be used before "/n" (and), as in, "/n THEHn" (and then).

The actor should learn to recognize this sound if he uses it. He should notice its unobtrusive production so that when he finds its use pointed out in a particular instance in a certain dialect, he will be able to give this sound a normal and natural interpretation. The American variety of glottal stop should not be as rich or full or strong as the Scottish type.

CHAPTER II

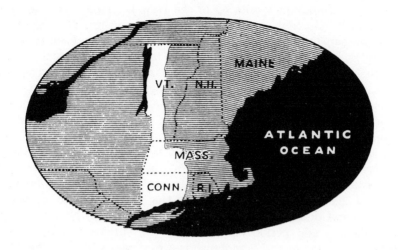

THE NEW ENGLAND DIALECT

CONTRARY TO POPULAR belief, the New England dialect is not spoken throughout the New England area. Actually it is to be found in the states of Maine, New Hampshire (except the mountain area), little more than half of eastern Vermont, the eastern half of Massachusetts, the extreme eastern strip of Connecticut, and Rhode Island. Most of the people in western New England which comprises the western half of Vermont, the western half of Massachusetts, and most of Connecticut speak General-American or a modified form of it.

The line of demarcation between the two sections begins at the uppermost pinnacle of the Green Mountains and proceeds south into the Berkshires between Daltu and Pittsfield, Mass., then turns east to the Worcester Hills, south to Athol, and then swings south to a sound about five miles west of New Sanders, Connecticut. This line bounds the limits of the so-called New England dialect in its westward expansion, with the exception of a few dialect islands in the Connecticut Valley.

This does not mean that only two dialects are spoken by the inhabitants of this section of the country. The New Haven, Connecticut dialect, for example, has many variances from the Boston type of New England dialect, as has Rhode Island. Fairfield County, in southwestern Connecticut is so close to New York City and the Hudson Valley that it has taken on much of their dialects and has even retained elements of the New Amsterdam Dutch. Certain districts in Maine know nothing of the New England dialect spoken by people in adjacent states. The speech of western New England is predominantly General-American with a few eastern New England carryovers, most of which are mentioned in the following text.

The dialect given here is typical of eastern New England speech and may be used in accordance with the variations given for historical or modern rural or coastal characters. A modern urban character should use only certain elements since a leveling-off process to General-American is gradually erasing many of the dialect variants. This is particularly true of the people in the industrial sectors of southern New England. The northern rural sections, however, and a number of districts such as Marblehead, Cape Ann, and Martha's Vineyard have continued to resist the movement to General-American and preserve many of the dialect features of New England.

Tradition and fiction emphasize in the shrewd Yankee trader resistance to change and a snobbishness that made him believe himself superior to "other folks." Add the traits of miserliness, hair-cloth restraint, and ultraconservatism, and temper the picture with admirable qualities — a desire to succeed by hard work, strength of will, and singleness of purpose. Of course, the resulting character is no more typical of all inhabitants of the region than are the characters of *Tobacco Road* typical Southerners. But it is not too broad a generalization to say that the traits mentioned are portrayed in varying degree in most New England characters — both historical and contemporary.

A great number of the early New England settlers came from Scotland and Ireland, as well as England and other countries. Contrary to popular belief, they were not all prim, pious Puritans. There were the usual obstreperous, earthy, irrepressible individuals found in any large group which migrates in wholesale fashion to settle a new country. Perhaps it was this ebullience on the part of some which brought forth the ultraconservative attitude on the part of others. This latter is a characteristic trait of the New Englander and affects not only his views on money — which eschews the waste of spending for fashion among other things, — but also his opinion of any "newfangled" ideas. The rocky, almost untillable New England soil must also have contributed to make the New England farmer, especially, a man of unemotional disposition.

Just as no one typical New Englander embodies all of the character traits, so no one speaker embodies all of the dialect elements. Each person in all the dialect regions is a law unto himself, and is guided by his own emotions or lack thereof, his background, desires, inhibitions, and frustrations.

LILT AND STRESS

The New Englander's almost unmoving adherence to tradition has resulted in the retention of speech variances that had their sources in the language of the original English settlers. As far back as the Revolution, Ben Franklin joshed the New Englanders about their pronunciation of "cow" as "keow." Many New Englanders still call a cow a "kyAoo," a result of the tendency toward nasalization and diphthongization which created the "New England twang" so derided by the British. The Cape Cod area has less nasalization than other New England communities.

As in Southern nasalization, the tongue arches up in the mouth, the middle of it rising until it almost touches the roof of the mouth. This same habit produces the palatalized "k" and "g" which are pronounced "ky" and "gy" by many speakers in the New England, Southern, and Mountain areas.

The pitch of the New England dialect is somewhat higher than General-American. The tempo varies from the Southern in that it is more rapid, although the tonal patterns of its lilt are similar to those observed in Tidewater Virginia and coastal North and South Carolina.

Ordinary statements of fact have an upward inflection similar to British, but this upward inflection is used in General-American for a question sentence. Coincidental with the reserved nature of the people, their speech mirrors their repressed uncertainties. A prosaic remark may be spoken with an air of caution. For example, "kAlAYt hi:z UHgUuhn" (ca'late he's a-goin') would have the following lilt:

"kA   Uuhn."
lAYt hi:z   gU
UH

It should be noticed that in the New England dialect the choice of words is also indicative of prudence. Rather than the definite, possibly provocative "I *know* he's going," the New Englander prefers the more indefinite, safer "I *calculate*." And the lilt seems to imply that his unvoiced thoughts are: "Ary thing might happen, t'aint for me to say for sartin, but sfars I know I ca'late he's a-goin'."

Even the simple "hAoodi" (howdy) is uttered with a certain
reservation:

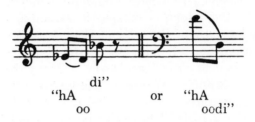

            di"
    "hA   or   "hA
        oo   oodi"

Although the Texan may also say "howdy" on two notes, as in
the second example above, his range is broader, and he imparts to
the word a sincere interest. To the New Englander the word is a
stylized form of greeting uttered with the customary mental reserva-
tions. The pitch pattern is narrow and tight; in certain respects it is
similar to British and Scottish.

There is a tendency, especially among the older folk, to overemphasize certain final syllables which, in General-American, are
usually unstressed, as in **"padid"** (padded) and **"bAHskit"**
(basket). In these words the final syllable receives almost as
much emphasis as the initial syllable. This highlights the speech
and disturbs what would otherwise be a definite drawl.

The almost staccato effect is further heightened by trans-
posing the accent in certain two-syllable words so that the primary
accent is placed on the first syllable instead of on the second, as
in **"ri:pOHuht"** (report) or **"di:trAHit"** (Detroit). (See also
"Unstressed Syllables," page 40.)

Altogether, there is a sharp, clipped quality to the speech
that emerges despite excessive elongation and diphthongization.
There is a dryness that almost crackles.

THE GLOTTAL STOP

Many New Englanders make use of the glottal stop (see **"The
Glottal Stop,"** page 24) especially in place of final "t" or "nt,"
so that "twant" (it was not) becomes "twAW/." For the New
England dialect, the glottal stop should not be as rich or as strong
as it is in Scottish, unless of course, the character is historical
with permanent Scottish background.

The glottal stop is represented in this book as "/" and examples
of its use will be found in the sections **"Grammar Changes"** and
"Typical Words and Phrases."

A reaction against the use of the glottal stop resulted in a
distinct and precise pronunciation of "t" by many New Englanders.

A final "t" is generally pronounced, by all, when it precedes an initial vowel word.

In learning the New England dialect, or any other regional American dialect, it must be remembered that this is not a foreign language, but one of the many variants of American speech. In the following section on **"Vowel Changes"** the explanations should be carefully studied before practicing the drill words. For example, under the "U" of "up" it will be noticed that although the symbol is given as "AW," a full, rich "AW" is not indicated. This dialect, like all others, requires sincere study and constant practice so that its reproduction may be smooth, understandable, and believable. Sounds that vary from the student's own speech should not be unduly stressed because of their novelty to the student.

VOWEL CHANGES

"AY" .... as in "make," "break," "they," etc.

In the New England dialect, this long "a" may be almost a pure "AY" sound, rather than the "AY-EE" of General-American. When unstressed, it often becomes "EH."

DRILL WORDS

mAYk	(make)	stAYt	(state)	lAYt	(late)
brAYk	(break)	prAY	(pray)	frAYd	(afraid)
THAY	(they)	shAYk	(shake)	hAYt	(hate)

HISTORICAL VARIATION: Historical characters or modern characters in rural or coastal Maine may use the variant "EH" as in "rEHdiOH" (radio) and "mEHbi" (maybe).

EXCEPTIONS: Many people, in rural areas, who have adopted the sound of "AY" continue to use "EH" for the common words "nEHkid" (naked) and "snEHk" (snake).

When "day" is used as a suffix, it is commonly pronounced "di" as in "hOlidi" (holiday).

"UH" .... as in "alone," "final," "sofa," etc.

In the rural speech of eastern New England, the initial unstressed syllable is usually dropped, as in "bAoot" (about), "lAood" (allowed), and "kAoont" (account). However, people in western New England, as well as those in larger eastern cities, generally retain the initial "UH."

The medial unstressed syllable may also be dropped, as in "fAHinli" (finally). For a further discussion of the medial unstressed "a," see **"Unstressed Syllables"** and **"Dropped Syllables."**

Although the change of final, unstressed "UH" to "i:" was found in many New England districts, it was, and still is, particularly in rural areas, especially common in the eastern half, as in "sOHdi:" (soda), "AHidi:" (idea), and "hi:ldi:" (Hilda). For the correct pronunciation of "i:" see "EE" on page 33.

The final, unstressed vowel may also become "UHr," when final in a sentence or when followed by an initial vowel word, as in "AnUHr UHn AHidUHr" (Anna and Ida). For a further discussion of this linking "r," see "R" under "Consonant Changes."

"AH" .... as in "father," "alms," "park," etc.

The typical pronunciation of this sound is "AA." It is produced by saying "A" (see Figure 1) with the mouth in the wider position of "AH" (see Figure 2).

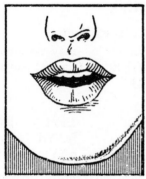

Fig. 1   Fig. 2

DRILL WORDS

fAATHUH	(father)	hAAdli	(hardly)
AAmz	(alms)	kAAdz	(cards)
pAAk	(park)	pAAti	(party)

stAAlUit	(starlight)
dAAknis	(darkness)
pAAtid	(parted)

This "AA" may be used generally for persons living in the nineteenth and twentieth centuries. It may also be used for people in western New England, in which case the "r" should be sounded, as in "kAArdz" (cards) or "stAArtid" (started).

HISTORICAL VARIATIONS: If the character to be portrayed lived in a rural district in the last quarter of the eighteenth century or the first half of the nineteenth century, he may use "AH." The urbanite, living in this same period, however, would generally use "AA."

In many rural sections, southeast of the Boston area, "AH" may be heard, as in "pAH:k" (park).

EXCEPTIONS: Rural New Englanders commonly pronounce "far" as "fU-UH" and "are" as "EH-UH."

"A:" .... as in "ask," "staff," "aunt," etc.

Both "AH" and "AA" may be used in these words, but the choice of either generally depends on the age and background of the character. The "AH" variant may be used by the rustic or "common" man living in the first half of the nineteenth century; the "AA" for the "elite" of the same period.

DRILL WORDS

AHsk	(ask)	lAHftUH	(laughter)
stAHf	(staff)	dizAHstUH	(disaster)
AHnt	(aunt)	grAHntid	(granted)

	brAHntch	(branch)
	dAHns	(dance)
	klAHsp	(clasp)

HISTORICAL VARIATIONS: In the eighteenth century, the "AA" variant was generally used by all. This sound was retained by most of the city people until the middle of the nineteenth century.

If the character to be portrayed is one of the "common" people, living from about 1850 to the present day, the "AA" sound should be used. If, however, the character is one of the older "elite," the "AH" is preferred.

Many modern New England urbanites use the General-American "A:" as in "dA:nsin pAAtnUH" (dancing partner). It will be noticed that although the "A:" is used in "dancing" the "AA" sound may still be retained in "partner."

EXCEPTION: In rural areas, "rather" is commonly pronounced as "rUTHuh."

"A" .... as in "bad," "am," "narrow," etc.

The New England "A" sound is much the same as it is in General-American except that it is often flatter and has a more nasal quality. As with most New England vowels, this sound is often drawn out a little longer than in General-American.

DRILL WORDS

bAd	(bad)	klAm	(clam)	hArUH	(harrow)
Am	(am)	hApi	(happy)	lAnd	(land)
nArUH	(narrow)	kAt	(cat)	mAtUH	(matter)

VARIATION: Before the sound of "sh" this vowel may become "Ai." There should be no break between "A" and "i" since "i" is merely a glide vowel sound. It is heard in words like "krAish" (crash) and "rAishin" (ration).

HISTORICAL VARIATION: If the character to be portrayed lived in the middle of the nineteenth century, or a little later, "AH" may be used, especially if the character lived in a rural district. Thus, General-American "A" words would become "hAHpi" (happy), "mAHtUH" (matter), "AHpl" (apple), and "lAHdUH" (ladder).

EXCEPTIONS: Certain common words are generally pronounced with "EH" as in: "hEHv" (have), "hEHz" (has), "kEHtch" (catch), "hEHd" (had), "kEHrij" (carriage), and "kEHn" (can).

"AW" .... as in "all," "fault," "wash," etc.

In the New England dialect, this sound generally becomes "AH," when not preceded by "w" nor followed by "r."

DRILL WORDS

AHl	(all)	kAHl	(call)	gAHntlit	(gauntlet)
fAHlt	(fault)	tAHt	(taught)	AHlUHz	(always)
hAHk	(hawk)	tAHk	(talk)	skAHld	(scald)

WHEN THE SOUND OF "w" PRECEDES THE GENERAL-AMERICAN "AW," THIS VOWEL SOUND GENERALLY CHANGES TO "O" IN THE NEW ENGLAND DIALECT.

DRILL WORDS

wOsh	(wash)	kwOril	(quarrel)	wOsp	(wasp)
wOtch	(watch)	wOrin	(Warren)	wOtUH	(water)
skwOsh	(squash)	wOrint	(warrant)	wOk	(walk)

HISTORICAL VARIATION: If the character lived in the early nineteenth century, the sound of "AA" may be substituted for words spelled with "au" or "ua" as in "sAAs" (sauce), "kwAAliti" (quality), and "hAAnt" (haunt). This variant may also be used for older rural characters of the twentieth century.

"AW" .... as in "off," "cough," "soft," etc.

When the General-American "AW" sound is spelled with "o," it is usually pronounced as "O" in the New England dialect.

DRILL WORDS

Of	(off)	bOstin	(Boston)	kOfi	(coffee)
kOf	(cough)	lOst	(lost)	lOng	(long)
sOft	(soft)	klOth	(cloth)	dOg	(dog)

VARIATION: Modern New Englanders are tending toward the use of "AW," especially those in western New England.

"AW" .... as in "more," "war," "forest," etc.

In the New England dialect, this "AW" sound is generally spoken far forward in the mouth so that it often sounds like "OH." It is elongated to "OHuh" because of the dropped "r." Because of the frequent "OH" quality given this General-American "AW," the "OH" symbol will be used. But a tensed "OH" sound should not be made.

DRILL WORDS

mOHuh	(more)	pOHuht	(port)	skOHuhtch	(scorch)
kOHuh	(core)	fOHuhs	(force)	mOHuhbid	(morbid)
fOHuh	(four)	shOHuht	(short)	pOHuhshin	(portion)

For words like "fOris" (forest, the following general rule may be applied:

*WHEN THE GENERAL-AMERICAN "AW" SOUND IS FOL-
LOWED BY THE SOUND OF "r" PLUS A VOWEL, IT IS
COMMONLY CHANGED TO "O" IN THE NEW ENGLAND
DIALECT.*

DRILL WORDS

sOri	(sorry)	flOridi:	(Florida)	lOril	(laurel)
pOrij	(porridge)	hOrid	(horrid)	fOrin	(foreign)
Orinj	(orange)	Origin	(origin)	dOris	(Doris)

EXCEPTION: When unstressed, "for" is commonly pronounced as "fUH."

"EE" .... as in "he," "easy," "treaty," etc.

This long "EE" sound is generally changed to "i:" which is a sound between "EE" and "i." It can be produced by tensing "i," that is, by saying "i" with the tongue tensed for "EE." When unstressed, "i" should be used.

DRILL WORDS

hi:	(he)	pAAti	(party)	pEHski	(pesky)
i:zi	(easy)	gri:si	(greasy)	kri:mi	(creamy)
tri:ti	(treaty)	sOfli	(softly)	fri:li	(freely)

HISTORICAL VARIATION: The character, especially if he is of Irish extraction, who lived in the eighteenth or nineteenth century may pronounce the final "eit" as "AY" as in "knsAYt" (conceit).

EXCEPTION: The words "creek" and "breeches" are commonly pronounced "krik" and "britchiz." The words "either" and

"neither" are generally "iTHUH" and "nUHTHUH" although
these may be replaced by "AAri" (ary) and "nAAri" (nary). Modern
New Englanders frequently say "EETHuh" or "AHiTHuh" (either);
and "nEETHuh" or "nAHiTHuh" (neither). The word "real"
is commonly "rAYl."

"EH" . . . . as in "bet," "said," "friend," etc.

Ordinarily, this sound is the same in the New England dialect
as it is in General-American.

DRILL WORDS

bEHt	(bet)	rEHdnis	(redness)
sEHd	(said)	shEHltUH	(shelter)
swEHp	(swept)	brEHkfis	(breakfast)

drEHtfl	(dreadful)
mEHdUH	(meadow)
sprEHd	(spread)

In a number of short or common words, rural speakers generally substitute the vowel sound of "i" especially before "d," "n,"
"s," or "t."

DRILL WORDS

ini	(any)	stidi	(steady)	yistUHdi	(yesterday)
yit	(yet)	frin	(friend)	UHgins	(against)
git	(get)	kitl	(kettle)	tchis	(chest)

EXCEPTION: The word "deaf" is commonly pronounced "di:f."

HISTORICAL VARIATION: The change of "i" for "EH" may
also be used for an urban character living in the eighteenth or
early nineteenth century.

"EH" . . . . as in "there," "chair," "dare," etc.

When followed by "r," this vowel sound is generally changed
to "AA" in New England dialect speech. When the "r" is dropped,
the sound becomes "AAuh."

DRILL WORDS

THAAuh	(there)	wEHlfAAuh	(welfare)
tchAAuh	(chair)	UHmAArikin	(American)
dAAuh	(dare)	stAAkis	(staircase)

skAAsli	(scarcely)
kAAlis	(careless)
bAAli	(barely)

EXCEPTIONS: The words "vary" and "Mary" are commonly
pronounced "vAYri" and "mAYri."

HISTORICAL VARIATIONS: If the character is an elderly person of the present day, living in a rural or coastal area, or if he is an historical character, "i:" may be used for certain common words, as in "tchi:UH" (chair), "ki:UH" (care), and "shi:UHz" (shares).

"I" . . . . as in "ice," "might," "strike," etc.

The sounds "AHi" and "Ui:" may both be used by one character speaking the New England dialect. If both sounds are to be used, the following general rule should be observed:

WHEN GENERAL-AMERICAN LONG "i" (I) IS FINAL OR IS FOLLOWED BY THE SOUNDS "f," "k," "p," "s," "t," or "th," IT MAY CHANGE TO "Ui:" IN THE NEW ENGLAND DIALECT.

DRILL WORDS

Ui:s	(ice)	hAHid	(hide)	prAHid	(pride)
mUi:t	(might)	tAHim	(time)	fUi:t	(fight)
strUi:k	(strike)	mAHin	(mind)	krUi:	(cry)

Either sound may be used separately by one character, whether modern or historical.

VARIATION: A variant sound is "AAi:" as in "lAAi:t" (light), "pAAi:k" (pike), "fAAi:n" (fine).

The variant "AWi:" may also be used, particularly for older rural or historical characters, especially those in the Cape Cod area. This variant may be used as in "sAWi:d" (side) and "tAWi:d" (tide).

EXCEPTION: The word "oblige" is commonly "bli:j."

"i" . . . . as in "it," "women," "busy," etc.

In the New England dialect, this "i" is sharper and more intensified than in General-American and approaches "EE" in quality. It will be represented here as "i:" as in "i:t" (it).

DRILL WORDS

wi:min	(women)	kni:pshn	(conniption)	li:tl	(little)
bi:zi	(busy)	fi:UHsli	(fiercely)	pi:g	(pig)
hi:m	(hymn)	ni:UHli	(nearly)	fri:lz	(frills)

HISTORICAL VARIATION: The variant "EH" may be used for certain common words, especially when the vowel sound is followed by "n" as in "sEHnts" (since), "rEHntch" (rinse), "spEHrit" (spirit), "EHf" (if), and "bEHn" (been).

"OH" .... as in "home," "rode," "tone," etc.

It is with the pronunciation of this long "o" (OH) sound that the New England dialect projects one of its most characteristic dialect variants. There has been much controversy regarding its true quality. For practical purposes it is represented here as "Uuh." The "U" (as in "up") is produced far forward in the mouth and is endowed with a slight "AW" flavor. The "uh" is a faint glide and should not be prolonged.

Although this "Uuh" is typical of the New England dialect, it cannot be sounded for all long "o" words. Its use is inconsistent, being generally found in "hUuhl" (whole) but seldom in "hOHl" (hole), in "stUuhn" (stone) but not in "tOHn" (tone); therefore, no absolute rule can be given. However, it may generally be used before "d" and "t" and in the following drill words:

DRILL WORDS

dUuhnt	(don't)	bUuhth	(both)	hUuhli	(wholly)
Uuhnli	(only)	hUuhmli	(homely)	bUuhn	(bone)
fUuhks	(folks)	mUuhst	(most)	rUuhd	(road)
shUuhn	(shone)	rUuhm	(roam)	nUuhn	(known)
smUuhk	(smoke)	strUuhv	(strove)	Uuhn	(own)
thrUuhn	(throne)	lUuhn	(alone)	mUuhn	(moan)

These words and their derivatives should be pronounced with "Uuh"; all others with "OH."

REGIONAL VARIATION: In rural areas of Connecticut, the glide "uh" is often dropped and only the "U" is used, as in "hUm" (home).

EXCEPTION: When the General-American "OH" sound is final and spelled "ow," it should be changed to "UH" for an historical or modern rural character, as in "wi:dUH" (widow).

"O" .... as in "bond," "hot," "stop," etc.

Generally, this "O" sound should remain the same as in General-American.

DRILL WORDS

bOnd	(bond)	trOli	(trolley)	shOt	(shot)
hOt	(hot)	prOpUH	(proper)	trOt	(trot)
stOp	(stop)	jOni	(Johnny)	lOt	(lot)

VARIATION: Some New Englanders, particularly those in rural areas, use the variant "AW" as in "tAWm" (Tom), "dAWl" (doll), or "rAWk" (rock).

EXCEPTION: The word "got" is usually pronounced as "gUt."

"OO" .... as in "food," "do," "soon," etc.

In the New England dialect, this "OO" is generally preceded by an "i" glide.

DRILL WORDS

fiOOd	(food)	triOOth	(truth)	skiOOl	(school)
diOO	(do)	shiOOt	(shoot)	tiOO	(two)
siOOn	(soon)	tiOOzdi	(Tuesday)	riOOlUH	(ruler)

REGIONAL VARIATION: Western New Englanders generally use "OO" as in "fOOd" (food).

EXCEPTIONS: The following words are generally pronounced with the "oo" of "good" rather than "OO" of "food": "broom" (broom), "room" (room), "proof" (proof), "koop" (coop), and "soon" (soon).

When stressed, "to" may be pronounced as "tOH" in the New England dialect, as in "zi:k di:dn nOH wUH tOH sAY" (Zeke didn't know what to say).

CHARACTER VARIATION: When a General-American "OO" word is spelled with "u" after the consonant sounds "d," "l," "n," "s," "t," "th," or "z," this vowel sound may remain "OO" as in "dOOti" (duty), "nOOmrUHs" (numerous), and "lOOk" (Luke).

"oo" .... as in "good," "wolf," "soot," etc.

The New England treatment of this sound falls between "oo" and "U." Since it is closer to the latter, it will be represented here as "U," and the sound should be produced from far forward in the mouth.

DRILL WORDS

gUd	(good)	bUl	(bull)	fUtsOHuh	(footsore)
wUlf	(wolf)	tUk	(took)	wUminli	(womanly)
sUt	(soot)	stUd	(stood)	pUdin	(pudding)

EXCEPTION: The word "butcher" is commonly pronounced as "bOOtchUH."

"yOO" .... as in "unit," "cube," "beauty," etc.

In General-American this sound is commonly pronounced as "yOO" when long "u" is spelled as "eau," "ew," "u," or "ue" after the consonant sounds "b," "f," "h," "k," "m," or "p" as in "beauty," "few," "human," and so forth. It is also used for initial "u" or "you" as in "use" or "youth."

In the older New England dialect, however, an "i" glide often replaced the "y" as in "fiOO" (few). In an unaccented position the vowel sound was often changed to "i", as in "AAgimint" (argument).

DRILL WORDS

biOOti	(beauty)	AkizEHshin	(accusation)
hiOObUt	(Hubert)	dispiOOdid	(disputed)
vAli	(value)	kiOOmilEHt	(accumulate)

piOOtUH	(pewter)
ri:fiOOz	(refuse)
skiOOz	(excuse)

CHARACTER VARIATION: In a medial stressed syllable, the variant "OO" may also be used, as in "UHmOOzin" (amusing) and "knfOOzin" (confusing), particularly if the character lived in the last half of the nineteenth century, or in rural areas in the early twentieth century.

EXCEPTIONS: Initial "u" or "you" words generally take "yiOO" as in "yiOOz" (use) or "yiOOth" (youth).

NOTE: For words like "new," "stupid," or "duty" refer back to "OO" as in "food."

"U" . . . . as in "up," "does," "just," etc.
    In the New England dialect, this "U" sound often has a slight "AW" flavor. This blending of the two sounds can be achieved by placing the lips in the pursed position for "AW" but pronouncing "U" instead. For our purposes this combination sound will be designated as "AW," but it must be remembered that a rich, full "AW" sound should not be used. If the "U" is spoken far forward in the mouth, the "AW" quality will be easily obtained.

DRILL WORDS

AWp	(up)	kAWntri	(country)
dAWz	(does)	mAWTHuh	(mother)
krAWm	(crum)	hAWntUH	(hunter)

kAWnstibl	(constable)
nAWthin	(nothing)
bAWjit	(budget)

CHARACTER VARIATIONS: If the character to be portrayed is historical and has a Scottish or Irish background, the variant "oo" may be used. This sound is like the "oo" of "good," but is produced from a more forward position in the mouth.
    If the character has an English background, the "U" should be further back in the throat so that it almost becomes "AH." This variant sound is commonly heard throughout Maine.

For a rural character, either modern or historical, the "U" sound should become "EH" under certain conditions. This change is usually made when the General-American "U" sound is between any two of the following consonant sounds: "j," "r," "s," "sh," or "tch"; or if the vowel sound is between one of the above-mentioned consonant sounds and "f," "h," "t," or "v."

DRILL WORDS

jEHj	(judge)	sEHtch	(such)	rEHsh	(rush)
jEHs	(just)	grEHj	(grudge)	shEHv	(shove)
hEHsh	(hush)	shEHt	(shut)	tEHtch	(touch)

"ER" .... as in "curb," "earn," "fern," etc.

The old-fashioned New England pronunciation of "ER" is "U:," and this sound is still heard, especially in rural areas or along the northeast coast. A Bostonian living in California for the past twenty years still retains the pronunciation of "ER" as "U:," as in, "fU:nitchUH" (furniture). In addition, his two younger children have somehow absorbed this New England pronunciation although their normal speech is General-American. The "U" should be produced from a forward position in the mouth, and there is sometimes a faint "ER" color to it. The (:) indicates that the following "r" sound is dropped and "U" should be drawn out.

DRILL WORDS

kU:b	(curb)	sU:tin	(certain)	hU:rt	(hurt)
U:n	(earn)	dU:ti	(dirty)	wU:k	(work)
fU:n	(fern)	fU:st	(first	shU:t	(shirt)

HISTORICAL VARIATIONS: For an historical, or older rural character, the variant "AA" may be used, if the vowel sound is spelled with "e" or "ea" as in "sAAtin" (certain), "sAAtch" (search), or "pAAsin" (person). For the correct pronunciation of "AA" refer back to "AH" as in "father."

Modern eastern New Englanders living in or near large urban centers usually pronounce this sound as "ER" as in "bERn" (burn) or "fERm" (firm). This "ER" sound is like the General-American "ER" except that the "r" is silent. Western New Englanders generally pronounce the "r."

EXCEPTION: When in an unaccented position, this vowel sound changed to "UH" as in "fAATHuh" (father).

"OW" .... as in "out," "cow," "house," etc.

In the New England dialect this vowel sound is often changed to "Aoo." This is a blend of the "A" of "bad" and the "oo" of "good," and it must be treated as a blend rather than as two individual sounds.

DRILL WORDS

Aoot	(out)	rAoodi	(rowdy)	hAoon	(hound)
kAoo	(cow)	bAoon	(bound)	sAooUH	(sour)
hAoos	(house)	shAoot	(shout)	prAood	(proud)

HISTORICAL VARIATION: An urban character of the nineteenth century may use "AHoo" as in "hAHoos" (house). Grammarians of the eighteenth and early nineteenth centuries preferred "AW-OO" as in "dAW-OOn" (down).

"OI" . . . . as in "oil," "boy," "noise," etc.

The older New England dialect of the eighteenth and early nineteenth centuries generally treats with this sound as "AHi." This is a blend of the General-American sounds "AH" (as in "father") and "i" (as in "it").

DRILL WORDS

AHil	(oil)	jAHin	(join)	AHistUHz	(oysters)
bAHi	(boy)	pAHint	(point)	pAHizn	(poison)
nAHiz	(noise)	brAHil	(broil)	spAHil	(spoil)

HISTORICAL VARIATIONS: Modern urban New England generally uses "AWi" as in "pAWint" (point), although "OHi" may also be used as in "pOHint" (point).

UNSTRESSED SYLLABLES

Much of the color of the New England dialect is achieved by the treatment of the unstressed syllables. This is particularly true of the old-fashioned New England rural speech.

MEDIAL UNSTRESSED SYLLABLES GENERALLY CHANGE TO "i" IN THE NEW ENGLAND DIALECT.

With this change to "i" the unstressed syllable receives slightly more stress than is customary in General-American.

DRILL WORDS

bAAgin	(bargain)	sU:kis	(circus)
pOkit	(pocket)	dEHpiti	(deputy)
wAgin	(wagon)	sijist	(suggest)

hAAnis	(harness)
Animil	(animal)
fAHinil	(final)

The unstressed "ow" endings are usually "UH" in rural New England, as in "fEHluh" (fellow) and "mEHdUH" (meadow). A modern character, living in a large city or in western New England should use "OH" as in "fOlOH" (follow).

When the General-American sound of "ER" is spelled "ar," "er," "ir," "or," "ur," or "yr" and is final or followed by a consonant in an unstressed syllable, the vowel sound may change to "UH" and the "r" should be dropped, as in "AHltUH" (altar), "mU:mUH" (murmur), "mAAtUH" (martyr), or "Aluhji" (allergy). However, when one of the above-mentioned combinations is followed by a vowel, the "UH" is dropped in favor of the sounded "r," as in "mU:mrin" (murmuring) and "shEHltrin" (sheltering).

The participle ending ("ing") which, in General-American is often unstressed or "UHn" should receive slightly more stress in the New England dialect, where it is commonly pronounced as "in" as in "diOOin" (doing), "pAHintin" (pointing), and "kAAtin" (carting).

DROPPED SYLLABLES

One of the most important elements in the New England dialect is the dropping of unstressed vowel sounds and syllables. It has made for such pronunciations as "kAlAYt" (calculate), "fAHinli" (finally), and "sEHp" (except).

It is almost possible to suggest that, whenever feasible, without making the word incomprehensible, the unstressed vowel or syllable be dropped completely. This could be applied both initially and medially.

Initially, for example, "UH" is often dropped in "bAoot" (about), "kAoont" (account), "twi:ks" (betwixt), "lAood" (allowed), "bi:liti" (ability),"kOmidAYt" (accommodate),"mU:riki:" (America), and "pAArintli" (apparently).

Medial "a" may also be dropped in an unstressed syllable, as in "jinli" (generally), "pti:kluh" (particular), and "yiOOzhuhl" (usual).

Initial "e" may be dropped in an unstressed syllable, as in "zAmin" (examine), "zAkli" (exactly), "fi:shint" (efficient), "stAblish" (establish), "skwAHiUH" (esquire), "tU:nil (eternal), "vAnjlis" (evangelist), and "skiOOz" (excuse).

Medial "e" may also be dropped in an unstressed syllable, as in "EHlfint" (elephant), "prAps" (perhaps), "i:ntris" (interest), "mEHmbUH" (remember), "sEHtri:" (etcetera), and "strAHbri" (strawberry).

Initial "i" is occasionally dropped when unstressed, as in "liOOminAYt" (illuminate), "mAjinAYshn" (imagination), "si:nOO-AYt" (insinuate). "stid" (instead).

Medial "i" is often dropped in an unstressed syllable, as in "drEHkli" (directly), "fU:ntchoo" (furniture), and "koorAHsti" (curiosity).

The "ile" ending is commonly stressed to "AHil," as in "hAWstAHil" (hostile), "fU:tAHil" (fertile), and "rEHptAHil" (reptile).

The "ine" ending becomes "AHin," especially among rural folk, as in "jinOO-AHin" (genuine) and "injAHin" (engine).

Initial "o" is often dropped in an unstressed syllable, as in "bli:j" (oblige), "fEHnd" (offend), "pOsm" (opossum), "pi:nyin" (opinion), and "pOHnint" (opponent).

Medial "o" is often dropped in unstressed syllables, as in "klEHk" (collect), "mEHmri" (memory), "pfEHsUH" (professor), "kAWmftibl" (comfortable), "plUi:t" (polite), "pli:smn" (policeman), "tmOrUH" (tomorrow), and "vli:shn" (volition).

Initial "u" is occasionally dropped, as in "li:siz" (Ulysses), and "brEHli" (umbrella).

Medial "u" is often dropped in unstressed syllables, as in "nAtril" (natural), "rEHptAYshn" (reputation), "pti:klUH" (particular), "kAlAYt" (calculate), "rEHglUH" (regular), "Akrit" (accurate), "Oklis" (occulist), "sprUi:z" (surprise), and "gAuhlis" (garrulous).

When "f," "k," "p," "s," or "t" comes before the dropped vowel, it would be impossible to pronounce them without sounding a slight puff of breath at the same time. This puff, however, should not be a full "UH" aspirate sound. It is merely a means of glide immediately to the next consonant sound, as in "ptEHk" (protect), "tmOrUH" (tomorrow), "sprUi:z" (surprise), and "knEHk" (connect).

The custom of dropping syllables is more noticeable when complete words are almost dropped, as in "wUdv" (would have), "s-hi:" (said he), "tAWTHuh" (the other), "AWn:i:th" (underneath), "twUHz" (it was), "zEHf" (as if), "twAWnt" (it wasn't), "twUuhnt" (it won't), "twUd" (it would), or "sUi:" (said I).

This makes for such phrases as:

> "twUuhn diOO tAHl."
> (It won't do at all.)

> "n zUi: wz sAYin"
> (and as I was saying)

> "gd i:vnin tyUH."
> (Good evening to you.)

Obviously, the dialect uses an overabundance of contractions. Practically all the contractions used in General-American colloquial speech can be used in the New England dialect except when the word is to be emphasized, as in "I **have** got it," instead of "I've got it," where the sense stress demands the complete word.

The word "of" (spelled "o" in eye-dialect) is frequently contracted to "uh" as in "mAWnth uh sAWndiz" (month of Sundays), "bAWntch uh grAYps" (bunch of grapes), and "lOt uh fAWn" (lot of fun). This is typical of the weak treatment given the word in General-American. But it is never so contracted if the following word is "a" or "an" as in "sni:p UHv UH gU:l" (snip of a girl) or "pi:s UHv UHn Orinj" (piece of an orange).

The following combinations may also be used: "AWnt" (on it), "i:nt" (in it), "kdv" (could have), "TH" (the), "AWnm" (on them), "sti:dUH" (instead of), "lUi:kzif" (like as if), "jEHvUH" (did you ever), and "ydv" (you would have). As in the last example, "ydv," it must be remembered that all three consonants are run together with as little of an aspirate "uh" separating them as is possible.

CONSONANT CHANGES

(Only the important consonant changes have been listed)

D — Final "d" is almost always dropped after "n" as in "lAn" (land).

Rural speech features a change from final "d" to "t" after "l" or "n," as in "hOHlt" (hold) or "spint" (spend).

When "d" is followed by the sound of long "u" (OO), it may change to "j" as in "jOOti" (duty) or "rijOOs" (reduce). The words "Indian" and "Indies" are commonly "i:njin" and "i:nji:z."

F — Medial "f" is often dropped from the word "AHtUH" (after) and from its compounds "AHtUHniOOn" (afternoon), "AHtUHwU:dz" (afterwards), and so so.

G — The New England hard "g" is usually pronounced from a more forward position in the mouth and is slightly palatalized. Ordinarily, in General-American this consonant is produced with the back portion of the tongue rising to touch the soft palate, the exact position depending on the quality of the vowel sound to follow (see Fig. 3). The New England "g," however, is produced with the tongue-palate connection considerably more to the front of the roof of the mouth (see Fig. 4). This results in the introduction of a slight glide "y" sound after "g," particularly in the speech of the old-time rural folk, when hard "g" comes before "AA," "A," or "U." This palatalized "g" will be written in our phonetics as

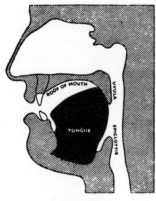

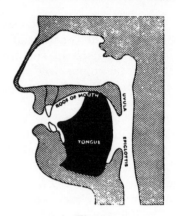

Fig. 3   Fig. 4

"gy," and it must be remembered that the "y" should be extremely light and serve only as a slight glide from the "g" to the following vowel sound, as in "gyAAdin" (garden), "gyAli" (galley), and "gyU:lz" (girls).

H — When "h" is initial and is followed by a "yOO" sound, it is often dropped, as in "yOOmin" (human), "yOOj" (huge), and "yOO" (Hugh). The "h" is often added to "ain't," making it "hAYnt."

K — This consonant, like hard "g," is palatalized (see Figures 3 and 4). It is produced from a more forward position in the mouth and adds a roughened "y" glide (see "G" above) when followed by "AA," "A," or "U:," as in "kyAAdz" (cards), "kyAt" (cat), and "kyU:l" (curl).

In such words as "AHst" (asked) and "vi:tlz" (victuals) the "k" is usually dropped.

L — When "l" is followed by "m," it may add an aspirate "uh" as in "EHluhm" (elm) or "fi:luhm" (film). An older character may also use this aspirated "l" in the word "gUluhp" (gulp).

The "l" is generally dropped in the words "AHrEHdi" (already), "wAAnit" (walnut), and "AHmUHs" (almost).

N — Words which end in the General-American "UHn" sound may change to "ing" in the New England dialect, as in "mAoonting" (mountain), "kU:ting" (curtain), and "kApting" (captain).

In rural speech, "chimney" is commonly pronounced as "tchi:mbli" and "cranberries" as "krAmbriz."

NG — The nasalized "ng" is generally dropped from a participial ending and replaced by a clearly pronounced "n," as in "pUdin" (pudding). This is especially frequent north of Boston and along the east coast.

The word "strength" and "length" may also be pronounced with a clear "n," as "strEHnth" and "lEHnth."

KW — The "kw" sound of "q" may drop the "w" as in" i:kUHl" (equal) and "trAngkil" (tranquil).

R — The typical New Englander, like the Southerner, is thought to drop all medial and final "r" sounds. This is not true in either case.

Initially, "r" is produced from a forward position in the mouth with the tongue tip pointing to the ridge behind the upper front teeth. This "r" is sharper and thinner than the General-American or Mountain "r."

When "r" is preceded by a vowel and followed by a consonant, it is usually dropped, as in "thU:ti" (thirty), "mAAtin" (Martin), or "lOHuhd" (lord). The vowel sound is slightly elongated to make up for the dropped "r."

Many old-fashioned New Englanders pronounce the prefix "pro" as though it were written "per," and in this way they avoid pronouncing the "r" as in "pU:vAHid" (provide) or "pU:diOOs" (produce). Western New Englanders sound the consonant as in "pUHrdiOOs" (produce).

When "r" is final in a word and is preceded by a pure vowel sound, it is usually dropped, as in "kAA" (car) and "sU:" (sir).

When "r" is final in a word and preceded by a diphthong, it is usually changed to "UH" as in "flAooUH" (flour) and "mOHuh" (more).

When "r" is final in a word and the following word begins with a vowel, a great many New Englanders pronounce the "r" lightly. It acts more as a glide than a full sound. However, for a real "down-East" New England dialect, this linking "r" should not be used, and the pronunciation of final "r" words should be as in "fOHuh AooUHz" (four hours) and "hU: AAm" (her arm).

Old-fashioned New England speech, and that of a great many modern New Englanders, features an excrescent "r" after a final, unstressed "UH" sound, as in "AHidi:UHr" (idea) and after a final "AH" sound as in "lAHr" (law). This excrescent "r" should be used only if the next word begins with a vowel, or if the "UH" or "AH" word is final, as in "THuh lAHr UHv THuh lAn" (the law of the land) and "TH AHidi:UHr UHv THAt AHidi:UHr" (the idea of that idea).

If the character to be portrayed had social aspirations and lived in the middle of the nineteenth century, particularly from 1840 to 1860, medial "r" between vowels may be dropped, as in "vEHi" (very), "kAAi" (carry), or "mAA-EEd" (married). This speech habit is sometimes used by modern eastern New Englanders, as in "pAAuhtrOOpUHz" (paratroopers).

People of western New England generally pronounce "r" initially, medially, and finally. Although some modern eastern New Englanders are gradually pronouncing preconsonantal "r's," inhabitants of certain districts—like Cape Ann, Martha's Vineyard, and Marblehead—are loathe to give in to the trend.

SH — Many down-Easters changed "sh" to "s" when it was followed by "r" as in "sri:k" (shriek) or "sri:l" (shrill). This was especially prevalent in Maine.

The word "rubbish" was, and is, commonly pronounced as "rAWbij."

T — If "t" is in an unstressed syllable and is preceded by the sound of "f," "k," "p," "n," or "s," it is often dropped, as in "zAkli" (exactly) or "kEHpn" (Captain). However, if "t" is followed by "er" or "ure," it is generally retained, as in "mAHstUH" (master) or "pAHstUH" (pasture).

Certain common words add "t" after "s," as in "UHkrOst" (across), or "wAHnst" (once).

TH — When in an unstressed adverb, conjunction, or pronoun, this voiced "TH" may be dropped, as in "tiOO UHvm" (two of them), or "mOHuhn hU: shAA" (more than her share).

V — A character who lived in the eighteenth or early nineteenth centuries may sound "w" for "v" as in "wi:tilz" (victuals), "wAAi" (very), or "wEHsil" (vessel). If used at all this variation should be retained especially for persons living in the coastal area, including Boston.

W — When unstressed, or part of the suffix "ward," the sound of "w" may be dropped, as in "THAoot" (without), "AHliz" (always), or "AHkUHd" (awkward).

WH — New Englanders, with the exception of many of the people of Boston and Cambridge, Massachusetts, commonly pronounce the initial "wh" sound as "w" as in "wEHn" (when) or "wAA" (where). People in Boston and Cambridge usually say "hwEHn" (when), and so forth.

GRAMMAR CHANGES

This section treats with the New England dialect spoken, in the main, by rural folk with little education. Their errors in grammar encompass practically the entire list of errors noted in the chapter on "The Common Speech." Naturally, the more educated the character, the fewer his errors.

In addition to the common errors listed previously, the New Englander is addicted to other verbal locutions that give flavor to the dialect speech. Many of these errors have been retained, and some of them were carried across the country by pioneers who migrated west and south.

New Englanders were especially partial to weak verb forms as in:

"UH nU::hd i: wUHz UH tchAWklhEHd!"
(I *knowed* he was a chucklehead!)
(I *knew* he was a dope!)

"kAWm AWp thi:k UHz bAAni klApUH."
(*Come* up thick as barney clapper.)
(The fog *came* up as thick as soured milk.)

Other weak verb forms will be found in the chapter **"The Common Speech."**

A characteristic and important error was the use of "be" in place of "am" or "are," as in:

"hAoo bi: yUH, wi:dUH stUuhn?"
(How *be* you, widow Stone?)
(How *are* you, widow Stone?)

"hi:z shAApUH n Ui: bi:."
(He's sharper than I *be.*)
(He's sharper than I *am.*)

"wi:l sEHt rUi:t wAA wi bi:."
(We'll set right where we *be.*)
(We'll sit right where we *are.*)

"dUuhnt si:m lUi:k THAY bi: tUH hUuhm."
(Don't seem like they *be* to home.)
(It doesn't seem as if they'*re* home.)

Although eastern New England seems to have used "be" generally in place of "am" or "are" and occasionally "is," many people in western New England reserved its use for dependent clauses only. Thus, while an eastern New Englander might say "I be a-goin," the western New Englander would say "I'm a-goin" or "I said I be a-goin."

In the negative, "aint" or "haint" was usually preferred, as in:

"THEHm ri:binz hAY/ yU:n, bi: THAY?"
(Them ribbons *hain't* yourn, be they?)
(Those ribbons *aren't* yours, are they?)

"EHf THAt AY/ THUH bi:tinis AHidi:!"
(If that *ain't* the beatenist idea!)
(If that *isn't* the most ridiculous idea!)

Lack of agreement between verb and subject was a common error, as in:

"wAAz THEHm bUuhts?"
(Where's them boats?)
(Where are those boats?)

The use of "twAW/," "twU:/," or "twAA/" for "it was not" or "it were not" is quite common in the dialect, as in:

"twAW/ nUH wAY uh diOOn i:t."
(*Twant* no way of doing it.)
(*That was* no way to do it.)

"twAW/ lUi:k jEHf tUH Akt AWp."
(*Twant* like Jeff to act up.)
(*It wasn't* like Jeff to misbehave.)

"Ui:d AdmAHuh tiOO fi: twAA/ fUH THuh rAYn."
(I'd admire to if *twant* for the rain.)
(I'd like to if *it weren't* for the rain.)

The use of "shUHd" (should) for "to" is generally favored after "want," as in:

"zi:k wAHnts yUH shUHd stOp kAAri:n AWn."
(Zeke wants you *should* stop carryin' on.)
(Zeke wants you *to* stop scolding.)

"hi wAHnts Ui: shUHd git THuh gAlisiz."
(He wants I *should* get the galluses.)
(He wants me *to* get the suspenders.)

"Ui: dUuhnt wAHnt yUH shUHd Ak sUH grAooti."
(I don't want you *should* act so grouty.)
(I don't want you *to* act so ill-tempered.)

The phrase "lUi:k tUH" (like to) is often substituted for "almost," as in:

"THuh pOHuh kri:tUH lUi:k tUH drAoondid."
(The poor creature *like to* drownded.)
(The poor fellow *almost* drowned.)

"hi lUi:k tUH bU:st iz bri:tchiz."
(He *like to* burst his britches.)
(He *almost* tore his breeches.)

When preceded by a query in indirect discourse, the dependent verb phrase "if I had" is often replaced by "did," as in:

"THAY AHst di:d UH si: im."
(They asked *did* I see him.)
(They asked *if I had* seen him.)

The substitution of "shouldn't wonder but what" in place of "I think" is common, as in:

"shUHdn wAWndUH bUHt wUt UH wi:l."
(*Shouldn't wonder but what* I will.)
(*I think* I will.)

"shUHdn wAWndUH bUHt wUt its flAWmidi:dl."
(*Shouldn't wonder but what* it's flummydiddle.)
(*I think* it's nonsense.)

Another common error substitutes "AWn" (on) for "of" in the phrases "of it" or "of them," as in:

"tiOO AWn UHmz nAWf fUH mi:."
(Two *on* 'em's 'nough for me.)
(Two *of* them are enough for me.)

"AY/ nEHvUH hi:UHd AWnt."
(Ain't never heerd *on*'t.)
(I haven't ever heard *of* it.)

Two numerals separated by "or" usually drop the "or," as in:

"tiOO thri: tAHimz UH kAlAYt."
(Two three times, I cal'late.)
(Two *or* three times, I guess.)

A distinctive habit in the New England dialect is the dropping of the pronoun subject when it is the initial word of the sentence, as in:

"tAHt skiOOl nUi: AWntUH tiOO yi:UH."
(Taught school nigh onto two year.)
(*I* taught school for almost two years.)

"lAAnd i:t rUi:t kwi:k tiOO."
(Learned it right quick, too.)
(*He* learned it quickly, too.)

There is also prevalent a reversal of certain phrases, as in:

"thi:ngks Ui: UHl hi:v tiOO."
(*Thinks I*, I'll heave to.)
(I'll heave to, *I thought*.)

"hAYn UHgUuhn sEHz Ui:."
(Hain't a-goin', *says I*.)
(I'm not going, *I said*.)

The substitution of "yUH" (you) for "yourself" is quite common, as in:

"git yUH UH lOHf UH brEHd."
(Git *you* a loaf of bread.)
(Get a loaf of bread for *yourself*.)

The verb "are" is often omitted after "wAAuh" (where), as in:

"wAA yUH gUuhn riOOf?"
(Where you goin', Rufe?)
(Where *are* you going, Rufus?)

The pronoun "yiOO" (you) is often introduced to give added emphasis, as in:

"THAts UH fAk yiOO!"
(That's a fact, *you!*)
(That's a fact!)

The use of the singular, in place of the plural, for quantitative words is common, as in:

"hi: drUuhv bAoot fOHuh mAHil dAoon."
(He drove about four *mile* down.)
(He drove about four *miles* down.)

"hAY/ bUHt AYti yi:UH UHgOn."
(Hain't but eighty *year* agone.)
(It was only eighty *years* ago.)

In a dependent clause, the adverb "ever" is placed before the subject, as in:

"THuh bi:tinis thi:ngimiji:g UHz EHvUH Ui: si:n."
(The beatenest thingamajig as *ever I* seen.)
(The most unusual thing *I ever* saw.)

Instead of using a definite negative remark, the New Englander is likely to temper the negative with the verb "seem," as in:

"kAHnt si:m tUH kAA."
(Can't *seem* to care.)
(I don't care.)

"kAHnt si:m tUH lUi:k i:m nOHhAoo."
(Can't *seem* to like him nohow.)
(I don't like him at all.)

The conjunction "unless" may be dropped in favor of "THAoot" (without), as in:

"Ui: wUuhnt gOH THAoot yiOO gOH tiOO."
(I won't go *'thout* you go too.)
(I won't go *unless* you go too.)

"dUuhnt sEHt AWp iTH mi: THAoot yUHd AdmAHuh tOH."
(Don't sit up with me *'thout* you'd admire to.)
(Don't court me *unless* you'd like to.)

TYPICAL WORDS AND PHRASES

Following is a list of some of the typical words and phrases that larded much of the New England conversation in the past. Many of these expressions are still heard, especially in rural areas.

"fAA gi:v mi: UH kini:pshin fi:t."
(*Fair* give me a conniption fit.)
(It *almost* made me wild.)

"hi: lAood UHz hAoo twU:/ rUi:t."
(He *'lowed* as how twant right.)
(He *thought* it wasn't right.)

"UH kAlAYt AWn kAWmin."
(I *ca'late* on comin'.)
(I *expect* to come.)

"mOHuhn Ui: kUHn tOHt UH fi:gUH."
(More'n I can *tote*, I *figure*.)
(It's more than I can *carry*, I *think*.)

"fEHl rUi:t plAWm i:ntUH TH bAAn."
(Fell *right plumb* into the barn.)
(It fell directly into the barn.)

"Ui: mAHin TH tAHim wi wint."
(I *mind* the time we went.)
(I *remember* the time we went.)

"kAAl fEHtcht TH dOg UH ki:k."
(Carl *fetched* the dog a kick.)
(Carl *gave* the dog a kick.)

"hi fEHtcht sAAri: AWp i:TH UHm."
(He *fetched* Sarah up with him.)
(He *brought* Sarah with him.)

"wOk AWp lOng UHv pAWpUH."
(Walk up *'long of* Puppa.)
(Walk up *with* Papa.)

"kAlAYt Ui:l wOK dAoon lOng tUH TH wAWf."
(Ca'late I'll walk down *along* to the wharf.)
(I think I'll walk down to the wharf.)

"Ui:l sEHt fUH: spEHl."
(I'll sit for a *spell*.)
(I'll sit for a *while*.)

"fi:tid hi:m rAYl prOpUH lUi:k."
(Fitted him *real proper* like.)
(It fit him *properly*.)

"hi:d li:vzUH i:t UHz wU:k."
(He'd *lievser* eat as work.)
(He'd *rather* eat than work.)

"twU: nUi: AWntUH fAHiv mAHil."
(Twere *nigh on to* five mile.)
(It was *nearly* five miles.)

"mEHbi THUH jEHj win tAWTHUH wAY."
(Maybe the judge went *t'other* way.)
(Maybe the judge went *the other* way.)

"UH bOdid bi: sAAtin tUH stAAv."
(A *body*'d be certain to starve.)
(A *person* would certainly starve.)

"AHiyi! liOOk di:d UH mAHstUH jOb."
(Ayah! Luke did a *master* job.)
(Yes! Luke did an *excellent* job.)

"hi: thEHngks UH mAHstUH sUi:t UH mAYri."
(He thinks a *master sight* of Mary.)
(He thinks a *great deal* of Mary.)

"THAY wUHz fAA si:li bAoot i:t."
(They was *fair* silly 'bout it.)
(They were *quite* silly about it.)

"hi: wUHz jEHs UHsEH/n kwUi:t lUi:k."
(He was just *a-settin' quiet-like*.)
(He was just *sitting quietly*.)

"lAHft sAYm UHz i:f i:t wUHz yiOOmin."
(Laughed *same as if* it was human.)
(It laughed *as though* it were human.)

"hi: dAWn i:t THAoot Ui:m mi:stUk."
(He done it *without* I'm mistook.)
(He did it, *unless* I'm mistaken.)

"di:dn AYm tUH tOHt i:t TH hUuhl wAY."
(Didn't *aim* to tote it the whole way.)
(I didn't *intend* to carry it the whole way.)

"i:t wUHz AHl lOng UH ji:mz wi:dUH wUmin."
(It was all *'long of* Jim's widow woman.)
(It was all *because of* Jim's widow.)

"lUkUH hi:UH! yiOO!"
(Look-a-here! you!)
(Look here! you!)

"hAY/ sOt Ui: AWn nAAri wAWn, AAri."
(Hain't *sot eye* on nary one, ary.)
(I haven't *seen* a single one, either.)

"hAYnt gOt nAAri nAWn."
(Hain't got *nary* none.)
(I haven't *any*.)

"hi:UHd tEHl hi dAAsn kAWm."
(Heerd tell he *dassn't* come.)
(I heard that he *didn't dare* come.)

"dUuhnt dAAs gOH THAoot Ui: tEHl grAnTHuh."
(Don't *dast* go without I tell gran'ther.)
(I don't *dare* go unless I tell grandfather.)

"kEHnt fUH TH lUi:f UH mi: AWnUHstAn."
(Can't *for the life of me* understand.)
(I can't understand it.)

"Ui:l thAngk yUH kAHinli tUH gOH."
(I'll *thank you kindly* to go.)
(Will you *please* get out.)

"hi:t plAWm smAkiti dAb i:ntUH i:t."
(Hit plumb *smackety-dab* into it.)
(I hit squarely into it.)

"kwi:k UHz EHvUH mUH di:nUH wUHz EHt."
(*Quick as* ever my dinner was et.)
(*As soon as* I ate my dinner.)

"bi:UHn UHz Ui:m hi:UH, lEHts gOH."
(*Being as* I'm here, let's go.)
(*Now that* I'm here, let's go.)

"kAHnt rUi:tli nOH fUH shUuh."
(Can't *rightly know* for sure.)
(I can't be sure.)

"hi: lEHt AWn i: wUHz AYlin."
(He *let on* he was ailin'.)
(He *pretended* he was ill.)

"drEHkli THAY kAWm AWp tUH AWs."
(*Directly*, they come up to us.)
(*Soon* they came up to us.)

"kAWm nEHks frAHidi Ui:l gOH."
(*Come* next Friday, I'll go.)
(**I'll go next Friday.**)

"bAk THi:s lEHtUH fUH grAmi, lAHij."
(*Back* this letter for grandma, Lige.)
(*Address* this letter for grandma, Lige.)

"gi:t AWfm THAt AAuh kri:tUH nAoo."
(Get off'm *that 'ere* critter now.)
(Get off *that* horse now.)

"hOHzi:zUH prOpUH fiOOl bAoot siOO."
(Hosea's *a proper fool about* Sue.)
(Hosea's *very fond* of Sue.)

"AAri wAWn uhl diOO."
(*Ary* one'll do.)
(*Either* one'll do.)

"wAWt i:n tAWngkit gAWt yUH sUH rAHilt AWp."
(What *in tunkit* got you so riled up.)
(What got you so angry.)

"THEHn AHl twAWnst shi AWp UHn dAHid."
(Then *all at oncet* she up and died.)
(Then, suddenly, she died.)

"Ui: gOt mi wAWn dAoon sEHluh."
(I got me one *down cellar.*)
(I have one *in the cellar.*)

"twAWnt nOH wAY UH diOOn UHt."
(*Twant* no way a-doing it.)
(*That wasn't* any way of doing it.)

"THEHts hi:zn UHn tAYnt yUuhn."
(That's *hisn* and it ain't *yourn.*)
(That's *his* and it isn't *yours.*)

"jAWn wUHz UH tAWlibl bi:g mAHn."
(John was a *tolerable* big man.)
(John was a *rather* big man.)

"jEHs tOlibl."
(Just tolerable.)
(**I'm pretty well.**)

EXCLAMATIONS

"bi: ji:gU:d!"	(Be jiggered!)
"bi: di:ngd!"	(Be dinged!)
"bi: blAood!"	(Be blowed!)
"wUi: yiOO!"	(Why, you!)
"Ui: swAAn!"	(I swan!)
"bUi: fAHiUH!"	(By fire!)
"ji: wi:dikUH!"	(Gee whittaker!)
"ji:hOsifAt!"	(Gehosephatt!)
"blOH mUH shU:t!"	(Blow my shirt!)
"wAAuh i:n tAWngkit!"	(Where in tunket!)
"wAWt i:n tAWngkit!"	(What in tunket!)
"hiOO i:n tAWngkit!"	(Who in tunket!)
"grAYshUHs EHvU:z!"	(Gracious evers!)
"nAWt bUi: UH jAWgfUl!"	(Not by a jugful!)
"gOdfri:!"	(Godfrey!)
"dAd blAYmdis!"	(Dad blamedest!)
"mUi: stAAz UHn bOdi!"	(My stars and body!)
"bUi: grAYshUHs!"	(By gracious!)
"shAH!"	(Pshaw!)
"wAWt i:n tAAnAYshUHn!"	(What in tarnation!)
"dUuhnt THAt bi:t AHl!"	(Don't that beat all!)
"ji:njUH!"	(Ginger!)
"tchAoodUH!"	(Chowder!)
"ji:riOOzilim kri:kits!"	(Jerusalem crickets!)

The following exclamations are used principally by women:

"lAH!"	(Lah!)
"lAn!"	(Land!)
"lAn sAYks!"	(Land sakes!)
"sAYks uhlAHiv!"	(Sakes alive!)

The exclamation "Ayah!" may be used to denote a number of different meanings. Like its modern General-American counterpart "yup," it can indicate doubt, agreement, interest, consent, or annoyance — depending on the inflection given it. It may be pronounced as "AHiyi/," "Ui:yi," "AAyi/," "AYuh/," or "EHuh/."

SIMILES

"UHz triOO UHz pri:tchin"
(as true as preaching)

"strAYt UHz UH gAWn bAAril"
(straight as a gun barrel)

"UHz THOH TH di:vil ki:kt i:m AWn i:nd"
(as though the devil kicked him on end)

"kiOOlz UH kAookAWmbUH"
(cool as a cucumber)

"sli:k UHz UH wi:sl"
(slick as a whistle)

"tchAWk tUH yUH vUi:tilz"
(chock to your vitals)

"di:fU:n UH kiOOt"
(deafer'n a coot)

"UHz mi:n UHz tU:ki bi:tUHz"
(as mean as turkey bitters)

"lUi:k AHl git Aoot"
(like all get out)

"li:k lUi:k UH ri:dl"
(leak like a riddle [sieve])

"tAWf UHz UH bAHilt Aool"
(tough as a boiled owl)

"fAHs UHz UH kAt i:n UH gAYl"
(fast as a cat in a gale)

"UHz bAd UHz AHl pUHzEHst"
(as bad as all possessed)

"brUi:t UHz UH bAWtin"
(bright as a button)

"krOs UHz sAm pAtch"
(cross as Sam Patch)

"i:zi gOHin UHz OHl ti:li"
(easygoing as old Tilly)

"gri:n lUi:k UH tchEHsi kAt"
(grin like a chessy [Cheshire] cat)

"hUuhmli UHz UH stUuhn fEHns"
(homely as a stone fence)

"mi:nUH n giOOs gri:s"
(meaner than goose grease)

"mOHuh AAuhz THuhn UH kAWntri stAWd hOs"
(more airs than a country studhorse)

"Od UHz di:ks hAtbAn"
(odd as Dick's hatband)

"pOHuh UHz jOHbz tU:ki"
(poor as Job's turkey)

"shAAp UHz UH mi:t Aks"
(sharp as a meat axe)

"slOHuh UHn stOk sti:l"
(slower than stock-still)

"sOf UHz mAWsh"
(soft as mush)

"sAooUH UHz swi:l"
(sour as swill)

"tAHl UHz UH bi:npOHl"
(tall as a beanpole)

"Ak lUi:k fUuhks"
(act like folks)

"bi:g UHz UH dAWtch AWvn"
(big as a Dutch oven)

"mAd UHz UH hOpUH"
(mad as a hopper)

"bi:g UHz AHl AootUH dOHuhz"
(big as all out-of-doors)

"UHz bliOO UHz kAAm wOtUH"
(as blue as calm water)

"krAYzi UHz UH liOOn"
(crazy as a loon)

"pAWfin lUi:k UH grAmpis"
(puffing like a grampus [whale])

"hApi UHz bi:n wOtUH"
(happy as bean-water)

"rUi:t UHz bi:n wOtUH"
(right as bean-water)

MONOLOGS

(From *Cap'n Bailey and the Widder Dyer** by Charles W. Burton)

My stars 'n' body! What a start you give me! Never supposed you'd get here ahead of me. Merry Christmas to you. Would of said it afore, only for you takin' the breath away from me. See ye got your stockin's hung up by the fireplace. Well, now, ain't that cute. A little doll same as there allus was when I was a little girl. 'N' here's some candy. Well, what on earth might this be down in the toe? That's where Grampa allus put a shiny new half-dollar. This is square, though. What is it? All done up nice. 'Tain't a joke, is it? Cap'n Zachariah U. Bailey! So that's what ye wanted with my old cameo ring! Ye wanted to match the size of it, you old flounder! Well, I could set right down and cry. All my days I've wanted a — a — Cap'n Zachariah Bailey! They must of given you the wrong ring. This one's an engagement ring. Well — now I *am* goin' to cry.

(From *Cap'n Bailey and the Widder Dyer** by Charles W. Burton)

One day in Gloucester's enough to tucker anybody out, now I'll tell ye. Spent nigh unto the hull blessed day tryin' to get somethin' to eat. I'n' Judge Burnside cal'lated on layin' in some rations. 'Bout the fust thing he thought of up thar in Gloucester was vittles. S'e, Bailey, a feller ought to be able to get a right good shore dinner up here where fish is so plentiful. Sye, dunno why not. S'e, wonder where's the best place to get a bite. Sye, I dunno. S'pose we do some inquirin', sye. Well, sir, fust I'd ask somebody, 'n' then Judge Burnside would, but seems like information's one thing them Gloucester folks ain't aimin' to give out. Ask any one on 'em where's a good eatin' place, 'n' all they'll say is, most any place. Fin'ly Judge Burnside cal'lates we might get further by askin' strangers, so he bore down on a fam'ly o' folks settin' in an autymobile. S'e, neighbor, we're spendin' the day in Gloucester. We'd like your advice on where to go for dinner, he says. Well, the feller drivin' the autymobile looked kind o' funny, 'n' he says well, if you're spendin' the day in Gloucester, ye might just as well eat in that place we just come outen. That's just what we did. Spent the day in Gloucester in that hotel waitin' to get served. We both ordered clam clowder 'n' baked lobster. Cal'lated we could eat the chowder while they was cookin' the lobster. 'Bout an hour after that Judge Burnside begun to fidget. 'Bout then a waitress sailed past with a decklo'd o' somethin'. Well, sir, next time that waitress hove in

* Reprinted with permission of Marshall Jones Company and Charles W. Burton sight, I hailed her. Sye, how about our clam chowder? Says she, what clam chowder? Sye that clam chowder we ordered when you was a little girl. Says she, clam chowder's all gone. How about some lobster stew, she says. Says she, will ye have coffee with your dinner or after? Sye, fetch in the coffee this afternoon; it keeps me awake if I drink it late at night. Long about three o'clock in the afternoon, what do ye s'pose she wanted to know? Wanted to know if we'd have coffee.

CHAPTER III

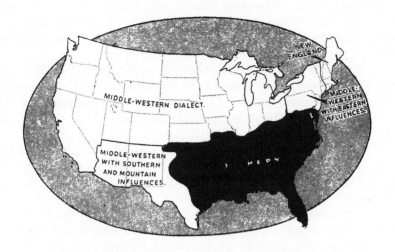

THE SOUTHERN DIALECT

ROUGHLY SPEAKING, there are three general dialects spoken in the South. These comprise what is commonly called the Southern dialect. Actors often erroneously use this hybrid speech for a character who lives anywhere in southern United States, thus making no distinction between lowland, mountain, or coastal areas. The three main dialect divisions of the South are as follows:

1. The general Southern dialect is spoken by approximately 30,000,000 persons in the southern low country, exclusive of the segregated mountain districts and of the Tidewater region. This includes the states of Maryland, West Virginia, Delaware (except the Delaware-Maryland-Virginia Peninsula and along the eastern coast to South Carolina), Kentucky, Tennessee, Alabama, Georgia, Florida, Louisiana, Arkansas, Missouri, Mississippi, southern Illinois, southern Ohio, southern Indiana, and Texas, excluding the southeast section.

2. The Mountain dialect is spoken in various sections of the Appalachian mountain range including the Great Smokies of Tennessee and North Carolina, the Blue Ridge Mountains of Virginia and West Virginia, the Cumberland Mountains of Kentucky and Tennessee, and in the Ozark Mountains of Arkansas and southern Missouri. These highland dialects are not necessarily spoken only by mountain dwellers. Infiltrations of the speech into the surrounding lowland sections have been made by migrants into adjoining and

sometimes distant sections, as, for example, into the flat lands of the Southwest; the cities Fort Worth and Dallas, Texas; the Piedmont area; the Delaware-Maryland-Virginia Peninsula; and even across water to the Chesapeake Bay islands. (See "The Mountain Dialect," page 148.)

3. The Tidewater dialect is spoken from the Delaware-Maryland-Virginia Peninsula down the eastern coast to South Carolina, with speakers to be found around Charlottesville and Richmond in Virginia and certain northern sections of the Shenandoah Valley. (See "The Tidewater Dialect," page 103.)

The above dialect divisions do not necessarily include the various Negro dialects spoken in the South. Certain Negro dialects on the order of the Gullah do vary widely from the general Southern. (See "The Negro Dialect," page 185.)

It can be seen that "a Southern dialect" is more — much more — than the actor has been led to believe. Radio, screen, and television actors should be especially cognizant of the regional dialects and should be fully capable of simulating them correctly. For their dialect interpretation is subject to criticism by listeners throughout the country, not merely — as in the theatre — by audiences in the city in which the play is performed. Certainly Southern gentlemen and their ladies would be startled to hear their counterparts on stage or screen drawl in the rhythm of Georgia crackers. They would be more than startled — they would probably be enraged.

The typical Southerner is inordinately proud of his Southern background and resents any attempts at Northern encroachments, particularly in regard to his pronunciation. Pride in his speech is reflected in his retention of it this long despite the fact that General-American Middle Western speech has influenced other dialect regions in the country, as New England, New York, and the West.

The Southerner has a traditionally long memory. Apochrypha has it that the deep South is still fighting the Civil War, or, as they prefer to call it, the War Between the States. From the viewpoint of a Northerner, the Southerner is easygoing and inclined to laziness. Yet, he can be violently active. He can erupt in a civil war just as the warm-blooded Spaniards, the revolution-loving Central and South Americans, and the pre-republic Mexicans. His unbalanced volatility is evidenced in his long-lived contumacy for the Negro and his envenomed hatred for the "damyankee" Northerner for having espoused the cause of a supposedly "inferior race sprung from the apes." He is often a fiery orator even when speaking to a friend about some minor cherished conviction. He resorts frequently to biblical phrases and incidents.

Customs die hard in the magnolia South. The "old families" are revered with almost monarchial awe. The wealthy Southerner prefers to live in a Colonial mansion that is reminiscent of his glorious past. The men of the old South were gentlemen with genteel manners who made of business a pleasure, in contrast with their Yankee compatriots who made of pleasure a business. In fact, the origin of "Southern hospitality" may be found in the curious social habits of the early Virginia planters who, according to W. E. Woodward, practically waited at the crossroads to waylay wearied travelers into weekends and fortnights of rest.

Finally, the men of the Old South were intense individualists. And in their willingness to grant that same privilege of individuality to others, they displayed traits of genuine friendship and helpfulness. On the whole, it may be said that Southerners are, at once, emotionally violent yet physically indolent, provincial yet worldly wise, educated but illogical, genteel yet barbarous.

The lower-class Southerner, however, presents another problem. The faults of his social superiors become magnified in him until they may become abnormalities. The representative "po' white trash" Southerner is traditionally shiftless. He is slow to thought and slow to speech but quick to violence. In his own words, he can be a "hell-raiser." Ordinarily, he is illiterate or, at best, inadequately educated. The rural folk of the submarginal lands, the tenant farmers, the millworkers, the "Tobacco Road" degenerates, all suffer from a kind of mass inertia. That they have remained so, from antebellum days, is not so much their fault as that of the prevailing caste system, an outmoded relic of the prebellum past to which much of the South remains steadfast.

Again the reader — particularly the actor — should be cautioned against portraying a "typical" character — Southern or otherwise. The characters may embody a few or many of the traditions and qualities mentioned in previous paragraphs, but he is, above all, an individual and should be interpreted as such.

LILT AND STRESS

From the foregoing it can be adduced why the speech of the Southerner is peculiarly representative of his character. The "upper-class" Southerner is proud of his speech and, therefore, more careful of his pronunciation. The "lower-class" Southerner, on the other hand, mirrors his indifference in his excessively drawled and slovenly speech, his elision of consonants, nasalization of vowels, and abundance of grammatical errors.

In all Southerners, though, speech is drawled, with lilt patterns gliding up and down the scale in musical cadences. The drawl is particularly noticeable at the end of a phrase or a sentence.

The voice levels, compared to those of the North, are more high pitched and nasalized, particularly among the less educated. There is a general tendency to speak from the forward part of the mouth.

The sentence "wEE di:n hEHv mUtch tAHuhm" (We didn't have much time) may be spoken with the following lilt:

tAH.

"wEE   mUtch   uhm"
         hEHv
     di:n

The final word "tAHuhm" (time) receives greatest stress, the highest note, and the drawl.

The tendency to speak slowly results in the stressing of words which are unstressed in General-American, as in "hEEz nAHt sOH: bAid" (he's not so bad) which may be spoken with the following lilt:

OH .

"hEEz   s   OH: .Aid"
        nAHt   bA.

In the above lilt the word "sOH:" (so) receives greatest stress and drawl, and "bAid" (bad) receives slightly less. Both words have greater stress than in General-American speech.

As seen in the above examples, the stressed word receives the greatest tonal variation. This must be produced without exaggeration or loudness.

There is a tendency to stress the initial syllable of a word, particularly a short word. This is especially noticeable in the lowlands near the mountain areas, and will be heard in such words as "gEEtAH:" (guitar), "sEEmEHuhnt" (cement), and "rEE:pAWuht" (report).

However, words ending with "ary," "ery," or "ory" usually take primary stress on the next-to-the-last syllable as in "sEH:krUHtEH:iri" (secretary), "sEHimitEH:iri" (cemetery), and "AWditAW:ri" (auditory). Secondary stress is given to the initial syllable. This undue emphasis on the next-to-the-last syllable gives words of this type more lilt than in Middle Western speech where only the initial syllable receives moderate stress.

Another important element that contributes to the distinctive Southern lilt is nasalization. This quality is particularly noticeable in the production of "A" and "OW" and also before "m," "n," or "ng." It results from a tendency to hold the center of the tongue close to the hard palate so that nasalization naturally follows. This habit is also common among highlanders and, in a more modified degree, among the Irish people.

THE SOUTHERN DRAWL

In Southern speech a stressed word becomes drawled, and the drawled word becomes diphthongized. Even in rapid conversation the drawl is so obvious as to make it almost a badge of Southern speech. This does not mean that every word should receive this treatment. Actually, the greatest amount of drawl and diphthongization is heard before a pause or at the end of a sentence although it is also a natural result of stress. Thus, the sentence "AH thAWwUHt AH koo:wUHd" (I thought I could) may be spoken with the words "thought" and "could" receiving stress and drawl. The final word, "could," however, has the greater stress, inflection, and drawl since it occurs before a pause.

The Southern drawl can be achieved in a number of ways.

1. The diphthongized vowel sound should be given its full treatment, particularly when stressed.
2. Certain vowels which are not normally diphthongized are followed by a glide vowel sound when drawled:

Vowel	adds	as in
"A"	"yUH"	"glA:iyUHs" (glass)
"AW"	"wUH"	"thAW:wUHt" (thought)
"EH"	"yUH"	"hwEH:iyUH" (where)
"i"	"yUH"	"THi:yUHs" (this)
"OO"	"wUH"	"mOOwUHn" (moon)
"oo"	"wUH"	"shoowUHd" (should)

The intrusive "w" and "y" sounds in the above drawl glides should not be given a full treatment. They must be light and almost inaudible.

3. Initial consonants should be produced with slightly more force than in General-American speech. This tends to slow up the speech by producing a slight aspirate after the consonant sound.

The aspirate must result naturally from the more forceful production of the consonant and must never be introduced as an independent vowel sound.

The drawl is directly responsible for many of the variant vowel sounds heard not only in the same section of the country, but in the same city, and even by the same person. The drawl produces so many shadings of one sound that it is impossible to list them all, but the important and typical variations are discussed in the following sections.

VOWEL CHANGES

"AY" .... as in "take," "break," "they," etc.

Ordinarily, this long "a" (AY) is pronounced as it is in General-American. But when this sound is stressed and final in a word, or in a stressed word of a sentence it is elongated to "AY:." This elongation is also commonly used before "k," "n," and "t," even when the word does not receive sense stress.

DRILL WORDS

tAY:k	(take)	nAYbUH	(neighbor)	AY:nt	(ain't)
brAY:k	(break)	tUHdAY:	(today)	lAY:t	(late)
THAY:	(they)	plAYst	(placed)	grAYd	(grade)

VARIATION: The variant "EH" may also be used particularly for a character from Alabama, North Carolina, the Shenandoah Valley, or Tennessee, as in "fEHth" (faith), "grEHt" (great), or "pEHtriUHt" (patriot). It is produced from a more forward position in the mouth than the General-American "EH."

Many speakers who use "AY" retain the variant "EH" for certain common words, as in "grEH:t" (great), "snEH:k" (snake), "plEHg" (plague), and "nEH:kid" (naked).

EXCEPTIONS: When the General-American "AY" sound is final and unstressed, it is pronounced as "i" as in "sERndi" (Sunday). The word "drain" is commonly pronounced as "drEEn."

"UH" .... as in "alone," "final," "sofa," etc.

Initially, this sound may be pronounced as in General-American, as in "UHbAoot" (about). However, some Southerners use the variant "AY" as in "AYgiUHnst" (against). The "UH" is preferred.

Medially, however, it is commonly changed to "i" in an unaccented syllable, as in "sERtin" (certain). In careless speech, it is often dropped as in "fAH:nl" (final). For a further discussion of this unstressed vowel sound see the section on **"Dropped Syllables."**

Finally, it should remain as in General-American, that is "UH" as in "sOHfUH" (sofa). However, if the character lives in a rural community, particularly near one of the mountain areas, he may use the variant "i" as in "sOHdi" (soda).

The article "UH" (a) is frequently pronounced as "AY" in formal speech, as in "fAWuh AY nAWminEE" (for a nominee).

Many actors erroneously add an intrusive "r" after "UH" as in "AH:diUHr" instead of "AH:diUH" (idea). See "R" under **"Consonant Changes."**

This "UH" may be added to many other vowel sounds and is an important factor of the "Southern drawl" (page 65).

DRILL WORDS

UHlOH-OOn	(alone)	kERtin	(curtain)
lAYzinis	(laziness)	biznis	(business)
dEHluhwEHuh	(Delaware)	kUluh	(color)

nAHlij	(knowledge)
gAH:din	(garden)
tchAHnUH	(China)

EXCEPTION: Many Southerners pronounce "always" as "AW-OOlwAYz."

"AH" .... as in "tar," "start," "park," etc.

Southerners generally give this "a" the same sound as in General-American. However, when the vowel is followed by "r" plus a final consonant, the "r" is replaced by a glide "uh" as in "pAHuhk" (park).

If the vowel sound is followed by "r" plus one or more syllables, the "r" is dropped, and the vowel is merely elongated, as in "stAH:tid" (started). This is also true if the vowel is followed by final "r" as in "kAH:" (car).

DRILL WORDS

dAHuhk	(dark)	kAHuht	(cart)
mAH:buhl	(marble)	stAHuht	(start)
dAH:luhn	(darling)	pAH:tnUH	(partner)

tAH:	(tar)
jAH:	(jar)
bAH:	(bar)

VARIATION: The variant "AW" may be used, especially for a character from Alabama, Arkansas, Louisiana, Mississippi, the Shenandoah Valley, southern Ohio and backwoods Florida — the Florida "cracker," as in "AWmi" (army).

"AH" .... as in "alms," "palm," "psalm," etc.

This sound generally remains the same, except that it adds

the "uh" glide, as in "AHuhmz," (alms), "pAHuhmz" (palms), or "sAHuhm" (psalm).

A great many Southerners, especially elderly people or those with little formal education, use the variant "A" as in "kAuhm" (calm), "bAuhm" (balm), or "kwAuhm" (qualm).

"A:" .... as in "ask," "draft," "aunt," etc.

This much-mooted vowel sound generally occurs before "f," "m," "n," or "s" plus a consonant; before "gh" when it has the sound of "f" (as in "laugh"); and before the "th" of "path." The Southerner ordinarily pronounces this vowel sound as "A:" which is the "A" of "bad" elongated. However, it is usually of slightly longer duration and, when drawled, adds an "i" glide, as in "pA:is" (pass), or "fA:istUH" (faster). This "A:i" usually has a distinct nasal quality.

DRILL WORDS

A:ist	(ask)	bA:iskit	(basket)
drA:ift	(draft)	pA:istchUH	(pasture)
A:int	(aunt)	lA:iftUH	(laughter)

kA:if	(calf)
sA:impl	(sample)
bA:ith	(bath)

VARIATION: Some Southerners use "A-EE" as in "hA-EEF" (half) or "pA-EEst" (past).

EXCEPTION: The word "can't" is commonly pronounced as "kAYnt."

"A" .... as in "bad," "narrow," "pal," etc.

The Southerner generally pronounces this vowel sound as "Ai" as in "bAid" (bad). When stressed, the first element "A" receives the emphasis. It has a distinct nasal quality, particularly before "m" or "n."

When drawled before "l," the sound "Ayuh" is used, as in "payuhl" (pal).

Words spelled "arrow" are usually pronounced with "A" as in "nArUH" (narrow), although older rural or historical characters may use "AH" as in "nAHrUH" (narrow).

kAit	(cat)	AyuhlbERt	(Albert)
pAitch	(patch)	spArUH	(sparrow)
lAind	(land)	frAijil	(fragile)

mAin	(man)
sAyuhl	(Sal)
hAit	(hat)

VARIATIONS: The variation "AH" may be used for a character from east-central Alabama, west-central Georgia, or rural Florida, as in "mAHn" (man).

The variation "A-EE" may also be used, particularly for a character from the deep South, as in "A-EEd" (add) and "hA-EEt" (hat).

NOTE: The contractions "AHm" (I'm) and "mAH" ('mI) are frequently heard in sentences, as in "mAH gOHuhn" ('m I going?) and "AHm gOHuhn" (I'm going).

"AW" .... as in "all," "off," "saw," etc.

This is one of the protean sounds in the South. It receives various pronunciations depending on its spelling, stress, and position in a sentence. Individual variants, however, are not confined to particular sections, nor even to a particular class of Southerner. The General-American "AW" has a sturdy definite quality, but when mouthed by a Southerner, it is elusive and personal rather than standard.

For this reason it is impossible to list all the variations, together with their variants. But for the purpose of this book the following distinctions are valid and may be used in whole or in part for a Southern character.

The "AW" used by the Southerner is produced from a forward position in the mouth and often has a slight "OH" flavor. When final in a word, or stressed, this "AW" sound is commonly elongated and diphthongized to "AW-OH." The first element, "AW," receives the emphasis while the "OH" serves as a light glide.

The use of "AW-OH" is particularly noticeable when the vowel sound is spelled with two letters, as in "thAW-OHt" (thought), "sAW-OHs" (source), and "sAW-OH" (saw).

When an "AW" sound is followed by "l," it is usually elongated and diphthongized to "AW-OO," as in "kAW-OOl" (call).

DRILL WORDS

dAW-OHg	(dog)	lAW-OH	(law)
kAW-OHfi	(coffee)	drAW-OH	(draw)
sAW-OHf	(soft)	drAW-OOl	(drawl)

AW-OOltUH	(alter)
bAW-OHstin	(Boston)
rAW-OHngli	(wrongly)

VARIATION: Some Southerners use the single "AW" sound, as in "AWf" (off) and "dAWg" (dog.)

EXCEPTION: The variant "Ai" is commonly used for words in which "AW" is spelled "au" as in "sAis" (sauce), "sAisi" (saucy), "hAint" (haunt), and "gAint" (gaunt). This variant should be used especially for a character of elementary education.

"AW" . . . . as in "more," "door," "pour," etc.

When the General-American "AW" sound is spelled with "o" and is followed by final "r" or by "r" plus a consonant, the vowel is pronounced as "AWuh," and the "r" is dropped, as in "mAWuh" (more), "bAWuhn" (born), and "fAWuht" (fort).

When "AW" is spelled with two letters, as "oa," "oo," or "ou," it generally has a decided "OH" quality and will be represented as "OHuh." The following "r" is dropped, as in "kOHuhs" (coarse), "flOHuh" (floor), and "kOHuhs" (course).

The words "morning" and "mourning" aptly illustrate these variant pronunciations, since the former is commonly pronounced as "mAWuhnUHn" and the latter as "mOHuhnUHn."

DRILL WORDS

fOHuh	(four)	pOHuh	(pour)
kAWuhd	(cord)	AWuhdUH	(order)
shAWuht	(short)	fAWuhm	(form)

dOHuh	(door)
sUHpAWuht	(support)
rEEpAWuht	(report)

VARIATION: The glide "uh" is often dropped in careless speech, especially by Southerners with little formal education as in "fOHtEEn" (fourteen) and "kAWn" (corn).

"AW" . . . . as in "forest," "moral," "horrid," etc.

When the General-American "AW" is followed by the sound of "r" plus a vowel, it is generally pronounced as "AH" as in "fAHrist" (forest), "mAHrUHl" (moral), "hAHrid" (horrid), and so on.

"EE" . . . . as in "he," "treat," "greedy," etc.

In a stressed syllable or word, this "EE" remains the same, as in "mEEzUHlz" (measles) or in the sentence "thrEEz UH krAood" (three's a crowd). The "EE" is of slightly longer duration before the sound of "tch" as in "prEE:tchUH" (preacher).

This vowel sound generally adds an "uh" glide before "l" particularly in short words, as in "fEEuhl" (feel) or "mEEuhl" (meal).

In an unstressed position, this long "e" usually is treated as a short "i" as in "dipEHnz" (depends) or "wiuhl shi dOO UHt" (will she do it?). This change to "i" also applies to final unstressed "y" which is pronounced as "EE" in General-American speech, as in "grEEdi" (greedy), "hEHvi" (heavy), or "AH:ti:uhlri" (artillery).

DRILL WORDS

fEElin	(feeling)	rEE:tch	(reach)
iniwAuh	(anywhere)	pEEpuhl	(people)
nEEtli	(neatly)	nEEdi	(needy)

bilEEv	(believe)
pEEuhl	(peal)
spEEdi	(speedy)

EXCEPTIONS: The words "either" and "neither" are generally pronounced as "EETHuh" and "nEETHuh."

The words "breeches" and "creek" are usually pronounced as "britchiz" and "krik."

The article "the" is usually pronounced as "THuh" even before an initial vowel word, as in "THuh Aipl" (the apple), "THuh UTHuh" (the other), or "THuh swEH:ng shi:UHft" (the swing shift).

NOTE: Many Southerners accent the prefix of a word, and in such cases the unstressed vowel sound becomes stressed, as in "dEEsEEv" (deceive) or "rEEpAWuht" (report). (See the section on "Lilt and Stress," page 63.)

"EH" .... as in "egg," "head," "said," etc.

There are several variations for this "EH" sound. For a modern character of good education, it is suggested that "EH" be used, as in "EHvri" (every), "EHg" (egg), or "hEHd" (head). When stressed, this sound is generally elongated to "EH:" as in "sEH:d" (said) or "brEH:d" (bread). When followed by "l," this sound usually adds an "uh" glide, as in "tEHuhl" (tell), "spEHuhl" (spell), or "mEHuhlt" (melt). The "uh" glide is particularly noticeable in short words when the sound of "l" is final or followed by a consonant. Thus, such words as "fEH:luh" (fellow) or "jEH:lis" (jealous) may use an elongated vowel sound rather than the "uh" glide.

DRILL WORDS

lEH:stUH	(Lester)	mEH:luh	(mellow)
EH:kstrUH	(extra)	shEHuhl	(shell)
vEH:trinz	(veterans)	plEH:zhUH	(pleasure)

rEH:st	(rest)
pEH:ski	(pesky)
iEH:li	(jelly)

VARIATIONS: The variant "AY:" may be used for an historical character or an elderly modern person, particularly one who lives in a rural community and has had little or no formal education. It is particularly common if the vowel sound is spelled "ea" or if it is followed by the consonant sound "d," "g," "k," "t," "j," or "sh" in a monosyllable, as in the following examples:

DRILL WORDS

mAY:zhUH	(measure)	nAY:k	(neck)
drAY:d	(dread)	frAY:t	(fret)
AY:g	(egg)	AY:j	(edge)

frAY:sh	(fresh)
lAY:g	(leg)
hAY:d	(head)

Although some Southerners, other than those listed in the above categories, use the "AY:" variant, it is not as common as it once was.

Some Southerners use the variant "i" in certain common words, particularly when the vowel sound is followed by "s" or "t" as in "tchist" (chest), "yit" (yet), "yistidi" (yesterday), or "git" (get).

EXCEPTION: The word "deaf" is frequently pronounced as "dEEf."

"EH" .... as in "friend," "sense," "temper," etc.

The most typical pronunciation for the short "e" (EH) sound before a nasal consonant is "i" as in "UHtimt" (attempt) and "mini" (many). When followed by "n" plus "d," "s," or "t," the vowel sound usually takes an "UH" glide, as in "fiUHnts" (fence) and "biUHnt" (bent). This "i" variant may be tensed to "i:" (see below).

When this short "e" (EH) sound is followed by the consonant sound "ntch," it is frequently pronounced as "i:" as in "bi:ntch" (bench) and "fri:ntch" (French). The symbol "i:" indicates a sound between "EE" and "i." It may be produced by holding the tongue in the tensed position for "EE" and pronouncing "i." The full, tense quality of "EE" should not be used. When stressed, this vowel sound usually takes an "i" glide, as in "dri:intch" (drench).

The above vowel variants for "EH" should have a distinct nasal quality. This nasalization will also facilitate the correct pronunciation of "i:."

DRILL WORDS

timpUH	(temper)	tri:intch	(trench)
jinrUHl	(general)	siUHnts	(sense)
tiUHndUH	(tender)	trimbl	(tremble)

limin	(lemon)
iUHnd	(end)
siUHnts	(cents)

VARIATION: Some Southerners use a nasalized "EH" which takes an "uh" glide when stressed or drawled, as in "mEHuhn" (men) or "sEHuhntri" (sentry). Because of its fronted nasalized production, "EH" sometimes has a slight "AY" quality.

"EH" . . . . as in "there," "bear," "Sarah," etc.

When "EH" is followed by "r," it is commonly pronounced as "A" in the South. Since the "r" is dropped, this "A" is further elongated into "Auh."

DRILL WORDS

THAuh	(there)	hwAuh	(where)	hAuh	(hair)
bAuh	(bear)	stAuh	(stare)	mAuh	(mare)
tchAuh	(chair)	fAuh	(fair)	tAuh	(tear)

VARIATIONS: This "A" is sometimes produced from a higher, more forward position in the mouth so that it becomes "AAuh" as in "bAAuh" (bear). (See page 30.)

For an historical character, or a modern character with little or no formal education, the variant "i:UH" should be used in such words as "ki:UH" (care), "tchi:UH" (chair), and "shi:IH" (share) and their derivatives.

EXCEPTION: The word "area" is commonly pronounced as "AYri:UH" in the deep South, but "Ari:UH" in the more northerly South.

"I" . . . . as in "time," "aisle," "fry," etc.

Almost always a faint diphthongal glide follows the Southern "AH" (for long "I") which is not a full "i" and will be designated here as "uh" so that the complete sound is generally "AHuh," as in "tAHuhp" (type). This light "uh" glide is especially noticeable when long "I" precedes a voiceless consonant — "f," "k," "p," "s," "t," or "th."

DRILL WORDS

lAHuhf	(life)	AHuhs	(ice)
lAHuhk	(like)	nAHuht	(night)
pAHuhp	(pipe)	pAHuhthUHn	(python)

nAHuhf	(knife)
sAHuht	(sight)
rAHuhp	(ripe)

It must be remembered that the "uh" glide is very light. When long "I" is stressed and before the above-mentioned consonants, it becomes "AH:uh" as in "spAH:uht" (spite).

Before a voiced consonant — "b," "d," "g," "j," "v," "z," or "TH" — the "uh" glide is dropped, as in "wAHz" (wise), "tAHgUH" (tiger), "rAHd" (ride), and "AHvi" (ivy). Under stress, this sound is elongated to "AH:" as in "lAH:j" (Lige) and "sAH:TH" (scythe).

When long "I" precedes "k," "m," or "n," the single element "AH" may be used when the word is unstressed, as in "tAHm" (time) or "fAHn" (fine). When stressed, however, the "uh" glide is added, as in "mAHuhl" (mile) or "nAHuhn" (nine).

When long "I" is final in a word, it is treated as "AH" as in "AH" (I), "mAH" (my), and "trAH" (try). Under stress it is elongated into "AH:" as in "frAH:" (fry) or "spAH:" (spy).

A point to remember is that the lips should be spread wider in pronouncing the Southern "AH" than when pronouncing General-American "I."

"I" . . . . as in "wire," "tired," "liar," etc.

When long "I" is followed by "r," it is generally pronounced as "AH:" and the "r" is dropped, as in "wAH:" (wire). When the "I" is stressed, the "uh" glide is added and the word becomes "wAH:uh" (wire). If the word is unduly drawled, a linking "y" connects the two elements, as in "wAH:yuh" (wire).

DRILL WORDS

tAH:d	(tired)	hAH:	(higher)	prAH:	(prior)
lAH:	(liar)	mAH:	(mire)	dAH:	(dire)
fAH:	(fire)	bAH:	(buyer)	ritAH:	(retire)

VARIATION: Although the above sound is preferred, a variant is "AW:" as in "tAW:d" (tired), "fAW:" (fire), and "wAW:" (wire).

"i" . . . . as in "it," "busy," "since," etc.

This short "i" is generally intensified to "i:" except when it occurs before a nasal consonant. This "i:" is more forward and constricted than General-American "i," but it does not quite approach the quality of "EE." When stressed, it becomes "i:UH" as in "li:UHv" (live), "THi:UHs" (this), "bi:UHzi" (busy), and "sti:UHtch" (stitch).

There are many variations for short "i" before the sound of "n" or "ng" so that the following rules must be considered as general and not specific. Although a number of Southerners retain "i:" in all their short "i" words, others use the following pronunciations.

WHEN SHORT "i" IS FOLLOWED BY THE SOUNDS "ntch," "ng-g," or "ng-k," IT IS INTENSIFIED TO A NASALIZED "i:."

DRILL WORDS

pi:ntch	(pinch)	i:ntch	(inch)
si:ng-gl	(single)	fi:ng-gUH	(finger)
ti:ng-kUH	(tinker)	spri:ng-kl	(sprinkle)

li:ntch	(lynch)
li:ng-gUH	(linger)
li:ng-k	(link)

IN A MONOSYLLABIC WORD, "ing" IS COMMONLY PRONOUNCED AS A NASALIZED "EH:ng" AS IN "thEH:ng" (*thing*).

DRILL WORDS

strEH:ng	(string)	brEH:ng	(bring)
sEH:ng	(sing)	klEH:ng	(cling)
stEH:ng	(sting)	kEH:ng	(king)

stEH:ng	(sting)
rEH:ng	(wring)
wEH:ng	(wing)

WHEN SHORT "i" IS FOLLOWED BY "n" PLUS ANY OTHER CONSONANT SOUND, IT IS COMMONLY PRONOUNCED AS A NASALIZED "EH:."

DRILL WORDS

sEH:nts	(since)	hEH:ndUH	(hinder)
rEH:ntch	(rinse)	EH:nsAHd	(inside)
prEH:nts	(prince)	pEH:ndUH	(pinder)

sEH:nsiUH	(sincere)
EH:ntris	(interest)
splEH:ntUH	(splinter)

Because this "EH:" sound is tensed and produced from an extremely forward position in the mouth, it sometimes takes on an "AY" flavor, as in "thAYng" (thing) and "rAYn̦tch" (rinse).

VARIATIONS: Some people, particularly from east-central Alabama, west-central Georgia, or the lowland area of the Smoky Mountains, use the variant "EH:" for "i" before "ntch," "ng-g," or "ng-k," as in "rEH:ng-kl" (wrinkle) or "klEH:ntch" (clinch).

The variant "A:" is also common, particularly among people with little formal education, as in "thA:ng" (thing) and "brA:ng" (bring). It has been observed particularly in Oklahoma although it is frequently used in other sections of the South.

NOTE: The participial ending "ing" is generally treated as "UHn," as in "sEH:ngUHn" (singing).

"i" .... as in "here," "clear," "cheer," etc.

When short "i" is followed by "r," it becomes "iUH" and the "r" is dropped, as in "hiUH" (here), "kliUH" (clear), and "tchiUH" (cheer).

Some Southerners tense "i" to "i:" particularly in words of two or more syllables, as in "kli:UHli" (clearly), "dri:UHri" (dreary), and "tchi:UHfl" (cheerful).

When drawled, the two elements may add a linking "y" as in "fiyUH" (fear) or "ti:yUH" (tear).

VARIATION: The variant "EHuh" is also commonly used, as in "nEHuh" (near) and "stEHuh" (steer).

"OH" .... as in "bone," "sew," "dough," etc.

When this long "o" sound is stressed, it is pronounced as in General-American with both elements of the diphthong ("OH-OO") present, but of course tenser and more forward in the mouth. This stressed "o" will be designated as "OH:."

When not unduly stressed in a word this vowel sound is almost a pure "OH" without the "OO" glide, and it will be designated here as "OH."

DRILL WORDS

sOH:jUH	(soldier)	hOH:tEHl	(hotel)
lOH:li	(lowly)	grOH:pUHn	(groping)
brOH:k	(broke)	slOH:li	(slowly)

sOH:bUH	(sober)
rOH:stUHn	(roasting)
hOH:pUHn	(hoping)

"O" .... as in "on," "bond," "Johnny," etc.

Either the General-American "O" (as in "bond") or "AH" (as in "fAHTHER" [father]) may be used for this vowel sound. In American speech these sounds are close to each other, and many people use them interchangeably. However, this sound will be designated as "AH" in this section.

DRILL WORDS

bAHnd	(bond)	prAHbli	(probably)
jAHni	(Johnny)	lAHbstUH	(lobster)
stAHp	(stop)	nAHmnEE	(nominee)

rAHbUH	(robber)
pAHkit	(pocket)
tAHni:k	(tonic)

VARIATIONS: A variant sound used by a great many Southerners is "AW," produced from a forward position in the mouth, as in "AWnis" (honest), "jAWni" (Johnny), and "bAWnd" (bond). This sound should not be as tense as the New York "AW."

For an older rural person, or an historical character, "drop," "crop," and "yonder" may be pronounced as "drA:p," "krA:p," and "yA:ndUH."

Many speakers in Alabama, Oklahoma, and the Shenandoah Valley, substitute "U" for "O," as in "bUm" (bomb), "stUp" (stop), and "pUkit" (pocket).

Many Southerners, especially from Alabama, intensify the "AW" variant for "O" to "OH" as in "OHn" (on).

NOTE: Generally, throughout the South, "on" is sounded as "AWn."

"OO" .... as in "food," "do," and "blue," etc.

Ordinarily, this sound is pronounced as in General-American. However,

WHEN SPELLED "eu," "ew," or "u" AND PRECEDED BY "d," "n," OR "t," "OO" is PRONOUNCED AS "iOO."

DRILL WORDS

niOO	(new)	ridiOOs	(reduce)
tiOOn	(tune)	stiOOpid	(stupid)
diOOti	(duty)	tiOOlip	(tulip)

stiOOdint	(student)
rEHzidiOO	(residue)
niOOmOH:ni	(pneumonia)

NOTE: A great many Southerners, however, often use an "iOO" substitute for "OO" when the word is spelled with letters other than those mentioned in the above rule, especially when the syllable is stressed or excessively drawled, as in "diOO" (do), "fiOOd" (food), and "giOObUH" (goober).

EXCEPTIONS: The words "broom," "room," "soon," "noon," and "hoof" may be pronounced either with "oo" or "OO." The word "coop," however, is almost always treated as "koop" in the South.

Plantation speech often pronounces "to" as "tOH:" when it is stressed. The word "ewe" is frequently "yOH:".

"oo" .... as in "good," "full," "soot," etc.

Generally, this sound may remain the same, except that the Southern "oo" has a tendency to be more fronted and tense than the General-American sound. It is usually diphthongized to "ooi" after "b," "k," or "p" and before "sh" as in "booish" (bush), "pooish" (push), and "kooishn" (cushion).

HOWEVER, WHEN THIS VOWEL SOUND IS PRECEDED AND FOLLOWED BY "f," "h," "k," "l," "p," "r," "s," OR "t," MANY SOUTHERNERS PRONOUNCE IT AS "U."

DRILL WORDS

pUt	(put)	fAWuhsUk	(forsook)	sUt	(soot)
rUt	(root)	fUlfi:l	(fulfill)	hUf	(hoof)
pUs	(puss)	pUlpit	(pulpit)	rUf	(roof)

This "U" variant is also produced from a more forward position in the mouth than the General-American "U." It is used principally, though not solely, by elderly people in the rural areas.

VARIATIONS: When "oo" is in an unstressed syllable and follows "d," "n," or "t," it may add a "y" glide as in "dyoorAY:shn" (duration).

People in the Shenandoah Valley, Virginia, and West Virginia frequently use "OO" in words like "pOOsh" (push) and "bOOsh" (bush).

In certain common words "oo" before final "r" becomes "OHuh" as in "shOHuh" (sure), "pOHuh" (poor), "kyOHuh" (cure), and "pyOHuh" (pure), and their derivatives. In rapid speech, the "uh" is dropped, as in "shOH" (sure).

"yOO" .... as in "unit," "cube," "beauty," etc.

The Southern treatment of this "yOO" sound usually remains the same as in General-American. In considerably drawled speech, it often takes a light "i" glide as in "byiOOti" (beauty).

Unstressed "yOO" may be changed to "i:" as in "pAWpi:lAYshn" (population) or to "UH" as in "mUHni:pUHlAYt" (manipulate).

Final "yOO" is often pronounced as "UH" as in "stAitchUH" (statue) or "kAWnti:nUH" (continue).

"U" .... as in "up," "lunch," "brush," etc.

A number of variations are to be found in the Southerner's treatment of this "U" sound. It is usually produced from a forward position in the mouth which, with some speakers, makes "U" so fronted as to have a slight "ER" quality. This "ER" is the symbol for the sound of "er" in "her" with the "r" silent.

WHEN "U" IS FOLLOWED BY "m" OR "n," IT IS COMMONLY PRONOUNCED AS A SLIGHTLY NASALIZED "ER."

DRILL WORDS

lERntch	(lunch)	sERmthin	(something)
pERmp	(pump)	sERndi	(Sunday)
kERntri	(country)	hERng-gri	(hungry)

lERmpi	(lumpy)
hERnt	(hunt)
jERmp	(jump)

Some people pronounce this short "u" (U) sound followed by a nasal consonant as "UER" particularly when it is stressed, as in "kUERntri" (country). The "U" receives the emphasis and "ER" is used as a glide.

WHEN "U" IS FOLLOWED BY "f," "k," "st," "sk," OR "t," IT IS GENERALLY ELONGATED TO "Uuh".

DRILL WORDS

kUuhf	(cuff)	dUuhski	(dusky)	nUuhkl	(knuckle)
lUuhk	(luck)	nUuht	(nut)	krUuhs	(crust)
rUuhs	(rust)	rUuhf	(rough)	trUuhs	(trust)

However, when "U" is followed by "sh," it takes an "i" glide, as in "brUish" (brush).

Some Southerners, particularly those in rural communities or near the mountain areas, make the following change:

WHEN "U" IN A MONOSYLLABIC WORD IS BETWEEN ANY TWO OF THE CONSONANT SOUNDS "j," "sh," "tch," "s," OR "r"; OR BETWEEN ONE OF THESE CONSONANT SOUNDS AND "f," "t," OR "v," THE VOWEL MAY CHANGE TO "EH."

This is particularly true of common words like "jEHs" (just), "hEHsh" (hush), "tEHtch" (touch), and "shEHt" (shut). As previously mentioned, this use of "EH" should depend on the age, education, and environment of the character.

Before all other consonant sounds "U" may be pronounced as it is in General-American, except that it should be produced from a more forward position in the mouth. It will be designated as "U" as in "Up" (up), "lUvli" (lovely), or "dUzn" (doesn't).

VARIATION: When "U" is followed by "sh" in monosyllabic words and their derivatives, it may become "UHr" as in "mUHrsh" (mush), "krUHrsh" (crush) and "blUHrsh" (blush). This variant should be used particularly for a character from the more northerly South, the Shenandoah Valley, or from eastern West Virginia. This pronunciation is also common in the words "fUHrs" (fuss) and "mUHrtch" (much).

EXCEPTIONS: A great many Southerners pronounce the prefix "un" as "AHn" as in "AHntriOO" (untrue). If the character is from the Shenandoah Valley or eastern West Virginia, however, the variant "AWn" should be used, as in "AWnsEHf" (unsafe).

"ER" . . . . as in "person," "hurt," "earn," etc.

There are two important variants for this General-American "ER" sound as used by the Southerner: "Ui" and "ER."

The sound of "Ui" should be used particularly for a character from Louisiana, Mississippi, North Carolina, and Tennessee. The "U" and "i" blend together and should not be pronounced as separate sounds. Many people tense the short "i" to "i:" as in "pUi:sn" (person). The actor should be careful not to substitute the sound of "OI" as in "oil."

DRILL WORDS

hUit	(hurt)	nUis	(nurse)	sUiv	(serve)
Uin	(earn)	pUis	(purse)	nUiv	(nerve)
fUis	(first)	wUik	(work)	Uin	(earn)

When this sound is final in a word, the "i" glide should be dropped, as in "hU:" (her) stressed and "hUH" unstressed.

Although "Ui" may also be used for a character from Alabama, Georgia, or South Carolina, a variant pronunciation, particularly in these sections is "ERi" as in "shERit" (shirt), "skwERil" (squirrel), and "tERinUHp" (turnip). Some speakers tense the "i" to "i:" so that the sound becomes "ERi:" as in "lERi:k" (lurk). The "i" should be dropped when the sound is final in a word, as in "fER:" (fur).

The "ER" may be heard generally throughout the South, though it is not as common in the deep South as it is in the more northerly South. This "ER" is the sound of "er" in the General-American word "her" (hER) except that the "r" is silent. Thus, the Southerner using this variant would say "hER" (her). When stressed or drawled, this sound becomes "ER:."

DRILL WORDS

fERn	(fern)	fERnis	(furnace)	bERd	(bird)
bERn	(burn)	pERtchis	(purchase)	wERth	(worth)
lERn	(learn)	pERsn	(person)	shERk	(shirk)

VARIATIONS: The single element "U" has been observed in the speech of many people, especially those from Arkansas and Oklahoma, so that "work" is pronounced as "wUk," and so on.

Some Southerners pronounce "ER" with a slight "r" quality so that it almost approaches the General-American sound.

EXCEPTIONS: The following should be used particularly for a character from the rural South:

CERTAIN COMMON "ER" WORDS WHICH ARE SPELLED WITH "e" OR "ea" ARE PRONOUNCED WITH "AH."

Examples of this general rule are: "lAHn" (learn), "sAHv" (serve), and "sAHtch" (search).

CERTAIN COMMON "ER" WORDS WHICH ARE SPELLED WITH "i," "o" OR "u" BEFORE "rs" ARE PRONOUNCED WITH "U."

Examples of this general rule are: "fUs" (first), "kUs" (curse), and "wUs" (worst).

"OW" .... as in "out," "cow," "proud," etc.

There are many variations of this "OW" diphthong in the South, but they vary more with individual speakers than with particular regions. The two most common basic pronunciations are "AHoo" and "Aoo." Either is acceptable, but the actor must guard against extreme nasalization if the character is of the "upper class." The "Aoo" sound is preferred.

DRILL WORDS

nAoo	(now)	prAOOd	(proud)	pAooUH	(power)
Aoot	(out)	AooUH	(hour)	dAoon	(down)
kAoo	(cow)	fAoon	(found)	lAood	(loud)

VARIATIONS: For variations, see the sections on regional speech and **"The Mountain Dialect."**

"OI" .... as in "oil," "boy," "voice," etc.

The Southern dialect usually retains the first element of this diphthong, "AW," but replaces the final "EE" element with an "i" glide, as in "bAW:il" (boil). The "i" indicates the typical elongation.

DRILL WORDS

AW:il	(oil)	injAW:i	(enjoy)
bAW:i	(boy)	bAW:ilin	(boiling)
vAW:is	(voice)	jAW:inUH	(joiner)

hAW:idn	(hoyden)
nAW:iz	(noise)
spAW:il	(spoil)

VARIATIONS: A variant for a character from the Shenandoah area is "AWr" as in "bAWrlin" (boiling). The use of this excrescent "r" must not be overdone however.

In the deep South, particularly in Louisiana, the variant "ERi" may be used, as in "ERil" (oil) and "vERis" (voice).

Older characters in rural areas may use "AHi" in certain common words like "pAHizn" (poison), "hAHist" (hoist), and "spAHil" (spoil).

UNSTRESSED SYLLABLES

In the South the speech habit of slurring unstresssed vowels makes for the substitution of short "i" for the "uh" sound heard in General-American, as in "dAyuhlis" (Dallas), "bA:iskit" (basket) and "mAH:kit" (market).

When an unstressed final syllable ends with the consonant sound "d," "f," "j," "k," "m," "n," "s," "t," "sh," "v," or "z," the preceding vowel is frequently pronounced as "i" as in "bAuhlid" (ballad), "bi:skit" (biscuit), "bAY:lif" (bailiff), "AuhlmUHnik" (almanac), "kAibij" (cabbage), "rEH:lish" (relish), and "rAHbin" (robin).

The unstressed "ow" endings of words are usually pronounced, in the South as "UH" as in "nArUH" (narrow), "fEH:luh" (fellow) and "pi:luh" (pillow).

When the final unstressed syllable ends in "om," the "o" is usually pronounced as "UH" as in "bAHtUHm" (bottom).

When the initial element of a final unstressed syllable is "t," and the final element is "n," the syllable is usually treated as "/n" as in "kAH/n" (cotton), "sER/n" (certain) and "kUi/n" (curtain). The "/" is the symbol for the glottal stop. In the above words it must not be as obvious as it is in the Scottish dialect. It should retain its usual General-American sound. (See "THE GLOTTAL STOP," page 24.)

When the initial element of a final unstressed syllable is "d" and the final element is "n," both the glottal stop and the sound of "d" are used. The "d," however, does not get its full sound. It is produced a fraction of an instant after the glottal stop, and it blends into the sound of "n," as in "blEE/dn" (bleeding). Here, too, the glottal stop must not be full and rich so that it pulls the "d" sound back into the throat. This "/dn" is a common sound in colloquial General-American speech and should give no difficulty to the average actor.

When the initial element of the final unstressed syllable is "s" or "z" and the final element is "n," the two sounds blend together as in "pAWizn" (poison) and "pERsn" (person).

When the participial ending "ing" is preceded by a vowel, the "g" is usually dropped and the "i" becomes "uh" as in "dOOuhn" (doing) and "sEE:uhn" (seeing).

After "r" the "ing" ending is often reduced to "n," as in "stER:n" (stirring) and "dAHktUHn" (doctoring).

When the "ing" ending follows a single "l," it drops the "g" and retains the "i" sound as in "bAY:lin" (bailing), "krA:iklin" (crackling), and "fi:dlin" (fiddling).

However, when the "ing" is preceded by a double "l," the "i" is pronounced as "uh" although the "g" is dropped, as in "kAW-OOluhn" (calling), "pUluhn" (pulling), and "fi:luhn" (filling).

When the "ing" ending is preceded by any other consonant (except "d," "l," "s," "t," and "z" which have been discussed above), the "g" is dropped and the "i" is changed to "UH" as in "stAHpUHn" (stopping), "li:vUHn" (living), and "kAW-OHfUHn" (coughing).

Words ending in unstressed "ian" usually treat this sound as "EEn" as in "plEE:bEEn" (plebian).

The "ville" ending in names of cities is usually pronounced as "vuhl" as in "dA:invuhl" (Danville), "nAHksvuhl" (Knoxville), and "A:ishvuhl" (Ashville).

Medial unstressed "e" is often pronounced as "i:" as in "ini:miz" (enemies), "bini:fit" (benefit), and "wimi:n" (women). This tensed

short "i" (i:) is common in the South and may be heard in many
places where "i" has been recommended.

DROPPED SYLLABLES

The following suggestions are to be used particularly in the
speech delineation of the "lower-class" Southerner, although a great
many educated people of the "upper class" also drop syllables, especially in colloquial speech.

Medial "a" and "o" are often dropped before "l," "n," or "r"
in an unstressed syllable, as in "vi:grUHs" (vigorous), "i:gnUHnt"
(ignorant), "klER:mbUHS" (Columbus), "jinli" (generally),
"A:inthni" (Anthony), and "knfEHdrit" (confederate).

Medial "i" is often dropped as in "AW-OHfsUH" (officer),
"AH:sh" (Irish), "fAWuhnUH" (foreigner), and "mA:Hs" (Morris).

Medial "e" and "i" are often dropped before "l," "n," or "r,"
as in "EHntERs" (interest), "gAuhlri" (gallery), "bAitri" (battery), "fAimli" (family), "mAY/nUHns" (maintenance), and
"EEvnUHn" (evening).

Medial "ery" is often dropped from "EHvUHbAHdi" (every-
body), "EHvUHhwAuh" (everywhere), and "EHvUHthUHn"
(everything).

Medial "u" is often dropped as in "rEHigluh" (regular),
"Aikrit" (accurate), and "pUHti:kluh" (particular).

Initial mute "a" is often dropped as in "bAoot" (about),
"lAHuhm klAHk" (alarm clock), and "kAoon" (account).

An initial syllable that contains a weak vowel sound in General-
American, is occasionally dropped in the South, as in "tAY:dUH"
(potato), "skEEdUH" (mosquito), and "fEHdrit" (Confederate).
See above pronunciation for "Confederate" where the "o" in the
initial syllable is dropped and the "k" and "n" blend together.
An itinerant snake-oil peddler in Asheville, North Carolina, was
heard to say "kAWrnfEHdrUHt" with an intrusive "r."

An "a" pronounced as ("UH") is often prefixed to an initial
syllable, especially by the uneducated and mountain folk. This is
particularly true of verbs, as in "UHtEHilin" (a-telling),
"UHdOOuhn" (a-doing), and "UHwAY/n" (a-waiting).

REVERSED SYLLABLES

Uneducated Southern speech, in particular, also features certain syllabic reversals of which the change of "re" to "er" (ER) is
the most common, as in "AY:pERn" (apron), "tchi:ldERn" (children), and "AuhlfERd" (Alfred).

SUBSTITUTED SYLLABLES

Many Southerners, particularly those with little formal education, substitute "ER" for "ro" as in "pERtEHik" (protect), "pERdiOOs" (produce), and "mAHuhkERfOHn" (microphone).

Medial unstressed "pen" is sometimes dropped in favor of "/m" as in "kAH/mtUH" (carpenter), "kOH/mhAYgn" (Copenhagen), and "tER/mtAHm" (turpentine).

CONSONANT CHANGES

(Only the important changes are listed.)

D — When "d" is preceded by "n" and followed by "l" or the sound of "z," it is often dropped, as in "kA:inuhl" (candle) and "hA:inz" (hands).

When "d" follows "l" or "n," it is often dropped, particularly in a final position, as in "kOHl" (cold), "tchAHlish" (childish), and "lA:in" (land).

When sounded, "d" is often produced with slightly more force than in General-American. Thus "d" sometimes has the sound of "t" when final, as in "tOHlt" (told) and "lA:int" (land).

In words like "idiot" and "Indian," "d" is sometimes changed to "j" as in "i:jUHt" and "i:njUHn."

G — In General-American, hard "g" (as in "go") is pronounced with the back portion of the tongue rising to touch the forward part of the soft palate (see Figure 5) the contact point depending on the quality of the vowel sound to follow.

The typical Southern "g," however, is produced with the tongue-palate connection more toward the front of the mouth (see Figure 6). This often results in the introduction of a "y" glide sound or a sort of roughened "UH" after "g."

When "g" is followed by an "AH" sound, it takes the "y" glide as in "gyAH:d" (guard). This change, however, is confined mostly to the older people and should seldom be used for younger, more modern speech. It would be inadvisable to add this "y" to "g" before any other sound but "AH" in Tidewater Virginia or Charleston, South Carolina. But in many other portions of the South and in the Southwest as well, the "y" is often added before "i," "A," and "EH" sounds but not before "AH."

Final "g" is almost always dropped from the "ing" participial endings, particularly in coastal Virginia. See **"Unstressed Syllables"** for a detailed discussion of this elision.

Lower-class Southerners, in particular, usually drop the "g" in such words as "lEHinth" (length) and "strEHinth" (strength).

H — The Southern dialect features a dropping of initial "h" in such words as "ERmbuhl" (humble) and "yOOmUH" (humor); however, the modern tendency is toward the sounding of "h" in these words.

The word "herb" is pronounced as "yAH:b" particularly by older rural speakers.

The sound of "h" is commonly added to "OH:vUHhAW-OOlz" (overalls), but its use in "hit" (it) and "hAYnt" (ain't) is generally restricted to mountain or rural areas.

K — Like hard "g" this consonant sound is also produced from a more forward position in the mouth by many Southerners. (See

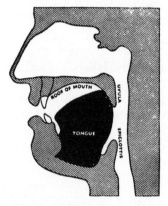
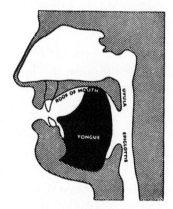

Fig. 5   Fig. 6

Figures 5 and 6.) The "y" glide may be used in such words as "kyAH:" (car), "kyAuh" (care), and "kyimistri" (chemistry). Many Southerners use the General-American "k" and "g," although there is a tendency to produce these sounds from a more fronted position.

Final "k" is often formed but not sounded fully in some sections of the South, particularly in Louisiana and Virginia.

L — When "l" is initial or between two vowels, the second of which is "uh," "i" or "EH," it is given a clear "l" (as in "lily") treatment. This clear "l" is different from the General-American sound in that it is a quick, tense flip of the tongue which lightly taps the forward part of the roof of the mouth, a fraction of an inch behind the upper front teeth.

People in the Delmarva area (Delaware, Maryland, Virginia) generally use a clear initial "l" although the dark "l" (as in "full") is common after "oo," "AW," and "AH."

When medial "l" is preceded by "EH," "A," or "i," and is immediately followed by a final consonant, the "l" is usually dropped in the Southern dialect and replaced by either "UH" or "oo," as in "fi:UHm" (film), "sEHoof" (self), and "hEHoop" (help).

Some Southerners drop "l" without using the "oo" or "UH" substitute, as in "sEHf" (self).

The dropped "l" is rarely heard in Delmarva speech, although it is frequent in the Tidewater area.

When final "l" is spelled "ll" after "EH," "A" or "i," the added "oo" sound may be used in place of "l" or in conjunction with "l" as in "yEHoo" or "yEHool" (yell).

The "l" is generally sounded in "AW:luhz" (always). This word may also be pronounced "AW:lwAYz." Some Southerners sound "l" in "sAyuhlmin" (salmon) and "sAyuhlv" (salve).

P — Initial "p" is often produced with slightly more force than in General-American.

Final "p" is sometimes sounded with such little force that although the lips are in position for "p" no sound is heard. This has been noticed particularly in Louisiana and Virginia.

R — It has always been a hard and fast rule among actors to drop all "r's" in the Southern dialect in the belief that this is a universal Southern habit. This practice persists in spite of the fact that a great many Southerners pronounce "r" in most positions, particularly inhabitants of the mountain districts, rural Florida, Kentucky, Tennessee, northern Alabama, western Virginia, the Delmarva area, the Shenandoah Valley, Arkansas, and western Texas.

A characteristic element of Delmarva speech is the pronunciation of "r" in all positions. In this area, "r" has more of its true quality than anywhere else in the South except the mountain and valley districts. But the Delmarva "r" does not approach the northern sound in tensity or duration, and it is not as fully sounded in a final position. Initially and medially, however, it is quite audible.

Some Southerners endow certain vowels with an "r" flavor. This has been noticed particularly in Oklahoma, northeastern Texas, western Virginia, the Shenandoah Valley, West Virginia, mountain areas, and the Delmarva area. The intrusive "r" coloring is usually limited to the "AW" sound, as in "AWuhrt" (ought) and "bAWuhrl" (boil).

Since the pronunciation or "r" is one of the characteristics of the Southern dialect, it is important that the following suggestions be observed:

When "r" is the initial letter in a word, it is pronounced as in General-American, although when stressed it is often of slightly longer duration.

When medial "r" is between vowels, it is usually pronounced, as in "vEHri" (very), "stAWri" (story), and "kAri" (carry). However, some Southerners, particularly in eastern Virginia and among less-educated people drop the "r" between vowels so that the words are pronounced as "vEH:i" (very), "stOH:i" (story), and "kA:i" (carry).

Before a consonant, "r" is generally silent, as in "snAWuht" (snort), "shER:t" (shirt), and "pAHti:shn" (partition).

A great many Southerners change "r" to an "uh" sound which is sometimes given an "r" coloring. This "uh" is also one of the elements that contributes to the Southern drawl, as in "pAHuhk" (park), "hAHuhd" (hard), and "fAWuhm" (form).

Many rural Southerners drop the "r" in "through" and "threw" and pronounce both words as "thOO" or "thiOO."

When an unaccented syllable is spelled with "ar," "er," "ir," "or," "ur," or "yr," it is often pronounced as "UH" as in "sUHdAHnik" (sardonic), "fuhlAWuhn" (forlorn), and "zEHfUH" (zephyr).

Final "r" is generally dropped when it is preceded by a pure vowel sound, and the vowel sound is prolonged to make up for the lost consonant, as in "mAW:" (more), "kAW:" (car), and "mi:" (mere).

Final "r" generally becomes "UH" when preceded by the diphthong "OW" (Aoo) as in "AooUH" (our).

The linking "r" before an initial vowel word should be used by a character who is careful of his speech in other respects. An example of this linking "r" is "mAW:rUHnmAW:" (more and more) in which the first "more" retains the "r" before the initial-vowel word "and," while the second "more" drops "r" since no vowel follows.

Many Southerners do not use this linking "r" and pronounce the above phrase as "mAW:UHnmAW:" (more and more). The linking "r" has been heard only occasionally in speakers from the Delmarva area or eastern Virginia.

Despite its use by many actors, the intrusive "r" after final "UH" as in "AH:diUHr" (idea) is not a common habit in the South and should not be used in delineating a Southern character. It is heard occasionally in the mountain areas.

S — In the South, with the exception of Louisiana, this consonant is not hissed as strongly as it is in General-American. Certain speakers, particularly those in Virginia, have a tendency to pronounce "s" with almost an "sh" quality.

The words "grease" and "greasy" are commonly pronounced with "z" in the South; and "Mrs." is "miziz" or in rapid speech "miz."

SH — When "sh" is followed by "r," it is sometimes sounded as "s" particularly in the Shenandoah Valley, West Virginia, eastern Virginia, and in the Tidewater area, as in "sril" (shrill) and "srimp" (shrimp).

Some Southerners, particularly in Virginia, give "sh" a slight "zh" coloring, as in "fAzhUHn" (fashion).

T — Initially, "t" is often produced with slightly more force than in General-American.

When medial "t" is between two consonants, the first of which is "k," "n," or "s," it is often dropped, particularly in informal speech, as in "Aiks" (acts), "twini" (twenty), and "tchEHsnUHt" (chestnut).

Medial double "t" is sometimes replaced by a light glottal stop, as in "gAH/n" (gotten), "si:/n" (sitting). (See page 83, also "The Glottal Stop," page 24.)

When double "t" is followed by "l," the tongue is in position for "t" but the "t" is not sounded, as in "rAi(t)lUH" (rattler).

When "t" is preceded by "s" and followed by "s," the "t" is dropped, as in "fi:s" (fists) and "rEHs" (rests). In words of this type, the final "s" is generally elongated.

Medial "t" between vowels often has the sound of "d" as in "lEHdUH" (letter) and "pAH:di" (party). This is also true when final "t" is followed by a vowel, as in "THAidUHwAY:" (that away) and "gidUHlAW-OHng" (get along).

Final "t" is often changed to "tch" when the next word begins with "h" or "y," as in "AootchiUH" (out here) and "lEHtchUH" (let you).

This change to "tch" is sometimes used when "t" is followed by long "u" pronounced as "yOO" in the South, as in "tchOOzdi" (Tuesday) and "tchOOn" (tune).

When final "t" is followed by an initial "d" word, the "t" is often dropped, as in "hwAH dAHi diOO" (what did I do).

Final "t" is often dropped after "f," "n," or "s" as in "sAW-OHf" (soft), "di:n" (didn't), an "wUis" (worst).

TH — This sound is often thickened, particularly by people in Louisiana, Virginia, and South Carolina, so that "this" is pronounced as "dTHi:s" (this). The tongue tip is placed behind instead of between the teeth. The word "with" is commonly sounded as "wi:th" rather than "wi:TH."

TCH — The final "tch" sound is sometimes pronounced as "j" as in "sA:inwi:j" (sandwich), "spi:nij" (spinach), and "AW-OHstrij" (ostrich).

V — In an unaccented position, final "v" is sometimes dropped, as in "fOH fAH tAHmz" (four, five times).

Older people, particularly those living along the coast, substitute "w" for "v" as in "wEHsl" (vessel) and "wA:i" (very).

W — In an unstressed syllable "w" is commonly dropped, as in "yERngERn" (young one) and "AW-OHkUHd" (awkward).

WH — Although some Southerners, particularly those in Virginia pronounce "wh" as "hw" as in "hwEHn," a great many, including a number of Virginians, drop the "h" and sound only "w" as in "wEHn" (when) and "wAHi" (why).

NG — Southerners generally pronounce a clear "n" rather than a nasalized "ng" in such words as "bAinkwEHt" (banquet), "hAinkUHtchi:f" (handkerchief), and "jAWnkwil" (jonquil).

The words "length" and "strength" are also commonly pronounced with "n" rather than "ng" as in "lEHnth" and "strEHnth."

Y — When a word begins with a vowel sound followed by "r" some Southerners, particularly elderly rural people, begin the word with a "y" sound, as in "yAHth" (earth).

GRAMMAR CHANGES

The average educated Southerner speaks with almost the same grammatical correctness as the average educated Northerner. Grammatical errors are universal rather than regional and vary according to the educational background of the speaker. See **"The Common Speech."**

Variants, however, are to be found in Southern speech, particularly in word usage. For example, Southerners may use the word "kAri" (carry) instead of "take" or "escort." The sentence, "kAri mi bAik tUH OH:l vUHji:ni:" (Carry me back to old Virginia) does not mean that the speaker expects to be actually carried. Nor does the sentence "kAri THi:s hyUH hAWuhs hOH:m" (Carry this here horse home) imply that the person is to hold the horse in his arms. It means, rather that the person will lead the horse home. Naturally, many Southerners use the word "take" and "lead" and so forth.

Also common among Southerners is superfluous use of the adverbs "here" and "there," as in:

"THi:s hyUH mAinz gOH:uhn."
(This **here** man's going.)
(This man's going.)

"THAit THA:uh gUi:lz mAHuhn."
(That **there** girl's mine.)
(That girl's mine.)

The indefinite article "an" is often replaced by "a" in the speech of many Southerners, as in:

"i:n UH AooUH."
(in *a* hour)
(in *an* hour)

An intrusive "for" is sometimes used after verbs showing desire and before an infinitive, as in:

"AH dOHn intin fUH hER dUH gOH:."
(I don't intend *for* her to go.)
(I don't want her to go.)

An expression indigenous to the entire South is the much-used and abused "yOO AW-OOl" (you-all), flaunted by many actors as an identifying Southern badge. It must be remembered that, in the main, the use of "you-all" is confined strictly to the plural. Actors who sieze on this expression as the *ne plus ultra* of the Southern dialect are advised to refrain from saying "THAits UH pERdi drEHs yOO AW-OOl AH wAuhn" (That's a pretty dress you-all are wearing.)

Although the expression may be directed to one person, the sentence should imply plurality. Thus, a speaker may say to a friend, "yOO AW-OOl sEE hUib yistidi" (you-all see Herb yesterday?) if the query is intended to include the friend and his family or the friend and other members of his household. That is why the simple greeting, "hA yAW-OOl" (how you-all?) usually provokes a recital of the health of the entire family.

The phrase may be pronounced with three different inflections, each with a super-fine distinction of meaning. When the "yOO" (you) is accented, as in "*yOO*-AW-OOl mUuhs kERm" (you-all must come), the implication is that the group of people gathered before the speaker are invited. When the "AW-OOl" (all), however is accented, as in "yOO *AW-OOl* mUuhs kERm," the implication is that everyone present, without exception, is invited. The contraction "yAW-OOl" (y'all) is used in the simple plural sense, as in "trAH if yAW-OOl kUHn kERm" (try if y'all can come).

Some Southerners, particularly those in the Ozark region and in rural Texas, do use this expression with almost as much freedom as the uninformed actor, but generally, throughout the South, its use should be restricted to include two or more persons.

Some Southerners have also been heard to say "AW-OOl UH yUH" (all of you) and even "AW-OOl UH yiOO-AW-OOl" (all of you-all). (Refer back to "AW" as in "all" for the correct pronunciation of "AW-OO.")

The substitution of "like to" for "almost" is as common all over the South as it was in Victorian Ireland to where its origin can be traced.

"AH lAHuhk tUH brOH:k mUH bAik."
(I *like to* broke my back.)
(I *almost* broke my back.)

There is a common supposition that the Southerner substitutes "they" for "there" as in "THAYz nOH tAHuhm" (there's no time). Actually, this is simply a matter of pronunciation. In the South, "there" is usually pronounced as "THAuh" but in rapid speech it may sometimes be mistaken for "THAYuh" (there) because the vowel sound receives a forward production and often a nasal quality. Some Southerners do say "THAY" (there) but these are generally older speakers living in the mountain areas.

In the same way, the weak form of "have" is commonly pronounced "UHv" and promulgates the erroneous supposition that "of" is substituted for "have," as in:

"kUHd mAHuhk UHv bAWild it"
(Could Mark have boiled it.)

This "UHv" is sometimes further reduced to "UH" as in:

"hi shUHd UH thAW-OHt."
(He should have thought.)

Instead of saying one "might be able to" do something, a common substitute is "might could" as in:

"AH mAHuht kUHd hEHuhp yUH."
(I *might could* help you.)
(I *might be able* to help you.)

"AH mAHuht kUHd wERk fAW yUH."
(I *might could* work for you.)
(I *might be able* to work for you.)

The most prevalent grammatical error is the misuse of verb forms, as in:

"wi hAiz plinti tAHuhm."
(We *has* plenty time.)
(We *have* plenty of time.)

"AH nOH:z rAHuht wEHyoo."
(I *knows* right well.)
(I *know* right well.)

The use of "study" for "think" is common in the South, particularly in the low country near the mountains, as in:

"gAWdUH stUdi AWn i:t fERis."
(Gotta *study* on it first.)
(I've got to *think* about it first.)

"AHm stUdi:n AWn diOOuhn it."
'I'm *studying* on doing it.)
(I'm *thinking* of doing it.)

The use of "none" for "at all," a form of double negative, is heard, as in:

"shUHdn hERit yUH nU-ERn."
(Shouldn't hurt you *none.*)
(Shouldn't hurt you *at all.*)

Other double negatives are common, as in:

"di:dn nOHbAHdi gOH:."
(*Didn't nobody* go.)
(Nobody went.)

"AY/ gAH/ nOH kAW-OOl bAW-OOlin mEE Aoot."
(*Ain't* got *no* call bawling me out.)
(He has no reason for bawling me out.)

"AH dOH nEHvUH gOH:."
(I *don't never* go.)
(I never go.)

The "but what" expression is frequent in the South, as in:

"AH dUHnOH bUHt wUHt AHl EEt sERm."
(I don't know *but what* I'll eat some.)
(I think I'll eat some.)

The substitution of "but" for "only" has also been observed, as in:

"AYn gAH/bUHt thUidi sAYnts."
(Ain't *got but* thirty cents.)
(I have *only* thirty cents.)

The use of "how come" for "why" is also prevalent, as in:

"hAkERm yUH AY/ nEHvUH grOHd kAW:uhn?"
(*How come* you ain't never growed corn?)
(*Why* haven't you ever grown corn?)

Emphasis is often made with the use of the word "sure," as in:

"AHd shOH hAY: tUH stAY hyUH."
(I'd *sure* hate to stay here.)
(I'd *certainly* hate to stay here.)

Instead of "very," Southerners are prone to use "right" as in:

"THAi/ wUHz rAHuht nAHuhs UH ji:m."
(That was *right* nice of Jim.)
(That was *very* nice of Jim.)

"i:ts rAHuht pERdi."
(It's *right* pretty.)
'It's *very* pretty.)

The expression "a right smart" is commonly used instead of "a great deal," as in:

"AH gAWdUH rAHuht smAHuht UH wERik."
(I got *a right smart* of work.)
(I have *a great deal* of work.)

"THAits UH rAHuht smAHuht UH mERni."
(That's *a right smart* of money.)
(That's *a great deal* of money.)

"THA:uhzUH rAHuht smAHuht UH rAY:n."
(There was *a right smart* of rain.)
(There was *a great deal* of rain.)

The phrase "a piece" is commonly used in place of "a way," as in:

"AH li:v UH li:dUHl pi:s Up THuh rOH:d"
(I live a little *piece* up the road.)
(I live a little *way* [distance] up the road.)

The expressions "that-a-way" (that way) and "this-a-way" (this way) are heard frequently throughout the South, as in:

"hi: wint THAidUHwAY:."
(He went *that-a-way*.)
(He went *that way*.)

"nEHvUH kUHd dOO it THAidUHwAY:."
(Never could do it *that-a-way*.)
(Never could do it *that way*.)

The word "powerful" is often used instead of "very." It is used in much the same way as the British "tremendously":

"THAi/ wUHz pAoofUHl gUd."
(That was *powerful* good.)
(That was *very* good.)

"i:ts UH pAoofUHl bi:g fi:sh."
(It's a *powerful* big fish.)
(It's a *very* big fish.)

The phrase "a power" may be used in the same way as "a right smart" or "a heap," but "a power" seems to indicate a tremendous or "powerful" amount. "A heap" seems to imply a slightly smaller quantity which, however, if put into a "heap" would be impressive. The phrase "a right smart" seems to indicate a shrewd amount — not too large, nor too small. The phrase "a smidgen" is the least amount, little more than a smudge.

Using these four expressions, an example sentence would be: "hi hAid UH pAooUH UH mERni UHn EEvin THOH hi giv UH hEEp AWn it UHwAY: hEE sti:ool hAid UH rAHuht smAHuht UH kAish ti:oo hEE dAH:d UHn THin THAuh wUHzn bUHd UH smi:jin lEH:f."

In regular spelling this sentence is: "He had a power of money, and even though he give a heap on it away he still had a right smart of cash till he died and then there wasn't but a smidgen left."

Another similar phrase is "a mess" used particularly in reference to food, as in:

"shi jEHs kUkt Up UH mEH:s UH brAY:d."
(She just cooked up *a mess* of bread.)
(She just cooked *a . lot* of bread.)

"mi:z brAoon shOHuh hAiz UH mEH:s UH diOOfERni:z."
(Mrs. Brown sure has *a mess* of dofunnies.)
(Mrs. Brown certainly has *a lot* of knick-knacks.)

In a sentence with two verbs, the second is often changed into an infinitive by the addition of "to" as in:

"AHl hAiv bAWb tUH gidi/ fAW yUH."
(I'll have Bob *to* get it for you.)
(I'll have Bob get it for you.)

"hi mAYd UHs AW-OOl tUH rAHuht Aoo nAY:mz."
(He made us all *to* write our names.)
(He made us all write our names.)

The use of the reflexive pronoun is common, as in:

"gAWdUH git mEE UH jAW:b."
(Gotta *get me* a job.)
(I have to *get* a job.)

The substitution of "to" for "at" is frequent, as in:

"AH wERik tUH jAWnz plEHis."
(I work *to* John's place.)
(I work *at* John's.)

The word "however" is sometimes used in place of "no matter how" as in:

"hAooEHvUH yUH dUuhz shEE dOHn lAHuhk i:t."
(*However* you does, she don't like it.)
(*No matter how* you do it, she doesn't like it.)

In expressing certainty, the phrase "for sure" is often used, as in:

"AHm gOHn bi mArid sERndi fUH shooUH."
(I'm going [*to*] be married Sunday *for sure*.)
(I'm going to be married Sunday!)

Heard frequently in Southern speech is the contraction "off'n" (off from) in place of "from" as in:

"AH tUk i:t AWfn im."
(I took it *off'n* him.)
(I took it *from* him.)

The contraction "out'n" for "out cf" is also used, as in:

"tAYk it Aoo/n THuh bAWks."
(Take it *out'n* the box.)
(Take it *out of* the box.)

An old favorite among Southerners is "nigh" or "nigh on to" instead of "almost" as in:

"i:ts nAHi AWntUH sERndAoon."
(It's *nigh on to* sundown.)
(It's *almost* sunset.)

"i:ts mAHuh/ nAHi AW-OOl bERind Aoot."
(It's *mighty nigh* all burned out.)
(It's *almost* all burned out.)

In the above example "mighty" is an intensive and the phrase "mighty nigh" means "very nearly." "Mighty" is also used in:

"THAits mAHuhdi nAHuhs AWn yUH."
(That's *mighty* nice on you.)
(That's *very* nice of you.)

"yUH mAHuhdi shAoo/n rAHuht AH wi:oo."
(You're *mighty shouting right* I will.)
(I *certainly* will.) or (You're *darned right* I will.)

Common to many Southerners is the use of "fixing" for "preparing," as in:

"AHm fi:ksn tUH gOH Aoot."
(I'm *fixing* to go out.)
(I'm *preparing* to go out.)

"AHm fi:ksn tUH diOO jEHs THAit!"
(I'm *fixing* to do just that!)
(I'm *preparing* to do just that!)

Rural Southerners, particularly, introduce the sound of "UH" (a) before present participles, as in:

"AHm UH gOHuhn hOH:m."
(I'm *a*-going home.)
(I'm going home.)

"mAW hi:UHd tAWm UHshAoo/n."
(Ma heard Tom *a*-shouting.)
(Ma heard Tom shouting.)

The words "briggety" and "feisty" are commonly heard. They both mean conceited, but the first infers a certain braggadocio and willfulness; while "feisty" usually implies an impulsive eagerness. Although the adjective "feisty" is heard particularly with reference to any small dog who acts with impudence beyond his size, it is also used toward people.

The word "briggety" is usually pronounced without the "r" (biggety) in the Southern lowlands away from the mountain areas.

"stAWp Aiktin sUH fAHisti!"
(Stop acting so feisty!)
(Stop acting like a smart-Alec!)

"hEEz shOHuh UH bi:gidi fEH:lUH."
(He's sure a biggety fellow.)
(He's certainly a show-off.)

Rural folk with little or no formal education use "done" for "have" or "has" as in:

"THAY dERn ki:oolt THuh li:l OH: fAHis dAW-OHg."
(They done killed the little old feist dog.)
(They've killed the little old doggy.)

"AH dERn tOH:l yUH tUH stAWp."
(I done told you to stop.)
(I've told you to stop.)

Another universal usage throughout the South is the reference to the time after twelve o'clock noon as "evening" rather than "afternoon" as it is in the Middle West.

The examples in this section should be used with discretion. Although some of the above changes have been used by educated Southerners, they should certainly not all be used. The actor, author, or director must have a complete picture of the character in mind so that the choice of words and grammatical correctness will be true to his family background, education, age, and so forth.

COMMON EXPRESSIONS

The following expressions are only a few of the most common. They may be used occasionally to salt up a line.

"hi:UHd tEHuhl UHz hAoo hi:d gAW-OHn."
(Heard tell as how he'd gone.)

"mUH hEHooth wUHz pOHli."
(My health was poorly.)

"AHv UH mAHuhn tUH gOH."
(I've a mind to go.)

"mUH yERngUHn tUk dAoon THuh fEEvUH."
(My youngun took down with the fever.)

"AH dOHn rAHuhtli nOH: hAoo lAW-OHng hEEz gAW-OHn."
(I don't rightly know how long he's been gone.)

"AHmOH lAW: i:m i:n kOHuht."
(I'm going to law him in court.)

"THAuhzUH pAH:zUHl UH min kEℝ:m."
(There was a parcel of men come.)

"hil stAin THAuh UH git ki:oot wU-Eℝn."
(He'll stand there or get killed, one [or the other].)

"i:t wUHz wEℝ:th UH sAHuht mOHuhn AH pAY:d."
(It was worth a sight more than I paid.)

"i:t wUHz brOH:k sAH gUHt shEHd UHv it."
(It was broke so I got shut [rid] of it.)

"lAW! hAoowi kA:id AWn tUH THuh hOH:dAoon."
(Law! how we carried on to the hoe-down.)

"AH mAHuhn THuh tAHuhm AH tUk si:k."
(I mind [remember] the time I took sick.)

"AH kAYn lAH AYtAWool."
(I can't lie a-tall.)

"THAis dAoon rAHuht kAHuhn UH yUH mAim."
(That's downright kind of you, ma'am.)

"AH AYms tUH gi/ mEE UH fAWuhm."
(I aims to get me a form.)

"li:sn Ai/ mi."
(Listen to me!)

"bUHt hEEz sUH AW-OOlfAH:d lAYzi."
(But he's so all-fired lazy!)

"AHm plEℝm bEEd Aoot."
(I'm plumb beat [tired] out.)

"EHvUH fOOool thEH:ng hApUHnz tUH mEE."
(Every fool thing happens to me.)

"AH gUHdUHm frAYish fUHm THuh stAWuh."
"I got them fresh from the store.)

"EHf shi krAHz pAY Eℝ nOH mAHuhn."
(If she cries, pay her no mind [attention].)

MONOLOGS

Why, looka you hyiah, Matty Briggs! yawls co'tin' a passel o'
trouble messin' 'round with no-count trash like Henny Davis. An'
ah hain' a-goin' t' stan' fo' it much longer, ah haint. Ah don't rightly
know what's took a-holt on y'. Why, eve'body knows he ain't never
had no gumption whatsoever. Folks say he ain't even fitten' t' roll
with a pig let alone go with honest people like y'awl. An' none o'
them hankers none t' be seen with him. I reckon they don't none o'
them has the gumption t' tell him off on account o' he's supposed t'
be a tough gangster. But don't git the idy ah'm afeered. Ah ain't
skeered o' none o' his kind. An' what's more, I'm a-gonna fight him
if'n hits necessary so's he don't git you mixed up with his dirty work.
You mah man! an' ah reckon the leas' ah kin do is see to it you stay
mah man — alive. Ah don't never hold with these po' li'l white-lilies
womenfolks what says t' let their men have they own fling a mite.
Ah got shed o' fellers like him oncet when they was after my brother
Willie. An' ah reckon ah kin do it again. 'specially fo' the man ah
love. An' ah do love y', Matty. Hain't nobody kin say ah don't.
Hain't nobody gonna take y' away f'm me — not even that lowdown, o'nry, scum o' the earth Henny Davis!

(From *The Great Big Doorstep** by E. P. O'Donnell)

Ahmo tell yall sm wunnerful nyews. Alla you good BYPU
baw-woys n girls listenin daown n Creepmo Counny. Ou ole friend
Miz Cholly Awmstid's rot (right) oucher (out here) on the platfawm.
Naow Ah thank (think) yall go (going to) rememba Miz Awmstid's
saw-woybean progum fum the fair at Jackson, an Miz Awmstid
wawnts us to say a lil in behalfa her saw-woybean progum befo we
git off the air. Creepmo Counny where some ou (our) most progressive
people lee-uv hadden sen in any saw-woybean pledges fofo (for four)
yeahs han runnin I understand. So folks Ahmo (I'm going to) talk
plain. No munkey bidness. We expeck all yall BYPU people daown
there to line up behind Miz Cholly. We wawnchalla (want you all
to) promise you go *taw-uk* saw-woybeans an *thank* (think) saw-
woybeans an *lee-uv* saw-woybeans n lessall heppum (help them) putt
this progum ova hundid per cent.

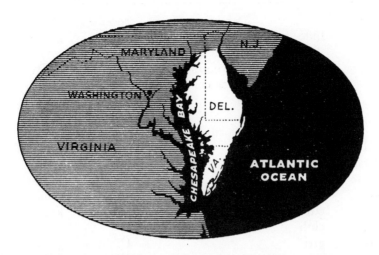

THE DELMARVA PENINSULA DIALECT

THE DELMARVA PENINSULA is made up of sections of Delaware, Maryland, and Virginia. The speech spoken here is also heard in many of the Chesapeake Islands off the Atlantic coast. It features a high pitch and a rapid tempo. Its most characteristic lilt pattern is a peculiar gallop of unequal rises and falls.

VOWEL CHANGES

Sound	as in	Pronounced	as in
AY	take	AY	tAYk
UH	alone	UH	UHlER-OOn
AH	father	AH	fAHTHEUhr
	farm (before "r")	AW	fAWrm
A:	ask	A:i	A:isk
	half (occasionally)	EH	hEHf
A	bat (stressed)	Ai	bAit
	crab (occasionally)	EH	krEHb
AW	dog	AW	dAWg
	more (before "r")	OHuh	mOHuhr
	small (before "l")	OHuh	smOHuhl
EE	three	EE	thrEE
	repeat (unstressed)	i	ripAY:t
	weak (spelled "ea")	AY:	wAY:k
	duty (spelled "y")	i	diOOti
EH	beg	EHi	bEHig
	fair (before final "r" or "r" plus a consonant)	ER	fER
	merit (before "r" plus a vowel)	U	mUrit

Sound	as in	Pronounced	as in
I	hide (before voiced and voiceless consonants)	AHi	hAHid
	sight (variant pronunciation before voiceless consonants)	ERi	sERit
i	miss	i:	mi:s
O	got	AH	gAHt
	on (only this word)	AW	AWn
OH	no	ER-OO	nER-OO
OO	do (unstressed)	OO	dOO
	do (stressed)	iOO	diOO
oo	took	oo	took
yOO	cute	yOO	kyOOt
U	club	U	klUb
ER	girl	U:	gU:l
	owner (final)	UHr	ER-OOnUHr
OW	now	Aoo	nAoo
	now	EHoo	nEHoo
OI	boy	AWi	bAWi
	boy (occasionally)	OHi	bOHi

The characteristic vowel changes in the Delmarva dialect are to be found in the pronunciations of "ER" for "EHr" as in "THER" (there) and in the substitution of a very fronted "ER-OO" for "OH" as in "spER-OOk" (spoke).

The "ER" symbol indicates the General-American pronunciation of the "er" of "hER" (her) except that there is no "r" sound, so that this word would be pronounced as "hER". This "ER" vowel sound, then, is suggested for the first element of the "I" and "OH" diphthongs. (See above.)

Application of the principles of drawl, syllabic elisions, and the treatment of unstressed syllables, etc. are to be made from the corresponding sections in the chapter on the general Southern dialect. For the consonant changes of an uneducated character, refer to the chapter on the Mountain dialect.

CONSONANT CHANGES

The most characteristic element in this dialect, as compared with general Southern, is its pronunciation of "r" in all positions. It should not be a tense "r" sound, however, particularly in a final position where the consonant is sounded lightly. Initially, and between vowels, the "r" should be quite audible. It should also be pronounced before a consonant. Linking "r" is not prevalent in this area and should be avoided.

Another characteristic change is the dropping of "h" in such words as "when" and "where" (wEHin, wER). The word "wharf," however, is commonly pronounced as "hwOHuhrf."

As in general Southern speech, "g" and "k" are frequently well fronted in the mouth, particularly by older people. Their treatment can be learned from the section under "G" and "K" in the consonant section of **"The Southern Dialect."**

The dropping of "l" heard so often in the South, as in "hEHoop" (help) is not a feature of Delmarva speech.

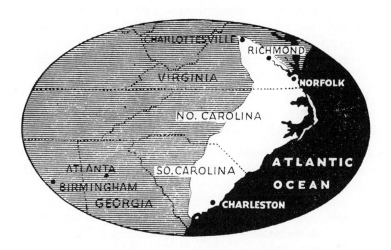

THE TIDEWATER DIALECT

THE TIDEWATER AREA includes southeastern Virginia, eastern North Carolina, and a little more than half of eastern coastal South Carolina. It follows the coast from slightly below Charleston, South Carolina, up to Norfolk, Virginia, where it slants upward to Charlottesville. Its western boundary is the Piedmont Arc, the foothills of the Appalachian Mountains.

The infiltrations of Mountain and General-American speech are to be found less in this area than in other sections of the South. This speech, particularly Virginia Tidewater, is more representative of the Southern dialect, as Northerners visualize it, than any of the other regional dialects.

The tendency to diphthongize vowels is less prevalent in the northern sections than in the southern sections. However, a vowel which is followed by a dropped "r" should be either elongated or followed by the "uh" glide, as in "fAH:" or "fAHuh" (far).

The speech is usually moderately pitched and has little nasalization. It is more evenly modulated than general Southern and has a pleasing, soft quality. There is usually a noticeable drawl before a pause, and initial syllables are frequently accented, as in "nER-OOvEHmbUH" (November).

VOWEL CHANGES

"AY" .... as in "make," "break," "they," etc.

Throughout the Tidewater area this long "a" (AY) sound may remain the same as in General-American. However, it must be remembered that a person who lives further south will have more of a drawled diphthongal quality in his pronunciation of "AY." This sometimes produces an "i" glide (AYi) noticed particularly before "g," "k," "l," and "n."

VARIATION: Many people in the Tidewater area use "EH" particularly before unvoiced consonant sounds, as in "fEHth" (faith), "pEH:tri:UHt" (patriot), and "shEHk" (shake).

EXCEPTIONS: The words "snake," "naked," and "great" are frequently pronounced as "snEHk," "nEHkid," and "grEHt."

"UH" .... as in "alone," "sofa," "final," etc.

Initially, medially, and finally this "UH" is usually treated as "UH." It is sometimes dropped initially, as in "bAoot" (about). See also **"Unstressed Syllables,"** page 82.)

"AH" .... as in "father," "arm," "calm," etc.

This "AH" may remain the same in production, but it is of slightly longer duration because of the dropped "r," as in fAHTHuh (father), AH:m (arm), and hAH:d (hard).

VARIATION: Many people, particularly in North Carolina, use "AA" as in "fAATHuh" (father), "hAAm" (harm), and "pAAt" (part). For the production of "AA," see page 30.

EXCEPTION: Words like "calm," "palm," and "balm" are commonly pronounced with "AA" as in "kAAm," "pAAm" and "bAAm."

"A:" .... as in "ask," "draft," "laugh," etc.

This sound may remain the same as in General-American. The "A" is as in "bad," and the (:) indicates elongation which, in General-American is "uh" but which becomes "i" in coastal speech. Thus, the Middle Westerner would say "Auhsk" while the person on the coast would say "Aisk" (ask) and "drAift" (draft).

VARIATION: The variant "AH" may also be used, but it should be reserved particularly for an older character.

"A" . . . . as in "bad," "am," "narrow," etc.

This vowel sound may remain the same except that it often takes an "i" glide when stressed, as in "bAid" (bad).

The variant "AH" is occasionally heard among elderly people, particularly in eastern Virginia, as in "hAHt" (hat).

When short "a" (A) is followed by double "r" (rr) plus a vowel, it is usually pronounced as "A" in the northern section as in "mAri" (marry) and "EHuh" in the southern section as in "mEHuhi" (marry).

"AW" . . . . as in "dog," "small," "long," etc.

For a modern character, the General-American "AW" may be used, as in "dAWg" (dog), "smAWl" (small), and "lAWng" (long).

However, many people in these areas use the variant "AH," particularly after "w" or before a nasal, as in "wAHsh" (wash), "wAHtUH" (water), "gAHn" (gone), and "lAHng" (long).

"AW" . . . . as in "forest," "four," "worn," etc.

When the General-American "AW" is followed by "r" or "rr" plus a vowel, this vowel sound is generally changed to "AH" by people in these coastal areas, as in "fAHrist" (forest), "AHrinj" (orange), "sAHri" (sorry), and "AHrijin" (origin).

When "AW" is followed by "r" final or plus a consonant, it is usually pronounced as "OHuh" as in "stOHuh" (store), "tOHuhn" (torn), "bOHuhn" (born), and "hOHuhn" (horn).

"EE" . . . . as in "we," "repeat," "very," etc.

When stressed, this vowel remains the same, but in an unstressed position it is changed to "i" as in "ripEEt" (repeat) and "vEH:i" (very).

"EH" . . . . as in "get," "fell," "ten," etc.

The actual sound of this vowel may remain the same as in General-American. Before "l," however, it is usually elongated to "EH:" as in "fEH:l," or it may take an "uh" glide as in "fEHuhl" (fell). The "l" is often dropped as in "fEH:" or "fEHuh" (fell) and "sEH:f" or "sEHuhf" (self).

The change of "EH" to "i" before a nasal consonant is only occasionally heard in this area, as in "tin" (ten). Its use is suggested only for a character of little education.

EXCEPTION: The word "again" is often pronounced as "UHgAYn."

"EH" .... as in "where," "hair," "bare," etc.

For a lighter dialect, "EH" may remain the same as in General-American" when followed by "r" as in "wEHuh" (where) and "hEHuh" (hair). The "r" of course is dropped in favor of the "uh" glide.

A more typical pronunciation, however, is "AA" as in "bAAuh" (bare) and "dAAuh" (dare). This "AA" is a sound between "AH" and "A" and may be achieved by producing the sound of "A" with the mouth and throat in position for "AH."

"I" .... as in "sigh," "side," "right," etc.

This vowel is pronounced as "AH" when final or followed by a voiced consonant, as in "AH" (I), "tAHd" (tide), "AHz" (eyes), "lAHvz" (lives), and "AHvi" (ivy). When stressed, this vowel sound is usually elongated to "AH:" as in "krAH:d" (cried).

When followed by a voiceless consonant, however, the variant "Ui" is used as in "rUit" (right), "mUik" (Mike), "pUip" (pipe), "Uis" (ice), and "lUif" (life). The "U" is the dominant sound, and the "i" is used only as a glide and must blend smoothly into the general sound. When in an accented syllable, only the "U" receives stress, as in "nU:it" (night).

"i" .... as in "it," "sit," "wish," etc.

This short "i" is usually intensified so that it almost becomes "EE." It will be designated here as "i:" and should be a sound intermediate between "i" and "EE" as in "i:t" (it), "fi:sh" (fish), and "si:t" (sit).

EXCEPTIONS: The words "whip" and "wish" are frequently pronounced as "wUHp" and "wUHsh."

"i" .... as in "here," "near," "dear," etc.

The typical pronunciation of this short "i" when followed by "r" is "EHuh" with the "r" dropped, as in "hyEHuh" (here), "nyEHuh" (near), "dyEHuh" (dear), klEHuh" (clear), and "tEHuh" (tear).

Short "i" may also be used, as in "fyiUH" (fear) and "miUH" (mere).

"O" .... as in "not," "shot," "hot," etc.

This short "o" (O) is usually pronounced as "AH" as in "nAHt" (not), "shAHt" (shot), and "hAHt" (hot).

The habit of speaking from a forward position in the mouth sometimes colors the "AH" sound so that it almost becomes "U" as in "tUm" (Tom), "bUm" (bomb), and "tUp" (top).

EXCEPTION: The word "on" is frequently pronounced as "AWn."

"OH" .... as in "no," "broke," "float," etc.

In the Tidewater area this "OH" sound is produced from a more forward position in the mouth. This frequently changes the sound to "ER-OO" as in "gER-OO" (go), "brER-OOk" (broke), and "flER-OOt" (float). The "ER" is the General-American sound of "er" in "her" with the "r" silent.

If the "OH" is produced from the front of the mouth, the "ER" coloration will result naturally. There should be no attempt to force the sound or exaggerate it.

"OO" .... as in "two," "moon," "food," etc.

This sound may remain the same, as in "tOO" (two) and "fOOd" (food). However, when spelled with "u," "ue," or "ew" and preceded by "d," "n," or "t," the vowel sound becomes "yOO" as in "dyOOti" (duty), "tyOOn" (tune), or "nyOO" (new). This "y" glide must be very slight and must not be given its full consonant pronunciation.

"oo" .... as in "took," "should," "foot," etc.

This sound remains the same, as in "took" (took), "shood" (should), and "foot" (foot).

The words "root" and "roof," however, are commonly pronounced as "rOOt" and "rOOf."

"oo" .... as in "poor," "your," "cure," etc.

When followed by "r," this vowel is pronounced as "OHuh" and the "r" is dropped, as in "pOHuh" (poor), "yOHuh" (your), and "kyOHuh" (cure).

"yOO" .... as in "use," "cute," "few," etc.

This sound remains the same, as in "yOOz" (use), "kyOOt" (cute), and "fyOO" (few).

"U" .... as in "up," "much," "fun," etc.

The sound of "U" should be produced from a forward position in the mouth as in "Up" (up), "mUtch" (much), and "fUn" (fun).

"ER" .... as in "work," "fur," "shirt," etc.

Essentially, this sound may remain the same as in General-American except that the "r" is frequently silent, as in "wERk" (work), "fER" (fur), and "shERt" (shirt).

The variant "U:" may also be used, although it is not as common, as in "wU:k" (work) and "shU:t" (shirt).

"OW" .... as in "house," "crowd," "out," etc.

The typical pronounciation of this sound is "Aoo" as in "krAood" (crowd) and "Aoot" (out). The "A" is not a flat sound; it usually tends toward "AA" as in "AAooUH" (hour) and "frAAoon" (frown). This pronunciation is not limited to one particular class, but seems to be used by most people regardless of their social or educational backgrounds.

Although many people use "Aoo" for all "OW" sounds, others make the following distinctions. When "OW" is followed by a voiced consonant, it is pronounced as "Aoo" as in "prAood" (proud), "tAoon" (town), and "hAooziz" (houses). This same pronunciation is common for final "OW" as in "nAoo" (now) and "hAoo" (how). But, when followed by an unvoiced consonant, this sound is pronounced as "ERoo" as in "ERoot" (out), "hERoos" (house), and "shERoot" (shout). This same pronunciation is sometimes used for final "OW" as in "nERoo" (now) and "hERoo" (how).

"OI" .... as in "oil," "boy," "join," etc.

This sound is usually pronounced "AW" as in "AWl" (oil) and "jAWn" (join). When final or stressed, it generally takes an "i" glide as in "bAWi" (boy) and "EHnjAWi" (enjoy).

CONSONANT CHANGES

As in Southern dialect speech, Tidewater also features forceful initial consonants. The general treatment of consonant sounds remains the same as in the South except for the following variations:

The "r" may be dropped between vowels, as in "vEH:i" (very), but care must be taken to elongate the vowel sound to make up for the elided consonant. Medial "r" is seldom dropped in Charleston, South Carolina, however.

An intrusive "r" is occasionally heard after "OI" as in "sAWrl" (soil). This has been noticed particularly in western Virginia.

Palatalized "g" and "k" are commonly used, particularly by elderly people. For a discussion of this, see "G," page 85, and "K," page 86.

There is a tendency, especially in careless speech, to drop unstressed syllables and to combine the two consonant sounds, as in "wAH:n:d" (wanted), "fAHnli" (finally), and "blEEv" (believe). These elisions are made even in short words such as "fm" (from), "sm" (some), and "n" (and) showing a tendency to glide on nasal consonants.

This elision is also common in phrases, as in "rAHd THAooUH kAHuh" (ride with our car).

For a further discussion of consonant and syllable changes, refer to corresponding sections in **"The Southern Dialect."**

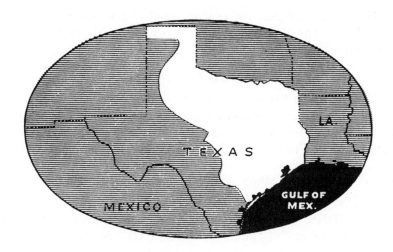

THE EAST TEXAS DIALECT

TEXAS IS THE LARGEST state in the Union, and according to the Texans, it is also the most beautiful and the greatest. As a group or individually, Texans are extremely |nationalistic and especially loyal to their beloved state.

Texas is a big state with big men, big cattle, big hats, and tall stories. The land is big and the people are big — in heart and in spirit. They are friendly, generous, and outspoken.

The typical Texas dialect is spoken by most Texans, but particularly by those in the eastern half of the state. Vowels are elongated; the tempo is slow with an almost monotonous intonation; there is distinct nasalization and a complete absence of tension in delivery. It is as relaxed a speech as can be found anywhere in America.

The Texas dialect is a combination of Southern and Mountain speech with an increasing infiltration of General-American. The educated "elite" have attempted to reduce the Texan's errors and make the speech closer to the Southern ideal, but this movement has made little headway, particularly in western Texas.

Texans in the eastern part of the state use a combination of the Southern and Mountain drawls (see pages 61 and 151), while west Texans generally speak with a "western drawl" (see page 299).

As in Southern and Mountain speech, there is a tendency to accent the initial syllables of words, particularly if they are short, as in "pOH:lEEs" (police), "dEEtrAWit" (Detroit), "dEEpinz" (depends), and "AHidi" (idea). (See also "Unstressed Syllables," page 118.)

It is suggested that the student study "The Southern Dialect" and "The Mountain Dialect" before beginning his study of "The East Texas Dialect."

VOWEL CHANGES

"AY" .... as in "take," "made," "ate," etc.

This vowel sound remains the same except that it is elongated to "AY:" and frequently adds an "i" glide when stressed and drawled, as in "tAY:ik" (take), "mAY:id" (made), and "lAY:it" (late).

Before "l" this vowel sound is generally drawled to "AYuh" as in "mAYuhl" (mail) and "rAYuhl" (rail).

EXCEPTIONS: Certain common words are generally pronounced with "EH" as in "nEHkid" (naked), "EHt" (ate), and "mEHk" (make).

"UH" .... as in "about," "final," "soda," etc.

Initially, this sound is generally dropped, as in "bAoot" (about), "bUuhv" (above), and "rAoon" (around).

Finally, this vowel sound changes to "i" as in "sOHdi" (soda), "EHuhli" (Ella), and "sOHfi" (sofa). For a lighter dialect, or for a modern character with good education the "UH" may be used, as in "AHidUH" (Ida) and "AHidiUH" (idea).

For the initial unstressed syllable, see the section on **"Unstressed Syllables."**

"AH" .... as in "far," "hard," "palm," etc.

When this vowel is followed by "r," it is usually pronounced as an elongated "AH:" and the "r" is dropped, as in "hAH:d" (hard), "fAH:m" (farm), and "AH:t" (art). This "AH" should be produced from back in the mouth; it is a deeper, richer sound than in General-American.

When followed by "lm," this sound is pronounced as "A:" in "kA:m" (calm), "pA:m" (palm), and "sA:m" (psalm).

VARIATION: Many Texans, particularly those in rural areas pronounce "AH" before "r" as "AW:" as in "pAW:t" (part) and "jAW:" (jar). People who use this pronunciation frequently add the sound of "r" as in "pAW:rk" (park). This "r" should not be tensed and strong, however.

EXCEPTION: The word "far" is frequently pronounced as "fER," particularly by those people who use the "AW" variant mentioned above.

"A:" .... **as in "ask," "dance," "fast," etc.**

This vowel sound remains the same. It is the "A" of "bAd" (bad) with slight elongation, as in "A:sk" (ask), "dA:ns" (dance), and "lA:f" (laugh). This sound has a nasal quality which is particularly noticeable before a nasal consonant. When stressed or drawled, it may take an "i" glide, as in "drA:if" (draft).

EXCEPTIONS: The words "aunt" and "can't" are commonly pronounced as "AY:int" and "kAY:int."

"A" .... **as in "bad," "man," "hat," etc.**

This sound remains the same except that it is frequently elongated to "A:" or drawled as "Auh" as in "bA:d" (bad) and "Auhl" (Al). It sometimes takes an "i" glide when stressed or drawled, as in "sA:id" (sad).

"A" .... **as in "narrow," "carry," "Harry," etc.**

The single "A" sound may be used in these words, as in "nArUH" (narrow), "kyAri" (carry), and "hAri" (Harry). When this sound is drawled, there is a tendency to include a faint "uh" glide, as in "mAuhrUH" (marrow).

"AW" .... **as in "dog," "cost," "taught," etc.**

This vowel sound should be lengthened into "AW:" as in "dAW:g" (dog), "kAW:st" (cost), and "tAW:t" (taught). It should be produced from a relaxed position farther back in the mouth.

An elderly or historical character may use "A" when this sound is spelled "au" and followed by "n" or the sound of "s" as in "hAntid" (haunted), "sAsij" (sausage), and "sAs" (sauce).

"AW" .... **as in "more," "short," "four," etc.**

Before "r" this vowel sound is generally pronounced as "OHuh" as in "mOHuh" (more) and "shOHuht" (short).

The "AW:" may also be used, preferably with a light "r" coloring, as in "mAW:rt" (Mort) and "fAW:rm" (form).

"EE" .... **as in "see," "meat," "easy," etc.**

When stressed, this sound remains the same, as in "sEE" (see) and "mEEt" (meat). When unstressed, it is usually changed to "i" as in "EEzi" (easy) and "rigAY:in" (regain).

"EH" .... **as in "cent," "egg," "sell," etc.**

Generally, the sound of "EH" may be used for all words. But its use is most consistent with careful speakers of average or better than average education. The following suggestions are made particularly for an older character, or a character with careless speech habits and little formal education. Some of these variants are used by the well-educated Texas, however, for certain of them are almost inherent in his speech habits.

The change of "EH" to "i" before a nasal consonant, for example, is common to most Texans, as in "sint" (cent), "tinnis" (tennis), "win" (when), and "UHsimbUHld" (assembled).

The pronunciations "lAY:g" (leg), "pAY:g" (peg), and "AY:g" (egg) are also commonly used by some people.

When followed by "l," this vowel sound, "EH," adds an "uh" or "yUH" glide when drawled, as in "sEHuhl" or "sEHyUHl" (sell).

Before all other consonant sounds the "EH" may remain the same, as in "kEHp" (kept), "EHvUH" (ever), and "tEHksis" (Texas).

EXCEPTIONS: The following words are frequently pronounced as "yit" (yet), "git" (get), "stidi" (steady), and "stid" (instead). These pronunciations should be used particularly for characters with little or no formal education.

The word "yes" is generally pronounced as "yA:s" or "yA:is."

"EH" .... as in "there," "care," "pair," etc.

When followed by "r," this vowel sound is generally pronounced as "Auh" if the "r" is dropped, as in "THAuh" (there) and "kAuh" (care). If the "r" sound is retained, the "uh" glide blends into the consonant, as in "pA-ER" (pair) and "stA-ER" (stare).

For a lighter dialect, "EH" may be used as in "wEHuh" (where) or "glEH-ER" (glare).

"I" .... as in "hide," "try," "time," etc.

This long "i" (I) is sounded as "AHi" as in "hAHid" (hide), "trAHi" (try), and "tAHim" (time).

In an unstressed position the personal pronouns become "UH" (I) and "mUH" (my).

"I" .... as in "fire," "wire," "hire," etc.

When followed by "r," long "i" (I) is generally pronounced as "AH:" as in "fAH:r" (fire) and "wAH:r" (wire). If the "r" is dropped, the pronunciation is "fAHuh" (fire) and "hAHuh" (hire).

The variant "AW:" may be used, particularly by a character who changes "AH" to "AW," as in "fAW:r" (fire) and "tAW:r" (tire).

"i" .... **as in "crib," "silk," "thing," etc.**

This sound may remain the same, except that when stressed, it takes an "UH" glide. This glide is particularly noticeable before "b," "d," "l," "m," or "n" as in "kriUHb" (crib), "hiUHd" (hid), "siuhlk" (silk), "hiUHm," (him), and "kntiUHnyUH" (continue). The glide must be very light and unobtrusive.

When "i" is followed by "nk" or "ng," a nasalized "EHi" is used, as in "thEHingk" (think) and "thEHing" (thing).

EXCEPTION: The word "whip" is commonly pronounced as "hwUp."

"i" .... **as in "near," "here," "clear," etc.**

When short "i" is followed by "r," it may become intensified so that it almost approaches "EE." This sound will be written as "i:" as in "nyi:r" (near) and "hyi:r" (here).

This sound is also frequently pronounced "EH" as in "klEHr" (clear) and "wEHr" (we're).

"O" .... **as in "rod," "bond," "on," etc.**

This vowel may be pronounced as "AH" as in "rAHd" (rod), and "bAHnd" (bond). People who use "AH," however, pronounce "on" as "AWn."

This same "AW" sound may be used as a variant, particularly in delineating a rural character, as in "stAWp" (stop) and "kAWni" (Connie).

"OH" .... **as in "bone," "grown," "no," etc.**

This sound remains the same, except that it receives greater elongation when drawled, as in "bOH:n" (bone) and "grOH:n" (grown).

The word "no" is commonly pronounced as "nAW:."

"OO" .... **as in "do," "new," "coop," etc.**

When spelled with "u" or "ew," and preceded by "d," "n," or "t," this vowel sound is preceded by a "y" glide, as in "dyOO" (dew), "nyOO" (new), "tyOOn" (tune), or "dyOOdi" (duty).

In all other words, this sound may remain "OO" as in "dOO" (do), "fOOd" (food), and "mOOn" (moon), although the variant "iOO" may also be used, as in "shiOO" (shoe).

EXCEPTIONS: The following words are generally pronounced as "koop" (coop), "diOO" (due), and "hoop" (hoop).

"oo" .... as in "put," "push," "hook," etc.

This vowel sound remains the same, as in "poot" (put) and "hook" (hook). But it generally takes an "i" glide when followed by "sh" as in "pooish" (push) and "kooishn" (cushion). When "oo" is followed by "l," the glide is usually "uh" as in "poouhl" (pull).

"oo" .... as in "sure," "poor," "cure," etc.

When followed by "r," this vowel sound should take an "UH" glide, as in "pooUH" (poor) and "shooUH" (sure). If the character is one who pronounces his "r's," this sound would be "ooUHr" as in "shooUHr" (sure).

However, many Texans, particularly those with careless speech habits, or little formal education, say "OH" as in "pOH" (poor), "shOH" (sure), and "pyOHli" (purely).

"yOO" ... as in "use," "few," "cube," etc.

This sound remains the same as General-American, as in "yOOz" (use), "fyOO" (few), and "kOOyb" (cube).

"U" .... as in "mud," "hungry," "touch," etc.

This vowel sound may remain the same as in General-American, except that when stressed, it takes an "uh" glide, as in "mUuhd" (mud) and "hUuhml" (humble).

If the character is elderly, or has little formal education, or lives in a rural district, the change to "EH" should be made in such words as "sEHtch" (such) and "shEHt" (shut). See "U" in **"The Southern Dialect,"** page 80.

If the character uses the "EH" variant for the words mentioned above, he should also use the "AW:" sound before a nasal sound as in "hAW:ng-gri" (hungry) and "wAW:n" (one).

"ER" .... as in "person," "hurt," "earn," etc.

For the average character, this sound should remain the same. If the "r" is used, it should be sounded lightly; if the "r" is dropped, the sound becomes "ER" as in "pERsn" (person), "hERt" (hurt), and "ERn" (earn).

Many Texans use the variant "U," particularly when "r" is followed by a vowel, as in "wUri" (worry), "hUri" (hurry), and "kUrij" (courage).

EXCEPTIONS: The pronunciation "gyAuhl" (girl) is frequently heard, but "hyERd" (heard) is used most consistently by elderly people with little formal education.

"OW" .... **as in "now," "crowd," "out," etc.**

This sound is generally pronounced as "Aoo" as in "nAoo" (now), "krAood" (crowd), and "Aoot" (out). When stressed, it becomes "A:oo" with the first element receiving the emphasis, as in "tA:oon" (town). This vowel sound has a distinct nasal quality.

"OI" .... **as in "boil," "boy," "roil," etc.**

This diphthong changes to "AWi" as in "bAWil" (boil), "bAWi" (boy), and "jAWin" (join).

For an elderly character, particularly one who lives in a rural area, the variant "AHi" should be used, as in "pAHint" (point), "sAHil" (soil), and "rAHil" (roil).

EXCEPTION: The pronunciation "rAHil" (roil) has been retained by many Texans who use "AWi" for all other words of this type.

CONSONANT CHANGES

(Only the important consonant changes have been listed.)

D — This consonant sound is frequently dropped after "n" as in "wUuhnER" (wonder), "skAinl" (scandal), and "kAinl" (candle).

G — This sound should be produced from a forward position in the mouth (Fig. 8), rather than back (Fig. 7). A common result of the fronted production is a "y" glide before the sounds "EE," "i," "EH," "AY," "A," or "Aoo" as in "gyiv" (give), "gyEHt" (get), "gyAY:in" (gain), and "gyAoon" (gown). (See Figures 7 and 8.)

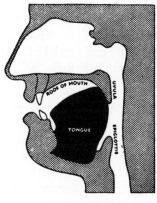
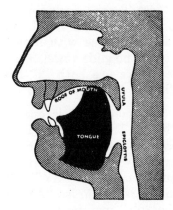

Fig. 7   Fig. 8

This fronted "g" also results in the peculiarity of Texas speech which changes the "g" almost into a "d" sound. This occurs only when "g" is followed by "l," as in "dlA:is" (glass) and "dlimps" (glimpse). This variant is important because it appears to be used by many Texans.

H — The sound of "h" is frequently dropped in favor of the "y" glide in the word "yi:UHr" (here) particularly in the phrase "km yi:UHr" (come here).

When the word "it" is in a stressed position, it is commonly pronounced as "hit" with an added "h." The word "overalls" frequently adds an "h" and is pronounced as "OH:vERhAWlz" by many Texans.

K — This consonant is produced from a forward position in the mouth so that a "y" glide naturally follows and the sound becomes "ky." This palatalized "ky" is common before "AY," "A:," "EH," or "Aoo" as in "kyAY:in" (can't), "kyA:bi:j" (cabbage), and "kyAoo" (cow). (See Figures 7 and 8.)

Like "g," this consonant is also affected by "l." When produced correctly, that is, forward in the mouth, "k" has a "t" quality before "l" as in "tlA:is" (class) and "tlAHim" (climb).

L — In most cases, this consonant sound is treated as in General-American. However, when "l" is preceded by a vowel and followed by a consonant, the full sound of "l" is not heard, as in "hEHoop" (help). After the first element "hEH," the tongue moves forward slightly, but it does not lift up to touch the roof of the mouth. The tip of the tongue remains slightly below the hard palate and slightly behind the upper front teeth, and the sound which results is the "oo" glide.

Most Texans, including the educated, use the "oo" or "UH" glide for "l" after a vowel and before a consonant. Many Texans, particularly those with little education, drop "l" completely and substitute no glide vowel, as in "sEH:f" (self) and "shEH:f" (shelf), while others use both "l" and the "uh" glide before "m", as in "EHluhm" (elm).

N — This consonant is one of the main reasons for the extreme nasality in Texas speech. It is so effective that, in rapid colloquial speech it is sometimes dropped completely, as is the French "n." Thus, the word "kAWfUHdis" (confidence) may be spoken with a distinctly nasalized "AW" and "i" but without the actual sound of "n." In the phrase "AY: gOH: tchAY:ij" (ain't gonna change), all the "n's" may be dropped and all the vowels nasalized.

NG — The participial ending "ing" is generally pronounced "in" as in "sEEin" (seeing) and "wAW:kin" (walking). However, when preceded by "d" or "t," the "i" is dropped, as in "fEE/dn" (feeding) and "si/n" (sitting). As usual, the "/" symbol represents the glottal stop. (See "The Glottal Stop," page 24.)

R — In Texas there are several variants in the pronunciation of this consonant caused by the two speech influences at work: that of the plantation South and that of the mountain South. The latter predominates.

When "r" is followed by a vowel, it is usually pronounced. Some Texans, particularly those with little formal education, drop "r" in such words as "thOO" (through), "thOH:" (throw), "thOH:t" (throat), and their derivatives.

When "r" is final in a word or precedes a consonant, it is either dropped, as in "EHvUH" (ever) and "hAW:d" (hard), or it is pronounced lightly so that it imparts more of an "r" coloring than a full pronunciation of the consonant sound. Texans who speak with the plantation dialect generally prefer to drop the "r," while those who are influenced by the Mountain speech retain its sound in a modified form.

The educated plantation people usually pronounce "r" between vowels, as in "vEHri" (very). There is a tendency among uneducated folk, particularly, to drop "r" between vowels, as in "vEH:i" (very). When the "r" is dropped, the preceding vowel sound should be elongated.

When "r" is final in a final unstressed syllable, it is generally dropped by those who are influenced by the plantation speech, as in "fAHTHuh" (father) and "pAY:ipUH" (paper). Others, particularly those influenced by Mountain speech, use an "r" flavor, making the sound "ER" as in "bAY:ikER" (baker) and "pAW:kER (Parker).

S — This consonant sound generally remains the same as in General-American except that it is usually pronounced as "z" in the words "grEE:z" (grease) and "miziz" (missus). The latter word is also pronounced as "mi:z" (missus).

T — Most Texans drop "t" after "k," "p," or "s" as in "fAik" (fact), "Ap" (apt), and "lAWs" (lost). If this pronunciation is used, the "k," "p," or "s" should be sounded very lightly without aspiration.

Medial "t" when followed by "l" is also dropped by many Texans, as in "mOH:sli" (mostly) and "EHgzA:ikli" (exactly). It is also dropped in such phrases as "lEH:s" (let us) and "lEH:mi" (let me).

When medial "t" occurs between vowels, it is frequently given a flapped treatment so that it sounds like "d" as in "wAHdUH" (water), "bidUH" (bitter), and "mOH:dsAHikl" (motorcycle).

The uneducated Texan frequently adds "t" after "n" or "s" as in "UHkrAW:st" (across) and "vAHrmint" (vermin).

TH — When unstressed, in colloquial speech, this voiced "TH" is frequently dropped, as in "AWnnis grAoon" (on this ground).

V — When the sound of "v" is immediately followed by a nasal sound, the result is "/m" as in "EE/m" (even), "gi/m" (giving), and "mOH:s U/m" (most of them). Most dialect writers suggest this sound by "bm" and write "ebm" for "even." Actually, the consonant "b" is not heard. In the word "even" for an example, pronounce the vowel sound "EE"; then immediately sound the glottal stop and "m." This glottal stop (/) must not be full and complete, as in the Scottish dialect. It is used as a result of forcing the sound of "m," and it must be produced simultaneously with "m." This change is predominant among Negroes, and many white Texans also use it in informal speech.

W — The consonant sound is often dropped in such words as bA:ikUHrdz" (backwards). "fAW:rd" (forward), and "sUuhmUHrz" (somewheres). The word "always" may be pronounced as "AWluhz" or "AWlwAY:z."

WH — The "wh" combination is usually pronounced as "hw" as in "hwEHn" (when) except in "why" which is always "wAHi" when stressed.

UNSTRESSED SYLLABLES

Colloquial Texas speech is lax in its pronunciation of unstressed syllables. The habit of dropping syllables contributes much to the characteristic drawl. The following sentences illustrate some of these tendencies:

"hi wUHz tAHuhd n AWnri tini rAY:it."
(He was tired and ornery at any rate.)

"tUHmAH: znUTHER dAY:i."
(Tomorrow's another day.)

"hwUtchUH gOH: dOO: THAoot AY:imi?"
(What are you going to do without Amy?)

In the above sentence, the word "gOH:" (going) has a distinctly nasal sound. (See **"N"** under **"Consonant Changes".**)

The following suggestions for unstressed syllables should be of considerable aid in achieving the smooth-flowing Texas dialect:

The prefix "be" is generally pronounced as "bUH" as in "bUHhAHin" (behind). The unstressed vowel sound may be dropped completely, particularly by uneducated Texans, as in "blAW:ng" (belong). However, if the character to be portrayed has a tendency to stress initial syllables, this prefix should be pronounced as "bEE" as in **"bEEhAHin"** (behind).

The prefix "re" when unstressed becomes "ri" as in "risEEv" (receive) and "ritERn" (return).

When the prefix "e" is unstressed, it may be pronounced as "i" as in "ilEHk" (elect) and "inUf" (enough), or it may be dropped as in "lEHk" (elect) and "nUf" (enough).

When "e" is in an unstressed prefix and followed by "r" plus a vowel, it may be dropped, as in "prA:ips" (perhaps), "srEEn" (serene), and "drAHiv" (derive).

Unstressed prefixes spelled "pre" or "pro" are usually pronounced as "pUH" as in "pUHpAuh" (prepare) and "pUHlAW:ng" (prolong). The pronunciation "pER" should be limited, in the main, to uneducated Texans who would say "pERtEHk" (protect) and "pERvint" (prevent).

When unstressed "i" is followed by two consonant sounds, it generally retains its pronunciation as "i" as in "distrEHs" (distress) and "distERb" (disturb). However, when followed by a consonant and a vowel, it usually is pronounced as "UH" as in "dUHjEHs" (digest) and "buhlAHksi" (Biloxi). The word "directly" is almost always pronounced as "drEHkli."

When the letter "i" follows "d," "p," or "t," it is usually dropped from the unstressed syllable, as in "mEHdsn" (medicine), "EHplAW:g" (epilog), and "sA:isfAHid" (satisfied).

Medial "o" in an unstressed syllable is usually dropped, as in "plAHit" (polite), "plEEs" (police), and "A:ikUHbAit" (acrobat).

Medial "er" and "or" are usually dropped when unstressed, particularly in compound words, as "wEHTHmAin" (weather man), "pEHpmint" (peppermint), and "mOH:dsAHikl" (motorcycle).

When medial "u" is unstressed, it is generally dropped, as in "Aiktchuhli" (actually) and "nAitchuhli" (naturally). The words "you" and "your" are commonly pronounced as "yUH" when unstressed.

The vowel sound in most unstressed final syllables, such as "al," "am," "ance," "bus," "ach," etc., is generally pronounced as "UH" as in "kli:rUHns" (clearance), "stUmUHk" (stomach), and "bAuhluhns" (balance).

Unstressed final "y" is pronounced as "i" as in "mUni" (money) and "sUndi" (Sunday).

Medial "e" in an unstressed syllable is usually dropped after "d" or "p" as in "AidkwUHt" (adequate) and "AiptAHit" (appetite).

The "es" ending is usually pronounced as "iz" when preceded by "j," "s," "z," "sh," or "tch" as in "hAooziz" (houses), "britchiz" (breeches), and "miziz" (missus). See variation in pronunciation of "missus" from p. 117.

Words ending "ed," "age," "ege," "edge," and "ach" are generally pronounced with an "i" vowel sound, as in "wAY:stid" (wasted), "kAHlij" (college), and "spi:nij" (spinach).

Final unstressed "ow" is usually pronounced as "UH" as in "bA:injUH" (banjo) and "bAHrUH" (borrow). When final "ow" is preceded by double "r," however, many Texans, particularly those with little formal education, drop the final vowel sound and elongate the preceding vowel sound, as in "bAH:r" (borrow) and "nA:r" (narrow).

Medial unstressed "er" is usually dropped, as in "A:ivrij" (average) and "bA:itri" (battery).

When "if" is in an unstressed position, it is frequently pronounced as "EHf," as in "EHf AHi UHz yOO" (if I was you). The phrase "it ain't" is usually "tAY:nt."

GRAMMAR CHANGES

The typical uneducated Texan is addicted to most of the grammatical errors listed in **"The Common Speech"** and more. He phrases his sentences with the grammatical indifference of a highlander. In many instances this is as it should be since mountain folk have migrated to Texas in fairly large numbers. Naturally, the more educated the character, the fewer his errors. But even well-educated Texans are not averse to "aint's," "taint's," and "shootinest, tootinest" superlatives.

Following are some of the common grammatical errors and changes. For a character whose background is the plantation South, see the grammar section in **"The Southern Dialect."** For a character whose background is one of the mountain areas, see the grammar section in **"The Mountain Dialect."**

The verb "done" is used superfluously for action which has already been completed, as in:

"hEE dUuhn win't hAW:g wAHil."
(He *done* went hog-wild.)
(He went berserk.)

"UH dUuhn bAW:t UH AWil kA:in."
(I *done* bought a oil can.)
(I bought an oil can.)

"hEEz dUuhn wint"
(He's *done* went.)
(He's gone.)

The verb "went" is frequently used in place of "gone" as in:

"hEEz wint hOH:m UHrEH/ng."
(He's *went* home, I reckon.)
(I think he's *gone* home.)

The use of "might" for "may" is common, as in:

"mAHid UH kyAri yUH hOH:m."
(*Might* I carry you home?)
(*May* I take you home?)

"UH mAHit wood"
(I *might* would.)
(I *may*.)

There is a preference for "ought" instead of "should," as in:

"AWd AHi tUH wUri?"
(*Ought* I to worry?)
(*Should* I worry?)

"AHi AWdUH rUuhsl Up sm grUuhb."
(I *ought* to rustle up some grub.)
(I *should* get some food.)

Comparatives and superlatives are frequently formed by suffixing "er" and "est" incorrectly, as in:

"hEEz kUuhm rAoon AWfnUH."
"He's come round *oftener*.)
(He's been over *more often*.)

"hEEz UH hEHuhlrAY:znUHs Uuhmbri!"
(He's the *hell-raisingest* hombre!)
(He's the *most unruly* man!)

There is a tendency to use "directly" instead of "as soon as," as in:

"kUuhm Aoot drEHkli yUH finish."
(Come out *directly* you finish.)
(Come out *as soon as* you have finished.)

"hEE lid UH shUuhk drEHkli yUH kUHm in."
(He lit a shuck *directly* you come in.)
(He ran out *as soon as* you came in.)

The use of "good" for "well" is also common, as in:

"UHm fEEluhn pERdi good."
(I'm feeling *pretty good*.)
(I'm feeling *well*.)

"UHm good thA:ingk yUH mA:im."
(I'm good, thank you ma'am.)
(I'm *well*, thank you ma'am.)

The word "without" is frequently used in place of "unless" as in:

"UH koodn, gOH THAood UH hEHd mUH tchA:ips."
(I couldn't go *'thout* I had my chaps.)
(I couldn't go *unless* I had my chaps.)

"kAY:n yUH kUuhm THAood UH hEHv tUH kAri yUH."
(Can't you come *'thout* I have to carry you.)
(Can't you come *unless* I take you.)

There is a tendency to use "all" after the interrogative pronouns "who" and "what" as in:

"hwUd AWl jUH dOO in dA:lis!"
(What *all* did you do in Dallas?)
(What did you do in Dallas?)

"hOO AWl UHz EHuh wiTH yUH?"
(Who *all* was there with you?)
(Who was there with you?)

The phrase "is all" is sometimes used at the end of a sentence. It is a shortened form of "that's all," as in:

"UH kUuhm Up fUH sm jERki iz AWl."
(I came up for some jerky, *is all*.)
(I came up for some dried beef, that's all.)

"UH jEHs krEEst UHm iz AWl."
(I just creased him, *is all*.)
(I barely wounded him.)

The expressions "want in," "want out," and so forth are fairly common, as in:

"hEE wAWnUHd Uuhp UHn hAoold lAHk AWl gidAoot."
(He *wanted up* and howled like all getout.)
(He wanted to get up and howled loudly.)

"THuh lidl fEHluh wAWnts Uuhp."
(The little fellow *wants up*.)
(The little boy wants to get up.)

The following expressions are frequently used in reply to an unheard question:

"hwitch?"
(Which?)
(What?)

"sEHz hwitch?"
(Says which?)
(What?)

Other typical Texan expressions are:

"hAoo kUuhm yUH thOH:d UHt Aoot?"
(How come you throwed it out?)
(Why did you throw it out?)

"shEEz UH gA:l EHt sEEd THuh shOO/n."
(She's the gal that seed the shooting.)
(She's the girl who saw the shooting.)

"AY:n nAri UH wUuhn kUuhm."
(Ain't nary a one come.)
(No one came.)

"UH mAY:d Aoot lAHik AHd lAW im."
(I made out like I'd law him.)
(I pretended I'd sue him.)

"yOOd bEHs gOH: nAoo."
(You'd best go now.)
(You'd better go now.)

"dOO UH gUuhdUH wAY:d AWn yUH?"
(Do I got to wait on you?)
(Do I have to wait for you?)

The expression "yOO AWl" or "yAW:l" (you-all) is almost always used by Texans. Although it may be directed to one person, particularly by rural Texans, its use should usually imply plurality, as in "UHm kUuhmin Up tUH yOO AWlz hAoos rAHit soon" (I'm coming up to you-all's house right soon).

MONOLOG

(From *Wolfville Folks** by Alfred Henry Lewis.)

While folks likes Riley, his pard Four-bar Bob is far from bein' a pop'lar idol. Not that he ever starts anythin', but because he always looks as though he's goin' to. He's one of them sour, dark, oncommoonicative sports, whose atmosphere, as Peets calls it, is nacherally repellant. I myse'f figgers thar's a streak of Injun in Four-bar, in which eevent your not likin' him none is explained. Cross-breeds that a-way is always vicious an' onsatisfactory, an' no gent of experience ever takes his guns off while one's in sight. No, I'm onable to fathom what's wrong with cross-breeds; an' yet somehow some'ers they shore hides the seeds of disaster in their constitootions. Sech puzzles in hoomanity is plumb hard to savey, an' for myse'f I only gets at it this yere fashion. Take a proper deck of fifty-two kyards; a handful of gents'll play all night with 'em, win an' lose their thousands, an' never no cloud to rise in the sky. Let some sech element as a fifth ace creep in, an' it's a stack of yellows to a white chip thar's a killin'. It's the same with people. Some folks it looks like is foaled with a fifth ace in their make-up — predestines storm-centers from the jump!

---

* Reprinted with permission of D. Appleton-Century Company, Inc.

CHAPTER IV

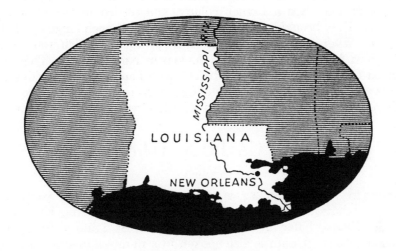

THE LOUISIANA-FRENCH DIALECTS

THREE BROAD TYPES of the French dialect are spoken by a great many inhabitants of Louisiana. These are the Cajun dialect, the Creole dialect, and the Gumbo dialect. The latter, Gumbo, is actually a patois of the French language itself, rather than a French dialect of the American language. It was the pidgin French of the Senegalese African slaves of New Orleans Colonial days and was used by the Negroes and their masters, the Creoles. Today, Gumbo is still being spoken by these Negroes although most of them converse in an American-Negro dialect highly colored with French vowel changes, lilt, and idiomatic expressions.

The Creole dialect of the American language was, and still is, spoken by New Orleans Creoles. There is a popular misconception that the Creole is a half-breed Negro. Actually, an American Creole is a person who was born in America of French or Spanish parents. Today, many of the young people of New Orleans speak as most Louisianians. But older Creoles, direct descendants of the French who first colonized New Orleans, converse normally in French and use a distinct French dialect in their American speech. The Creole French is that of the South of France, from which many original settlers of New Orleans came, and it differs markedly from the language spoken in other provinces, particularly the Paris, Normandy, Picardy, and Saintonge districts. From these regions came the original colonizers of Canada.

125

These Canadian French — the Acadians — were driven out of Canada by the British in 1755. After many tribulations, they arrived in Louisiana, then a French colony, and settled in the Mississippi Delta. They brought with them the peculiar French language dialect of the seventeenth and eighteenth centuries which was quite different from the French then spoken in New Orleans. They were called Cajuns and the Cajun dialect is still spoken by their descendants. Because of its derivation Cajun speech is distinct from the French-American dialect spoken by the Creoles of New Orleans.

THE CAJUN DIALECT

THE CAJUN DIALECT is spoken in the Louisiana parishes of Acadia, Allen, Beauregard, Calcasieu, Cameron, Evangeline, Iberia, Jefferson Davis, La Fayette, St. Landry, St. Martin, and St. Mary. Cajun is also spoken in a number of communities in the following parishes: Ascension, Assumption, Iberville, Jefferson, Orleans (including the city of New Orleans), Pointe Coupee, Plaquemines, St. Bernard, St. Charles, St. James, and West Baton Rouge. East of the Mississippi, Cajun is spoken in Livingston Parish, especially at French Settlement, and in the southern portions of St. Tammany and Tangipahoa. Cajun is also heard in Avoyelles and Rapides and occasionally in Natchitoches (town and parish) and in Rambin in the De Sota parish.

The name "Cajun" (generally pronounced "kAHzhEHn" by the natives) stems from "Acadia" which was the name of Newfoundland before it was taken over by the British. Since their Canadian days, the Cajuns have been an industrious, friendly, and wholesome people. They were primarily farming folk, and for this reason they preferred to settle in the primitive bayous and prairies of Louisiana rather than remain in New Orleans with the Creoles. In addition to reasons stated before, their choice of occupation has resulted in an important variance in the French-American dialect. Because of their democratic ideals they lived closely with the Indians and Negroes. Therefore the Cajun dialect contained a great many Negro inflections, pronunciations, words, and idiomatic phrases. In New Orleans, the Creoles remained particularly aloof from the Negroes, insisting that they retain their slave status. Their French dialect, as a result, was influenced more by the speech habits of the white Southerner.

Cajun speech, for example, includes such Negro words and pronunciations as: "shOHnUf" (sure enough), "lEHs" (let's), "dEHblmint" (devilment), "rEHntch" (rinse), "Aks" (ask), "EHf" (if), "jis" (just), "pOHk" (pork), "bOHd" (board), "AYg" (egg), "sEHns" (since), "rEHkn" (reckon), "yi:d" (heard), "yOH" (your), "yOHsEHf" (yourself), "hUkUuhm" (how come), "plUm" (plumb), "yAWndUH" (yonder), "kEHtch" (catch), "hAWs" (horse), "UH" (of), "git" (get), "tmAW:" (tomorrow), "hAW:" (horror), "hisEHf" (himself), "kyA:" (care), "dUuhn gAWn" (done gone) and "UH mEHs UH" (a mess of).

Thus, it would be correct to interlard the speech of the Cajuns with a great many of the words and phrases to be found in the section on **"The Negro Dialect."** The pronunciation of these words and phrases, for the most part, would be in the Negro dialect, distinct from the dialect changes listed in the following sections.

At the same time, Cajuns use a considerable number of French words in their speech. Following is a list of some of these words and phrases to be used as often as possible without making the dialect too thick: *"oui"* (yes), *"bien"* (good), *"mais"* (but), *"m'sieu"* (mister), *"cherie"* (darling), *"comment"* (how?), *"demoiselle"* (miss), *"pardon"* (pardon me), *"mais non"* (no!), *"il est bon heur"* (it is early), *"il dit"* (he said), *"hé quoi"* (what!), *"grand"* (tall), *"adieu"* (goodbye), *"c'est vrai"* (it is true), *"qu'est-ce c'est"* (what is it?), *"comme ca"* (like that), and *"la bas"* (down there).

There is a tendency to give slightly heavier stress to the final syllable of words, as in "mEHbEE" (maybe) and "brAkfAHs" (breakfast). At the same time, prefixes frequently receive primary stress, as in **"bifOH"** (before) and **"kAWndTHEEyoo"** (continue).

The lilt is less brisk than the general French-American dialect since it has been softened somewhat by the Southern drawl. But the habit of pronouncing stressed words with individual syllabic emphasis persists to a great degree.

VOWEL CHANGES

"AY" . . . . as in "take," "break," "make," etc.

This vowel sound is generally pronounced as "EH" as in "dTHEHg" (take), "brEHg" (break), and "mEHg" (make).

"UH" . . . . as in "along," "machine," "lima," etc.

Initially, this sound is frequently dropped, as in "lOHng" (along).

Medially, when stressed, this "UH" is pronounced according to the letter. Thus, "mUHshEEn" (machine) receives the unstressed "UH" treatment in General-American, but in Cajun if the first syllable receives stress, the pronunciation is "mAshin" (machine). In the same way, the General-American word "kUHnskript" (conscript) becomes "kAWnskrEEp" in Cajun. If the "UH" sound remains unstressed, it is generally dropped, as in "bloon" (balloon) and "bliv" (believe).

"AH" . . . . as in "park," "dark," "calm," etc.

When this vowel sound is followed by "r," it is generally pronounced as "AW," as in "pAWg" (park) and "dAWg" (dark). When followed by "lm," the sound may remain the same, as in "kAHm" (calm).

"A:" . . . . as in "ask," "aunt," "grass," etc.

This sound may remain the same as in General-American, as in "A:s" (ask) and "grA:s" (grass). The word "aunt" is frequently pronounced as "AYn" but the French word *"tante"* is also used.

"A" . . . . as in "bad," "hat," "carry," etc.

This vowel sound may remain the same, as in "bAdTH" (bad), "hAdTH" (hat), and "kAri" (carry).

A variant pronunciation is "AH" as in "bAHdTH" (bad) and "hAHdTH" (hat).

"AW" . . . . as in "call," "off," "dog," etc.

This vowel sound generally remains the same as in General-American, as in "kAWl" (call), "AWf" (off), and "dTHAWg" (dog). Some Cajuns use a more fronted, pursed "Aw" which gives the sound an "OH" coloring.

"AW" . . . . as in "more," "torn," "shore," etc.

When followed by "r," this vowel sound is usually pronounced as "OH" as in "mOH" (more), "dTHOHn" (torn), and "shOH" (shore).

"EE" . . . . as in "see," "treat," "crazy," etc.

Although "EE" may be used, many Cajuns prefer "i" particularly when the sound is unstressed, as in 'si" (see) and "dTHridTH" (treat).

A final "y" is almost always pronounced as "i" as in "krEHzi" (crazy).

"EH . . . . as in "get," "said," "bread," etc.

This sound is frequently pronounced as "AY" as in "gAYdTH" (get), "sAYdTH" (said), and "brAYdTH" (bread). The variant "A" may also be used, particularly before "n" as in "sAns" (cents). The "n" indicates that "n" is dropped and the preceding vowel "A" receives a nasalized treatment.

"EH" .... **as in "pair," "hair," "chair," etc.**

When followed by "r," this sound is generally pronounced as "Auh" and the "r" is dropped, as in "pAuh" (pair), "hAuh" (hair), and "tchAuh" (chair).

"I" .... **as in "ice," "hide," "sight," etc.**

This sound is generally pronounced as "AHi" as in "AHis" (ice), "hAHidTH" (hide), and "sAHidTH" (sight).

"I" .... **as in "fire," "wire," "tire," etc.**

When followed by "r," this sound is usually "AHuh" as in "fAHuh" (fire), "wAHuh" (wire), and "dTHAHuh" (tire).

"i" .... **as in "mistake," "little," "kill," etc.**

This vowel sound is frequently pronounced as "EE" as in "mEEzdTHEHg" (mistake), "lEE:l" (little), and "kEEl" (kill).

For a lighter dialect, "i" may be used.

The word "been" is frequently pronounced as "bin."

"i" .... **as in "near," "fear," "tear," etc.**

When followed by "r," this vowel sound is usually pronounced "i" as in "ni" (near), "fi" (fear), "and "dTHi" (tear). If the word is stressed, an "UH" glide is frequently added, as in "diUH" (dear).

"O" .... **as in "on," "hot," "lot," etc.**

This vowel sound is generally pronounced as "AH" as in "hAHdTH" (hot) and "lAHdTH" (lot). The word "on" however, is frequently pronounced as "AWn" or "AWn," although "AHn" and "AHn" are also heard. (See **"N"** under **"Consonant Changes."**)

The variant "AW" may also be used as in "nAWt" (not).

"OH" .... **as in "road," "hope," "stone," etc.**

When initial or medial and not followed by a nasal consonant, this sound may remain the same, as in "rOHdTH" (road) and "hOHb" (hope).

When followed by a nasal consonant, this sound is usually pronounced as a nasalized "AW." This sound should be produced from the forward part of the mouth. The symbol used for this nasalized vowel sound is "AWn" as in "bAWn" (bone), or "AWm" as in "hAWm" (home). The "n" or "m" indicates that the consonant sound is dropped and the preceding vowel nasalized. See **"M"** and **"N"** in **"Consonant Changes."**)

When final and spelled "ow" in words of more than one syllable, this sound is usually pronounced as "uh" as in "fEHluh" (fellow) and "yEHluh" (yellow).

"OO" .... as in "food," "shoot," "do," etc.

Many Cajuns pronounce this long "u" (OO) sound as "oo" as in "food" (food), "shoodTH" (shoot), and "dTHoo" (do).

"oo" .... as in "good," "could," "stood," etc.

This vowel sound may remain the same as in General-American, but it should be produced from a more forward position in the mouth. This forward production frequently gives it the quality of "ER" which is the sound of "er" in the General-American pronunciation of "hER" (her) with the "r" silent. This sound is like the sound of "eu" in the French words *"fleur"* or *"neuf."* Thus many Cajuns say "gERdTH" (good), "kERdTH" (could), and "sdTHERdTH" (stood).

A variant of this forward "oo" is "OO" as in "pOOdTH" (put) and "fOOl" (full).

"oo" .... as in "your," "sure," "pure," etc.

When followed by "r," this sound is usually pronounced as "OH" with the "r" dropped, as in "yOH" (your), "kyOH" (cure), and "pyOH" (pure).

"yoo" .... as in "use," "cute," "beauty," etc.

Although this sound may remain the same as in General-American, some Cajuns use the variant "yoo" as in "yooz" (use), "kyoodTH" (cute), and "byoodTHi" (beauty).

The word "bayou" is generally pronounced as "bAHiyUH."

"U" .... as in "up," "hug," "hunt," etc.

Although "U" may be used, it should not be used consistently. The variants "AW" and "ER" are frequently heard, and all three sounds may be used by one speaker.

It is suggested that "U" be used occasionally to lighten the dialect, that "AW" be used before all consonant sound except nasals, and that "ER" be used before nasals, as in "Ub" (up), "hAWg" (hug), and "hERnt" (hunt). (See **"M"** and **"N"** in **"Consonant Changes."**)

"ER" .... as in "work," "turn," "first," etc.

This sound may be pronounced as "U: as in "wU:g" (work), "tU:n" (turn), and "fU:s" (first). A variant pronunciation is "ERi" as in "wERig" (work).

"OW" .... as in "out," "loud," "shout," etc.

This sound is generally pronounced as "AH" as in "AHdTH" (out), "lAHdTH" (loud), and "shAHdTH" (shout).

"OI" .... as in **"boy," "noise," "spoil,"** etc.

This sound is usually pronounced as "AWi" as in "bAWi" (boy), "nAWiz" (noise), and "spAWil" (spoil).

The variant "AHi" is sometimes heard in "kwAHin" (coin), "kwAHil" (coil) and "twAHil" (toil).

CONSONANT CHANGES

(Only the important consonant changes have been listed.)

B — There is a tendency to sound final "b" almost like "p" as in "kAHp" (cob). The substituted "p" sound should not be fully aspirated, however.

Medial "b" is occasionally pronounced as "v" as in the word "vAjdTHuhvuhlz" (vegetables).

D — Final "d" is sometimes so forcibly pronounced that it takes on a "t" quality, as in "kEEt" (kid). The substituted "t" sound should not be fully aspirated, however.

Generally, "d" is pronounced with the tip of the tongue touching the back of the front teeth. This gives it a thickened quality which will be represented as "dTH" as in "dTHAHi" (die) and "hEEdTH" (hid).

Initial "d" often changes to "j" when followed by "ue," "u," or "eu" as in "joo" (due), "jook" (duke), and "joos" (deuce).

Final "d" is almost always dropped when preceded by "l" or "n" as in "OHl" (old) and "spAn" (spend).

The sound of "d" is usually dropped from such words as "kERndTH" (couldn't) and "hwERndTH" (wouldn't).

F — This consonant sound may remain the same, except that when it is final in a word and followed by an initial-vowel word, it is generally pronounced as "v" as in "EEv AH gOH" (if I go).

Many Cajuns have difficulty with "f" and produce instead a sound similar to the "h" of the General-American word "hwI" (why). This sound, which will be designated here as "hf," may also be compared to the sound made when blowing out a candle. Thus, many Cajuns say "hfEEl" (feel) and "sAWhf" (soft). The lips should remain slightly parted and should not assume the position for "f."

G — This sound generally remains the same as in General-American. (Fig. 9). However, final "g" is frequently pronounced as "k" when the next word begins with a vowel, as in "bEEk OHl" (big old).

Initial "g" often takes a palatal "y" glide, as in "gyAWdTHuhn" (garden) (Fig. 10).

H — Like the French, the Cajun dialect features a dropping of initial "h" as in "U:uh" (her) and "AWm" (home).

However, when initial "h" is pronounced, many Cajuns give it a gutteral "kh" sound, as in "khwAH" (why), "khoo" (who), and "khyEH" (here). This "kh" is like the "ch" in the Scottish word "*loch*" or the German word "*ich*."

An initial "h" or "kh" is frequently added to initial-vowel words, particularly "hEEn" (in) and "hEEdTH" (it).

J — Many of the older Cajuns retain the French "zh" sound for "j" as in "EHzh" (age) and "zhERmp" (jump).

K — Final "k" is often so weakly sounded that it takes on a "g" flavor as in "lAHig" (like). This is also frequently true of medial "k" as in "lAWgi" (lucky).

Initial "k" frequently takes a "y" glide, as in "kyAuh" (care). (See Fig. 10.)

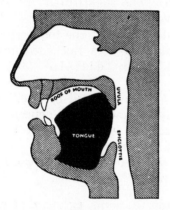
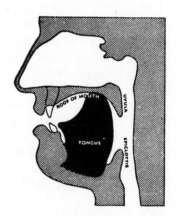

Fig. 9   Fig. 10

L — Initial "l" is sounded as in General-American.

Medial "l" is generally dropped in words like "sEHf" (self), "AWrAHidTH" (all right), "AWmOHs" (almost), and so forth.

Final "l" is frequently dropped, as in "pEEp" (people) and "dTHAv" (devil). This is a carry-over from the French language as spoken by the Cajuns.

The word "children" is often pronounced as "tchirUHn."

M and N — Initially, these consonants are pronounced as in General-American.

Medially and finally, under certain conditions, these consonant sounds may be dropped and their preceding vowel sounds nasalized. Nasalization can be achieved by keeping the soft palate in a relaxed, lowered position so that the throat passage is open and the vowel sound can pass out through the nose. (See Figures 11 and 12.)

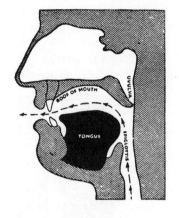 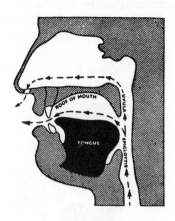

Fig. 11   Fig. 12

WHEN A VOWEL IS FOLLOWED BY "m" OR "n" PLUS ANOTHER CONSONANT, THE "m" OR "n" IS DROPPED AND THE PRECEDING VOWEL SOUND NASALIZED.

The symbols "m" and "n" will be used to designate the dropping of the consonant sound and the nasalization of the preceding vowel sound. Examples of the above rule are: "AWnli" (only), "pAnsEEl" (pencil), and "lEEmp" (limp).

When a nasal consonant is followed by "d" or "t," these consonants may also be dropped, as in "brAHn" (brand) and "pEHn" (paint).

WHEN FINAL "m" OR "n" IS FOLLOWED BY AN INITIAL-VOWEL WORD, THE "m" OR "n" SHOULD BE RETAINED AND THE PRECEDING VOWEL SOUND NEED NOT BE NASALIZED.

Examples of the above rule are: "khAWm EEz" (home is) and "tAn Agz" (ten acts). A great many Cajuns nasalize the vowel sound but pronounce "m" or "n." This is also a carry-over from the pronunciation in their original French.

NG — The "ing" participial ending is frequently pronounced as "EEn" (in) in which the vowel sound is nasalized and the "n" is dropped, as in "gAW-EEn" (going).

P — Final "p" is sounded with so little aspiration in Cajun that it takes on a "b" quality, as in "kAb" (cap). The full sound of "b," however, should not be used.

R — Initial "r" is usually sounded as in General-American. A great many Cajuns in the country parishes and small towns give it a slight tongue-tip trill (see Fig. 13), while others, especially in the Teche region, and in St. Martinville particularly, use a uvular trill (see Fig. 14). Both pronunciations are carry-overs from the French language.

Some Cajuns who had difficulty sounding the uvular "r" substitute a sound similar to "w," (Figs. 13 and 14), as in "wEEp"

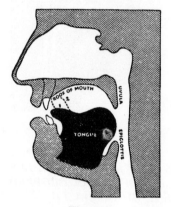 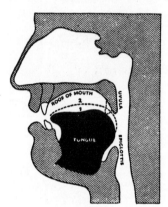

Fig. 13   Fig. 14

(rib), "kwAk" (correct), and "dwiwi" (dreary). Cajun speakers have been heard to use all three pronunciations of "r" in their speech. But the normal General-American "r" may be used primarily, while the others may be used to vary a characterization, especially when other Cajun dialects are being used in the script.

The pronunciation of medial and final "r," however, has been definitely affected by Southern and Negro speech. When medial "r" precedes a consonant, it is usually dropped, as in "AW:dTH" (heart) and "kAuhfuhl" (careful). There is little tendency to substitute the "uh" drawl sound for the dropped "r" which is characteristic of the Southern white. Rather there is a preference for a normal or sustained vowel sound without the drawl which is characteristic of the Southern Negro.

When medial "r" follows a consonant in a word of more than one syllable, it is often dropped, as in "pUHdoos" (produce) and "pAWpuhli" (properly). This tendency follows the Negro rather than the white habit.

The word "from" is frequently pronounced as "fUHm."

Medial "r" is also dropped between vowels, as in "vA:i" (very) and "mAH:EEj" (marriage).

Final "r" is always dropped, following the Southern tendency, as in "fOH" (for) and "fAW:mUH" (farmer). Older Cajuns sometimes pronounce final "er" as "AY" as in "mEEsdTHAY" (mister) and "fAW:mAY" (farmer).

Following the Negro rather than the Southern white pronunciation, Cajuns drop the "UH" substitute for final "r" in one-syllable words, as in "dTHOH" (door) and "mOH" (more). In multi-syllable words "UH" is substituted for final "r" as in "sEEnsiUH" (sincere) and "ripAuh" (repair).

As in the Southern dialect, Cajun drops the "r" completely when preceded by "OH" or "AW" as in "sdTHOH" (store) and "kyAW" (car). When preceded by "i" or "A," the "r" is dropped in favor of the "UH" substitute as in "niUH" (near) and "hAuh" (hair).

Although final "r" is generally dropped, many Cajuns who use a considerable amount of French in their speech often sound it with a uvular or tongue-tip trill.

S — Medial and final "s" almost always have a "z" quality, as in "bEHzbAWl" (baseball) and "mOHz" (most).

Occasionally the initial "s" is changed to "z" as in "zmAWl" (small) and "zOH" (so).

When followed by the consonant sound of "y" the "s" may be pronounced "sh," as in "mEEshyoo" (miss you).

SH — The word "shrimp is often pronounced as "swEEmp." This is an example of the "r" *grasseyé*, which is sounded by holding the mouth in position for "r" and pronouncing a light "w."

T — This consonant sound is generally thickened into "dTH" as in "dTHAHidTH" (tight) and "dTHAHim" (time). This "dTH" quality is produced by pronouncing "t" with the tongue-tip touching the back of the upper front teeth.

Final "t" is almost always dropped in Cajun when it is preceded by the sound of "f," "k," "l," "n," "p," or "s" as in "fAHk (fact), "sAWf" (soft), "hAWl" (halt), "rAn" (rent), and "fAHs" (fast).

As in the Negro dialect, "t" is often dropped in "dTHAHs" (that's) and "lEEl" (little).

The Cajuns frequently drop final and medial "t" in the pronunciation of compound words as "AHsAHi" (outside), "dTHEEdTHbEE" (tidbit), and "lERgAH" (lookout).

The word "turtle" is sometimes pronounced as "tU:kl."

TH — This sound is changed to the thickened "d" (dTH), as in "bAWdTHuh" (bother) and "dTHEEs" (this).

When unstressed, it is frequently dropped, as in "EH" (they).

TH — The unvoiced "th" is changed to the thickened "t" (dTH) as in "dTHEEn" (thin).

V — Initially and medially between vowels, this consonant often is pronounced as "bv," as in "dAbvuhl" (devil). The "bv" sound is produced by pronouncing "b" with the lips in a slightly open position.

W — Because there is no "w" in the original French language, many Cajuns pronounce it with extra force. This frequently adds an initial "h" sound as in "h-wU:g" (work) and "h-wEE" (we). As a result of the French influence, an intrusive "w" sound is frequently sounded before "oi" as in "kwAHin" (coin).

WH — Most Cajuns pronounce only the "w" in this "hw" combination, as in "wAuh" (where) and "wAHi" (white).

X — In words in which this consonant is pronounced as "ks" in General-American, it is frequently sounded as "gs" in Cajun, as in "AgspAg" (expect). When pronounced as "gz" in General-American, it is frequently sounded as "ks" as in "AksAHmp" (example).

Y — Many Cajuns add an initial "h" before initial "y" as in "h-yAdTH" (yet) and "h-yAluh" (yellow).

TCH — Older Cajuns sometimes substitute "sh" for this sound, as in "kAHsh" (catch).

UNSTRESSED SYLLABLES

Unstressed syllables in the Cajun dialect are generally treated as in the Negro. There are a few variations, however. Many Cajuns pronounce final "ing" as "EEn" as in "gOHEEn" (going); others simply use "UHn" as in "gOHuhn" (going).

Many Cajuns also substitute "EE" for the Southern "i" in unstressed final syllables, as in "h-wAHlEEs" (Wallace) and "sU:fEEs" (surface).

There is also a tendency to drop the final syllable of a multisyllable word if it ends with "l" or "ion" as in "pEEp" (people) and "pOHzEEsh" (position).

Medial unstressed syllables are often dropped completely, as in "jAndTHmUHn" (gentleman), "ERnsdTHAHn" (understand), and "brAWdTHEEnlAW" (brother-in-law).

GRAMMAR CHANGES

The grammatical errors typical of the Cajun dialect give it a distinct flavor. Although many errors of the Negro and the uneducated white Southerners are to be found, there are also errors that particularly characterize the Cajun dialect speech.

For example, the past tense is seldom used when the present tense is possible, as in:

"EE dTHAl mEE fOH dTHoo gOH."
(He *tell* me for to go.)
(He *told* me to go.)

"dTHEH rAHidTH mEE mAni lAdTHuh."
(They *write* me many letter.)
(They *wrote* many letters to me.)

The past tense is also formed by prefixing "been" to a present-tense verb, as in:

"yoo bin dTHrAH mEHg mEE mAHdTH."
(You *been try* make me mad.)
(You *tried* to make me mad.)

"AH bin h-wU:g AWl dTHAH dTHAHim."
((I *been work* all that time.)
(I *worked* all that time.)

The use of "what for" for "why" is also distinctive, as in:

"wAHdTH fOH yoo kAWl."
(*What for* you call?)
(*Why* did you call?)

The word "what" is also substituted for "that" or "who" as in:

"wAuh EEs dTHEE dTHrAs wAHdTH yoo mEHg?"
(Where is the dress *what* you make?)
(Where is the dress *that* you made?)

"dTHEE mAHn wAHdTH nOH."
(The man *what* know.)
(The man *who* knows.)

The preposition "to" is often omitted from the infinitive, as in:

"AHm gAWn mEHg mAHsEHf dTHEE AHdTH."
(I'm going *make* myself the hat.)
(I'm going *to make* myself a hat.)

The above example illustrates the habit of using "the" for "a'
or "an." The article may also intrude when unnecessary, as in:

"AHm dTHEE hfool AH rAkUHn."
(I'm *the* fool, I reckon.)
(I'm *a* fool, I reckon.)

"EEdTH lERg lAHig dTHEE mAWni."
(It look like *the* money.)
(It looks like money.)

The auxiliary verb is often dropped in the Cajun dialect, as in:

"wAHdTH yoo dTHoo nAH?"
(What you do now?)
(What *will* you do now?)

"yoo sEEn kOHz yoo frEHdTH."
(You sing 'cause you 'fraid.)
(You *are* singing because you're afraid.)

There is also prevalent a substitution of "one" used as an intensive for "a" or "an" as in:

"EEz wERn fAHin mAHn!"
(He's *one* fine man!)
(He's *a* fine man!)

The phrase "don't got but" is frequently used in Cajun, as in:

"AH dTHAWn gAWdTH bAWdTH dTHAn sAns mEE."
(I *don't got but* ten cents, me.)
(I have only ten cents.)

A comparative may be formed by adding "more" to an already comparative form, as in:

"mAH hAWs mOH bAdTHuh AHz dTHAHdTH."
(My horse *more better* as that.)
(My horse is *better* than that.)

Many Cajuns also add "est" to superlatives, as in:

"hEE dTHEE bAsdTHuhs tchAHl."
(He the *bestest* child.)
(He's the *best* child.)

The use of the reflexive pronoun is also common in Cajun speech, as in:

"mEE AHi kAHn gOH."
(*Me,* I can go.)
(I can go.)

"Us wEE blEEv yoo rAHidTH."
(*Us,* we believe you right.)
(We believe you are right.)

One of the most identifying characteristics of Cajun grammar is the use of the reflexive "me" at the end of a sentence, as in:

"AH EHn gAWEEn Aks yoo nOH mOH mEE."
(I ain't going ask you no more, *me.*)
(I'm not going to ask you any more.)

Another repetition occurs in beginning the sentence with a pronoun and ending the same sentence with the logical noun subject, as in:

"EE AWl dTHAHim smOHg mAH AWnk."
(He all time smoke, *my uncle.*)
(*My uncle* always smokes.)

There is a constant repetition of names, as in:

"EE brEEng pAWl bAWdTH pAWl pAWl EE drAHn pAWl."
(He bring *Paul,* but *Paul, Paul* he drown, *Paul.*)
(He brought Paul, but Paul drowned.)

The word "that" is used frequently, as in:

"dTHAH dTHAHim dTHEH gOH dTHoo dTHAHdTH bAHyoo."
(*That* time they go to *that* bayou.)
(Then, they went to the bayou.)

The past tense is sometimes formed by using "was" with a present tense verb, as in:

"wEE wAWz wAWg bAHg soon."
(We *was walk* back soon.)
(We *walked* back, soon.)

"AH wAWz gOH hOHm AWrAdi."
(I *was go* home already.)
(I *went* home.)

The double negative is commonly used, as in:

"wAdTHuh dTHAWn mEHg nOH dTHEEfUHns."
(Weather *don't* make *no* difference.)
(The weather makes *no* difference.)

"AH EHn gAWdTH nOH plEHs."
(I *ain't* got *no* place.)
(I have *no* place.)

Also prevalent in Cajun speech is the substitution of "don't got" for "haven't" or "hasn't" as in:

"EE dTHAWn gAWdTH nOH mOH bAdTHuh bOHdTH."
(He *don't got* no more better boat.)
(He *hasn't* a better boat.)

"AH dTHAWn gAWdTH fAHn klOHz."
(I *don't got* fine clothes.)
(I *haven't* fine clothes.)

Except in the instances noted previously, articles are generally omitted from most Cajun speech, as in:

"AH mEHg hOHl plEHs klEEn."
(I make whole place clean.)
(I cleaned *the* whole place.)

"yoo nEEdTH pirAWg nAH?"
(You need pirogue now?)
(Do you need *the* boat now?)

With modifying numbers the singular is preferred to the plural, as in:

"AH gOH fAHiv dTHAHim."
(I go five *time*.)
(I went five *times*.)

"hEE wAWg dTHAn mAHil."
(He walk ten *mile*.)
(He walked ten *miles*.)

The use of "at" with "where is" is also common, as in:

''wAuhz EHdTH dTHuh plEHs?"
(Where's *at* the place?)
(*Where is* the place?)

"wAuhz dTHuh jAWb EHdTH?"
(Where's the job *at?*)
(*Where's* the job?)

The phrase "used to couldn't" is frequently used to indicate some past inability, as in:

"AH yooz dTHuh kERn smOHg."
(I *use to couldn't* smoke.)
(I wasn't able to smoke.)

MONOLOGS

(From *The Great Big Doorstep** by E. P. O'Donnell.)

Patience is the admiraless thing you got. Take a look at me, and don't lose courage. Dave Tobin might come back tomorrow, or maybe some day before the river goes down and Emilien Ferdu sells his caddle and comes out the marsh to hole the meetin and pass the resolution. If he don't, I got plans, me, playin aroun in my head. Sometimes my head is spinnin aroun with plans like a piano stool, and maybe you think it ain goin no place, but while I'm turnin, I'm goin up or down like a piano stool, Duck. This mornin I'm goin up. The bess plan I got is a big-big plan, and that plan is to let what's gunna happen happen. Somethin's gunna happen to change our luck. So don't get excited.

(From *The Great Big Doorstep** by E. P. O'Donnell.)

I wonder what Poison Ivory's gunna do with this house when we leave. I bet he leaves it rot. The place where my chirren was born, two twins and a chile. He'd leave it rot to spite me, jiss to see me pass every day and watch it fall to pieces. It's gunna rot and tremble on its knees, like, down and down a stick at the time. A house got to have people to stay alive, hot meals and voices. . . .

* Reprinted with permission of Houghton Mifflin Company.

EH, Lord! A lamp in the window and a man sleepin on the porch! A house dies and falls when the people leave. It's like they take away the strank of the house when they go. Even a boat dies, like, when the owner pulls it asho and forgits it, I notice. A sad thing to see.

(From *The Great Big Doorstep** by E. P. O'Donnell.)

Listen, don't go. Kiss me goo-bye, eh? Don't you wunt me to kish you goo-bye? I ain gunna hurt you. I been waitin for you. Watsa matter with me? Do I smell like swimps and sulphur? Do I need a shave and do I roll cigarette with brown paper? Am I got something the matter with me? Me, I give you some advice. When I blow the whistle in the night, you come out. You let me take care you, sweedart. Then you gunna keep out of trouble, yes, because listen, the first man come along — boom! you gunna fall down. Because why? Because you good-hearted, ain't you? You donno how to say no. Somebody treat you nice, you dunno how to say no. That's why you better let me take care you, stay out of trouble. You know why I wunna get you, me? For spite. Your sister turn me down. Me! I wunna show her I can get somebody else right in the same house, by God. Ain't that swell? So you gunna be my pal. Please. We gunna have fun. And me I take care of you nice. No trouble if you be my pal. Now you gunna lemme kish you, sweedart. I never talk so much in my life. Kiss me.

THE NEW ORLEANS CREOLE DIALECT

THE CREOLES ARE THE descendants of the original French settlers of New Orleans. They came from a different part of France than the Cajuns and as a result, their dialect speech varies in the following respects:

There is practically no Negro influence in Creole. The speech of modern young Creoles is almost entirely free of the French influence and tends toward the Louisiana Southern type. But the older Creoles — and especially those in the history of New Orleans — speak with a definite French accent, similar, in a great degree, to the Cajun.

Simple French words and phrases like *"oui"* (yes), *"ma chére"* (my dear), *"c'est trés bien"* (it is very well), *"mais"* (but), and *"non"* (no) should be used when possible, but only if their meaning is clear.

---

* Reprinted with permission of Houghton Mifflin Company.

Other French words and phrases will be found in the section dealing with the Cajun dialect.

For the most part, the vowel changes used in Cajun may be used for Creole, except those which are a result of Negro influence. The following specific variants from Cajun are to be observed, however:

VOWEL VARIANTS

"AY" .... as in "aid," "mate," "they," etc.

This long "a" (AY) sound is changed to "EH" as in Cajun, but Creoles tend to elongate it more, as in "EHdTH" (aid) and "zEH:" (they).

"EH" .... as in "get," "tell," "bed," etc.

Although many Creoles substitute "A" for this sound, as in "gAdTH" (get), a great many also use "AY" as in "gAYdTH" (get), "vAY:" (very), and "AWnrAYdTH" (hundred).

"I" .... as in "ice," "mile," "tied," etc.

This vowel sound is generally changed to an elongated "AH:" as in "AH:s" (ice) and "mAH:l" (mile).

"U" .... as in "sun," "luck," "just," etc.

This vowel sound is usually "AW" before a nasal consonant, as in "sAWn" (sun) and "AWndTHEEl" (until). Before other consonant sounds, it is changed to "ER" as in "lERgi" (lucky) and "bERdTHAWn" (button).

The word "just" which is pronounced as "jiz" by many Cajuns, is usually pronounced as "jERz" or "jAWz" by Creoles.

"EE" .... as in "leave," "seem," "free," etc.

This vowel sound is frequently changed to "i" as in "liv" (leave), "sim" (seem), and "fri" (free).

CONSONANT VARIANTS

(Only the important consonant changes have been listed.)

H — This consonant sound sometimes precedes initial vowel words, as in "hAWnli" (only).

K — The palatalized "ky" sound is often used by Creoles, as in "kyAuh" (care) and "kyAWdTH" (card). (See page 132, figure 10.)

The word "ask" is usually pronounced as "AHs" in Creole rather than the Cajun "Aks" which was taken over from the Negro dialect.

L — As the Cajun, the Creole dialect drops final "le" as in "pip" (people) and "dTHrERb" (trouble). The word "little" is usually pronounced as "lEEdTH" by the Creoles rather than the Negro "lEEl" of the Cajuns.

M and N — These consonants usually give a nasal quality to the preceding vowel sound. For a detailed discussion see "M and N" on page 132.

R — The most important consonant variant is to be found in the Creole pronunciation of "r." The most popular "r" used in historical times was the French "r" *grasseyé*. This is a softened and only slightly rasping untrilled version of the French uvular "r." This "r" *grasseyé* may be achieved by holding the mouth in position for "r" and pronouncing a light "w." In this way, the "r" has a considerable "w" quality, but it must not have the full "w" sound, although the "w" symbol is used for this "r" *grasseyé*, as in "fwAn" (friend), and "wAHbEEdTH" (rabbit).

This "r" *grasseyé* should be used particularly by a character who has retained the use of French words in his American dialect speech.

Final "r" is generally dropped, as in "fAH:'" (fire) and "yAWndUH" (yonder).

Final "er" is sometimes pronounced as "EHr" as in "nAvEHr" (never) and "brERzEHr" (brother), or as "EH" as in "nAvEH" (never) and "brERzEH" (brother).

Between vowels, "r" is frequently dropped, as in "Avi" (every), "vAY:" (very), "mAY:" (Mary), and "pAlAH:z" (paralyze).

After a consonant, "r" is usually pronounced except when in a prefix, as in "pUHvAH:dTH" (provide) and "pUHdTHoos" (produce).

SH — Many Creoles use "s" for "sh" as in "sAHl" (shall) and "fAHsAWn" (fashion).

T — There is a tendency to drop final "t" when the next word begins with a consonant, as in "mAH: dTHrAH:" (might try) and "pAW fUHm" (apart from).

th — Although many Creoles use the dentalized "t" (dTH) for this sound, as in "pAHdTH" (path), a great many others use "s" as in "pAHs" (path).

TH — Some Creoles use the dentalized "d" (dTH) as in "dTHEEs" (this), while others use "z" as in "zEEs" (this).

TCH — Many Creole speakers substitute "j" for final "tch" as in "wEEj" (which) and "tchUj" (church). However, when medial "tch" follows a consonant sound, it is often changed to "sh" as in "pEEgshoo" (picture) and "AHgshool" (actual).

GRAMMAR CHANGES

The New Orleans Creoles had more education than the Cajuns. Hence, the errors they made are not as grave. There are, however, some typical changes that give the dialect a distinct flavor. Some of them are:

The auxiliary verb is often omitted, as in:

"vi: gAWn fAWl soon."
(Vera going fall soon.)
(Vera *is* going to fall soon.)

The elision of "to" in the above example is also common.
The present tense is often preferred to the past, as in:

"oo dTHAYl yoo dTHAHdTH."
(Who *tell* you that?)
(Who *told* you that?)

"AH dTHrAH: dTHoo sdTHAWb."
(I *try* to stop.)
(I *tried* to stop.)

As in the Cajun, the personal pronoun is frequently used as an intensifier, as in:

"mi AH gOH si."
(*Me,* I go see.)
(I'll go and see.)

"zAHdTH mAHn i nOH zi dTHroo."
(That man, *he* know the true.)
(That man knows the truth.)

There is also a tendency to substitute "what" for "who" as in:

"yoo min dTHi rEEj mAHn wAWdTH dTHAH:dTH?"
(You mean the rich man *what* died?)
(You mean the rich man *who* died?)

The word "that" is often used unnecessarily as an intensive, as in:

"nAWdTH ivn dTHAHdTH jOH!"
(Not even *that* Joe!)
(Not even Joe!)

The use of "those" for "the," "these," or "this" is also common, as in:

"zOHs mAHn EEs rAH:dTH."
(*Those* man is right.)
(*This* man is right.)

"AH dTHAWn si dTHOHs gU:l."
((I don't see *those* girl.)
(I don't see *the* girl.)

The substitution of "don't" for "am not," "is not," or "are not" is frequent, as in:

"AH dAWn gAWn gOH."
(I *don't* going go.)
(I *am not* going to go.)

"i dAWn kAWm EHn?"
(He *don't* come, eh?)
(He *isn't* coming, huh?)

The use of "for why" instead of "why" is common, as in:

"fOH wAH: yoo AHs mi?"
(*For why* you ask me?)
(*Why* do you ask me?)

Confusion of verb forms also occurs in the misuse of plural for singular verbs and vice versa, as in:

"shi hAW nAWdTH pyoo wAH:dTH!"
(She *are* not pure white!)
(She *is* not pure white!)

"zOHs mAHn EEs kAWmEEn."
(Those *man* is coming.)
(Those *men* are coming.)

The singular is preferred to the plural in nouns, as in:

"AH dTHAYl EEm fEEvdTHi dTHAH:m."
(I tell him fifty *time.*)
(I told him fifty *times.*)

"ERs wi rAH:dTH dTHoo mAH:l."
(Us, we ride two *mile.*)
(We rode two *miles.*)

MONOLOG*

Fo' why you come 'ere, *hein?* You wan' mek *scandale* fo' me, you. H'ever'wan know you mek love wees Mimi Coche two wik h'ago. Mebbe so you mek *scandale* fo' 'er *famille* too. To come 'ere, *c'est* no right. Me, I no wan' talk wees you no more, me. Wan seeng I say, me. Ees zees—you ween ze 'eart of my lee'l girl, 'elene. Ees bikause you 'ave ze 'eart of ze *artichaud* — a lif fo' h'ever'wan. You mek fine talk wees Tante Marie — she tell me so. You mek fine talk wees *ma femme*—she tell me so. You mak fine talk wees h'all my fran' bikause you wan' mek ze h'impression on me, on Theophile Baudine. On no! not Theophile Baudine! Ees bikause I know you fo' what you h'are, *M'sieu* Yankee. Ees bikause I know firs' you mek marry wees my lee'l girl, zen you gat you 'an' on 'er *argent*, zen you stil eet an' you go phtt! away — an' my leel' girl'ss 'eart she ees brawk. No, *M'sieu*. You ass' fo' my girl'ss 'an', I no geeve, so *you* gat mad. H'eef I geeve, h'an' you leave 'er, so *I* gat mad, me. Hein! better you gat mad.

---

*With permission of the author, Evan Thomas.

CHAPTER V

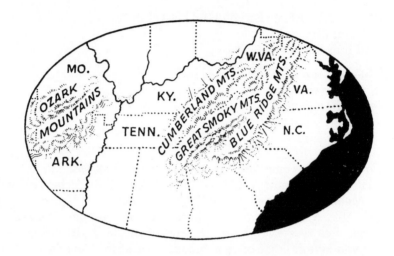

THE MOUNTAIN DIALECT

A LANKY HILLBILLY sprawling indolently on the ground, his rifle in one hand and a plug of tobacco in the other; his gaunt wife plowing or cooking or mending or spinning; granny "settin' " in the doorway of the shack sucking slowly on a corn pipe; the children, and they are legion, darting half-clothed in and out the brush — this is the average person's exaggerated picture of the highlander and his family. The actor who interprets these people solely as ignorant, superstitious, indolent, uncouth oafs who "shine" for business and "feud" for pleasure is guilty of producing caricatures, but not characters.

These mountain people may not be "citified" or have a great deal of "book-larnin'," but they have many qualities which are too often overlooked by actors. They are a colorful, exhilarating, exasperating folk who can be obstinately silent, brilliantly talkative, cruel and kind, spirited and lazy, but who are at all times basically democratic, trustworthy, courageous, and kind. The sincere actor would be wise to study these people in relation to their own surroundings rather than permit his urban surroundings to influence his judgment.

The exact history of the highlanders is not known, but it is believed they came mainly from the British Isles during the latter part of the eighteenth century. They settled principally in the Great Smoky Mountains of Tennessee and North Carolina, the Cumberlands of Tennessee and Kentucky, the Blue Ridge Mountains of

Virginia and West Virginia. Some of them moved west and settled in the Ozark Mountains of Arkansas and Missouri. Their speech is not restricted solely to these mountainous areas, however. Elements of the dialect are heard in Fort Worth and Dallas, Texas, northeastern Oklahoma, the Delaware-Maryland-Virginia peninsula, and the Piedmont, as well as in the more immediate lowland regions.

The highlanders themselves have changed little in two hundred years. They are a hardy people who have built their own homes, who have made their own clothes and the cloth that went into those clothes and even the thread that went into the cloth. They have had to be hardy to survive. There were no doctors within easy reach so they relied on herbs to cure their maladies. There was no formal education so they relied on nature to teach them and learned many things the city person does not. Hardships were ameliorated by the abundance of sweet, fresh air, the clear running water in the stream, the freedom of movement and of thought — all dear to the heart of the highlander.

Today they are still hemmed in by the mountains they love. Chicago or New York is as remote to them as Europe. A person who ventures forth into the lowlands is spoken of as having gone "abroad." A person from the lowlands who comes up into the mountains is spoken of as a "foreigner," an "outlander," or one of the "outlandish." These references to strangers are not meant to be derogatory.

Highlanders are slow to "confidence" a stranger until he has proven worthy of their trust. Asked a direct question, they will seldom give a direct answer. On the other hand, they feel it their right, almost their duty to query the stranger who comes into their mountain community. If the stranger is unfriendly, there will, of course, be no talk. Highland folk are proud and sensitive. They are quick to perceive the slightest half-wink of ridicule, but they can give back as good as they get, and often better.

It must be emphasized that for several hundred years they have lived alone. And they have liked it. It is only in the last fifty years that civilization has swept them up in her smothering embrace. For the most part, they are awed, bewildered, and a little uneasy about her charms. There will be a struggle before they completely slough off their old life in favor of more streamlined superstitions, "boughten" clothes, and time-saving gadgets.

This struggle is evidencing itself also in their speech, which is being slowly influenced by the radio, teachers, and more frequent contact with people in the lowlands. The older folk retain their own dialect speech, but the younger people are gradually adopting the dialect pronunciations of their teachers or co-workers. A high-school girl who had left the mountains and was living with her family in a midwestern city, spoke very good General-American English when she was among her schoolmates. But, at home, she was heard to use the dialect speech of her parents.

The dialect given in this chapter may be used for a character from any of the mountain areas, since the speech of most highland folk is essentially the same. The variants are more individual than regional, and one person may even pronounce the same word in several ways.

INTONATION AND STRESS

Highland speech is heavily and frequently stressed. Stressed words are usually "sung" on a comparatively high note. The general melody is soft and plaintive with a noticeable nasal quality. This nasalization must not be exaggerated however, it must not be so obvious that it develops into a whine.

The General-American sentence, "There isn't any sense in it," would be spoken by the Middle Westerner with moderate inflection and with the word "sense" receiving the accent on one note.

In the highlands, this same thought, expressed as "THAYn nA-ERi bi:UHdi siUHns i:uhn it" (There ain't nary bit of sense in it) would be spoken:

In this sentence, the least stress is given to the words "THAYn" (there ain't) and "it" (it), and the greatest stress to "i:uhn" (in).

The same sentence could also be spoken as:

The variant in this inflection gives "siUHns" (sense) the prime stress and the highest note. Prime stress in highland speech is more forceful than in General-American. This does not mean that the accented word must be spoken loudly. On the contrary, the typical highlander speaks in a quiet, almost confidential manner.

The constant, heavy accent resolves itself into a measured beat which gives a feeling of inevitability to the speech of the mountain people. This is further heightened by an upward lilt at the end of a sentence which gives the impression that the speaker has more to say. For example, the sentence "hEE shOH-ER UHz UH sli:UHk UHn" (He sure was a slick one) may be spoken as:

```
                                               UHn"
                                          UHk
                                    sli:
                              UH
                      UHz
     "hEE         ER
           shOH
```

Naturally, all highlanders do not speak alike. They do not use the same tempo, nor stress the same words. But, generally, the tempo is moderately fast, slowing down to a drawl before a pause; the stress is marked; the speech is toward the front of the mouth; nasalization is particularly noticeable before "m" or "n"; there is a tendency to speak in a minor key.

Initial-syllable stress is common, particularly in two-syllable words such as **"pOH:lEEs"** (police), **"sEEmiUHnt"** (cement), and **"gi:tAH-ER"** (guitar). (See also "Unstressed Syllables.") The stressed syllable generally takes the higher note.

Compound phrases frequently take heavy stress on both words, as in: **"grA-EEni woo:mUHn"** (granny-woman), **"rAH:dn kri:UHtER"** (riding creature), and **"EHuhvER tAH:m"** (every time).

Throughout the above examples, it may be noticed that stressed syllables are also diphthongized. This habit results in what is known as the Mountain drawl. In essence, it is like the Southern drawl (see page 61), except that the latter is not highlighted by the typically insistent stress of Mountain speech.

DRAWL AND DIPHTHONGIZATION

The Mountain drawl is generally reserved for the word or phrase before a pause. This pause may occur within a sentence as well as at the end of one. Diphthongization is also usual when a word is stressed, particularly if the word is short. The sentence "AH spi-shind i: dAHoon it" (I suspicioned he done it) may receive stress on the words "spi:shind" and "dAHoon," but generally only "dAHoon" would be drawled.

The drawl naturally disturbs the vowel sound in a word, so that it may be either elongated or diphthongized. For example, the word "gaily" (meaning "spirited" or "healthy"), is generally pronounced as "gAYli" when unstressed. When it is drawled, however, it may be pronounced as "gAY:li," "gAYuhli," or "gAYyuhli." In the first pronunciation, the "AY" sound is simply elongated; in the second, the "AY" is followed by a slight "uh" glide; and in the third, the "AY" is followed by a slight "yuh" glide.

This "uh" glide should be no greater than in the General-American pronunciation of the word "AdUHd" (added). It will be represented in small letters ("uh") or capitals ("UH"), but it must always be a faint, slight sound and should not be sounded as "U" (as in "up").

All vowel sounds are not diphthongized with the same glides, although "uh," "yuh" or "oo" are generally used before "l" as in "mAYuhl" (male), "gAyuhl" (gal), or "sti:ool" (still). (See **"L"** in "Consonant Changes.") A vowel which is diphthongized is stressed on the first element, and the glide is used merely as a link to the next sound.

Diphthongization for particular vowels sounds have been noted in the section on "Vowel Changes." The student must guard against mouthing the sounds so that the words become distorted. It must be remembered that although American speech varies in certain regions, it is still basically American speech. The vowel and consonant changes must be practiced carefully and constantly until they can be produced naturally and with no feeling of strangeness.

Although the typical highlander speaks with a rhythmic beat, hits the initial consonants forcefully, distorts vowel sounds, drops prefixes, adds suffixes, and generally breaks every rule in the modern grammar book, his is an independent nature, even when it comes to speaking. Therefore, although the material in this chapter gives many authentic vowel and consonant changes, plus variations, it cannot give them all.

VOWEL CHANGES

"AY" .... as in "take," "break," "they," etc.

This sound usually remains the same except that when it is drawled, it is of slightly longer duration than in General-American and will be represented as "AY:."

When "AY" is followed by "l," the drawl is more pronounced, and an "uh" or "yuh" glide may be used.

DRILL WORDS

tAY:k	(take)	frAYuhl	(frail)
brAY:k	(break)	nAYuhl	(nail)
THAY:	(they)	tAYuhl	(tail)

frAY:	(fray)
tAY:dERz	(potatoes)
AY:min	(aiming)

VARIATION: The variant "A-EE" may also be used, as in "prA-EEd" (prayed), "mA-EEd" (made), and "tchA-EEnj" (change). The first element (A) must blend smoothly into the second (EE) so that there is no break between them.

EXCEPTIONS: Unless stressed, the suffix "day" is pronounced as "di" as in "sAHoondi" (Sunday).

The following words are commonly pronounced as: "nEHkid" (naked), "grEHt" (great), "drEEn" (drain), "nAuhp" (nape), "sti:pl" (staple), and "gri:dER" (grater).

"UH" .... as in "alone," "sofa," "final," etc.

Initially, this sound is often dropped, as in "bAoot" (about). If used, it should have more of the quality of the glottal stop (/) (see "The Glottal Stop," page 24) than the full "UH" which is it given in General-American.

In a final, unstressed position, this "UH" is commonly changed to "i:" which is a sound between "EE" and "i."

Medially, "UH" is often dropped, but for a full discussion of the medial unstressed syllable see "Unstressed Syllables," page 167.

DRILL WORDS

lOH:n	(alone)	sOH:fi:	(sofa)
kAoont	(account)	AH:di:	(idea)
piER	(appear)	sOH:di:	(soda)

kyOOz	(accuse)
pAuhpi:	(pappy)
pAH:sm	(opossum)

"AH" .... as in "father," "arm," "palm," etc.

When followed by "r," this sound may remain the same as in General-American, except that it should be produced from farther back in the throat. When stressed, it will be designated as "AH." The "r" which follows this vowel is of a richer quality than the

General-American sound. The tongue should be a little farther back and more tensed.

When followed by "lm," this vowel is commonly pronounced as "AA" which becomes "AAuh" when drawled, as in "pAAuhm" (palm). This "AA" is produced by saying the "A" of "bad" (see Figure 15) with the mouth and throat in the more open position of "AH" (see Figure 16) as in "father."

 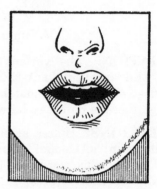

Fig. 15   Fig. 16

The word "father" is not given in the following drill words since most highlanders prefer the word "dAuhdi:" (daddy). If used, "father" is generally pronounced as "fAHTHER."

DRILL WORDS

AH:ERm	(arm)	kyAH:ERd	(card)
pAH:ERk	(park)	smAH:ERt	(smart)
kAAuhm	(calm)	lAH:ERd	(lard)

hAH:ERt	(heart)
stAH:ERt	(start)
dAH:ERk	(dark)

VARIATION: The variant "AW" may be used before "r" as in "smAW:ERt" (smart) and "tAW:ER" (tar).

The variant "Auh" may be used before "lm" as in "bAuhm" (balm) and "sAuhm" (psalm).

EXCEPTIONS: The following words are commonly pronounced as "pAAuhsl" (parcel), "pAAtrij" (partridge), "gAAgl" (gargle), "kAW:ERbn" (carbon), and "fERTHER" or fUTHER" (farther).

"A:" .... **as in "ask," "draft," "laugh," etc.**

This sound is generally pronounced as "A-EE" with the first element, "A," receiving the stress and blending immediately into the "EE" sound. There is usually a distinct nasal quality to this diphthong, particularly before "m" and "n."

DRILL WORDS

A-EEst	(asked)	pA-EEth	(path)
drA-EEf	(draft)	dA-EEns	(dance)
lA-EEf	(laugh)	kA-EEf	(calf)

pA-EEs	(past)
plA-EEnt	(plant)
brA-EEntch	(branch)

EXCEPTIONS: The words "can't" and "aunt" are frequently pronounced as "kAYnt" and "AYnt." The word "rather" is generally "rUTHER."

"A" .... as in "mash," "drag," "candy," etc.

This short "a" (A) is usually produced with the stem of the tongue closer to the roof of the mouth than in the General-American production of the sound. The highlander's "A" is also more fronted and has a distinct nasal quality, particularly before nasal consonants.

WHEN SHORT "a" IS FOLLOWED BY THE CONSONANT SOUND OF "k," "m," "n," "ng," "s," OR "sh," IT IS GENERALLY PRONOUNCED AS "A-EE."

This is the same sound that occurs in the "ask" words discussed above. The "A" receives the stress, and the "EE" is used as a glide to the next sound.

DRILL WORDS

bA-EEk	(back)	sA-EEng	(sang)
hA-EEm	(ham)	gA-EEs	(gas)
mA-EEn	(man)	krA-EEsh	(crash)

A-EEshvuhl	(Asheville)
bA-EEnjUH	(banjo)
A-EEspERn	(aspirin)

When short "a" is followed by "l," it may take either the "uh" or "yuh" glide as in "sAuhlit" (salad) or "Ayuhl" (Al).

Before all other consonant sounds "A" may be used, as in "bAd" (bad) and "hAt" (hat). When stressed, or drawled, the "uh" or "yuh" glide may be added.

VARIATIONS: Certain common words are frequently pronounced with "EH" as in "kEHtch" (catch), "THEHt" (that), and "gEHTHER" (gather).

EXCEPTIONS: When a verb is spelled with "amp," either final or before an unstressed syllable, the short "a" is often pronounced as "AH" as in "stAHmp" (stamp), "trAHmpl" (trample), and "pAHmpER" (pamper).

"A" . . . . as in "carry," "marry," "narrow," etc.

When short "a" is followed by double "rr" plus a vowel, it is generally pronounced as "AA." This sound is between the General-American "A" and "AH," and it is produced by holding the mouth in the open position for "AH" and sounding "A" (see Figures 15 and 16, page 154). Students who have studied the New England dialect will find the production of this sound familiar.

DRILL WORDS

kAAri	(carry)	spAArUH	(sparrow)
mAAri	(marry)	hAAri	(Harry)
nAArUH	(narrow)	bAAri	(Barry)

bAAruhl	(barrel)
kAA-ERn	(carrion)
mAArUH	(marrow)

VARIATION: The variant "AH" may also be used, as in "hAHrUH" (harrow).

"AW" . . . . as in "law," "cross," "song," etc.

There are many slight variations for this "AW" sound. People differ in pronouncing it; authorities differ in recording it. Therefore, the following rules must be considered general, but for the purpose of this book they are valid.

WHEN THE GENERAL-AMERICAN "AW" SOUND IS SPELLED WITH "a" OR "o" FOLLOWED BY "l" OR "s" PLUS A CONSONANT, IT IS OFTEN PRONOUNCED AS "AH-OO."

Both elements of this diphthong "AH-OO" seem to be relaxed and given almost equal value, as in "bAH-OOl" (ball), "krAH-OOs" (cross), and "tAH-OOk" (talk).

WHEN THE GENERAL-AMERICAN "AW" IS SPELLED "au," "aw," OR "ou" IT IS COMMONLY PRONOUNCED AS "AH-OO."

Thus, the following words would be "sAH-OO" (saw), "fAH-OOlt" (fault), and "fAH-OOt" (fought).

It must be remembered that when this "AH-OO" is in an unstressed syllable, it must not be given its full value.

DRILL WORDS

sprAH-OOl	(sprawl)	hAH-OOk	(hawk)
kAH-OOt	(caught)	lAH-OOst	(lost)
bAH-OOlz	(bawls)	sAH-OOs	(sauce)

sAH-OOsER	(saucer)
dAH-OOdER	(daughter)
fAH-OOl	(fall)

Before other consonants, a tense, forward "AW" may be used. This "AW" has a slight "OH" quality and when drawled becomes "AW-OH" as in "sAW-OHng" (song). In the diphthong, which is used principally in monosyllables, the first element "AW" is produced from farther back in the mouth so that it has an "AH" quality. Thus, "dAWg" (dog), when unstressed, sounds almost like "dOHg," and "dAW-OHg" (dog), when drawled, sounds almost like "dAH-OHg."

VARIATIONS: The second elements of the above diphthongs may also be pronounced as "oo" as in "brAHoot" (brought) and "fAWoog" (fog).

The words "hog" and "fog" are variable and have been heard pronounced with all the above variant sounds.

Some people pronounce "AW" as "A" when it is preceded and followed by "s" as in "sAsij" (sausage) and "sAsi" (saucy).

EXCEPTIONS: When the "AW" sound is spelled "au" and is followed by "n," it is commonly pronounced as "A" or, when drawled, "A-AY" as in "hAnt" (haunt) and "gA-AYnt" (gaunt).

CAUTION: The diphthongs in this section must be produced subtly, inobtrusively, and without exaggeration.

"AW" . . . . as in "forest," "short," "war," etc.

The following general rules show the tendency to replace "AW" before "r" with other vowel sounds:

WHEN GENERAL-AMERICAN "AW" IS FOLLOWED BY "r" PLUS A VOWEL (NOT "y"), OR "rr" PLUS A VOWEL (INCLUDING "y"), OR "r" PLUS "m" OR "n," IT IS OFTEN CHANGED TO "AH."

DRILL WORDS

fAHrist	(forest)	flAHridi:	(Florida)
sAHri	(sorry)	AH-ERnj	(orange)
tAHrmint	(torment)	tUHmAHrUH	(tomorrow)

	lAHruhl	(laurel)
	bAHri	(borrow)
	stAHrm	(storm)

*WHEN GENERAL-AMERICAN "AW" IS FOLLOWED BY
FINAL "r," OR "r" PLUS A CONSONANT OR "y," IT IS
OFTEN CHANGED TO "OH."*

DRILL WORDS

mOH-ER	(more)	fOH-ERs	(force)
rOH-ER	(roar)	dOHri	(dory)
kOH-ERd	(cord)	glOHri	(glory)

	swOH-ERd	(sword)
	pOH-ERk	(pork)
	stOHri	(story)

NOTE: See "R" under consonants for explanation of the change of "r" to "ER" before a consonant, as in "mOH-ER" (more), but not before "r" followed by a vowel sound, as in "stOHri" (story).

EXCEPTION: The word "foreigner" may be pronounced as "fERnER" or "fAWrnER".

"EE" . . . . as in "see," "evening," "really," etc.

This sound generally remains the same, as in "sEE" (see) and "EEvnin" (evening). Before "l," however, an "uh" glide is added, as in "fEEuhl" (feel) and "stEEuhl" (steal).

VARIATIONS: For "EE" words spelled with "ea" some highlanders prefer the older pronunciation "AY" as in "rAYli" (really), "jAYnz" (jeans), "grAYs" (grease), and "lAYswAH:z" (leastwise).

EXCEPTIONS: The words "lief" and "neither" are commonly pronounced as "liv" and "nUooTHER."

The word "crick" seems to be more frequently pronounced as "krEEk" in the Ozark and Smoky regions and as "krik" in the Blue Ridge and the Cumberlands.

"EE" . . . . as in "gaily," "county," "pretty," etc.

Final "y," which is sounded as "EE" in General-American, is usually pronounced as "i," although some speakers use the intermediate "i:" sound.

DRILL WORDS

bAHdi	(body)	jinERli	(generally)
kAooni	(county)	pERdi	(pretty)
kUHntrAri	(contrary)	spAHisi	(spicy)

pyOOni	(puny)
gAYyuhli	(gaily)
fAHisti	(feisty)

EXCEPTION: In the word "every," the final "y" is usually dropped, as in "EHvERhwiUHn" (whenever) and "EHvERthEHng" (everything).

"EH" . . . . as in "pen," "fresh," "head," etc.

In Mountain speech, this short "e" (EH) sound vacillates with almost every breath that bears it. Not only does it change in length, but it may also change in quality and color. Certain general rules follow for the more stable variations.

WHEN THE SHORT "e" (EH) SOUND IS FOLLOWED BY "m" OR "n" IT USUALLY CHANGES TO "i."

This "i" should be produced toward the front of the mouth and should have a noticeable nasal quality. The nasalization should not be burlesqued. When stressed or drawled, this "i" will be represented as "iUH" using the "UH" glide.

DRILL WORDS

piUHn	(pen)	iUHnjUHn	(engine)
siUHnt	(sent)	UHgiUHn	(again)
hwiUHn	(when)	wiUHnt	(went)

tiUHmpER	(temper)
liUHmUHn	(lemon)
iUHnithEHng	(anything)

WHEN THE SHORT "e" (EH) SOUND IS FOLLOWED BY THE CONSONANT SOUNDS "d," "g," "j," "sh" OR "zh," IT OFTEN CHANGES TO "AY."

DRILL WORDS

hAYd	(head)	frAYsh	(fresh)
lAYg	(leg)	mAYzhER	(measure)
AYj	(edge)	brAYd	(bread)

AYg	(egg)
bAYd	(bed)
plAYzhER	(pleasure)

VARIATIONS: The variant "A" may be used for words following the above rules, as in "hAd" (head), "frAsh" (fresh), "rAglER" (regular), "plAzhER" (pleasure), "mAn" (men), and "mAmri" (memory).

The "A" sound also occurs before "ll" as in "yAl" (yell). "mAlER" (mellow), and "yAlER" (yellow).

The variant "EH" may also be used for the above words as well as all others, but unlike the General-American pronunciation, the highlanders produce their sound from a more forward position in the mouth.

EXCEPTIONS: In certain common words "EH" becomes "i" before "s" and "t" as in "yistUHdi" (yesterday), "git" (get), and "yit" (yet).

"EH" . . . . as in "very," "parent," "where," etc.

When "EH" is followed by "r," two important variants are used in Mountain speech.

WHEN THE "EH" SOUND IS SPELLED WITH "e" BEFORE "r," THE VOWEL AND CONSONANT SOUNDS COMBINE AND ARE PRONOUNCED AS "ER."

This "ER" is the sound of "er" in the General-American pronunciation of "hER" (her). The Mountain "r" is usually stronger and richer than in General-American.

DRILL WORDS

vERi	(very)	hAEEkbERi	(hackberry)
hwER	(where)	UHmERiki	(America)
tERuhbuhl	(terrible)	shERif	(sheriff)

THERbAoots	(thereabouts)
tchERi	(cherry)
jERikOH	(Jericho)

WHEN THE "EH" SOUND IS SPELLED WITH "a," "ai," "ea," OR "ua" BEFORE "r," IT USUALLY CHANGES TO "AA."

This "AA" has already been discussed under "A" as in "carry."

DRILL WORDS

pAArint	(parent)	AAr	(air)	skAAr	(scare)
kAArluhs	(careless)	swAAr	(swear)	bAAr	(bear)
skwAAr	(square)	hAAr	(hair)	stAAr	(stare)

VARIATION: The variant "i" is sometimes used, particularly by old people, as in "kiER" (care) and "shiERf" (sheriff).

EXCEPTIONS: The word "where" may be pronounced as "wAAr" or "wER"; "there" may be "THAAr" or "THER."

"I" .... as in "like," "my," "iron," etc.

This vowel sound which is usually "AH-EE" in General-American becomes an elongated "AH:" in Mountain speech.

DRILL WORDS

lAH:k	(like)	hwAH:t	(white)
mAH:	(my)	kAH:nli	(kindly)
AH:ERn	(iron)	fAH:ERd	(fired)

mAH:di	(mighty)
rAH:fl	(rifle)
pAH:n	(pine)

VARIATION: Some highlanders use an "i" glide after "AH:" as in "lAH:ik" (like) and "kAH:inli" (kindly).

The variant "AAi" may also be used, as in "lAAik" (like) and "kAAinli" (kindly).

"i" .... as in "trip," "since," "bring," etc.

This short "i" is generally intensified to "i:" in Mountain speech. When stressed or drawled, it often becomes "ii:" as in "trii:p" (trip). The first element is the normal short "i," and the second element is the tensed "i:" which almost becomes "EE."

Before "l" the "uh" glide is often inserted, as in "hi:uhlz" (hills).

When unstressed, short "i" may remain the same.

DRILL WORDS

tri:p	(trip)	tchi:uhldERn	(children)
hi:t	(it)	hAWspi:tl	(hospital)
sti:uhl	(still)	diskUHmfi:t	(discomfit)

vi:uhlyUHn	(villain)
gi:tAH-ER	(guitar)
fi:sh	(fish)

Although the tensed "i:" is frequently heard before the nasal consonants, the variant "EH:" is suggested as being more typical of the dialect.

This "EH" should have a distinct nasal quality, but the actor
should guard against overemphasizing this feature.

DRILL WORDS

sEHns	(since)	EHvERthEHng	(everything)
brEHng	(bring)	lEHng-kERn	(Lincoln)
rEHntch	(rinse)	flEHngUHn	(flinging)

pEHn	(pin)
sprEHng	(spring)
strEHng	(string)

VARIATION: For a lighter dialect, short "i" may be used throughout, but it should be produced from a forward position in the mouth.

EXCEPTIONS: The following words are commonly pronounced as:
"pERdi" (pretty), "vAH:grUHs" (vigorous), "hwoop" (whip), and
"sEHt" (sit).

"i" .... as in "hear," "queer," "near," etc.

The short "i" is generally retained before "r" as in "fiER"
(fear), "hiER" (hear), "niER" (near), and "kwiER" (queer).

When the "r" is followed by a vowel, however, the "i" is often
dropped, as in "mERuhkl" (miracle) and "sERp" (syrup).

VARIATION: Many highlanders pronounce short "i" as "AA"
as in "kwAAr" (queer), "rAAr" (rear), "hAAr" (hear), and "klAAr"
(clear).

"OH" .... as in "stone," "moan," "fellow," etc.

This vowel sound generally remains the same except that when
it is stressed or drawled it receives greater elongation than in
General-American, as in "stOH:n" (stone), "mOH:n" (moan), and
"hOH:tEHl" (hotel).

Thus, the following words are commonly pronounced as
"AArUH" (arrow) and "nAArUH" (narrow). However, many high-
landers drop the final vowel sound completely and sound "r" as
"ER" as in "AA-ER" (arrow) and "spAA-ER" (sparrow).

WHEN THE FINAL "OH" SOUND IS UNSTRESSED AND PRECEDED BY ANY CONSONANT SOUND (EXCEPT "r"), IT IS GENERALLY TREATED AS "ER."

DRILL WORDS

fEHuhlER	(fellow)	wi:dER	(widow)
mAY:dER	(tomato)	yEHuhlER	(yellow)
bEHuhlER	(bellow)	fAHlER	(follow)

hAHlER	(hollow)
skEEdER	(mosquito)
pi:uhlER	(pillow)

Many highlanders give almost equal stress to both syllables of a two-syllable word. In such cases final "OH" should retain the "OH" sound, as in "AH-OOtOH" (auto) and "sOH:lOH" (solo).

"O" . . . . as in "rod," "hospital," "on," etc.

This sound is commonly pronounced as "AH" or "AHuh" when stressed.

DRILL WORDS

bAHuhb	(Bob)	tAHuhluhbuhl	(tolerable)
bAHuhdi	(body)	bAHuhTHER	(bother)
tAHuhnik	(tonic)	mAHuhnstrUHs	(monstrous)

gAHuhblER	(gobbler)
fAHuhtch	(fotch)
swAHuhlER	(swallow)

VARIATION: Many highlanders use the variant "AW" particularly before "g," "k," "m," "n," "s," or "z" as in the following examples:

DRILL WORDS

stAWk	(stock)	pAWsUHm	(opossum)
mAWk	(mock)	hAWspitl	(hospital)
tAWm	(Tom)	wAWnt	(want)

jAWn	(John)
rAWzn	(rosin)
AWn	(on)

EXCEPTIONS: The following pronunciations are used, particularly by elderly people: "krAp" (crop), "drAp (drop), and "yAndER" (yonder).

"OO" . . . . as in "food," "true," "do," etc.

This sound may remain the same as in General-American, except that when stressed it should receive greater elongation, as in "fOO:d" (food), "trOO:" (true), and "dOO:" (do).

Many highlanders use an "i" glide before "OO:" as in the following examples:

DRILL WORDS

fiOO:d	(food)	briOO:t	(brute)
triOO:	(true)	kiOO:n	(raccoon)
diOO:	(do)	friOO:t	(fruit)

priOO:v (prove)
miOO:n (moon)
shiOO:t (shoot)

WHEN THE GENERAL-AMERICAN "OO" SOUND IS PRE-CEDED BY "r" AND FOLLOWED BY A VOWEL, IT IS GENER-ALLY PRONOUNCED AS "ER."

This "ER" sound is like the "er" of "hER" (her) in General-American except that the "r" is silent as in "hER" (her). It should be produced from the front of the mouth and is used in words like "rER:nt" (ruined) and "krER-l" (cruel).

WHEN THE GENERAL-AMERICAN "OO" IS SPELLED "u," "ue," OR "ew" AND IS PRECEDED BY "d," "n," OR "t," IT TAKES A "y" GLIDE AND BECOMES yOO."

According to the above rule, the following words are pronounced as "tyOOn" (tune), "nyOO" (new), and "dyOO" (due). The "t" and "d" often blend into the "y" glide so that they become "tch" and "j" respectively, as in "tchOOlip" (tulip) and "jOOti" (duty).

EXCEPTIONS: The words "hoop," "coop," and "soon" are commonly pronounced with the "oo" of "good" and become "hoop," "koop," and "soon."

"oo" . . . . as in "book," "put," "during," etc.

This sound generally remains the same as in General-American except that it should be produced from a more forward position in the mouth. When stressed, it will be designated as "oo:" as in "boo:k" (book), "poo:t" (put), and "poo:dn" (pudding).

WHEN THE "oo" SOUND IS FOLLOWED BY "r" FINAL OR "r" PLUS ANOTHER CONSONANT SOUND, IT IS GENER-ALLY PRONOUNCED AS "OH."

In words following the above rule, the "r" sound becomes "ER" as in "shOH-ER" (sure), "pOH-ERli" (poorly), "yOH-ER" (your), "pyOH-ER" (pure), and "kyOH-ER" (cure).

EXCEPTIONS: The following words are commonly pronounced as "sUuht" (soot), "joorin" (during), "tUook" (took), and "shUook" (shook).

"yOO" . . . . as in "use," "music," "puny," etc.

As in General-American, a "y" glide is used before long "u" (OO) when it is the initial letter of a word, or when the preceding consonant sound is "b," "f," "g," "h," "k," "m," or "p," as in "yOOz" (use), "myOOzik" (music), and "pyOOni" (puny).

Highlanders give greater force to their initial consonants, and this often creates a slight "i" glide before the "y" in a stressed word, as in "hiyOOmin" (human), "miyOOl" (mule), and "biyOOgl" (bugle).

This sound is often changed to "UH" or dropped completely from a word. For a discussion of these changes see **"Unstressed Syllables."**

"U" . . . . as in "up," "nut," "country," etc.

When unstressed, this sound generally remains "U" as in General-American but it should be produced from a forward position in the mouth. Under stress, or drawl it becomes "Uoo" as in "nUoot" (nut). This "oo" is like the "oo" in "book" and it, too, should receive forward production. But it must be remembered that the "oo" is a glide and as such should be unobtrusive.

DRILL WORDS

Uoop	(up)	mUoosl	(muscle)
mUootch˙	(much)	sUoopER	(supper)
shUooks	(shucks)	lUooki	(lucky)
	kUoot	(cut)	
	kUoopl	(couple)	
	lUoov	(love)	

WHEN GENERAL-AMERICAN "U" IS FOLLOWED BY "m," "n," OR THE SOUND OF "ng," IT FREQUENTLY CHANGES TO "AHoo."

The two elements of this diphthong must blend together smoothly.

DRILL WORDS

kAHoontri	(country)	bAHoontch	(bunch)
hAHoong-gri	(hungry)	hAHoombl	(humble)
pAHoong-kn	(pumpkin)	rAHoonUHn	(running)
	plAHoom	(plumb)	
	gAHoon	(gun)	
	hAHoont	(hunt)	

The variant "AWoo" may also be used before nasal consonants, as in "wAWoon" (one), "plAWoondER" (plunder), and "jAWoomp" (jump).

VARIATIONS: The variant "EH" may be used when short "u" (U) is between any two of the consonant sounds "j," "sh," "tch," "s," or "r" as in "jEHuhj" (judge), "sEHuhtch" (such), "rEHuhsh" (rush), and "jEHuhs" (just).

This "EH" may also be used between one of the above-mentioned consonant sounds and "t" or "v" as in "tEHuhtch" (touch), "shEHuhv" (shove), and "shEHuht" (shut).

EXCEPTIONS: The following words are sometimes pronounced as "gERsh" (gush), "pERp" (pup), and "fERs" (fuss).

"ER" . . . . as in "her," "learn," "first," etc.

This sound is fundamentally the same in Mountain speech as it is in General-American. However, the highlander's "r" is richer and fuller so that the complete "ER" sound has a distinctive quality. The tongue should be more tensed in the production of this sound.

The forceful production of a preceding consonant sound may produce an "uh" glide before this vowel sound, as in "tchuhERtch" (church) and "kuhER" (cur). If used, this "UH" glide must be very light and in no way interfere with the dominant "ER" sound.

WHEN A GENERAL-AMERICAN "ER" WORD IS SPELLED WITH "e" OR "ea," MANY HIGHLANDERS CHANGE THIS SOUND TO "AA."

The "AA" sound has been discussed under "A" as in "carry." The actor must be careful not to force this sound into undue prominence. If he cannot produce this sound gracefully and easily, he may use the variant "AH."

The above rule applies to such words as "lAArn" (learn), "vAArmint" (vermin), "pAArsn" (person), "sAArtch" (search), "sAArtn" (certain), "pAArfikt" (perfect) and "sAArv" (serve).

EXCEPTIONS: Certain common words spelled with "i," "o," or "u" often drop the "r" before "s" and change the vowel sound to "U" as in "fUoos" (first), "wUoos" (worse), and "bUoost" (burst).

"OW" . . . . as in "out," "cow," "proud," etc.

Mountain folk generally pronounce this sound as "Aoo" with the "oo" acting as a glide from "A" to the following consonant sound.

DRILL WORDS

Aoot	(out)	kyAoonti	(county)
kyAoo	(cow)	shAoot	(shout)
prAood	(proud)	stAoot	(stout)

nAoo	(now)
hAoon	(hound)
hAoodi	(howdy)

When this sound is followed by "r," the "oo" glide blends into the following consonant sound, and the pronunciation becomes "A-ER" as in "sA-ER" (sour), "pA-ER" (power), and "skA-ER" (scour).

"OI" .... as in "oil," "boil," "toil," etc.

This diphthong is commonly pronounced as "AWi" by Mountain people. The "AW" should be produced from a forward position in the mouth, and the "i" should serve as a glide.

DRILL WORDS

AWil	(oil)	jAWin	(join)	tchAWis	(choice)
bAWil	(boil)	bAWi	(boy)	nAWizi	(noisy)
tAWil	(toil)	pAWint	(point)	spAWil	(spoil)

VARIATIONS: The variant "AHi" may also be used, particularly for an elderly character, as in "bAHil" (boil), "jAHin" (join), and "hAHist" (hoist).

UNSTRESSED SYLLABLES

The highlander's use of heavy and frequent stress on the accented syllables of a word often results in giving almost full stress to an unaccented syllable. Although the word "hOHtEHl" (hotel) is pronounced with the same sounds in both Mountain and Middle Western speech, it does not receive the same stress. People in the Middle West accent only the second syllable "tEHl" and generally pronounce it on a higher note than the unstressed first syllable "hOH."

People in the mountains, however, tend to place almost equal stress on both syllables and usually give "hOH:" the high note and "tEHl" the lower note. This practice of stressing initial unstressed syllables is found also in words like **"rEE:pOH-ERt"** (report), **"dAH:rEHkt"** (direct), **"AH:di:"** (idea), **"Auhdmi:t"** (admit), **"di:skUHmfi:t"** (discomfit), and **"dAEE:gAWn"** (doggone). In two-syllable words of this type, the initial syllable may receive primary stress and the second syllable secondary stress rather than have equal stress on both elements. The word "kUHntrAAri" (contrary), however, is commonly stressed on the second syllable only.

When "ent" is part of a suffix, it usually receives almost equal stress as the first syllable. This is particularly true of three-syllable words like **"sEHtlmiUHnt"** (settlement), **"kAWnfidiUHnt"** (confident), and **"A-EEksidiUHnt"** (accident).

Final "ville," however, receives little or no stress, as in "nAWksvuhl" (Knoxville) and "A-EEshvuhl" (Asheville).

When an unstressed final syllable ends with the consonant sound "d," "j," "k," "n," "s," "t," "sh," or "v," the preceding vowel is usually pronounced as "i" as in "sAyuhlit" (salad), "mAArij" (marriage), "dERik" (derrick), "nAWgin" (noggin), "prAWmis" (promise), "bA-EEskit" (basket), "li:krish" (licorice), and "Ai:ktiv" (active).

When the final unstressed syllable is spelled "ite," it is commonly pronounced as "AH:t" as in "fAY:vERAH:t" (favorite); when spelled "ate," it becomes "AY:t" as in "grAuhjiAY:t" (graduate).

When the initial consonant of a final unstressed syllable is "t" and the final consonant is "n," the "t" is often dropped in favor of the glottal stop (/), and the syllable becomes "/n" as in "mAW:ER/n" (Martin). (See **"The Glottal Stop,"** page 24.)

When the initial consonant of a final unstressed syllable is "d" and the final consonant is "n," both the glottal stop and the sound of "d" are used, as in "gyAH:ER/dn" (garden). This final "/dn" syllable should cause no difficulty as it is a common pronunciation throughout most of the United States. There need be no conscious attempt to produce the glottal stop as it will occur naturally if no vowel sound is introduced between "d" and "n."

When the initial consonant of a final unstressed syllable is "s," "sh," "v," or "z" and the final element is "n," the two sounds blend together, as in "pERsn" (person), "mi:shn" (mission), "Uoovn" (oven), and "pAWizn" (poison).

The participial ending "ing" is reduced to "uhn" (in') when preceded by a vowel, as in "diOO:uhn" (doing). This is similar to the Southern treatment, but it must be remembered that stress is important in Mountain speech and gives the necessary distinction to some words which might otherwise be pronounced the same in highland and lowland areas.

When the "ing" ending is preceded by "r" the two sounds ("r" and "n") blend together, as in "dAWktERn" (doctoring) and "wAA:ERn" (wearing).

Medial unstressed vowels are pronounced as "UH" or "i," the

latter being sometimes tensed to "i:." There is no definite rule which can be given for the exact use of either since the choice seems to be an individual matter and may often depend on the mood of the speaker. Thus, "Kentucky" has been heard as "kUHntUooki" and "kintUooki." On the other hand, a character who believes that a word should be pronounced as it is spelled, would say "kAY:ntUooki" (with the accent on the first syllable).

Another feature of Mountain speech is the dropping of an unstressed vowel, and sometimes a complete syllable, particularly before or after "l," "n," and "r" as in "fA-EEmli" (fam*i*ly), "prAWbli" (prob*a*bly), "fEHlni" (fel*o*ny), "EHvERbAHdi" (every-body), and "tERbuhl" (terr*i*ble).

When "i" is followed by another vowel, it is usually dropped, as in "kyoorUHs" (curious) and "jiOOluhs" (Julius). This is also true of the medial unstressed "yOO" sound which drops the "y" and changes "OO" to "UH" as in "AH:ERgUHmiUHnt"ʃ(argument), and "grAuhjuhl" (gradual). When the unstressed "yOO" sound is followed by unstressed "l" or "r," it may be dropped completely, as in "pERti:klER" (particular) and "fi:grin" (figuring).

An initial unstressed syllable is often completely dropped, as in "tAY:dERz" (potatoes), "kAH-OOl" (recall), and "spAH:z" (despise).

REVERSED SYLLABLES

In an unstressed syllable when "r" follows a consonant and precedes a vowel, it is generally pronounced after the vowel, as in "tchi:ldERn" (children), "AuhlfERd" (Alfred), and "pERtEHk" (protect).

CONSONANT CHANGES

(Only the important consonant changes are listed.)

Initial consonants of stressed syllables are pronounced more forcefully than in General-American.

B — In the unstressed "mble" ending, the "b" is often dropped, as in "brA-EEml" (bramble).

D — Final "d" is usually dropped after "l" and "n" as in "kOH:l" (cold) and "friUHn" (friend).

As in General-American, final "d" is sounded as "t" after the consonant sounds "f," "k," "p," "s," "sh," "tch," or "th" as in "fi:kst" (fixed) and "wERkt" (worked). However, it may also be sounded as "t" after "l" or "n" as in "spi:uhlt" (spilled) and "lAArnt" (learned).

In a final unaccented position, when preceded by an unstressed vowel sound, "d" is also pronounced as "t" as in "bAuhlit" (ballad).

When followed by the intrusive "y" glide, the "d" and "y" blend to form "j" as in "grAuhjuhl" (gradual).

F — This sound is usually dropped in "AuhtER" (after) and its compounds.

G — Hard "g" is sometimes dropped when preceded by the nasal "ng" sound so that the General-American word "Ang-grEE" (angry) is usually pronounced by mountain folk as "A-EEngri."

Many highlanders pronounce hard "g" from a more forward position in the mouth so that it becomes colored with a slight "y" glide (Fig. 18), as in "gyAH-ERd" (guard). This glide is used par-

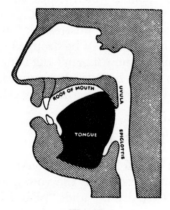

Fig. 17

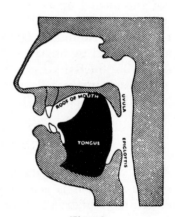

Fig. 18

ticularly by elderly people and is generally restricted to "g" followed by the sound of "AH."

H — As in General-American, personal pronouns are pronounced without the "h" when in an unstressed position in a sentence, as in "jAWn gi:v UHm UH rAYuhl nAH:s tAH:m" (John gave him a real nice time).

An "h" is generally prefixed to "it" and "ain't" so that they become "hi:t" and "hAY:nt."

Like all consonant sounds in Mountain speech, "h" has greater force, when stressed, than in General-American.

K — This consonant is usually produced from a more forward position in the mouth than in General-American (Fig. 17). Before front vowels it may take a "y" glide, as in "kyAH:ER" (car) (Fig. 18).

The word "asked" may drop the "k" (A-EEst) or place it before the "s" (A-EEks).

L — As in General-American, the consonant "l" has two sounds, dark and clear. There is no change in dark "l," but the clear "l" is distinctly different from the Middle West sound. It should be a tense, quick flip of the tongue which lightly taps the forward part of the hard palate just a fraction of an inch behind the teeth. This clear "l" is particularly noticeable when preceded by a vowel and followed by the sounds "i," "ER," or "A" as in "si:li" (silly), "swAWlER" (swallow), and "bERlAp" (burlap).

When "l" is in an unstressed position and followed by "b," "f," "m," "p," or "v," it is generally dropped and replaced with "oo" as in "sEHoof" (self), "fi:oom" (film), and "hEHoop" (help). If "l" is sounded, it should still retain the "oo" glide, as in "mEHoolvin" (Melvin).

If "l" is sounded before "m," however, the two consonant sounds are separated by a light "uh" glide, as in "EHluhm" (elm).

The word "walnut" is commonly pronounced "wAW-ERnUHt."

N — This consonant sound is often added to "EHf" (if) so that it becomes "EHfn" and to "Aoot" (out) so that it becomes "Aoo/n."

R — The highlander's "r" is a stronger, more distinctive sound than General-American (see Fig. 19). The tongue may be in its normal

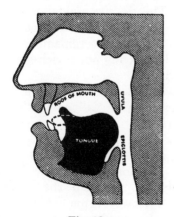

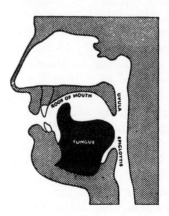

Fig. 19   Fig. 20

position but it should be more tensed. Many highlanders, however, give the tongue tip more of a backward curl (Fig. 20). This consonant is always sounded except in certain words where it is followed by the sound of "s," "t," or "TH" as in "wUoos" (worse), "pAAtrij" (partridge), and "fUooTHER" (further).

The "r" may also be dropped in "thOHt" (throat), "thOH:" (throw), and "thiOO" (through).

Final "r" is always sounded, and an intrusive "r" is common for the endings "o," "ow," and sometimes "a" as in "fEHlER" (fellow), "tAY:dER" (potato), and "lAH:mER" (lima).

An intrusive "r" is also common after the sound "AW" and in place of "U" as illustrated in the sentence, "THAt AAr fEHoolER UHz shOH-ER fERsi bAoot iz vi:tlz win i: wUHz Uoop in THuh nAW-ERfAW-ERk hAW-ERspitl" (That there fellow was sure fussy about his victuals when he was up in the Norfolk hospital). (See "U" as in "up," page 165.)

When "r" is followed by a consonant, it is generally pronounced as "ER" as in "stAH-ERt" (start), "pi-ERt" (pert), and "kOH-ERs" (course). This "ER" rather than "r" is the natural result of the tense "r" quality in the highlands.

The "ER" sound is frequently introduced before final "n" in an unstressed syllable, as in "woo:mERn" (woman) and "hEETHERn" (heathen).

S — The following words are commonly pronounced as "rEHntch" (rinse), "pEHntchERz" (pincers), "li:krish" (licorice), "nAArvish" (nervous), and "gli:mpsh" (glimpse).

T — When "t" is followed by an unstressed vowel plus "n," it is usually replaced by a slight glottal stop (/) as in "kAW/n" (cotton). (See "The Glottal Stop," page 24.) This is a common practice in informal speech throughout most of the United States and should cause no difficulty to the actor. But it must be remembered that the glottal stop in American regional speech is not a rich and complete sound as it is in the Scottish dialect.

Medially, and particularly between two vowel sounds, "t" is flapped lightly so that it resembles a faint "d" as in "bi:gidi" (biggity) and "pAH-ERdnER" (partner).

When double "t" is followed by "l," the tongue is in position for "t," but the "t" is not sounded, as in "sEH(t)lER" (settler).

When "t" is in an unstressed position and is preceded and followed by "s," the "t" is usually dropped and the preceding vowel elongated, as in "rEH:s" (rests). However, many highlanders, particularly elderly people retain the older pronunciation of "stUHs" in forming plurals, as in "nEHstUHs" (nests) and "pOH:stUHs" (posts).

After "f," "k," or "s," the "t" is often dropped, as in "zA-EEkli" (exactly), "sAW-OHf" (soft), and "fA-EEs" (fast).

After "f," "n," and "s," the sound of "t" is sometimes added, as in "kli:ft" (cliff), "sAArmint" (sermon), and "wAHoonst" (once).

Some highlanders retain the older pronunciations of "tERkl" (turtle) and "bri:kl" (brittle) in which "t" is replaced by "k."

When followed by the "y" glide, "t" is often sounded as "tch" as in "tchOOn" (tune) or "dOH:ntchUH" (don't you).

The "t" is generally sounded in "AWftUHn" (often).

TH — In an unstressed position "TH" may be dropped from pronouns, adverbs, and conjunctions as in "UHn iUHn" (and then), "EEvn OH" (even though), "lAH:k is" (like this), and "bi:gERn hiUHm" (bigger than him).

The word "moths" is commonly pronounced as "mAW-OHz."

th — Unvoiced "th" is occasionally changed to "t" when preceded by "n" or "r" as in "AH-ERtER" (Arthur) and "mAHoonts" (months).

The sound of "th" is generally added to "hAH:t-th" (height).

tch — The "ture" ending, which is generally pronounced as "tchER" in General-American, retains the sound of "t" in highland areas, as in "pA-EEstER" (pasture).

V — When "v" is followed by "n" in an unstressed syllable, the "v" becomes glottalized, and the "n" changes to "m" as in "Uoo/m" (oven), "lEHuh/m," and "i:/m" (even). The glottal stop (/) must not be produced as a separate element. The lips are closed for "m" immediately after the vowel sound is produced, and then the glottal stop is used to force the "m" sound. This use of the glottal stop is common in lax speech throughout the United States and should offer no difficulty to the actor, providing he does not try to overemphasize the sound.

W — This consonant sound is usually dropped in "AW-OHkERd" (awkward), "bA-EEkERdz" (backwards), "AH-OOluhz" (always), and "frEEkUHnt" (frequent).

The "w" sound is frequently heard in "swOH-ERd" (sword), "kwAH:l" (coil), "kwAH:n" (coin), "swinj" (singe), and "swi:vuhl" (shrivel).

Y — A "y" glide is frequently sounded before an initial vowel which is followed by "r" as in "yAHrn" (earn), "yAHrth" (earth), and "yAHrb" (herb).

Z — A final "z" sound is usually given to "bAi:kERdz" (backward) and "nOH:wAY:z" (noway).

WH — Although the single "w" sound is frequent, as in "win" (when), "hw" may also be used, as in "hwin" (when).

NG — Medial nasalized "ng" is usually sounded as "n" in such words as "strEHnth" (strength), "hAnkUHtchi:f" (handkerchief), and "lEHnth" (length).

SH — When initial "sh" is followed by "r," it may be pronounced as "s" particularly if the character is elderly, as in "sri:uhl" (shrill) and "srAood" (shroud).

GRAMMAR CHANGES

One of the most typical habits of the highlander is his fondness for redundancy. This is not peculiar to Mountain folk alone, but it is used more consistently and fully by them than by people in other regional areas. Some of the more common compounds are: "hAoon dAW-OHg" (hounddog), "mA-EEn pERsn" (man person), "kAoo briOOt" (cow brute), "bAH:bl boo:k" (bible book), "rAH:fl gAHoon" (rifle gun), "grA-EEni woo:mUHn" (granny woman), "ki:d UHv UH bAWi" (kid of a boy), "tiOOth diUHnis" (tooth dentist), and "bi:skit brAYd" (biscuit bread).

This practice is not limited solely to nouns, as illustrated by the following examples:

"AH jinERli yOOzhli srAoond hit."
(I *generally, usually* surround it.)
(I *usually* go around it.)

"hi/ wUHz jis UH smAH-OOl pyOOni li:dl OHl thEHng."
(It was just a *small, puny, little old* thing.)
(It was just a *small* thing.)

Like the Cockney, the highlander adds "er" to comparative forms as in:

"AH di:srimEHmbER witch wUHz wERsER."
(I disremember which was *worser*.)
(I don't remember which was *worse*.)

The adverb "more" may also be employed in forming the comparative of words that generally add "er", as in:

"bAH-ERbs mOH-ER pERdi UHn jAY:n."
(Barb's more *pretty* than Jane.)
(Barbara's *prettier* than Jane.)

The superlative is usually formed by suffixing "est" to the adjective, rather than adding the word "most" as in:

"hi/ wUHz THuh tERblis frAY ivER AH sEEd."
(Hit was the *terriblest* fray ever I seed.)
(It was the *most terrible* brawl I ever saw.)

The adverb "vERi" (very) is seldom used by the highlander who prefers more vital intensives, such as:

"THAY-ER mAH:di klEHvER fOH:k."
(They're *mighty* clever folk.)
(They're *very* friendly people.)

"AHd bi rAH:t prAood tUH gOH."
(I'd be *right* proud to go.)
(I'd be *very* glad to go.)

"hi/ shOH-ER wAAr UH tERbuhl goo:d mEHs UH vi:tlz."
(Hit sure were a *terrible* good mess of vi:tlz.)
(It was a *very* good dinner.)

"pAuhps pA-ERfuhl A-EEshi."
(Pap's powerful ashy.)
(Dad's *very* angry.)

Quantity is commonly expressed by the following terms:

"hi/ wUHz nOHrAYdid rAoon THuhd i: hAd UH pA-ER UH kA-EEsh mAHooni."
(Hit was norated round that he had *a power of* cash money.)
(It was told that he had *a great deal of* money.)

"wEEuhnz EHd UH hEE:p UH tchi:kinz."
(We-unz ate *a heap of* chickens.)
(We ate *a great many* chickens.)

"AH gUt mi: UH sAH:t UH rEHdn Uoop tUH diOO."
(I got me *a sight of* redding up to do.)
(I have *a lot of* cleaning to do.)

"AHd UH hEE:p sAH:t rUTHER gid UH soon stAH-ERt."
(I'd a *heap sight* rather git a soon start.)
(I'd *much* rather get an early start.)

"THAArz UH rAH:t smAH-ERt UH hAH-ERdnis twiks UHs."
(There's *a right smart of* hardness 'twixt us.)
(There's *a great deal of* ill-feeling between us.)

"hAYn EHt bUHd UH mEE:zli OH:l smi:UHjin."
(Hain't et but a measly old *smidgen*.)
(I've eaten only a *very small* piece.)

"wi gUt ri:UHmpshinz UH hA-EEm:EEt."
(We got *rimptions* of ham-meat.)
(We have *plenty* of ham.)

The conjunctions "that" and "than" and the pronoun "who" are commonly replaced with "as" as in:

"AH dOHn nOH UHz AH ivER kAWnfi:diUHnst im."
(I don't know *as* I ever confidenced him.)
(I don't think *that* I ever believed him.)

"jAWnz THuh wAHoon UHz AYgd im AWn."
(John's the one *as* egged him on.)
(John's the one *who* prodded him to do it.)

"drUTHER dA-EEns UHz EE:t."
(Druther dance *as* eat.)
(I'd rather dance *than* eat.)

Demonstrative pronouns are commonly followed by "here" or "there" as in:

"THi:sn hyERz gOH:n bi: UH rAH:t goo:/dn."
(This'n *here's* goin' be a right good 'un.)
(This one's going to be a very good one.)

"fEHtch mi: THAt THAAr kAookUoombER."
(Fetch me that *there* cowcumber.)
(Bring me that cucumber.)

"AH AYn mUootch UH: fiOOl bAoot THim THAr snAuhps."
(I ain't much of a fool 'bout them *there* snaps.)
(I'm not very fond of string beans.)

The prefix "uh" (a) is frequently used before verbs ending in "ing" as in:

"AH AYn UH hER/n fER yUH."
(I ain't *a-hurting* for you.)
(I don't need you.)

"AHm UH gi/n tUH it."
(I'm *a-gitting* to it.)
(I'm getting to it.)

"hEEz UH hAHlERn mA-EEstER."
(He's *a-hollering* master.)
(He's hollering a great deal.)

"hits UH kUoomin AWn tUH rAY:n."
(Hits *a-coming* on to rain.)
(It's beginning to rain.)

The use of this extra "UH" (a) is sometimes heard before or after other parts of speech, as in:

"hi: wiUHnt THAuhdUHwAY:."
(He went *that-a-way.*)
(He went that way.)

"AHv UH kUoom fER THuh rEEsEEt."
(I've *a-come* for the receipt.)
(I've come for the recipe.)

The possessive pronoun is usually followed by "own" which is contracted to "'n" as in:

"AH nOH:d in rEE:zn hit wAAr hi:zn."
(I knowed in reason hit were *his'n.*)
(I was almost positive it was *his.*)

"THAt li:dl OH:l fAH:s dAW-OHgz hERn."
(That little old feist dog's *her'n.*)
(That small, ill-tempered dog is *hers.*)

The reflexive pronouns "himself" and "themselves" are usually changed to "hi:zsEHoof" (himself) and "THEHrsEHoofs" (theirselves) with the primary accent on the last syllable.

"hi: wUHz jis UH spUoodn rAoon bAH hi:zsEHoof."
(He was just a-spudding round by *hisself.*)
(He was just ambling along by *himself.*)

"THAY trEEd THuh kOOn THEHrsEHoofs."
(They treed the 'coon *theirselves.*)
(They treed the raccoon *themselves.*)

Superfluous negatives are common, as in:

"nOHbAHdiz nivER spAHd im nOHhAoo."
(*Nobody's never* spied him *nowhow.*)
(*Nobody's* ever seen him anyway.)

"hAYnt nivER hiERd nOH sEHtch UH thEHng."
(*Hain't never* heard *no* such a thing.)
(I've *never* heard such a thing.)

Future time is commonly indicated by the use of "kUoom" (come), as in:

"wi: AY:mz tUH git shEHd UHv it kUoom grA-EEs."
(We aims to git shet of it *come grass*.)
(We plan to get rid of it *in the spring*.)

"AHm fi:ksin tUH stAH-ERt kUoom frAH:di."
(I'm fixing to start *come Friday*.)
(I intend to start *next Friday*.)

One of the most characteristic and colorful grammar changes is the use of an adjective or a noun as a verb, as in:

"shi: pERdid hERsEHoof Uoop sUoom."
(She *prettied* herself up some.)
(She made herself *pretty*.)

"wAHntchUH mUootch mi: stEHd UH fAH-OOl/n mi?"
(Why'ntyuh *much* me 'stead of *faulting* me?)
(Why don't you praise me instead of *finding fault* with me?)

"hi/ plAYzhERd im tUH sEE ER sUH gAY:li."
(Hit *pleasured* him to see her so gaily.)
(It gave him *pleasure* to see her so healthy.)

"AHl mUoosl it Uoop fER yUH."
(I'll *muscle* it up for you.)
(I'll *lift* it up for you.)

"THEHdAAr bUook diERuhl mEE:d UHs fER UH spEHool."
(That'ere buck deer'll *meat* us for a spell.)
(That deer will furnish us with meat for a while.)

"Est" is often added to the present participle for use as a superlative adjective, as in:

"mAi:giz THuh wERkinUHs woo:mERn AH nOH:."
(Maggie's the *workingest* woman I know.)
(Maggie is a *hard-working* woman.)

"Aoolz THuh sEHnginUHs mA-EEn UHn THuh kAooni."
(Al's the *singingest* man in the county.)
(Al is the *best singer* in the county.)

The adjective form is generally used instead of the adverbial, as in:

"shi: tUook AWn tERuhbuhl."
(She took on *terrible*.)
(She grieved a great deal.)

"hi: sAHt Uoop tER rAglER."
(He sot up to her *regular*.)
(He courted her *regularly*.)

Compounds are sometimes reversed, as in:

"AHool nAY:m UHt EHvERwiUHn yUH sAY:."
(I'll name it *everwhen* you say.)
(I'll mention it *whenever* you say.)

"tAY:k EHvERwi:tch pOH:k yUH kUHn yOOz wUuhst."
(Take *everwhich* poke you can use worse.)
(Take *whichever* paper bag you can use best.)

A qualifying "like" is often added to words, as in:

"hi: jis sEHt THAAr kAH:nli wi:shfuhl lAH:k."
(He just sat there kindly *wishful-like*.)
(He sat there rather *wistfully*.)

"AHv bEHn lOH:nsUHm lAHk THAoot yUH."
(I've been *lonesome-like* without you.)
(I've been *lonesome* without you.)

When "like" is used as a verb, it is frequently followed by "for" before an infinitive, as in:

"AH dOH:n lAH:k fER yUH tUH grEEn si:UHs."
(I don't *like for* you to green Sis.)
(I don't want you to tease Sis.)

"wEEuhnz UHd lAH:k fER jAWn tUH kUoom."
(We'uns would *like for* John to come.)
(We would *like* John to come.)

The personal pronouns "we" and "you" are often followed by "ones" which is contracted to " 'uns" as in:

"wEEuhnz UHz hER/n sUthin tERbuhl."
(*We'uns* was hurting something terrible.)
(*We* were aching terribly.)

"win dUH yOOuhnz rEHkin yuhl git bA-EEk?"
(When do *you'uns* reckon you'll get back?)
(When do *you* expect to get back?)

The use of "you-all" and "we-all" is also frequent, but it seems more prevalent among people who have had contact with the lowland areas.

The use of "AWn" (on) for "of" is common, as in:

"AH-OOl AWn UHm hiERd THuh gi:v Aoot."
(All *on* 'em heard the give-out.)
(All *of* them heard the announcement.)

"THEHts THuh bEE/nUHs tAY:l AH ivER hiERd AWn."
(That's the beatenest tale I ever heard *on*.)
(That's the most amazing lie I ever heard *of*.)

The use of the singular instead of the plural in nouns modified by numbers is also common, as in:

"AHv hEHd THEHt hER/n nAH AWn tUH tOO yiER."
(I've had that hurting nigh on to two *year*.)
(I've had that pain almost two *years*.)

"gUHt mi: tOO thrEE pAA-ER UH brOHgA-EEnz."
(Got me two three *pair* of brogans.)
(I have two or three *pairs* of heavy shoes.)

Some words are used only in the plural form, and often that form is incorrect, as in:

"AH gi:v Aoot trAH:n tUH git ini bAY:kin pAoodERz."
(I gave out trying to get any baking *powders*.)
(I stopped trying to get any baking *powder*.)

"AHd shOH-ER AdmAH-ER tUH hEHv THEHt tEEthbrEHsh."
(I'd sure admire to have that *teethbrush*.)
(I'd certainly like to have that *toothbrush*.)

Incorrect verb forms are common, as in:

"AH hOH:pt im bA-EEk iz lEHdER."
(I *holped* him back his letter.)
(I *helped* him address his letter.)

"shi: tAYkn THuh pEHkERwoo:d hOH:m."
(She *taken* the pecker-wood home.)
(She *took* the woodpecker home.)

"kAYn snUk OHvER UHn dri:ngkt hi:d AH-OOl."
(Cain *snuck* over and *drinked* it all.)
(Cain *sneaked* over and *drank* it all.)

"hEEz dAHoon bEHn dAY:d fER UH rAH:t goo:d spEHoo."
(He's *done been dead* for a right good spell.)
(He's *been dead* for a long time.)

The use of "done" is reserved for action which has already been completed, as in:

"AH dAHoon kAH-OOld it tOO im."
(I *done called* it to him.)
(I *mentioned* it to him.)

"AH dUHn dAHoon it."
(I *done done* it.)
(I *did* it.)

The phrase "What did you say?" is frequently replaced by the single word "wi:tch" (which?).

The interrogative pronoun "wUuht" (what) is often followed by "AH-OOl" (all) as in:

"wUuht AH-OOl wUuhz THEHt blAY:md thEHng?"
(*What-all* was that blamed thing?)
(*What* was that thing?)

The phrase "dUHnOH bUHt wUt" (don't know but what) is sometimes used instead of "think", as in:

"dUHnOH bUHt wUuhd AH wi:ool."
(Don't know *but what* I will.)
(I think I will.)

"dUHnOH bUHt wUuhd i:z dAHoon wi:UHnt."
(Don't know *but what* he's done gone.)
(I think he's gone.)

A personal pronoun is frequently inserted after the subject noun, as in:

"sOO shi: hEHd THuh mUooligrUoobz AWnt."
(Sue, *she* had the mullygrubs on it.)
(Sue was sulky about it.)

"rAuhf hEE li:vd bA-EEk yA-EEndER Up OHvER THAAr."
(Ralph, *he* lived back yander up over there.)
(Ralph lived over there.)

The preposition "Auht" (at) is redundantly used, particularly in questions, as in:

"wAAr i:z i: Auht?"
(Where is he at?)
(Where is he?)

The verb "li:sn" (listen) is commonly followed by "at" rather than "to" as in:

"li:sn UHt THEHt tOHdfrAH-OOg hAHlER."
(Listen *at* that toad-frog holler.)
(Listen *to* the toad croak.)

COMMON EXPRESSIONS

It is not possible to list all the expressions common to the high-lander; nor is it within the province of this book. The following examples are offered because they are typical and colorful. However, the actor or the writer must guard against an overabundance of these phrases, particularly when portraying a modern character.

One expression still in general use is "AH wUoodn tchOOz ini" (I wouldn't choose any). This is similar to the Middle Westerner's "I don't care for any" and is used in declining an offer of food.

Other examples are:

"AHool tEHoo yUH fER wAH: AH dAHoon it."
(I'll tell you *for why* I done it.)
(I'll tell you *why* I did it.)

"shUooks yUH kAYn hA-EEndili blAY:m ER."
(*Shucks,* you can't *handily* blame her.)
(*Shucks,* you can't *honestly* blame her.)

"hAoodi mAYk yERsEHoof plAYz/nt."
(*Howdy, make yourself pleasant.*)
(*Hello, make yourself at home.*)

"AHool trAH: tinjAWi yUH."
(I'll try to *enjoy* you.)
(I'll try to *entertain* you.)

"hi: li:t UH rA-EEg fER hOH:m."
(He *lit a rag for home.*)
(He *ran home.*)

"hi: li:t Aoot krAH-OOs THuh mAYdER."
(He *lit out* 'cross the meadow.)
(He *hurried out* across the meadow.)

"AHd tAY:k it kAH:nli EHf yUH woo:d."
(I'd *take it kindly* if you would.)
(I'd *appreciate it* if you would do so.)

"AHm plAHoom bEE:d Aoot."
(I'm plumb *beat out.*)
(I'm absolutely *exhausted.*)

"hi:ts Uoop AWn yA:EEndER pAHint."
(It's up on *yander* point.)
(It's up on *that* point.)

"hEEz UH pAH:n blA-EEngk tAY:l tEHoolER."
(He's a *point-blank* tale teller.)
(He's an *outright* liar.)

"hi: kOH-ERst THEHt bEE: rAH:t tUH THuh bEEgAHoom."
(He *coursed that bee* right to the *beegum.*)
(He *followed that bee* right to the *beehive.*)

"fAH hEHd mUH rUTHERz AHd gOH dAH:rEHkli."
(If I had my *rathers* I'd go directly.)
(If I had my *choice* I'd go right away.)

"AHm UH plAHoom fOOuhl bAoot shOH-ERt swEEtnin."
(I'm *a plumb fool about short-sweetening.*)
(I'm *very fond of sugar.*)

"hi:z sUH bri:gUHdi AH lAH:k tUH brAY:nd im."
(He's so *briggoty* I like to brained him.)
(He was so *haughty* I almost hit him.)

"sAHooniz gUHt THuh drAH: gri:nz."
(Sunny's got the *dry grins.*)
(Sunny has an *embarrassed smile.*)

MONOLOGS

(From *The Glass Window** by Lucy Furman.)

Hit hain't often lightning strikes in the right spot. Hit's more gen'ally apter to strike wrong. I hain't seed hit fall right sence Heck was a pup. But this time hit went spang, clean, straight to the mark. I allow both needed killing and needed hit bad. I know Bill did! Well, hit's a sight of satisfaction to see jestice fall — kindly cheers a body up and holps up their confidence in the running of things. I'll say this much for Him — God Almighty is a pyore puzzle and myxtery and vexation of sperrit a big part of the time; but now and again, oncet or twicet maybe in a long lifetime, He does take Him a notion to do a plumb thorough, downright, complete, ondivided, effectual good job!

---

* Reprinted with permission of Little, Brown and Company.

(From *The Trail of the Lonesome Pine** by John Fox, Jr.)

I've knowed that tree since I was a little girl — since I was a baby. Sister Sally uster tell me lots about that ole tree. She used to say hit was curious that hit should be 'way up here all alone — that she reckollected it ever since *she* was a baby, and she used to come up here and talk to it, and she said sometimes she could hear it jus' a whisperin' to her when she was down home in the cove. She said it was always a-whisperin' 'come — come — come!' an' atter she died, I heerd the folks sayin' as how she riz up in bed with her eyes right wide an' sayin' 'I hears it! It's a-whisperin' — I hears it — come — come — come!' The Red Rox said hit was the sperits, but I knowed what they told me that she was a thinkin' o' that ole tree thar. But I never let on.

(From *The Glass Window*† by Lucy Furman.)

Them renters of his'n I hain't never got acquainted with; they hain't belongers here — jest blowed in one day about corn-planting time in Aprile. I seed 'em go down one morning about sunup, the man big and stout, with a poke on his back and a babe on one arm, the woman pore and puny and all drug-out from packing tother baby. Most people in these parts don't confidence strangers and furriners, but Uncle Tutt, though he's hard on the Lord, allus was saft-hearted to folks; and he tuck pity-sake on 'em and allowed they could stay and crap for him, and give 'em 'steads and kivers and cheers and sech-like gear. They allowed their name was Johnson, and they come from Magoffin. Hit's quare, folks being that fur from home; hit's quare, too, they don't never put foot off'n the place. But maybe hit's right. I'll lay the woman's right anyways—she's as good-countenanced as ever I seed.

---

* Reprinted with permission of Charles Scribner's Sons.
† Reprinted with permission of Little, Brown and Company.

CHAPTER VI

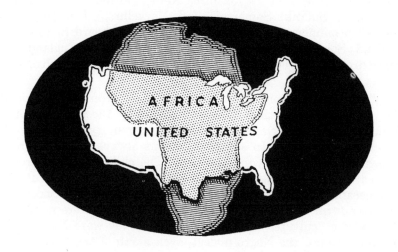

THE NEGRO DIALECT

To a great degree, the Negro dialect, as it is spoken over practically the entire United States, is similar to the Southern dialect as spoken by the uneducated whites. The similarity is so striking that some people believe it impossible to distinguish between a Negro and a white Southerner when only their speech is heard.

Actually, however, certain variants may make for a difference. The quality peculiar to the Negro voice enriches vowel sounds that may be phonetically similar to their Southern prototypes. This vocal distinction will be treated more fully under the section on "Lilt and Stress." There is also a difference in syntax. The Negro's grammatical solecisms are, in many instances, confined to Negro speech. Another variant is a more lax pronunciation of consonants by Negroes than by Southern whites. There is too, a tendency among Negroes to nasalize certain vowel sounds to such an extent that the following consonants are completely dropped. Finally, the Negro is addicted to certain locutions that are typically Negro.

The general Negro dialect is almost the same today as it was in the early plantation days when the Negroes learned their speech from their British-American masters. Roots of the Negro pronunciation are to be found not only in the speech of cultured Virginians, but also in the pre-Revolution British dialects. The

Negro pronunciation "hAYd" (head), for example, is to be found in the dialect speech of Devonshire, Kent, Norfolk, Northampton, Lancashire, Suffolk, Somerset, and Yorkshire. The supposedly Negroid pronunciation "gwyne" (going) is still heard in the South Midland, Southern, and South Western dialects of England. The Negro dropped "r" is nothing more than an extended British dropped "r."

This continuation of the Negro dialect from early Colonial days to the present time is accounted for by the fact that, until recently, the Negro was not given an opportunity to improve his speech by education. In addition, he was always forced to live in segregated sections, beyond the pale. The children, while growing up, heard little but Negro speech and continued to speak it after they became adults. Even when the Negro was finally accorded a primitive form of primary education, his teachers were not whites who spoke a "cultured" Southern dialect. They were Negroes who continued to use the Negro dialect, even north of the Potomac and the Mason and Dixon Line.

Recent developments have proved that, given the opportunity, the Negro can throw off his traditional dialect. For example, domestics who "live in" their place of employment for a number of years have been heard to use the same speech as their employers. A family in the Bronx may have a Negro maid who speaks with a typical Bronx dialect. The Harlem Negro speaks with a general Southern Negro dialect which has been well-watered with General-American pronunciations. The dropped "r" between vowels, for instance, is current mainly in the South. The consonant elisions of the Northern Negro are similar to those made by the Northern white. The educated Negro exhibits few dialect traits. If anything, he may roll his "r" sounds with an extra flourish as though compensating for the traditional loss of "r." However, there is still present the tendency to drawl certain vowel sounds together with the peculiar Negro voice quality and the soft, lush, musical lilt that is his speech heritage.

That the Negro has overcome many of the faults attributed to him, as a race, is obvious from the eminent position he has achieved in modern life as compared to his social position only a few years ago. The Negro has proved that his traditional indolence was more than a throwback to his historical lack of vigor and initiative in tropical Africa. It was a natural reaction to enforced slave labor that netted him no more than a meager sustenance, a precarious livelihood, and an uncertain future with no possibility of improving himself. It was only human for the Negro to loaf on a job that was distasteful, humiliating, and unremunerative. Understandably, he desired a way of life that was reserved for others more fortunate than he only by accident of birth.

The Negro's unbounded faith in religion was a direct result of his enslavement. The white man's religion offered a joyous world in the hereafter regardless of creed or color. His freedom-hungry existence and his natural love of music, both for singing and dancing, found a ready outlet in his religion.

With the end of slavery and with the discarding of many of the Jim Crow color bars, especially in the North, the Negro is coming into his own. His traditional laziness has vanished in many instances, so that his labors can be directed to his own benefit and for the assurance of his future. He can work as hard as his white companion if he is assured an equal pay check. His religion is being tempered by his emergence as a social entity. He is permitted to join labor unions. His vote, as a group, is sought because it is often necessary for a decision.

Gradually, the Negro is emerging from the miasma of slavery days which dogged him even after the Civil War — and still dogs him in certain benighted sections. It is obvious that the Negro is still backward where he is being curtailed by the anomalous condition of post-Civil War slavery or its substitutes. And, in the same way, in these hinterland sections, his speech is still heavily Negroid and definitely dialectal. The dialect speech of the Gullah Negroes, like the speech of white mountaineers, is accounted for by their seclusion from the world.

The Negro dialect is basically the same over the entire country. Northern Negroes are simply transplanted Southern Negroes or the children of transplanted Southern Negroes. Regional variants are to be found, in the main, where there are regional variants in the speech of the white folk. For example, the speech of the East Texas Negro is heavily colored with infiltrations of Mountain speech, although it stems from the plantation type. The dialect speech of Virginia and Carolina Negroes is closer to the plantation aristocratic type. While the speech of the Negroes in the Middle West has been especially affected by General-American, the Harlem Negro has taken on many characteristics of New York speech.

But there is an underlying Negro dialect basic to most Negro speech, and it is this basic dialect that will be discussed in this chapter. Certain variants such as Gullah, spoken in the Sea Islands off the Atlantic coast and the dialect spoken by Negroes in the Caribbean Islands will be treated separately.

The following material, then, can be considered as being representative of most Negro speech in the United States, within the limits of regional colorations. Certain of these outstanding variants will be mentioned in the text to be used in regional character variations.

LILT AND STRESS

There is a quality to the lilt of most Negro speech that defies exact scientific analysis. It is that strange *something* with which Negro speech is endowed. It is a rich, musical quality that gives an effect of softness, lushness, liquidity, and color. And although the lilt of Negro speech runs the gamut of musical pitch — for the Negro voice ranges, at times, from the cackling, high-pitched falsetto to the full rumbling bass — the same melodious character is still evident.

The source of this quality is as yet undiscovered. There is a theory that the configuration of the Negro skull is responsible — that the wide nasal orifice combined with enlarged sinuses contributes to advantage of large resonance chambers. Another theory proposes that the answer may be found somewhere in the aboriginal background of the guttural African dialects. An American carry-over from the original African speech is the habit, common to many Negroes, of raising the blade of the tongue to the point where the soft palate joins with the hard palate. In addition to changing the character of the spoken sounds, this unusual tongue-blade elevation tends to color them with a resonance that might be the Negro musical quality.

Another reason for this soft, pleasing speech may be that the Negro has been conditioned to relax. His walk is frequently a shuffle; his actions are slow-moving; his thought processes are deliberate; and his speech is correspondingly slow, deliberate, and drawled. This habit of relaxation results in speech that is at once melodious, full-throated, full-toned and possessing overtones that may be the secret of the Negro lilt.

Finally, this melody is coupled with another musical quality: rhythm. The Negro's inherent sense of rhythm is evidenced in his speech as well as in song. There is a rhythmic beat to his speech that carries his words along in rippling patterns of sound. The wide range of pitch can be easily observed in the treatment of "AH kA:in dOO dA:it" (I can't do that) which may be spoken with the following lilt:

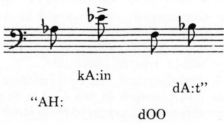

kA:in

dA:t"

"AH:

dOO

The query "hAH:oomAH gwAH:n gyidit" (How am I going to get it?) may be spoken with the following lilt:

"hAH:oomAH gwAH:n gyi
dit"

The word "gyit" (get) receives both the high note of the sentence and the greatest amount of stress.

The syllabic stress in words generally follows that of the region in which the Negro lives. Thus, Southern Negroes, in particular, are wont to give initial syllable stress to such words as **"hOH:tEHl"** (hotel) and **"sEE:mint"** (cement), although this habit has been frequently heard in the speech of Negroes in the North and other sections.

AFRICAN INFLUENCES

Before discussing the actual dialect changes, it may be enlightening to the student to examine some of the African influences that have contributed to the Negro dialect. The African Negroes who were blackbirded by slave traders to the West Indies and then to the South, as slaves, were almost all members of tribes that spoke some form of Bantu dialect — Bena, Duala, Jaunde, Kongo, Chuana, Shambala, Suto, Teke, Zulu, Luganda, Swahili, Kafir, etc. Thus they had a common background in the production of sounds in their own African language. And they have retained many of these speech habits to the present day.

The African language has more guttural consonants and nasalized vowels than American. As a result, the Negro still tends to keep the blade of the tongue higher in the mouth than does the white man. This placement generally makes for closer vowel sounds. The vowels "EE," "EH," and "A" are thus colored with an "AY" flavor. It also accounts, in part, for the lax sounding or actual dropping of consonants.

A number of other elements may suggest reasons for certain Negro dialect variants. Some of them may indicate that, instead of being completely influenced by white Colonial speech (which, in turn was influenced by Scottish, Irish and British), the Negro may have contributed much to the white Southern speech and may be responsible for many Southern dialect variants.

The extreme nasalization of both Southern and Negro speech has no base in the original Scottish, Irish, or British dialects, except in Cockney. But the few Cockneys who came over in Colonial days as indentured servants could hardly have contributed their nasalization to any great degree. Extreme nasalization before "m" or "n" is practically universal in the many-branched African language. As a matter of fact, its use is important enough to change the meaning of a word. For instance, the African word "*dAW*" means "belly" in the Ewe dialect. But when nasalized, "*dAWn*," it means "to be weak." The reasons for extreme nasalization of "ain't" as "AY*n*" and "can't" as "kAY*n*" among American Negroes may be found in African conditioning factors.

The dropping of the "n" after "AY" in the above examples may have been the result of another African speech habit. In the Effik dialect the word "he" is pronounced as "AYnyAY" but in rapid speech the initial "AY" is nasalized and the "n" is dropped, so that actually the word is sounded as "AY*ny*AY."

Both the Southern and Negro dialects have unstable "EH" and "AY" sounds and "OH" and "AW" sounds. These pairs of sounds each belong to a single phoneme in the Zulu African dialect. They are used interchangeably according to the quality of the vowel sound in the succeeding syllable. The American Negro may say "bEHd" or "bAYd" (bed), "mAYk" or "mEHk" (make), and so forth. These speech habits, so evident in current Negro dialect, may certainly have found their source in earlier African speech.

In the same way, the sounds of "EE" and "i:" in the Effik dialect belong to one phoneme.

Both the Southern and Negro dialects tend to drop "l" in such words as "self" and "careful." When "l" is sounded in Southern speech it is usually a clear "l" such as is heard in "Lily." Again, although "l" is occasionally dropped in other dialects of the British Isles, only the Cockney dialect features the dropping of "l". However, in the Effik, Twi, and Fante dialects of the African language there is no "l," and other African dialects which use "l" prefer the clear type rather than the dark.

The substitution of "b" for "v" by many Negroes may be accounted for by the fact that there is no "v" sound in the African language. The closest approach to it is the bi-labial "bv" sound similar to the Spanish pronunciation. The Negro treatment of "have" as "hab" and "river" as "ribUH" can be explained quite easily by this African source. The Gullah Negro, however, has retained the "bv" sound.

The sounds of "th" and "TH" are not to be found in any African dialect with the exception of Swahili, and then only in Arabic loan words. The Negro substitution of "t" and "d" for these sounds then is quite understandable.

But, perhaps the most persistent vestigial remains of the original African language is to be found in the Negro's pronunciation of "h." The African language features a peculiar pronunciation of its "h" sound. In its many dialects, the "h" is followed immediately by a roughened "kh" sound (as in the Scotch "*loch*" and the German "*ich*"), especially when "h" is followed by an "i" sound as in "hkhiUH" (here). Because of the instability of the final vowel sound, this word is also pronounced as "hkhyAH" or "hkhyEH."

This same roughened palatal sound is to be found in the Southern and Negro pronunciations of "k" and "g" (see "Consonant Changes"). The Virginia pronunciation of "k" as "ky" and "g" as "gy" may be attributed to the same source that introduced these palatal sounds into early New England speech. The Negro also has a source for his palatalized "g," "h," and "k" and it is his African forebears. In the Chuana dialect, for instance, "k" is pronounced before front vowels with a palatalized "y" sound, almost a "ky." The Negro not only pronounces "here" as "hkkiUH," "garden" as "gyAWdn," and "card" as "kyAWd," but he also adds the "y" to such words as "fyAH (fair), "byEH" (beer), "pyEH" (pair), and "pyi:UHz" (appears).

Finally, the Negro intonation can be traced directly to African sources. There is a quality in the Negro lilt that is distinctive. There is a wide vocal range that glides from a low-pitched guttural to a high-pitched falsetto. The Caucasian pitch, in comparison, is pedestrian and almost a monotone. The reason may be found in the fact that most African language dialects, like the Chinese language, use varying tone levels to indicate variant meanings of the same word. The Zulu dialect uses nine such tonal changes. Semantic changes are brought about by modified tone levels as in the word "*bona*" which means "they," when pronounced with a rising inflection, and "see" when given a falling tone.

It is not the purpose of this book to determine the degree to which African speech has, or has not, influenced the Negro dialect. But, the preceding material should give the student a better understanding of the vowel and consonant changes that follow. It must be remembered that sounds which may be new to the student are familiar to the Negro who speaks with the dialect. Therefore, there must be a sincere attempt to produce these new sounds naturally and without exaggeration.

VOWEL CHANGES

"AY" .... as in "take," "break," "they," etc.

Ordinarily, the Negro dialect treats with this long "a" as in General-American, except that there is a noticeable tendency to elongate it to "AY:" when stressed, as in "tAY:k" (take). Before "l" the sound becomes "AY:uh" as in "bAY:uhl" (bale) and "rAY:uhl" (rail).

DRILL WORDS

brAY:k	(break)	nAY:bUH	(neighbor)
dAY:	(they)	tAY:dUHz	(potatoes)
lAY:bUH	(labor)	kwAY:nUHd	(acquainted)

krAY:t	(crate)
stAY:k	(steak)
krAY:zi	(crazy)

VARIATIONS: Louisiana Negroes frequently substitute "EH:" as in "strEH:t" (straight) and "gEH:l" (gale).

In Virginia, "EE" is sometimes used, as in "dEE" (they), "brEEk" (break), and "plEEgd" (plagued).

EXCEPTIONS: Certain common words are almost always pronounced with "EH" even by many educated Negroes. These words are "snEHk" (snake), "mEHk" (make), "EHt" (ate), "grEHt" (great), "nEHkid" (naked), "tEHk" (take), "brEHk" (break), and "shEHk" (shake).

"UH" .... as in "alone," "sofa," "final," etc.

Initially, this sound is usually dropped, as in "bAoot" (about) and "nUdUH" (another).

Medially, it is frequently dropped, as in "fAH:nli" (finally) and "jinli" (generally). For a more detailed discussion, see **"Unstressed Syllables."**

Finally, this sound is usually the same as in General-American.

DRILL WORDS

lAWng	(along)	sOHfUH	(sofa)
bUv	(above)	kyOObUH	(Cuba)
lOH:n	(alone)	nAinUH	(banana)

sUmpshUHn	(assumption)
fi:ksyAY:dUHd	(asphyxiated)
strAHluhji	(astrology)

VARIATION: Final "UH" may also be changed to "i:" as in "AH:di:" (idea), "sOHfi:" (sofa), and "sOHdi:" (soda).

"AH" .... as in "father," "dark," "calm," etc.

This sound remains the same as in General-American. It may be elongated to "AH:," but it should not be diphthongized.

DRILL WORDS

fAH:dUH	(father)	bAH:bUH	(barber)
dAH:k	(dark)	pAH:di	(party)
kAH:m	(calm)	hAH:dli	(hardly)

pAH:m	(palm)
lAH:d	(lard)
pAH:k	(park)

VARIATIONS: Many Negroes, particularly those in Virginia, Harlem, east Texas, New Orleans and surrounding Louisiana use the variant "AW" before "r" as in "hAW:luhm" (Harlem), "tAW:" (tar), and "pAW:luh" (parlor).

"A:" .... as in "grass," "draft," "aunt," etc.

This sound occurs in most words in which short "a" is followed by "ff," "ft," "nch," "nce," "nt," "sk," "sp," "ss," "st," or "th," and in the Negro dialect it is generally pronounced as a nasalized "A:" sound. When in a stressed position, this vowel is pronounced as "A:i" with the first element stressed and the second element used as a glide. This nasalized "A:i" frequently imparts a suggestion of "AY."

DRILL WORDS

grA:is	(grass)	bA:iskit	(basket)
drA:if	(draft)	dA:ins	(dance)
A:in	(aunt)	lA:iftUH	(laughter)

klA:isp	(clasp)
lA:is	(last)
pA:ith	(path)

VARIATIONS: Virginia Negroes generally pronounce this vowel sound as "AH" as in "lAHf" (laugh) and "pAHs" (past).

In Louisiana, some Negroes use the variant "AW" as in "mAWsUH" (master), "lAWf" (laugh), and "rAWt (wrath). This variant "AW" sound should be used only before "f," "s," or "th."

"A" .... as in "am," "bad," "narrow," etc.

This vowel sound generally remains the same except that it is of slightly longer duration, as in "bA:d" (bad). Before "m" or "n" the vowel sound should have a distinct nasal quality which frequently produces an "i" glide, as in "mA:in" (man).

DRILL WORDS

nA:uh	(narrow)	nA:tchli	(naturally)
glA:d	(glad)	bA:tchluh	(bachelor)
bA:k	(back)	bA:dUH	(batter)

sA:li:	(Sally)
vA:lid	(valid)
hA:im	(ham)

VARIATION: Virginia Negroes frequently use the variant "AH" as in "glAHd" (glad) and "bAHkUH" (tobacco).

EXCEPTIONS: Short, common words are usually pronounced with "EH" when they are in an unstressed position, as in "hEHd" (had), "bEHd" (bad), and "hEHv" (have).

"AW" .... as in "all," "off," "talk," etc.

This vowel sound generally remains the same except that it is elongated to "AW:" as in "kAW:t" (caught).

Virginia Negroes, however, frequently use the variant "AH" as in "AHl" (all) and "blAHng" (belong).

"AW" .... as in "more," "floor," "corn," etc.

When this vowel sound is followed by final "r" or "r" plus a consonant, it is usually pronounced as "OH:" in the Negro dialect. Some speakers give this sound an "AW" coloring.

When followed by "r" plus a vowel, the sound of "AW:" is used, as in "AW:jin" (origin).

DRILL WORDS

mOH:	(more)	fAW:is	(forest)	pOH:	(pour)
flOH:	(floor)	AW:inj	(orange)	shOH:t	(short)
kOH:n	(corn)	kAW:is	(chorus)	fOH:	(four)

VARIATIONS: Virginia Negroes usually use the "uh" glide when "OH" is followed by "r" final or "r" plus a consonant, as in "kOHuhn" (corn) and "dOHuh" (door).

Northern Negroes generally use the "AWoo" variant, as in "bAWoon" (born) and "stAWoo" (store).

Southern Negroes, in particular, may use the "AH" variant before the sound of "r" plus a vowel, as in "fAH:is" (forest).

EXCEPTIONS: The following words are frequently pronounced as "hA:int" (haunt), "gA:int" (gaunt), "sA:is" (sauce), "fU:" (for), and "jERdn" (Jordan). Although "wasn't" is usually pronounced as "wAHnt," Louisiana Negroes tend to say "wU:nt."

"EE" .... as in "he," "treat," "people," etc.

When stressed, this sound is generally elongated, as in "trEE:t" (treat). Before final "l" however, it is diphthongized to "EEuh" as in "fEEuhl" (feel).

In a final unstressed position and spelled with "y," the "i" sound is used as in "kwEE:zi" (queasy). For a further discussion of this sound, see **"Unstressed Syllables."**

DRILL WORDS

pEE:pl	(people)	nEEuhl	(kneel)
nEE:dUH	(neither)	nEE:d	(need)
mEE:li	(mealy)	swEE:t	(sweet)

prEE:tch	(preach)
sEE:m	(seem)
lEE:v	(leave)

VARIATION: Some Negroes, particularly those in Virginia use the "iEE" glide for stressed syllables, as in "miEE" (me) and "miEEt" (meat).

Negroes in the deep South use the variant "AY" for the words "rAYuhl" (real) and "blAY:t" (bleat).

Because of French Creole and Cajun influences, many Louisiana Negroes sound "EE" as "i" as in "simz" (seems), "grit" (greet), and "filz" (feels).

"EH" .... as in "bet," "sell," "friend," etc.

Before most consonants, this vowel sound remains the same, as in "bEHt" (bet) or "bEH:t" (bet) when stressed.

However, before "b" or "l" an "uh" glide is frequently used, as in "wEEuhb" (web) and "sEHuhl" (sell). (See **"L"** in **"Consonant Changes."**)

When "EH" is followed by "m" or "n," it is usually changed to a nasalized "i" as in "limUHn" (lemon) and "frin" (friend).

DRILL WORDS

bEH:d	(bed)	pEHuhbl	(pebble)
mEH:t	(met)	fEHuhluh	(fellow)
lEH:k	(elect)	swEHuhl	(swell)

triml	(tremble)
bintch	(bench)
jinli	(generally)

EXCEPTIONS: The following are common: "AY:g" (egg), "lAY:g" (leg), "hAY:d" (head), "yAuhluh" (yellow), "yAis" (yes), "sti:d" (instead), "git" (get), and "yit" (yet).

"EH" .... **as in "care," "there," "pair," etc.**

Before "r" this vowel sound usually changes to "A:" as in "kA:" (care) and "dA:" (there). An "uh" glide may be used, particularly when the vowel sound is drawled, as in "pA:uh" (pair) and "hA:uh" (hair).

VARIATIONS: Some Negroes, particularly in Louisiana, Mississippi, South Carolina, and Virginia use the variant "AH:" as in "pAH:" (pair), and "fAH:" (fair).

"I" .... **as in "ice," "fine," "my," etc.**

In the Negro dialect, this sound ordinarily becomes an elongated "AH:" as in "fAH:n" (find).

Under stress, however, an "i" glide may be added particularly before "f," "k," "p," "s," and "t" as in "nAH:is" (nice).

DRILL WORDS

mAH:	(my)	spAH:dUH	(spider)
AH:is	(ice)	rAH:it	(right)
trAH:	(try)	pAH:ip	(pipe)

tAH:ik	(tyke)
hAH:d	(hide)
frAH:	(fry)

EXCEPTION: The word "oblige" is frequently pronounced as "UHblEEj" or "blEEj."

"i" .... **as in "it," "fish," "string," etc.**

Short "i" is generally tensed to "i:" particularly in a stressed syllable. This "i:" lies between "i" and "EE."

When short "i" is followed by "nk" or "ng," except in a participial ending, it is usually pronounced as "EH," particularly by Southern Negroes.

DRILL WORDS

wi:mUHn	(women)	strEHng	(string)
fi:shi	(fishy)	sEHng	(sing)
bi:zi	(busy)	thEHng-k	(think)

li:uhl	(little)
kri:sp	(crisp)
i:ntch	(inch)

VARIATIONS: Some Negroes, particularly those in Texas, use a nasalized "EHi" before "nk" or "ng" as in "rEHing" (ring) and "pEHing-k" (pink). This nasalized "EHi" should be produced from a more forward position in the mouth and should be as close to a nasalized "AY" as possible.

Other Negroes, particularly in Louisiana, use a nasalized "A" before "nk" or "ng" as in "thAng" (thing) and "sprAng-kl" (sprinkle).

EXCEPTIONS: The following words are frequently pronounced as "EHf" (if), "tEHl" (until), "woosh" (wish), "hwoop" or "hwUp" (whip), "hit" (it), and "sEHnts" (since).

The word "pretty" is variously pronounced as "pERdi," "pU:di," "pidi," or "poodi."

The word "hymn" is often pronounced as "hAH:m" especially in Louisiana.

"i" .... as in "near," "here," "miracle," etc.

When followed by final "r" or "r" plus a consonant, this short "i" sound takes an "UH" glide to replace the dropped "r" as in "niUH" (near), "fiUHsli" (fiercely), and "wiUH" (we're).

When short "i" is followed by "r" plus final "y," the "i" is tensed to "i:," the "r" is dropped, and the "y" is pronounced as "i" as in "wi:i" (weary) and "dri:i" (dreary).

When short "i" is followed by "r" plus a vowel, with the exception of "i" in the "ing" participial ending, it is frequently pronounced as "ER:" as in "sER:p" (syrup) and "mER:kl" (miracle). Some Negroes, particularly those in the deep South, use "U:" as in "sU:p" (syrup).

When short "i" is followed by "r" plus "ing," the vowel sound remains the same; the "r" is dropped; and the "uh" glide is used, as in "fiUHn" (fearing).

VARIATION: Some Negroes, particularly those in Louisiana, Texas, and Virginia, use the variant "EH" before final "r" or "r" plus a consonant, as in "nyEHli" (nearly), "hyEH" (here), and "yEH" (year).

EXCEPTION: The word "spirits" is frequently pronounced "spEH:ts" particularly by the Southern Negro, and the word "here" is often "hyU:."

"OH" .... as in "bone," "sew," "no," etc.

The Negro dialect generally drops the second element of "OH-OO" so that it becomes a pure "OH" as in "bOHn" (bone). Even when stressed, this vowel sound is usually lengthened rather than diphthongized. In this section, the lengthened "OH" will be represented as "OH:" as in "dOH:pi" (dopy).

DRILL WORDS

bOHt	(both)	nOH:hwA:	(nowhere)
lOHn	(alone)	jOH:kUH	(joker)
sOH	(sew)	spOH:z	(suppose)

pOH:smUHn	(postman)
pOHlEE:smUHn	(policeman)
AWdUHmOH:bEEl	(automobile)

VARIATIONS: Some Negroes, particularly those in Texas, use an "oo" glide before "l" as in "gOHool" (gold) and "hOHool" (whole). The "uh" glide is also used, particularly in South Carolina, as in "mOHuhs" (most) and "tOHuhn" (tone).

EXCEPTIONS: The word "no" is usually pronounced as "nAW," although many Virginia Negroes say "nAH."
    The word "Creole" is generally pronounced as "krEEyAWl" by Louisiana Negroes.
    The word "gwAHin" (going) frequently uses an intrusive "w" sound.

"O" .... as in "bond," "Johnny," "on," etc.

This vowel sound is generally pronounced as "AH" which is a little deeper and of slightly longer duration than the "O" of General-American.

DRILL WORDS

bAHn	(bond)	gAHli	(golly)	stAHp	(stop)
jAHni	(Johnny)	hAHluh	(hollow)	pAHli	(Polly)
hAHt	(hot)	bAHuh	(borrow)	gAHt	(got)

VARIATIONS: The variant "AW" is frequently used, particularly by some of the Negroes in Louisiana, Mississippi, and South Carolina, as in "bAWks" (box) and "kAWntrAk" (contract).

EXCEPTIONS: The word "on" should be pronounced as "AWn" and "drop" as "drAp" particularly by Negroes in the South.

"OO" .... as in "food," "do," "new," etc.

This vowel sound generally remains the same. However, when spelled "u," "ue," "ew," or "eu" and preceded by "d," "t," or "n," the vowel sound becomes "yOO," as in "nyOO" (knew). This added "y" glide is common among Southern Negroes, especially in Virginia, the Carolinas, Louisiana, and Texas. In the North, however, and particularly in the Middle West this "y" glide is rarely added.

DRILL WORDS

fOOd	(food)	nyOOdl	(noodle)
dOO	(do)	dyOOdi	(duty)
trOO	(true)	tyOOb	(tube)

nyOOrAHdUHs	(neuritis)
ridyOOs	(reduce)
tyOOzdi	(Tuesday)

EXCEPTIONS: The following words are frequently pronounced with "oo" rather than "OO": "koop" (coop), "room" (room), "soon" (soon), "roof" (roof), and "broom" (broom).

The word "chew" is usually pronounced as "tchAW."

"oo" . . . . as in "good," "wolf," "full," etc.

This sound is usually pronounced as in General-American except that it is elongated to "oo:" as in "goo:d" (good). See **"Unstressed Syllables"** for additional treatment of this sound.

DRILL WORDS

loo:k	(look)	foo:l	(full)
hoo:d	(hood)	woo:lf	(wolf)
poo:sh	(push)	shoo:d	(should)

footsOH:	(footsore)
koo:shn	(cushion)
boo:kshEHoof	(bookshelf)

VARIATIONS: Some Negroes use the variant "U" when this vowel sound is preceded and followed by "f," "h," "k," "l," "p," "r," "s," or "t" as in "pUt" (put), "lUki hyEHuh" (look at here), and "tUk" (took).

"oo" . . . . as in "sure," "pure," "your," etc.

When followed by final "r," this vowel sound generally changes to "OH" as in "shOH" (sure), "pyOH" (pure), and "yOH" (your). This pronunciation is also true of derivatives of such words, as in "shOHli" (surely), "pOHli" (poorly), and "kyOHd" (cured).

When followed by medial "r," this vowel sound usually remains the same, except that it is elongated, as in "dyoo:in" (during). The "y" glide in the above word is frequently added after "d," "n," and "t." (See "D" and "T" under **"Consonant Changes."**)

VARIATION: Some Negroes, particularly in Virginia, retain the "oo" sound before "r" as in "shooUH" (sure) and "pyooUH" (pure).

"yOO" .... as in "unit," "cube," "beauty," etc.

This sound is pronounced as it is in General-American. Medially, however, it is usually changed to "i" when unstressed, as in "AW:gimint" (argument).

Some Negroes, particularly in South Carolina and Georgia, add "n" to initial "yOO" as in "nyOOz" (use) and "nyOOnAHdid" (United).

"U" .... as in "up," "love," "lunch," etc.

This sound varies considerably in the Negro dialect. Ordinarily, though, it is a more relaxed, less tense sound than in General- or Southern-American.

> *IN MONOSYLLABLES, THE VOWEL SOUND "U" ADDS AN "uh" GLIDE BEFORE "b" OR "d" AS IN "rUuhb" (rub) AND "sUuhdz" (suds).*

The above general rule should be applied particularly to stressed words in a sentence.

> *THE VOWEL SOUND "U" IS FREQUENTLY CHANGED TO A NASALIZED "ER" BEFORE "m" OR "n" PLUS A CONSONANT AS IN "rERmp" (rump) AND "lERntch" (lunch).*

To produce this "ER" sound, pronounce "hER" (her) without sounding the "r" so that the word becomes "hER" (her). The "ER" should have a distinct nasal quality. This nasalization is frequently so pronounced that the following consonant sound is obliterated, as in "stERnt" (stunt).

DRILL WORDS

tUuhb	(tub)	ERng-kl	(uncle)
lUv	(love)	fERni	(funny)
dUz	(does)	sUpUH	(supper)

sERmtAH:m	(sometime)
kERntri	(country)
trERngk	(trunk)

VARIATIONS: Some Negroes use "Uoo" before nasal consonants, as in "bUooml bEE" (bumblebee) and "pUoontch" (punch).

The prefix "un" is generally pronounced as "AWn" as in "AWnlEHs (unless) and "AWnti:l" (until).

Many Negroes change "U" to "EH" in certain monosyllabic words in which the vowel sound is between any two of the consonant sounds "j," "sh," "tch," "s," or "r;" or between one of the foregoing consonant sound and "f," "t," or "v" as in "jEHs" (just), "tEHtch" (touch), and "brEHsh" (brush).

Some Negroes, particularly those in Louisiana, substitute a nasalized "EH" for the vowel sound in the prefix "un" as in "EHntAHd" (untied).

Tennessee Negroes frequently pronounce "hurry" as "hEH:i."

EXCEPTIONS: The word "such" may be pronounced as "sitch" except by Texas Negroes who say "sEHtch."

The word "cover" is often sounded as "kivUH" or "kyivUH," and "hungry" is almost always sounded as "hAW:ng-gri" with a nasalized "AW" sound.

"ER" .... as in "curb," "earn," "fern," etc.

A number of variations exist for the pronunciation of this sound in the Negro dialect. In all of them, however, the "r" is dropped.

One variant changes "ER" to "Ui" as in "hUid" (heard). This is a blending of the "U" of "up" (up) and the "i" of "it" (it). The actor should guard against pronouncing this sound as "OI."

This "Ui" sound should be used particularly for Negroes of Virginia, Louisiana, Texas, and New York.

DRILL WORDS

kUib	(curb)	pUil	(pearl)	bUigluh	(burglar)
Uin	(earn)	dUidi	(dirty)	wUid	(word)
fUin	(fern)	nUis	(nurse)	wUikUH	(worker)

VARIATIONS: Another popular variation, especially in monosyllables, is an elongated "U:" as in "gU:l" (girl). This may be used particularly for the Georgia, Texas, or Virginia Negro.

Still another variant treats with "ER" as "ER" as in "hA:mbERgUH" (hamburger).

A great many Negroes, particularly those in Virginia, use "ER" with an "uh" glide as in "bERuhd" (bird).

When this vowel sound is spelled with "e" or "ea" it may be pronounced as "AH," particularly by an elderly Negro, as in "sAH:v" (serve) and "lAH:n" (learn).

EXCEPTIONS: Many Negroes, both old and young, use the variant "U" for words spelled with "o," "i," or "u" before "rs" as in "wUs" (worse), "fUs" (first), and "nUs" (nurse). The use of

"U" in words of this type is common even though the speaker may use "ER" or "Ui" for other words which take a General-American "ER" sound. Thus, the speaker may say "fUs wERd" (first word) or "wUs wUik" (worst work).

The word "girl" is often pronounced as "gA:l", "gyAuhl," or "gEHl," but it may also be pronounced according to the above suggested variants.

The word "sir" is usually sounded as "sU" or "sUH."

Final "er" is pronounced as "UH" as in "bOH:dUH" (border).

"OW" . . . . as in "out," "cow," "house," etc.

The Negro seldom flattens this diphthong into "Aoo" as in "dAoon" (down). Instead he usually treats it with an elongated "AH:" plus the "oo" glide, as in "hAH:oos" (house).

DRILL WORDS

AH:oot	(out)	bAH:oonri	(boundary)
kyAH:oo	(cow)	kyAH:ooni	(county)
lAH:oo	(allow)	sAH:ookrAH:ood	(sauerkraut)

grAH:oon (ground)
nAH:oo (now)
shAH:oot (shout)

VARIATIONS: The variant "U-OO" is frequently used by eastern Negroes, particularly those in Virginia, as in "shU-OOt" (shout). The two elements must blend together with no break between them. The "U" is produced from the throat, and the "OO" is produced from a forward position in the mouth with the lips in a fairly tense position.

"OI" . . . . as in "oil," "boy," "noise," etc.

This diphthong is usually pronounced as "AWi" by most Negroes, especially in the North.

DRILL WORDS

bAWi	(boy)	vAWis	(voice)
AWil	(oil)	injAWi	(enjoy)
nAWiz	(noise)	pAWint	(point)

brAWiluh (broiler)
AWistUH (oyster)
spAWild (spoiled)

VARIATION: The variant "AHi" may be used particularly for elderly or rural Negroes whose speech has been heavily influenced by Mountain speech, such as the Texas, Louisiana or Piedmont Negro. This sound is used as in "pAHint" (point) and "bAHil" (boil).

Some Negroes, particularly those who live in New York City use the variant "ERi" as in "nERiz" (noise) "jERint" (joint).

UNSTRESSED SYLLABLES

Much of the flavor of the Negro dialect is achieved by the indifferent treatment of unstressed syllables. The elision of initial syllables is particularly frequent.

Initial unstressed "a" is usually dropped, as in "lAW:ng" (along), "bAH:oot" (about), "sEHp" (accept), and "thAW:di" (authority).

Medial "a," when unstressed, may be dropped completely or changed to "UH" as in "fAH:nli" (finally), "tOH:dz" (towards), "jinli" (generally), "mEH:skn" (Mexican), "prAH:vUHt" (private), and "pA:kUHj" (package).

Final unstressed "a" or "ia" is usually pronounced as "i:" as in "nyOOmOH:ni:" (pneumonia), "EHksri:" (extra), and "sAri:" (Sarah).

Initial unstressed "e" is usually dropped, especially in a prefix, as in "lEHktrik" (electric), "zA:mUHn" (examine), "zA:kli" (exactly), "vA:njlUHs" (evangelist), and "lAH:jUH" (Elijah).

Medial unstressed "e" may be dropped completely or changed to "UH" as in "fAW:n" (foreign), "mi:zri" (misery), "lAH:sUHns" (license), "di:fUHns" (difference), and "pAHkUHt" (pocket).

Initial unstressed "i" is usually dropped, as in "mA:jUHn" (imagine), "ni:shl" (initial), and "sti:d" (instead).

Medial unstressed "i" is either dropped or changed to "UH" as in "ri:jnuhl" (original), "lOOzA:nUH" (Louisiana), "fUintchUH" (furniture), "drEHkli" (directly), "AWfUHs" (office), "dUHvAH:d" (divide), and "mUHstAY:k" (mistake).

Final unstressed "y" is usually changed to "i" as in "ini" (any), "plini" (plenty), "bA:tri" (battery), and "mERni" (money). Some Negroes shade this "i" sound to "EH" as in "plEHnEH" (plenty) and "bA:trEH" (battery).

Initial unstressed "o" is also dropped, especially in a prefix, as in "blAH:j" (oblige), "pi:nyUHn" (opinion), and "pOH:nUHn" (opponent).

Medial unstressed "o" is either dropped or changed to "UH" as in "tAY:dUHz" (potatoes), "klEHk" (collect), "kOHknU/" (coconut), "mEHmri" (memory), "pUHvAH:d" (provide), and "spi:gUH/" (spiggot).

When unstressed, initial "u" is often dropped, especially in a prefix, as in "lEHs (unless), "brEHluh" (umbrella), and "li:sUHz" (Ulysses).

Medial unstressed "u" is often dropped, or changed to "UH" as in "rEHgluh" (regular), "A:krUHt" (accurate), "sprAH:z" (surprise), "nA:tchuhl" (natural), and "nA:tchli" (naturally).

Final unstressed "u" is sometimes changed to "i:" as in the word "AH:gi:" (argue).

It can be seen from many of the above examples that not only are vowels dropped from unstressed syllables, but entire syllables may be elided. This, too, is typical of the dialect and makes for much of its flavor.

When final unstressed "en," "on," "an," or "in" is preceded by "t," the vowel sound is dropped; the "t" is replaced by the glottal stop (/), and the "n" is nasalized, as in "kAH/n" (cotton) and "sA:/n" (satin). (See "T" in **"Consonant Changes"** and also **"The Glottal Stop"** on page 24.)

Final unstressed "ow" is usually pronounced as "UH" as in "wi:dUH" (widow) and "fEHuhluh" (fellow). When "ow" is preceded by "r," however, it is often dropped, together with the "r" sound and the preceding vowel is considerably elongated, as in "fU::" (furrow), "bAH::" (borrow), and "tUHmAH::" (tomorrow). This is also the case when final unstressed "er" or "or" is preceded by "r" as in "wA::" (wearer) and "hAW::" (horror).

When a final unstressed syllable is spelled with "an," "en," "on," or "ing" and is preceded by "d," "f," "k," "s," or "z," the vowel is dropped, and the two consonant sounds are blended together, as in "gyAH:dn" (garden), "lA:fn" (laughing), "mAY:kn" (making), "dUzn" (dozen), and "lEH:sn" (lesson).

When the participial ending "ing" follows most other consonants, it is usually changed to "UHn" as in "kOHmUHn" (combing), "bAWiluhn" (boiling), and "sOHpUHn" (soaping).

When the participial ending "ing" is preceded by a vowel sound, only the "n" is sounded, as in "trAH:n" (trying), "bAHoon" (bowing), and "bEE:n" (being).

When the participial ending "ing" is preceded by "n," the "ing" is pronounced as an elongated "n:" as in "lEE:n:" (leaning), "fAH:n:" (finding), and "mOHn:" (morning). However, when the word is heavily stressed in a sentence, the "ing" ending is pronounced as "UHn" as in "mOHnUHn" (morning).

There is also evident in the Negro dialect a tendency to run words together, as in "dyUdUH" (the other) and "yAsUHndEE:d" (yes indeed).

CONSONANT CHANGES

(Only the important consonant changes are listed.)

Negro speech is so relaxed that its consonant sounds are usually slurred or dropped completely. One Negro speaker, recorded on a transcription from an audience participation radio show, dropped almost all his consonants when he said, "i: OH nOH dA:" (he don't know that). A modified form of consonant elision should be used since it is an identifying characteristic of the Negro dialect as distinct from the Southern dialect. The actor should guard against a profuse use of consonant elisions however.

D — Final "d" is usually dropped after "l" or "n" as in "kOHl" (cold) and "lA:n" (land).

When final "d" is in the past tense ending of a verb, it may be changed to "t" after "l" or "n" as in "ki:lt" (killed) and "bUint" (burned).

Medial "d" is usually dropped after "n" and before "l" or "z" as in "kA:nl" (candle) and "hA:nz" (hands).

Some Negroes, particularly in Louisiana and South Carolina, change "d" to "g" before "v" as in "AgvA:ins" (advance).

When "d" is followed by the long "OO" sound spelled with "u," it usually changes to "j" as in "jOOdi" (duty). The word "Judas" is sometimes pronounced as "jOOjUHs."

When medial "d" is followed by an unstressed "i" sound plus another vowel, it may also be pronounced as "j" as in "kOH:jUHn" (accordian) and "mEE:jUHm" (medium). This change to "j" is also found in phrases like "di:jUH" (did you) and "woo:jUH" (would you).

The word "corner" is often pronounced with an extra "d" as in "kOH:ndUH" particularly by Southern Negroes.

F — This consonant sound is frequently dropped in the word "A:idUH" (after) and its compounds, such as "A:idUHwUHdz" (afterwards).

G — A palatalized hard "g" is frequently used in the South, particularly in the Carolinas, Kentucky, Tennessee, Texas, and Virginia. This sound is produced by sounding "g" with the juncture of the tongue blade and hard palate in a more forward position (Fig. 22) than in General-American (Fig. 21). This forward production of

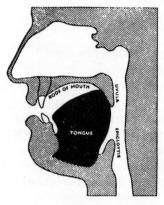

Fig. 21

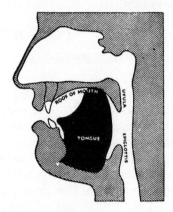

Fig. 22

"g" makes for a faint "y" glide sound following it, as in "gyAH:dn" (garden), "gyi:t" (get), and "gyA:luhsUHz" (galluses).

H — This consonant sound is frequently dropped in such words as "yOOmUHn" (human) and "yOOmUH" (humor). It may also be dropped in other initial "h" words, particularly when the word is in an unstressed position, as in "iz" (his), "OHm" (home), and "U:" (her). The initial "h" is not dropped as consistently as in the Cockney dialect, and it is suggested that the actor reserve this elision for unstressed words which are run together, as in "AH:nOH winEEz gOHn bEE hOHm" (I don't know when he's going to be home.)

J — The word "just" is often pronounced with an initial "d" as in "dis" or "dEHs."

K — This consonant like "g" (see Figures 21 and 22) is also produced from a more forward position in the mouth so that a slight "y" glide results, as in "kyAH:dz" (cards), "kyA:" (care), and "kyi:/n" (kitten). This palatalized "k" is heard particularly in the speech of Negroes of the Carolinas, Kentucky, Tennessee, Texas, and Virginia.

The word "ask" may be pronounced as "A:is," "A:ist," or "A:ks."

L — When "l" is preceded by "EH" and followed by "f" or "p," it is usually dropped, as in "sEH:f" (self), and "hEH:p" (help).

When preceded by "EH," "A," or "i" and followed by "b," "k," "m," "v," or "w," the "l" is dropped in favor of an "oo" glide, as in "AoobUit" (Albert), "si:ook" (silk), "fi:oom" (film), "si:oovUH" (silver), and "AW:ooz" (always).

The pronunciations "AkUHhAWl" (alcohol) and "jEH:nmUHn" (gentleman) are frequently heard.

N — This consonant contributes much to the nasalization found in the Negro dialect. A vowel preceding "n" should be nasalized, as in "trAY:n" (train). The symbol "n" indicates that the preceding vowel is nasalized and the "n" dropped. Many Negroes nasalize the preceding vowel and retain "n" as in "trAY:nn" (train).

Nasalization may be achieved by keeping the throat passage open so that the vowel sound travels up through the nose (see Figure 23 and 24). In practicing nasalization, a small mirror may

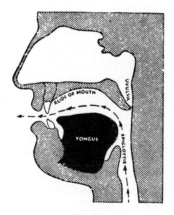
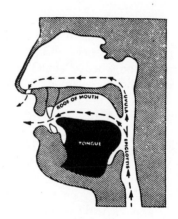

Fig. 23   Fig. 24

be held under the nose so that the actor will know when he is nasalizing correctly by the foggy appearance of the mirror.

Complete nasalization, in which the consonant sound is nasalized completely, as in "AY:n gOHn tchAY:nj" (ain't going to change), is used consistently in rapid Negro speech, but it would be unintelligible for theatrical work. Therefore, the dropping of "n" should be used with discretion, although the preceding vowel sound retains its nasalization.

Final "n" is frequently changed to "m" when preceded by "p" or "v" which receive the glottal treatment, as in "hA:/m" (happen) and "sEH:/m" (seven). (See **"The Glottal Stop,"** page 24.)

The change of "n" to "m" is sometimes made in such words as "mi:lyUHm" (million), "bihAH:m" (behind), and "kAWmUHsAY:shn" (conversation).

NG — The sound of "n" is substituted for "ng" in such words as "strEHnth" (strength) and "lEHnth" (length).

Some Negroes, particularly in Louisiana and Texas, use an added "k" sound, as in "strEHng-k" (strength), and "blAWng-k" (belong).

For the final "ing" participial ending, see **"Unstressed Syllables."**

P — Medial "p" is frequently changed to "b" when followed by a voiceless consonant, as in "bA:btAH:z" (baptize) and "EHbsm" (epsom). The "b," however, should not receive its full sound; that is, it should not be sounded as forcefully as it is when in an initial position.

R — Initially, "r" is pronounced as in General-American.

When "r" follows an initial consonant, it is also pronounced, as in "trAH:" (try) and "brEHng" (bring). Exceptions are to be found in the words "thOO" (through), "thOHt" (throat), "thOH:" (throw), and sometimes "nAWsuhlz" (nostrils).

When "r" is in the prefix "pro" or "pre," it is usually dropped, as in "pUHvAH:d" (provide) and "pUHzEHn" (present).

When "r" is preceded by a vowel and followed by a consonant, it is dropped, as in "hAH:t" (heart) and "gU:l" (girl). Usually, the vowel sound is elongated to make up for the dropped "r."

Throughout almost the entire South, with the exception of the educated Negroes, "r" is dropped between vowels, as in "vEH:i" (very) and "kA:id" (carried). Negroes in the North, and especially those living in large cities, tend to pronounce this "r" although a great many uneducated Negroes prefer to drop it.

There is practically no linking "r" in Negro speech. Thus, since final "r" is usually dropped, it remains dropped even though the next word begins with a vowel, as in "OH:vUH i:t" (over it).

Some Negroes, particularly those influenced by Mountain speech, use an intrusive "r" after "AW" as in "wAWrsh" (wash) and "hAWrspidl" (hospital). This "r" should not be as rich as the Mountain "r," however. It should be a lightly-sounded "r" which imparts the flavor of the consonant rather than the full sound of it.

The "r" may also be dropped from such words as "fUHm" (from), "sA:di" (Saturday), "di:fUHn" (different), "tchi:lUHn" (children), "EHvi" (every), and "mi:stUHs" (mistress).

S — When final "s" is followed by an initial "y" sound, it is frequently pronounced as "sh" as in "di:shyi" (this here) and "lA:ishyi" (last year).

SH — Some Negroes, particularly in the Tidewater area, the Shenandoah Valley, West Virginia, and Louisiana pronounce this sound as "s" when it is followed by "r" as in "swi:mp" (shrimp) and "swi:ngk" (shrink). (For the correct pronunciation of "w" in the above examples, see "R," page 144.)

Medial "sh" is sometimes pronounced as "s" as in "fi:st" (fished).

T — Final "t" is usually dropped after "f," "k," "p," or "s" as in "sAW:f" (soft), "A:k" (act), "dAHp" (adopt), and "mOH:sli" (mostly).

Between vowels or before "l," "t" is usually changed to "d" as in "bEH:dUH" (better) and "bAH:dl" (bottle).

However, when "t" is final or followed by an unstressed vowel plus final "n," it is sometimes treated as a glottal stop (/). In producing the glottal stop, the glottis, at the back of the throat, is closed off by the back of the tongue as it rises to meet the soft palate. The stop is momentary and the next sound breaks through the closure in a mildly explosive manner. This slight explosion, which is sometimes compared with the sound produced when clearing one's throat, is the glottal stop. Whisper the sentence, "I am at Al's," and forcibly emphasize each initial vowel sound. Notice that a sound, similar to a slight cough preceded each initial vowel. This is the glottal stop as it should be used in the Negro dialect for such words as "kAH/n" (cotton), "fA:/n" (fatten), "si:/n" (sitting), and so forth. It should be used particularly for the New York Negro.

The glottal stop can be observed in use in the following phrases:

"AY:n A/ sU/m"	(Ain't that something.)
"twAW/ nU/n"	(It wasn't nothing.)
"dAWg bAH/ mi"	(Dog bite me!)
"AY/ gAH/ nOH"	(Ain't got no . . .)

Some Negroes add an extra "t" after final "s" as in "twAH:st" (twice), "krAW:st" (across), and "klOH:st" (close).

When "t" is followed by an "OO" sound, spelled "u" or "ue," it frequently takes a "y" glide, as in "tyOOn" (tune) or "tyOOzdi" (Tuesday). Many Negroes, however, change the "ty" to "tch" as in "tchOOn" (tune) or "tchOOzdi" (Tuesday).

The word "turtle" is sometimes pronounced as "tUkl" particularly by Southern Negroes.

TH — This voiced "TH" is usually changed to "d" as in "di:s" (this), "dOH:z" (those), and "dA:t" (that).

Medially, it is often dropped in such words as "bAY:z" (bathes), "klOH:z" (clothes), and "rEE:z" (wreathes).

Medially, between vowels, it usually changes to "d" as in "wEHdUH" (weather) and "UdUH" (other).

Initially, it is frequently dropped in rapid, colloquial speech, as in "kAW:l A/ mA:n" (Call that man) and "AY: woodn wAHn A/ dAW:g" (They wouldn't want that dog).

Some Negroes, particularly those in Northern cities, use "TH" as in "brUTHUH" (brother).

th — Unvoiced "th" usually changes to "t" as in "tEHngk" (think) and "tAW:t" (thought).

Another variation, observed especially in Louisiana, Tennessee, Texas, and the Georgia-Alabama dialect of Uncle Remus, changes "th" to "f" as in "mAHoof" (mouth), "frOH:t" (throat), "brEH:f" (breath), and "trOOf" (truth). This "f" should not have the full sound it has when used initially.

The word "something" is usually pronounced as "sU/m."

V — There has been noted, particularly in the Carolinas, Kentucky, Louisiana, Texas, and the Georgia-Alabama dialect of Uncle Remus, the change of final "v" to "b" as in "hA:b" (have) and "li:b" (live). This is also true of derivatives of such words, as "lUbli" (lovely). The substituted "b" sound should not be given its full pronunciation. It is either sounded lightly, or the lips may be put in position for "b" without sounding it. The latter production should be used especially when the sound occurs at the end of a sentence.

When a Negro uses this change, he does not always apply it to all words but generally only to those words in which final "v" is followed by a word beginning with "b," "f," "m," "n," "p," "r," "s," "t," "v," or "w" as in "li:b fAH:n" (live fine), "hA:b nOH" (have no), "li:b rAH:t" (live right), and "sAY:b vEH: mU:tch" (save very much).

Final "v" is often dropped, as in "gi: mi:" (give me) and "nEH:mAH:n" (never mind).

The words "evening," "over," "oven," and "heaven" are frequently pronounced "EEbnin," "OHbUH," "U/m," and "hEH/m." In the word "heaven" the first syllable "hEH" should be pronounced; then the mouth should be closed for the production of "m" which should be forcefully produced by means of the glottal stop (/). A similar production should be used for "U/m" (oven).

Some Negroes, particularly in Louisiana, change initial "v" to "w" as in "wEH:i" (very.) and "wUis" (voice).

W — This consonant sound is often dropped from such words as "oo:mUHn" (woman), "fOH:d" (forward), "tOH:dz" (towards), and "A:idUHdz" (afterwards).

It is often added, though not as frequently as most actors believe, in the words "gwAHin" (going), "kwAH:l" (coil), "kwi:shn" (cushion), and "twEHl" (until). The use of "w" in these words is rarely heard among Northern Negroes.

WH — The "wh" combination is usually pronounced as "hw" by Southern Negroes, as in "hwA:" (where) and "hwin" (when). Words like "hOO" (who) naturally retain only the "h" sound.

Northern Negroes, particularly those in the Middle West, pronounce "wh" as "w" as in "wA:" (where) and "wAH:" (why).

Y — This consonant sound is often added initially to such initial-vowel words as "yU:th" (earth), "yi:UH" (ear), and "yAH:b" (herb).

A slight "y" glide is frequently used after "g," "h," "k," "m," and "n," as in "gyAY:t" (gate), "hyU:" (here), "kyA:ndi" (candy), "myi:ook" (milk), and "nyi:li" (nearly). This glide is more common after "g" and "k."

Virginia Negroes, in particular, use the "y" glide before "AH" in almost all words, as in "dyAH" (there), "hyAH:" (here), "nyAH" (near), and "myAH" (mere).

Z — Many Negroes change medial "z" to "d" before "n" as in "dUdn" (dozen), "kUdn" (cousin), and "bi:dnUHs" (business).

GRAMMAR CHANGES

There are no rules of grammar in the lexicon of the poor, uneducated Negro. His choice of words, therefore, is rich in a varied display of errors. Those listed in **"The Common Speech"** may be used almost in their entirety with considerable additions, as in "i:z yUH i:z UH i:z yUH AY:/" (Is you is or is you ain't?).

The prevailing conjugation of "to be" is:

"AH i:z"	(I is)	or	"AHz"	(I's)
"yOO i:z"	(you is)	or	"yOOz"	(you's)
"hEE i:z"	(he is)	or	"hEEz"	(he's)
"Us i:z"	(us is)	or	"UsUHz"	(us's)
"yOO AWl i:z"	(you all is)	or	"yAWlz"	(y'all's)
"dAY: i:z"	(they is)	or	"dAY:z"	(they's)

Examples of the above conjugations are:

"AH i:z kUmn!"   "AHz hyU: bAWs."
(I *is* comin!')   (I'*s* here, boss.)
(I *am* coming!)   (I'*m* here, boss.)

"yOO i:z mA:d!"   "yOOz lAY:t."
(You *is* mad!)   (You'*s* late.)
(You *are* mad!)   (You *are* late.)

"hEE shOH i:z hyiUH!"   "hEEs UHgOH:n."
(He sure *is* here!)   (He'*s* a-going.)
(He *is* here!)   (He'*s* going.)

"Us i:z bOHf trAH:in!"   "UsUHz nEHbUH dERn."
(Us *is* both trying!)   (Us'*s* never done.)
(We *are* both trying!)   (We *are* never done.)

"yOO AWl i:z gOH:n!"   "yAWlz mAH:di prAH:ood."
(You-all *is* going!)   (Y'all'*s* mightly proud.)
(You *are* all going!)   (You *are* all very proud.)

"dAY: i:z dAY:d!"   "dAY:z fAH:in."
(They *is* dead!)   (They'*s* fine.)
(They *are* dead!)   (They *are* fine.)

The phrase "he am" is seldom used by Negroes, as in "hEE A:m hyiUH" (He am here).

The use of "wEE AWl" (we-all) is current as in "wEE AWlz gOH:n" (we-alls going). Louisiana Negroes, in particular, sometimes use "Us AWl" (us-all) as in "Us AWlz yOOmn" (us-all's human.)

There is also a preference in Negro speech for the present tense of a verb, so that, "hEE rERn hOHm" (He run home) and "hEE sAY: nU/n" (He say nothing) are used instead of "hEE rA:n" (he ran) or "hEE sAY:d" (he said). However, when the past tense is used to indicate completed action, many Negroes affix a preceding "done" to the verb, as in:

"hEE dERn di:d UHd AWrEHdi."
(He *done did* it already.)
(He *did* it already.)

Many Negroes, particularly those with little education would use "done done" instead of "done did" as in:

"hEE dERn dERn UHd AWrEHdi."
(He *done done* it already.)
(He *did* it already.)

In the same way, many Negroes would use the following variations:

"AH dERn gAY:v UHt bA:k."
(I *done gave* it back.)
(I *gave* it back.)

"AH dERn gi:v UHt bA:k."
(I *done give* it back.)
(I *gave* it back.)

Many Negroes, particularly in Louisiana, use "I'm" for "I've," as in:

"AHm gAH/ mEE UH mA:n."
(I'*m* got me a man.)
(*I've* got myself a man.)

A preference for "does" instead of "do" is prevalent, as in:

"dUz yUH grEE dUH jAWin?"
(*Does* you agree to join?)
(*Do* you agree to join?)

"hwA: dUHz wi gOH hwin wi gOH:z?"
(Where *does* we go when we goes?)
(Where *do* we go when we go?)

A universal error substitutes the third person singular of a present-tense verb for the first person, as in:

"AH gi:ts mAH:di tAH:d."
(I *gits* mighty tired.)
(I *get* very tired.)

"AH klEEnz AH dU:s AH skrUuhbz."
(I *cleans*, I *dusts*, I *scrubs*.)
(I *clean*, I *dust*, I *scrub*.)

"Us gyi:ts tchi:/luhnz."
(Us *gits* chitlins.)
(We *get* chitlings.)

A popular error made by most Negroes is the substitution "they" for "there," as in:

"AY:z sU/m fUni bAH:ood UHt."
(*They's* something funny about it.)
(*There's* something funny about it.)

"AY AYn nOH yOOs trAH:n."
(*They* ain't no use trying.)
(*There's* no use trying.)

The above error may be accounted for by the fact that "there" is almost always pronounced as "dA:" with the vowel sound nasalized. This nasalization brings the vowel sound close to "AY:," and as such it is frequently pronounced. Thus, what appears to be an error in grammar may be simply a variation in dialect speech. A similar explanation may be true for the use of "of" instead of "have" which is common to many Negroes. The weak forms of "have" and "of" are both "UHv" so that "AH woo:d UHv gAW:n" may be interpreted as "I would have gone" or "I would of gone."

Another error, found mostly in the speech of Southern Negroes, although a great many older Northern Negroes use it, is the addition of "s" or "es" to a plural word, as in:

"tEHk kyA: dEHm pOHsiz."
(Take care them *postses*.)
(Take care of those *posts*.)

"mAH fEEts UHz tAH:d."
(My *feets* is tired.)
(My *feet* are tired.)

Many Negroes, including those in the North, form the past tense of a verb by adding "ed" to a present-tense verb, as in:

"AH tEHld UHm nAHtUH."
(I *telled* him not to.)
(I *told* him not to.)

"AY gi:vd UH/ tUH mi:."
(They *gived* it to me.)
(They *gave* it to me.)

The double negative, and even the triple negative, is frequently used, as in:

"AY di:n nOHbAHdi sEE UHt."
(They did*n't nobody* see it.)
(*Nobody* saw it.)

"AYn̲nEHvUH gAH/ nOH jAWb nOHhAH:oo."
(*Ain't never* got *no* job *no*how.)
(I *never* had a job.)

"dAYn̲ nOH yOOs krAH:n."
(There *ain't no* use crying.)
(There's *no* use crying.)

The addition of "all" after "what" is found in the speech of many Negroes, as in:

"wUdAWl AY hA:z tUH dOO?"
(What *all* they has to do?)
(What do they have to do?)

The use of "fixing" for "preparing" or "planning" is also common to Negro speech, as in:

"AH wUHz fi:ksUHn fUH dUH tEH: yUH."
(I was *fixing* for to tell you.)
(I was *planning* to tell you.)

"yOO fi:ksUHn tUH gOH nAH:oo?"
(You *fixing* to go now?)
(Are you *preparing* to go now?)

The redundant use of a reflexive personal pronoun is common, as in:

"gAHdUH fAH:n mEE UH gyA:uhl."
(Got to find *me* a girl.)
(I have to find a girl.)

"gyi:/ yUH AH:oodUH hyEH:."
(Get *you* out of here.)
(Get out of here.)

"lEHs Us gyi:t."
(Let's *us* git.)
(Let's go.)

The dialect also features many such past-tense verb forms as "flang" (flung), "brang" (brought), "thunk" (thought), "clomb" (climbed), "knowed" (knew), "kotched" (caught), "shuck" (shook), "swole" (swollen), and "tuck" (took).

The superlative is frequently formed by adding "est" to superlative forms, as in "bEHsUHs" (bestest) and "mOHsUHs" (mostest). The comparative generally adds "er," as in "wU:sUH" (worser) and "pAWpyuhluh:" (popularer).

The auxiliary verb is often omitted from Negro speech, as in:

"nAH:oo yUH tAW:kn."
(Now you talking.)
(Now you're talking.)

"hOO dA:t?"
(Who that?)
(Who *is* that?)

"AH goo:d UHz hi:m."
(I good as him.)
(I'm *as* good as he is.)

A confusion of prepositions substitutes "on" for "of" as in:

"fOH: AWn UHm"
(four *on* them)
(four *of* them)

There is also current a substitution of "is" for "do" as in:

"i:z yUH wAWnUH gOH:?"
(*Is* you want to go?)
(*Do* you want to go?)

The word "ain't" is commonly used in a negative statement, as in:

"AH AYnOH wAH:."
(I *ain't* know why.)
(I *don't* know why.)

"i:d AYn loo:k rAH:it."
(It *ain't* look right.)
(It *doesn't* look right.)

A substitution of "which" for "who" is also heard, as in:

"dUH fEHuhluh wi:tch kUoom yEH."
(The fellow *which* comes here.)
(The fellow *who* comes here.)

There is also to be found in the dialect speech, a use of "did" for "had" as in:

"di:d AH nOH AHdUH wint."
(Did I know, I'd a went.)
(*Had* I known, I'd have gone.)

The intrusion of an unnecessary "at" after "where" is frequently used, as in:

"wA: A:d i:z dAY?"
(Where *at* is they?)
(Where are they?)

The substitution of "gin" for "gave" is quite common among Southern Negroes but rare in the North, as in:

"AH gi:n UHd UH shUv."
(I *gin* it a shove.)
(I *gave* it a shove.)

There is also current a substitution of "at' for "to" after "listen," as in:

"li:sn A:di:m!"
(Listen *at* him!)
(Listen *to* him!)

COMMON PHRASES

An expression common to most Negroes, but rapidly declining in use in the north, is the phrase "you-all." It may be variously pronounced as "yAWl," "yOO AWl," "yAWoo," or "yAW." Southern white speakers generally reserve its use to indicate plurality. But Negroes use it both plurally and singularly, as in:

"hAHkUm yAWlz tAH:d?"
(How come *you-all's* tired?)
(Why are *you* tired?)

"yAWlz gAHdUH kUoom."
(*You-all's* gotta come.)
(*You-all* must come.)

Many Southern Negroes also use "us-all" or "we-all" as in:

"Us AWlz gi:/n OHl."
(*Us-all's* gettin' old.)
(*We're* getting old.)

"wEE AWl kAYn wUk hAWd."
(*We-all* can't work hard.)
(*We* can't work hard.)

The use of "how come" for "why" is also popular, as in:

"hAHkUm yUH AYn gAWn yit?"
(*How come* you ain't gone yet?)
(*Why* haven't you gone yet?)

To emphasize a statement, a Negro will often use the phrase "at all," as in:

"AH dOHn gi:dUHt AYtAWl."
(I don't get it *at all*.)
(I don't understand it.)

The phrase "please, sir" or "please, ma'am" is often interpolated into a Negro's speech, a throwback to slavery days, as in:

"ki:n AH gOH plEE sUH?"
(Can I go, *please, sir?*)
(May I go, sir?)

"i:z dAY nUf wU:k plEEz mA:m?"
(Is they enough work, *please, ma'am?*)
(Is there enough work, ma'am?)

The "absolute truth" is almost always phrased as the "gospel truth" as in:

"yA:zUH dA:s gAWspuhl trOOt!"
(Yes sir! that's *gospel truth!*)
(Yes sir! that's absolutely true!)

The phrase "ever which way" is often substituted for "in all directions" as in:

"hi rERn AWf EHvUH wi:tch wAY:."
(He run off *ever which way.*)
(He ran off in all directions.)

Like the Southern and Mountain people, the Negro is addicted to the phrase "like to" instead of "almost" as in:

"AH lAH:ik tUH ki:l UHm."
(I *like to* kill him.)
(I *almost* killed him.)

The use of "fitten" for "suited" or "entitled" is also to be found in Negro dialect speech, as in:

"hEE AYnn fi:/n tUH bi sEE:n."
(He ain't *fitten* to be seen.)
(He's in no *condition* to be seen.)

"yAY/ fi:/n tUH bi blEH:st."
(You ain't *fitten* to be blessed.)
(You aren't *entitled* to be blessed.)

The words "lowdown," "worthless," and occasionally "ornery" are used by many Negroes to indicate utter worthlessness or depravity, as in:

"yOO lOHdAH:oon OH:nri wU:tlUHs trA:ish."
(You lowdown, ornery, worthless trash.)

The Southern Negro in particular still uses the expression "hush your mouth" for "be quiet" or "shut up" as in:

"hEHsh yOH mAH:oof wi:n AH OHrAY:ts."
(Hush your mouth when I orates.)
(Be quiet when I speak.)

The use of "twAHn," "twAWn," or "twOHn" (the latter particularly in Virginia) is still current for "it wasn't" as in:

'twAWn nOH yOOs!"
(*Twan't* no use!)
(*It wasn't* any use!)

"twAWn/ mAH:n"
(*Twan't* mine!)
(*It wasn't* mine!)

Almost every Negro is partial to the use of "this here" and "that there" as in:

"di:shyEH kAH:n AY:nOH goo:d."
(This *here* kind ain't no good.)
(This kind is no good.)

"dA dA: bi:g mAH:oof mA:n."
(That *there* big mouth man.)
(That man with the big mouth.)

The use of "mind" for "remember" is also current, as in:

"yUH mAH:n win AH gAHdUHt?"
(You *mind* when I got it?)
(Do you *remember* when I got it?)

The noun "mind" is also frequently used in place of "attention" as in:

"dOHn pAY nOH mAH:n tUHt."
(Don't pay no *mind* to it.
(Don't pay any *attention* to it.)

The phrase "out of" is usually pronounced as though it were "outen" as in:

"tAYkUHt AH:oodn mAH wAY:."
(Take it *outen* my way.)
(Take it *out of* my way.)

The phrase "fool head off" is frequently appended to a verb to indicate an extreme amount of action, as in:

"AY lA:if dAY fOOl hAYd AW:f."
(They laugh they fool head off.)
(They laughed their fool heads off.)

Many Negroes still use "every last one" for "all of you," as in:

"EHvi lA:is wERn UH yUH gAHdUH trAH:."
(*Every last one* of you gotta try.)
(*All* of you must try.)

The use of "call" for "reason" is also found in the dialect speech, as in:

"AYnOH kAW:l fOH yUH dUH bi mA:d."
(Ain't no *call* for you to be mad.)
(There's no *reason* for you to be angry.)

Many Southern Negroes still use the word "study" rather than "think," as in:

"gAHdUH stUuhdi bAH:oodUHt."
(Gotta *study* about it.)
(I have to *think* about it.)

A popular phrase is "had my druthers" for "had my choice," as in:

"fAH hAd mUH drUdUHz AHd gOH:."
(If I had my *druthers*, I'd go.)
(If I had my *choice*, I'd go.)

For "pretend" the Negro often uses the phrase "play like," as in:

"lEHsUHs plAY lAH:ik wi gOH:."
(Le's us *play like* we go.)
(Let's *pretend* we're going.)

INTERJECTIONS

As with popular phrases, interjections change with the times. At present, especially in the North, there is a craze for so-called "jive-talk" which has contributed many popular phrases and interjections, not only to Negro speech but to the speech of many other American groups as well. But these will have their day and fade in popularity leaving, perhaps, a few deep-rooted idioms to join the ranks of other such interjections which are now part of the Negro idiom, such as:

"mA:in!"	(Man!)
"lOH:di!"	(Lordy!)
"shOHnUf!"	(Sure enough!)
"AYn dA:/ sUoo/m!"	(Ain't that something!)
"AH bi dAW:gAW:n!"	(I'll be doggoned!)
"dAW:g bAH/ mi!"	(Dog bite me!)
"dAW:g mAH kA:ts!"	(Dog my cats!)
"AYnUH/ dUH trOOf!"	(Ain't it the truth!)

MISPRONUNCIATIONS

Another important factor contributing to the color of Negro dialect speech is the malaprop quality of the mispronunciations in the Negro's lexicon. The Negro frequently resorts to twisted and garbled versions of sesquipedalian words, an addiction that has made for much of the supposed humor in the Negro dialect. For example, a Negro may say, "hAH:ooz yOH kOHpUHrAWsti sUHgAY:shAYt kUoomn lAWng" (How's your coporosity sagaciate coming along?), or "AH prAWmUHs tUH fOHsEHk UHm fOH AWl UdUHz twEHl dEH:t dOO Us dEE:pAWt" (I promise to forsake him for all others until death do us depart).

A judicious sprinkling of such malapropisms may salt a characterization to a certain degree, but a surfeit of them would lose the distinctive flavor and make the speech incomprehensible. Following is a list of some of the malformed words:

"UpsEHtmin"	"upsetment"	(upset)
"sEEsdUHd"	"ceaseded"	(deceased)
"AY:jUHbuhl"	"ageable"	(aged)
"ri:tchkrA:t"	"richcrat"	(aristocrat)
"jOObUHnAY:dUHd"	"jubenated"	(rejuvenated)
"tOObAWnkuhlOOsi"	"tubonkuloosi"	(tuberculosis)
"shEE mAY:uhl"	"she-male"	(female)
"bUstikAYdUHd"	"busticated"	(broke)
"si:sti:fkUHt"	"sistificate"	(certificate)
"pUHzA:kli"	"perzackly"	(exactly)
"kwi:zUHfAH:"	"quizzify"	(quiz)
"sprEHsUHfAH:"	"spressify"	(specify)
"i:nsUoo"	"insult"	(consult)
"kUHmi:t"	"commit"	(permit)
"rEHkUHmAH:zAYdid"	"recognizated"	(recognized)
"nOHshnmint"	"notionment"	(notion)
"rEEkAYzhUHn"	"recasion"	(occasion)
"prEEzis"	"presist"	(persist)
"hAH:sUHmEHbUH"	"howsomeber"	(however)
"li:ni:mUHm"	"linimum"	(liniment)

MONOLOGS

(From *Black Cameos* by H. Emmet Kennedy.)

        I ain' beggin' none y'all to b'leeve wat I'm tellin yuh. I'm des natchally tellin' y'all wat I seen happen. Y'all kin do like yuh like 'bout b'leevin', but wat I'm tellin' yuh 's

Gawd dyin' truth fum hyeah to heaven, des like I seen de thing
happen wid dese same two wide-open Afficky eyes. 'Twas one
Saddy evenin', an' I was settin' down to mahself on top a sack o'
I'ish potatoes in Mistuh Cholly Groos sto'-room; an' right scattuh-
cawnduh fum whah I was settin' dey had a b'ahl of gin wat had a
fawcet wat was leakin'. An' 'twan' say 'zackly leakin' neithuh, but
des drippin' slow, drap fo' drap. Well, I was settin' dah, watchin' it
drippin', wen fus' thing I knowed, who come lopin' 'cross de flo, fum
behin' de ba'hl in de cawnduh but one li'l ole long-tail mice. 'E
ain' paid me no 'tenshun, but runned ove' to whah de fawcet was
drippin', an' licked out 'is tongue good as 'e felt an' got 'im a tas'e o'
de gin drippin' fum de fawcet. I des look at 'im, an' I say: Now yuh
tell me! Ef dat mice ain' got sense de same as people! Lickin' out 'is
tongue to ketch dat gin drippin' fum de fawcet! Yas, Lawd, hit look
like dat gin mus' bin gi'n 'im relish fo' flavuhs, 'cause soon's 'e done
swalluhd de fus' drap 'e licked out 'is tongue to git 'im anothuh drap.
Yas, 'e look like 'e make up 'is min' 'e gwine lap 'is lickuhs to 'is
sattaffacshun long's nobody ain' meddle 'im. An' I des set dah
watchin' 'im, 'cause I was indaquiztun to see wat 'e gwine do nex'.
Well, yuh know I breathes hahd. So 'e mus' bin hyeahed me breathin',
so dah whah 'e turned roun' an' seen me watchin' 'im den 'e runned
out in de middle 'o de flo', an' fus' thing I knowed, Mistuh Mice
had sprunged up in de aih an' landed squah on top de bah'l o' gin.
I book at 'im an' I say: Lawd! now wa's dis dumb beas' gwine do
nex'? An' 'e mus' bin un'stood what I say. 'Cause 'e look me direck
in de face, an' 'e commence wallin' 'is eyes all 'roun' de room: den
'e reah'd back on top dat bah'l o' gin, an' bless Gawd, dat mice look
at me an' say des as plain as ef 'e was people: Now show me dat
damn tom cat say 'e wan' fight!

(From *Darker Brother** by Bucklin Moon)

I ain sure, Birdie. I don't know what I did then. I reckon I like
tuh git out in the country someplace. We could have us some
chickens an grow cowpease an collards. We could go fishin and be in
the sun. Yuh like that, Birdie? Yuh wusn brought up like I was,
Birdie. I never seen uh pair of shoes til just before I came up here.
It sure pretty down there. I know all that, Jim Crow and all the
rest. Yuh know the difference, Birdie? Up here they let me come
to the front door and they call me Mr. Johnson. Only when I mention
job they slam the door in my face. Down there they say "Nigger, get
on round tuh the back door." Then 1 get fed up good.

---

* Reprinted with permission of Doubleday, Doran and Co.

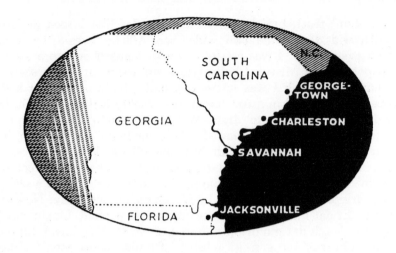

THE GULLAH DIALECT

EVEN THE PHONETICIANS who deny the existence of regional American dialects do agree that the Gullah Negro dialect is one of the few American dialects they recognize. It is spoken by the Negro inhabitants of the Sea Islands and those along the coast of Georgia and South Carolina from about Georgetown through the cities of Charleston and Savannah and south along the coast of Georgia to the northeast coast of Florida.

The Negroes here are, for the most part, descendants of slaves brought over from the west coast of Africa, the exact location of which is unknown. The derivation of the name "Gullah" is also doubtful though some believe it came from the Angola tribe of Negroes. These original African slaves, whatever their place of birth may have been, took on the speech of their white masters which was a combination of the lower-class English of the seventeenth and eighteenth centuries with Scotch-Irish infiltrations. Actually, they took on the phonetic gloss of English pronunciation but retained the primitive African spirit of delivery together with many African words. And because of their segregated, isolated island habitat, they retained their older speech despite the changes being wrought in the speech of neighboring regions. To this day, even the younger generation uses this African version of seventeenth century English. Indeed, it can be posited that certain aspects of Gullah are more correct English than General-American. The most extreme form of the Gullah dialect is to be found in the speech of the Negroes living in the Edisto Island and in the Cumbahee section.

It would be impossible to add to the admirable characterization on the Gullah Negro as made by Reed Smith. He stated that the Gullah Negro is, at once "unbelievably primitive, childlike, excitedly religious, ignorant, illiterate, humorous, shrewd, shiftless beyond expression, superstitious, unstable, likable, loyal, gifted with picturesque speech, humble, kindly, generous, good-natured and entirely without malice." Like most Negroes, they are reserved when conversing with whites. In fact, with whites, their dialect is not so thick as it is in ordinary conversation among themselves.

LILT

The Gullah dialect is characterized by a strange lack of the typical Negro drawl. Instead, the delivery is rapid, almost staccato. Syllables are clipped off sharply rather than being elided fuzzily, as is the case with the speech of the average Negro. There is a choppiness to the speech that makes for a sort of crackling delivery. In its rapidity and fluctuations, it may be compared to the quacking of the cartoon character, Donald Duck. This quality brought about the belief that the origin of the Gullah Negroes was to be found along the west coast of Africa, south of Sierra Leone, where records reveal the existence of a tribe of Negroes known as the "Qua-Qua's," so called because of the duck-quacking character of their native speech.

That the spirit of the Gullah lilt derives from African sources is a fact not to be questioned. Research has proved that the source of most of the African words still used in the dialect can be traced to the Umbundu branch of the Bantu dialect. This is one of the many African dialects that uses a system of tonal inflection to indicate changes in meaning, grammar, and mood. And although these tonal changes are not as evident now in the English dialect of the descendants of the original African slaves, they have remained in the speech to a certain extent. Thus, today, the Gullah dialect is further characterized by a decidedly wide range of tonal patterns, even wider than in the average Negro dialect. In spite of the rapid utterance of their speech, there is an indefinable musical quality very reminiscent of the original African intonations.

On the whole, the speech of the Gullah Negro is pitched low. It has the full resonance typical of Negro speech, and its rhythmical quality mirrors the love of rhythm so inherent in the Negro psyche. However, because of the wide range, the low pitch can, and does, rise to an extremely high pitch that is intensified with the addition of nasalization.

For example, the sentence "EE EHn lib i nUH mOH" (He ain't live here no more) would show a sudden rise on the word "live," and the entire sentence would be spoken as:

DROPPED SYLLABLES

The authentic Gullah dialect, as used among the people themselves, would be of such a nature that it would be entirely incomprehensible to other than Gullah ears. This is the result of a number of factors. The Gullah system of grammar, for example, is most primitive. It has been often characterized as being a sort of Pidgin English. In addition many words are used in a sense foreign to the actual American meaning of the words. Then again there are many African words found in the dialect. The Gullah habit of dropping consonants, especially in places where the meaning of the word becomes obscured, as in "tin" (sting), adds to the obfuscation. But, most serious of all, is the dropping of entire syllables.

The prefix of a word is almost always lopped off, as in "spAHiz" (despise), "tUn (attend), "spOHz" (suppose, expose), "stUd" (instead), "trAHk" (attract), "prUs" (oppress), "gAAd" (regard), "tUmp" (contempt), and "mAHi" (admire).

To add to the confusion, many Gullah speakers, in trying to affect better speech, substitute a "re" or "ex" for these ordinarily dropped prefixes, as in "rEEsplAYn" (explain), "rEEsAHid" (decide), "rEEpOHz" (expose), "EHkswAHis" (advice), and even "rEEmOHnyUH" (pneumonia).

Gullah speakers also drop medial and final syllables, even when the sense becomes completely obliterated, as in "wUsnUbUH" (worse than ever), "EEgnUHn" (ignorant), "shUm" (see 'em), "mAHnUHzbuhl" (manageable), and "kUmbEE" (Cumbahee).

Before going into the subject of grammar changes and other elements contributing to the Gullah dialect, it would be best to examine the vowel and consonant changes at this time.

VOWEL CHANGES

Sound	as in	Pronounced		as in
AY	make	EH	(particularly in common words like "break," "snake," etc.)	mEHk
	chase	AY	(sometimes)	tchAYs
UH	alone		dropped initially	lOHn
	sofa	U		sOHfU
AH	part	AA	(when followed by "r" or "lm," see "AH," page 30)	pAAt
	calm	AH	(sometimes)	kAHm
	father	AH		fAHdUH
A:	task	AH		tAHs
A	man	AH		mAHn
	back	EH	(occasionally)	bEHk
	and	EH	(usually)	EHn
AW	call	AW		kAWl
	lost	AW		lAWs
	short	OH	(before "r")	shOHt
	off	AH	(frequently in this word)	AHf
	water	AH	(when preceded by a "w" sound)	wAHdUH
EE	heat	EE		hEEt
	heat	i	(occasionally)	hit
EH	help	EH	(generally)	hEHp
	bed	AY	(in certain words spelled with "e" or "ea"; see "EH," page 195)	bAYd
	instead	i	(sometimes; see "EH," page 195)	stid
	deaf	EE	(exception)	dEEf
	breakfast	U	(exception)	brUkfUs
	yellow	A	(exception)	yAluh
	there	EH	(before "r")	dEH
I	side	AAi		sAAid
	like	U	(occasionally)	lUk
	I	UH	(particularly when unstressed)	UH
i	it	i		it
	fish	EE	(often)	fEEsh
	fish	U	(occasionally)	fUsh
	spirit	EH:	(before "r")	pEH:t

Sound	as in	Pronounced		as In
O	not	**AH**		nAHt
	not	**AW**	(variant)	nAWt
	upon	**U**	(particularly when un-stressed)	pUn
	drop	**A**	(exception)	drAp
OH	home	**OH**	(sometimes with an "AW" flavor)	hOHm
	going	**U**	(exception)	gUn
OO	food	**OO**		fOOd
	too	**OH**	(also "yOH" for "you")	tOH
oo	good	**oo**		good
	good	**U**	(occasionally)	gUd
yOO	few	**iOO**		fiOO
	use	**yiOO**		yiOOz
yoo	pure	**yOH**		pyOH
U	fun	**U**		fUn
	unfit	**AW**	(when initial in prefix)	AWnfit
	judge	**EH**	(See "U," page 200)	jEHj
	just	**i**		jis
ER	girl	**U**		gUl
	girl	**EH**	(variant)	gEHl
	number	**UH**	(when final)	nUmbUH
OW	now	**AH**		nAH
	now	**AHoo**	(variant)	nAHoo
	now	**U**	(occasionally, particularly when unstressed)	nU
	cow	**OH**	(also in "sow")	kOH
OI	join	**AHi**		jAHin
	join	**AWi**	(occasionally)	jAWin

CONSONANT CHANGES

Most of the consonant changes of the Gullah dialect are listed below. But all of them should not be used consistently if the speech is to be understood. Some compromise must be made between audibility, understandability, and authenticity.

In the Gullah dialect, consonant elisions are characteristic, and many word meanings are completely erased in the process. The actor, therefore, must be judicious as to his choice of consonant elisions so that the meaning of the word will be clear either from the context of the sentence or from the portion of the word that is retained.

B — Initially, this consonant sound remains the same as in General-American. Medially and finally, however, it usually takes a "v" coloring so that the actual sound becomes "bv" in our phonetics. This "bv" sound is like the Spanish sound in "hAHbvAHnAH" (Havana) and is produced with the lips not quite touching each other in the center while "b" or "v" is sounded, as in "hAHbv" (have) and "rUbvUH" (rubber).

Medial "b" is often dropped, especially when preceded by "m" as in "nUmUH" (number), "sUmuhl" (assemble), and "timuhl" (thimble).

D — When followed by a "y" glide, initial or medial "d" is often changed to "j" as in "jOO" (due), "EEnjin" (Indian), and "jooUH" (endure). Obviously, this last example would be completely obscured if pronounced exactly as in Gullah, so the actor would retain the dropped prefix and pronounce the word as "injooUH" (endure).

Medial "d" is often dropped when unstressed after "l" and "n" as in "tchiluhn" (children) and "kAHnuhl" (candle).

Final "d" is generally dropped, especially after "l" or "n" as in "lAHn" (land) and "fAAin" (fine).

When not dropped, final "d" is frequently changed to "t" as in "tOOpit" (stupid) and "AAilUnt" (island).

F — This consonant is also produced with the lips instead of with the lips and teeth as in General-American. The result is a sound that sometimes appears to be "f" and other times "v." The sound can be reproduced by shaping the lips for "w" but sounding "f." The result is similar to the forceful sound of "h" in "hwEHn" (when). The symbol "f" will be retained, but the "h" treatment should be used when it can be produced naturally.

G — As in the general Negro dialect "g" is palatalized in Gullah speech. See page 205 for a detailed description of this process.

H — Occasionally "h" is added to an initial vowel word, as in "hinjin" (Indian) and "hAHisUHz" (oysters).

In rapid speech "h" is frequently dropped as in "im" (him), "EE" (he), and "OHl" (hold).

K — The palatalization of "k" is also found in Gullah. See page 206 for a detailed discussion.

Some speakers sound "k" lightly so that it takes on a "g" flavor.

The word "ask" is frequently pronounced as "AHks."

L — Medial "l" is frequently dropped, especially when it is preceded by "EH," "A," or "i" and is followed by "b," "f," "m," "p," "v," or "w" as in "AHbUt" (Albert), "hEHp" (help), and "fim" (film).

Final "l" is often dropped, especially in the "le" ending where it is usually replaced with "oo" as in "trUmoo" (tremble) and "pEEpoo" (people).

M — When final, "m" is often dropped with the extreme nasalization of its preceding vowel sound, as in "hAHkUm" (how come?).

N — The nasalization of "n" contributes greatly to the nasal quality of the Gullah speech. The vowel before "n" should be nasalized, and unless the word meaning is obscured, the "n" should be dropped, as in "gUn" (going) and "tchEHnj" (change).

When a word begins with "y," an initial "n" is often added as in "nyOOt" (youth) and "nyUn" (young).

NG — This combination is generally pronounced as "n" as in "finUH" (finger), "lUnt" (length), and "trUn" (strength). The last example illustrates the futility of adhering too strictly to the exact pronunciation. The word "strength" would be difficult to understand if reproduced exactly. Therefore, it is best to sound the word as "strUnt" and depend on its context to give it full meaning.

P — When "p" is preceded by "m," it is often dropped, as in "kAHm" (camp), "hAHmUH" (hamper), and "sAHmoo" (sample).

Final "p" is often dropped when preceded by "s" as in "klAHs" (clasp) and "wAWs" (wasp).

R — The Gullah "r" sound is considerably affected by its African origin. The African "r" pronounced like the French "r" *grasseyé* (see page 144) sounds very much like "w" because of its extreme frontal production. The Gullah generally restricts his use of his "r" to the initial position in a word, although he sometimes uses it medially between vowels. Thus, "very" may be pronounced as "bvEHi" or "bvEHri," and "marry" may be "mAHi" or "mAHri."

A great many Gullah speakers also drop "r" after a consonant, as in "bUdUH" (brother) and "pOObv" (prove). The "r" should not be dropped in short words like "krAAi" (cry) or the meaning of the word would be obscured.

Medial "r" between vowels often receives the single-flap British treatment which results in a sound similar to "d," as in "hUdi" (hurry). A full-flavored "d" should not be used.

S — An initial "s" is sometimes sounded before a word beginning with the sound of "k" or "t" as in "skwEHshn" (question), strAHm" (tramp), and "skrAHootch" (crouch).

When initial "s" is followed by the sound of "k," "p," or "t," it is usually dropped, as in "kAHtch" (scorch), "plAHsh" (splash) and "tAHn" (stand).

Initial "s" is often pronounced as "sh" as in "shishUH" (such a) and "shUm" (see 'em).

When final and followed by the sound of "y," this consonant is frequently pronounced as "sh" as in "dishyi" (this here).

SH — Initial "sh" is often changed to "s" when followed by "r" as in "srim" (shrimp) and "srUbv" (shrub). (See "R," page 144.)

T — When initial or medial "t" is followed by "OO," it is often changed to "tch" as in "tchOObv" (tube), "tchOO" (two), "grAHditchOOd" (gratitude), and "tchOOl" (tool). This change is more frequent in "OO" words that take a "y" glide and are spelled with "u" or "ue."

Medial double "t" (tt) is often dropped, as in "bAH:l" (bottle), "rAH:n" (rotten), and "bAH:m" (bottom). The vowel sound is usually of slightly longer duration to make up for the dropped consonant sound. Some Gullah speakers change "t" to "d" as in "bidUH" (bitter) and "bAHdUHm" (bottom).

Medial "t" between vowels is often changed to a light "d" as in "kyAHduhlAWg" (catalog), and "sidifAAid" (citified). This change is also common with final "t" particularly when it is followed by an initial vowel word, as in "sid AWn" (sit on) and "kAHd AHood" (cat out).

Final "t" is generally dropped when preceded by a consonant sound, as in "AHk" (act), "pEHn" (paint), and "kAWs" (cost).

TH — This consonant sound is pronounced as "d" as in "dUH" (the), "widUH" (wither) and "bAYd" (bathe).

Occasionally a flapped "d" is used so that the resulting sound resembles a flapped "r" as in "tUrUH" (t'other).

th — This consonant sound is pronounced as "t" as in "tink" (think), "piti" (pithy), and "pAHt" (path).

ts — Medial "ts" is often pronounced as "tch" as in "kUtchEE" (curtsy), "flAWtchUHm" (flotsam), and "tEHtchUHn" (Stetson).

tch — Medial "tch" before "ure" is often sounded as "d" as in "kridUH" (creature), "pAHsdUH" (pasture), and "lEHkdUH" (lecture).

Final "tch" is sometimes sounded as "sh" as in "shishUH" (such a).

V — The confusion in the exact pronunciation of this sound may be attributed to the fact that it is pronounced bi-labially instead of labiodentally. Thus, instead of allowing the lower lip to touch the upper teeth in the pronunciation of "v," the lips should be close together but not touching. There is generally a slight opening in the center of the mouth. This sound is represented in our phonetics as "bv" as in "ribvUH" (river) and "libv" (live). (See "B.") Because of its elusive quality, this sound has been variously reported as "b" as in "bUri" (very), "w" as in "wAHis" (voice), and sometimes "v" as in "vAAin" (vine).

W — Initial "w" is often dropped before "oo" as in "ood" (would) and "oomUHn" (woman).

Medial "w" is often dropped in such words as "fAWdz" (forwards) and "AHdUHz" (afterwards).

An intrusive "w" is frequently used before "oi" as in "kwAHin" (coin), "gwAHin" (going), and "kwAHil" (coil).

WH — This combination sound is generally pronounced as "w" as in "wEH" (where) and "witch" (which).

Y — This consonant sound is often added initially when a word begins with "ea" as in "yUt" (earth) and "yUn" (earn).

When the "yOO" is initial, it is sometimes preceded by "n" as in "nyOOz" (use), "nyOOnAAid" (United), and "nyOO" (you).

A "y" glide is sometimes used when one word ends with a vowel sound and the next word begins with a vowel, particularly "i" or "EH" as in "EH yiz" (they is) and "EE yEHd" (he ate).

ZH — This sound is frequently changed to "j" as in "mAYjUH" (measure), "plAYjUH" (pleasure), and "vijUHn" (vision).

Z — When final and followed by the sound of "y," this consonant is frequently pronounced as "zh" as in "dEEzhyi" (these here).

GRAMMAR CHANGES

It is with the peculiar grammatical changes that the Gullah dialect becomes ambiguous. Like Pidgin English, with which it has been compared, it uses the simplest of constructions. As reported by Reed Smith, the sentence "UH yEHdi yUHm bUHdUH yEHn shUm" (I yeddy 'um but I ain't sh'um) could be interpreted in sixty-four different ways.

		it			it
I	hear	her	but I	didn't	her
		him			him
	heard	them		don't	them

One construction is made to serve where a dozen are necessary in ordinary English. The use of "UHm" (um), for example, so prevalent among most primitive speakers of English — Chinese,

South Sea Islanders, African Negroes, Eskimos, and Indians — is
to be found in Gullah as well. Here, it is used in place of the objective
forms of all third-person pronouns, as in:

"UH tOHl UHm."
(I told *'um.*)
(I told *her.*)

"yUH shUm?"
(You sh'*um?*)
(Did you see *him?*)

"wAA EE dUnUHm?"
(Why he done *'um?*)
(Why did he do *it?*)

"UH shUm gOH."
(I sh'*um* go.)
(I saw *them* go.)

In the same way, the word "he" (pronounced as "EE") is used
for all the third person singular personal pronouns in the nominative
case, as in:

"EE gyid pAWntAHp dEE kyAAd."
(*He* git 'pon top the cart.)
(*He* got on top of the cart.)

"EE lif UHm hAHn."
(*He* lift 'um hand.)
(*She* raised her hand.)

"EE yEHn bvUk."
(*He* ain't work.)
(*It* won't work.)

The word "he" may also be used for a pronoun in the objective
case when this pronoun is stressed, as in:

"EE gibv EE EHkswAAis."
(He give *he* exwice.)
(She gave *her* advice.)

The pronoun "he" may also be used for "they" as in:

"EE lEHd EHnEE?"
(*He* late, enty?)
(*They're* late, aren't they?)

Most inanimate objects and all animals are designated as "EE" in Gullah, as in:

"EE fAWl dAHoon."
(*He* fall down.)
(*It* fell down.)

"grAHb uhHOHl EE hAWluh."
(Grab a-hold *he* halter.)
(Grab hold of *its* halter.)

Possessive pronouns are also supplanted by the ever-present "EE," as in:

"EE tEHg EE tchAAil."
(He take *he* child.)
(She took *her* child.)

"gibv UHm EE miOOl."
(Give 'um *he* mule.)
(Give him *his* mule.)

"tEHl UHm EE wUt."
(Tell 'um *he* worth.)
(Tell them *its* worth.)

The possessive is also indicated with "him," "we," "us," "you," "them," as in:

"EE kUm wEE hAHs EHntEE?"
(He come *we* house, enty?)
(He came to *our* house, didn't he?)

"EE tUk im gUl wEH."
(He took *him* girl 'way.)
(He took *his* girl away.)

"Us plEHs iz bUn."
(*Us* place is burn.)
(*Our* place burned down.)

"tOHd OOnUH OHn nyAHm."
(Tote *you* own nyam.)
(Carry *your* food.)

"EE mEHg dEHm OHn klOHz."
(He make *them* own clothes.)
(She makes *their* clothing.)

Possessive is also expressed by the use of the nominative or objective personal pronoun, as in:

"AH nEHm mOHs."
(*I* name Morse.)
(*My* name is Morse.)

"mEE hAWs EE blAAin."
. (*Me* horse he blind.)
(*My* horse is blind.)

Simple reflexive pronouns are used, as in:

"EE mEHg EEsEHf bigUHdi."
(He make '*eself* biggety.)
(He made *himself* big-headed.)

"Us bAA UHt wEE OHn sEHf."
(Us buy it *we own self.*)
(We bought it *ourselves.*)

"EE sin dEHmsEHf."
(He sing *themself.*)
(They sang by *themselves.*)

"EE wAHnUHm fOH dEH OHn sEHf."
(He want 'um for *their own self.*)
(They want it for *themselves.*)

The nominative and objective cases are often confused and reversed, as in:

"dEHm gibv dishyi tUH wEE."
(*Them* give this here to we.)
(*They* gave this to us.)

The demonstrative pronoun "those" is seldom used, but others are:

"dAH dEH mAHn him hAHluh."
(That there man *him* holler.)
(That man hollered.)

"dEHm gUlz yEHdi yUHm."
(*Them* girls heard it.)
(*Those* girls heard it.)

"dEHm dEH prAWgz iz pAYnUHd."
(*Them there* pirogues is painted.)
(*Those* boats are painted.)

"dishyi tAAim UH gOHz."
(*This here* time I goes.)
(*This* time I'm going.)

"dEEzhyi gOObUHz iz mAAin."
(*These here* goobers is mine.)
(*These* peanuts are mine.)

Repetitive words are to be found in Gullah, as in:

"dAHz shishi tAWk."
(That's *she-she* talk.)
(That's *woman's* gossip.)

"dEH dEH im gOH!"
(*There there* him go!)
(*There* he goes!)

In Gullah all tenses of a verb are generally served by the present tense, as in: "EE kUm bAHk." This could mean any one of the following combinations:

$$\left.\begin{array}{l} \text{he} \\ \\ \text{she} \\ \\ \text{it} \end{array}\right. \left\{\begin{array}{l} \text{comes} \\ \text{came} \\ \text{is coming} \\ \text{has come} \\ \text{had come} \\ \text{will come} \end{array}\right\} \text{back.}$$

When compound forms of the past tense are used, the present-tense stem verb does not add the declension ending, but it does take a preceding "UH" sound, as in:

"EE bin UH gOH dEH."
(He been *a-go* there.)
(He *went* there.)

"EH bin UH sid AWl dEH."
(They been *a-sit* all day.)
(They've been *sitting* all day.)

The future is usually indicated with "going," as in:

"UH gwAHin tEHluhm."
(I *gwine* tell 'um.)
(I'm *going* to tell her.)

"EE gwAHin gibv UHm EE hAWs."
(He *gwine* give 'um he horse.)
(He's *going* to give him his horse.)

Finality in actions is expressed with "done," as in:

"dUH mAHn dUn pAHs."
(The man *done pass.*)
(The man *has passed.*)

"That" is often replaced by "for," as in:

"him tingk fUH EE gOH."
(Him think *for* he go.)
(He thinks *that* she went.)

The pronouns "what," "who," and "whom" are usually supplanted by "wUH" (what), as in:

"wUH dUH nEHm im?"
(*What* the name him?)
(*What's* his name?)

"dUH mAHn wUH nOH."
(The man *what* know.)
(The man *who* knows.))

"wUH yUH wAHn?"
(*What* you want?)
(*Whom* do you wish?)

"wUH dAHt?"
(*What* that?)
(*Who's* that?)

An important characteristic is the use of a noun as a verb, when the sentence would ordinarily be constructed with a predicate adjective, as in:

"him plAYjUH UHm AWlUHz."
(Him *pleasure* 'um always.)
(He always makes her *happy.*)

Instead of "and" or "than," the word "nUH" (nor) is frequently used, as in:

"him nUH Us gOH."
(Him *nor* us go.)
(He *and* I are going.)

"mOH bEHdUH wAWk nUH rUn."
(More better walk *nor* run.)
(It's better to walk *than* run.)

As can be seen in the above example, the comparative "more better" is used. Also, in use are such superlatives as:

"him dUH wUsUHs oomUHn!"
(Him the *worsest* woman.)
(She's the *worst* woman!)

"EE dUH bEHsUHs dAWg."
(He the *bestest* dog.)
(He's the *best* dog.)

The pronouns "you" and "your" are pronounced variously as:

"OOnUH mEHkUHm good."
(*Oona* make 'um good.)
(*You* make it good.)

"yOOnUH tEHk EE AAm."
(*Youna* take he arm.)
(*You* take his arm.)

"wOOnUH AHks mEE dAHt."
(*Woona* ask me that.)
(*You* asked me that.)

The preposition "to" is often supplanted with "for," as in:

"UH kUm fUH sEE AWtOO dEHm."
(I come *for* see all two them.)
(I came *to* see both of them.)

"him nOH hAH fUH fOOl UH mAHn."
(Him know how *for* fool a man.)
(She knows how *to* fool a man.)

The word "along" is often substituted for "with," as in:

"EE gOH lAWng dUH mAHn."
(He go *'long* the man.)
(He went *with* the man.)

"UH gOH lAWng UHm."
(I go *'long* 'um.)
(I'll go *with* them.)

For "as if" Gullah speakers substitute "same like":

"sEHm lAAk EE bUn mAHd."
(*same like* he been mad)
(*as if* he were angry)

For "on" the Gullah often uses "upon" as in:

"him trOH UHm pAWn dUH flOH."
(Him throw 'um *'pon* the floor.)
(He threw it *on* the floor.)

The word "ain't" is used quite often in Gullah and is pronounced as "EHn" or "yEHn" depending on whether it is preceded by a consonant or a vowel, as in:

"him EHn UH gOH dEH."
(Him *ain't* a-go there.)
(He *isn't* going there.)

"dEH yEHn UH kUm nAHoo."
(They *ain't* a-come now.)
(They *won't* come now.)

However, a very popular expression in Gullah is the use of "EHntEE" (ain't he) used as in: "EHntEE yUH shUm" which can mean "Haven't you seen him?" or "Don't you see them?" or "Aren't you seeing her?" or "Won't you see us?" and so forth.

At the same time, "EHntEE" may be used much as the French use *"n'est ce pas"* or the Germans *"nicht war,"* as in, "yUH shUm EHntEE" which can mean:

$$\text{You} \begin{cases} \text{saw} \\ \\ \text{see} \end{cases} \begin{cases} \text{her} \\ \text{him} \\ \text{it} \end{cases} \begin{cases} \text{didn't you?} \\ \text{don't you?} \\ \text{do you?} \end{cases}$$

The word "yEHdi" often heard in the dialect means "hear" or "heard" as in "UH yEHdi UHm" which can mean:

$$\text{I} \begin{cases} \text{hear} \\ \\ \text{heard} \end{cases} \begin{cases} \text{it} \\ \text{him} \\ \text{her} \\ \text{them} \end{cases}$$

COMMON WORDS AND PHRASES

Word	Pronounced	Meaning
task	tAHs	a unit of measure
all two	AWtOO	both
soon	sOOn	early
study	stEHdi	to think
buckra	bUkrUH	white
goober	gOObUH	peanut
two time	tOO tAAim	second
three time	trEE tAAim	third
peruse	pEErOOs	saunter
master	mAHsUH (when used alone)	
Master Tom	mAHs tAWm (used with name)	
hoist	hAHis	lift
evening	EEbvnUHn	afternoon
'posit your word	pAHsit yOH wUd	take an oath
first fowl crow	fUs fAHl krOH	early morning
this May gone	dis mAY gAWn	last May
this May coming	dis mAY kUmUHn	this coming May
t'other	tUdUH	the other

AFRICAN WORDS USED

buckra	a white man
goober	a peanut
cooter	a turtle
okra	a vegetable
nyam	to eat
yam	sweet potato
ki!	an exclamation
oona or *youna*	you or your
plat-eye	an evil spirit

MONOLOG

(From *The Captain* by A. E. Gonzales.)

One time, Debble meet 'Ooman duh paat'. Debble is uh berry mannussuble man wid 'Ooman, so, w'en 'e shum 'e t'row 'e tail obuh 'e aa'm, same lukkuh 'e bin cloak, en' mek'um uh berry stylish bow. De 'Ooman toss 'e head, 'e grin, 'e ketch 'e frock by de bottom with all two 'e han', 'e hice'um up to 'e knee, en' 'e drap'um un low cutchy, 'cause him en' Debble git 'long berry well, berry well!

Attuh de time uh day done pass, de Debble ax de 'Ooman how 'e mek'out 'long de man; w'edduh 'e done l'aa'n how fuh manage de man, en' fetch'um to 'e han'. De 'Ooman laugh. "Budduh," 'e say. "Hukkuh you kin ax me dat? Enty you l'aa'n me how 'seitful? Enty you show me how fuh do 'um? Enty uh folluh yo' exwice? Uh got de man gwine! 'E dunno w'ich way 'e duh gwine — but 'e gwine my way, enty?"

"Tell me how you do'um," de Debble say.

"Uh got good ecknowledge how fuh fool de man. Uh got 'tring tie 'pun de man, en' w'en we git to de fawk uh de road, weh one de road lean one side, en' t'odduh road lean t'odduh side — w'en Uh git to da' place, ef Uh gwine one road, Uh pull de 'tring fuh lead de man een de t'odduh road. W'ichebbuh road Uh want, Uh pull de man een de road wuh Uh yent want, 'cause de stubbunt creetuh so cuntrady en' haa'dhead, ef him see me foot lean fuh one road, him foot fuh lean to de t'odduh one, 'cause him t'ink man fuh hab 'e own way. Him eegnunt to dat! So dat how Uh gitt-um fuh trabble my road, en' de man nebbuh know weh 'e duh gwine, but 'e ben' 'e neck en' pull de load, jiz' ez sattify ez ox wuh done bruk!"

THE VIRGIN ISLANDS DIALECT

ALTHOUGH THEIR ANTECEDENTS were also African slaves, the West Indian Negroes are almost a race apart from the North American Negroes, both in temperament and dialect. The American Negro generally gives the impression of being happy-go-lucky, carefree, and easygoing while the West Indian Negro is traditionally surly, arrogant, shrewd, moody, and vindictive. This may be the result of the almost inhuman treatment the early slaves received at the hands of Dutch, British, and Danish slave-holders in the West Indies. It may also be accounted for by the fact that the original African slaves were members of different African tribes. The Virgin Islands Negroes, for example, originated from the Amina tribe along the west coast of Africa. This was a warlike, proud tribe of Negroes who never accepted their slavery and sparked many of the slave insurrections in the West Indies.

The dialects spoken in the West Indian Islands are varied. The Dominican Negro has been influenced by Cockney speech so that, today, his American dialect has a definite Cockney flavor. The Monteserrat Negro, on the other hand, patterned his speech after that of his Irish overseers. The word "you" is pronounced by them as "yiz" which is a definite Irish treatment. Cuban, Porto Rican, and Dominican Republic Negroes use *Papirmiento*, a form of Spanish, while Negroes in Martinique, Guadeloupe, and Haiti use a *bâtard* form of French. On the islands of St. Thomas, St. John, and St. Croix, purchased by the United States from Denmark, the Negroes speak English. These three islands comprise the Virgin Islands.

This English, however, is a far cry from American English. Danish occupation left its stamp on the speech. This is particularly evident in the dialect speech of the St. John and St. Thomas Negroes who usually accent the final syllable of a word regardless of its proper treatment in English. As in Gullah, the influences of African speech are still evident, not only in pronunciation but also in the use of certain African language words such as *buckra* (white man) and *joombee* (jumby-ghost).

VOWEL CHANGES

	as in	Pronounced		as in
AY	make	**EH**	(particularly in such common words as "take," "naked," "hate," etc.)	mEHk
	sail	**AY**		sAYl
UH	about		(dropped initially)	bAHt
	woman	**i**	(in unstressed syllable)	oomin
AH	art	**AH**		AHrt
A:	ask	**AH**		AHks
A	man	**AH**		mAHn
AW	ball	**AH**	(also before "r" or after "w" as in "short" and "watch")	bAHl
	more	**AW**	(variant before "r" final or plus a consonant)	mAW
EE	we	**EE**		wEE
	city	**EE**		si:tEE
EH	head	**AY**	(in many common words such as "leg," "dead," "bed," etc.)	hAYd
	never	**EH**	(variant particularly before consonant sounds other than "n" or "r")	nEHbvAH
	cent	**A**	(before "n")	sAN
	where	**AH**	(before "r")	wAH
I	nice	**AWi**		nAWis
	I	**AH**		AH
i	give	**i:**		gi:
	until	**EH**	(exception)	tEHl
	nigger	**AY**	(exception)	nAYgAH
o	on	**AH**		AHn
	drop	**A**	(exception)	drAp
OH	don't	**OH**		dOHn
OO	who	**OO**		hOO

Sound	as in	Pronounced		as in
oo	could	U		kUd
yOO	cube	yOO		kyOOb
U	one	AH	(generally)	wAHn
	young	oo	(exception)	yoong
	just	EH	(see "U," page 200)	jEHs
	such	i		sitch
ER	sir	AH		sAH
	water	AH	(final unstressed syllable)	wAHtAH
OW	pound	AH		pAHn
	down	oo	(exception)	doon
OI	boy	ooEE		booEE

CONSONANT CHANGES

B — This consonant sound is often confused with "v." Actually, it is the same "b" as pronounced in Gullah, a sort of "bv" combination as in the Spanish. (See "B," and "V," pages 229 and 231.) This makes for such pronunciations as "bvAHn" (burn), "kAHbvAHj" (cabbage), and "tAHbv" (stab).

D — Final "d" is generally dropped when preceded by "n," "s," or "l" as in "lAHn" (land), "fAHs" (fast), and "kOHl" (scold).

Final "d" is also often dropped following a vowel, as in "fEE" (feel) and "gU mAHrnin" (good morning).

Medially, it is sometimes changed to "t" as in "sAHtin" (sudden).

F — This is a bilabial sound made with both lips instead of with the lower lip placed against the upper front teeth. In producing this bilabial "f," there should be a small central opening between the lips and through this the air should be forced out. The resulting sound is similar to the "h" of the word "hwEHn" (when). This sound may be used initially, medially, and finally, as in "fAHn" (fun), "AHfin" (often), and "sAYf" (safe).

This sound is generally dropped in the word "AHtAH" (after) and its compounds.

G — Hard "g" is usually palatalized, as in "gyAHrdi:ng" (garden). (See "G," page 85.)

K — This consonant sound is also palatalized, as in "kyAHt" (cart). (See "K," page 86.)

The word "ask" generally reverses the "k" and is pronounced as "AHks."

L — This consonant sound is frequently dropped from words like "sEHf" (self) and "hEHp" (help).

NG — This participial ending "ing" is generally pronounced as "in" as in "wi:lin" (willing).

On the other hand, final "n" is frequently sounded as "ng" as in "kAHpti:ng" (captain), "sAHrti:ng" (certain), and "vAHrji:ng" (virgin).

R — The consonant "r" receives a mixed treatment. Initially, of course, it is always sounded, although many give it the "r" *grasseyé* treatment which imparts to it the "w" flavor. (See "R," page 144.)

Medial "r" is sounded after a consonant, as in "trAWi" (try).

When medial "r" is preceded by a vowel and followed by a consonant, it may be pronounced or dropped, as in "shAHrt" (short) and "hAHnis" (harness).

Final "r" is dropped, as in "nEHbvAH" (never) and "fAH" (far).

S — Initial "s" is frequently dropped before the sounds "k," "p," or "t" as in "ki:m" (skim), "pEEd" (speed), and "tAHn" (stand).

Final "s" is sometimes pronounced as "sh" as in "kAHtlAHsh" (cutlass).

T — Final "t" is generally dropped after "k," "l," "n," "p," or "s" as in "fAHk" (fact), "gyi:l" (gilt), "AHn" (aunt), "AHp" (apt), and "fAHs" (fast).

Final "t" is also often dropped when preceded by a vowel, as in "wAH" (what) and "nAH" (not).

When final "t" is pronounced, it is usually sounded so forcibly that a definite aspirate "UH" sound results, as in "dAHtUH" (that) and "kAHtUH" (cut).

Medial "t" is often dropped after "l," "n," or "s" as in "hAHlAH" (halter), "sAnAH" (center), and "fAHsAH" (faster).

TH — This sound is generally pronounced as "d" as in "dAHt" (that), "fAHdAH" (father), and "bAYd" (bathe).

th — This sound is generally pronounced as "t" as in "ti:nk" (think) and "pAHt (path).

V — Like "b" this sound is pronounced bilabially (see "B" and "V," pages 229 and 231). An attempt should be made to pronounce "b" without allowing the center of the lips to touch. This sound is written in our phonetics as "bv" as in "ri:bvAH" (river), "sAHrbvis" (service), and "bvAHrEE" (very).

Final "v" is sometimes dropped, as in "gi:" (give) and "li:" (live).

W — Initially, this consonant is often dropped in "oomin" (woman).

Z — Medially, between vowels, this consonant sound is sometimes pronounced as "s" as in "mi:sAHbAHl" (miserable).

GRAMMAR CHANGES

The pronoun "me" is preferred in the nominative case rather than "I," as in:

"mEE hAHbv gAHt."
(*Me* have got.)
(*I* have.)

"mEE gi: dEE mAHn mAHnEE."
(*Me* give the man money.)
(*I* gave the man money.)

The objective "me" is also used in preference to the possessive "my," as in:

"hAHn mEE pAY OHbvAH."
(Hand *me* pay over.)
(Hand over *my* pay.)

The pronoun "he" is used even when "she," "it," or "they" is indicated, as in:

"AHtAH EE gOH."
(After *he* go.)
(After *she* went.)

"EE dOHn lAWik UHm."
((*He* don't like 'um.)
(*They* don't like it.)

The use of "um" for "it" is also common to Virgin Island **Negro** speech, as in:

"mEE sEE UHm kAHm kwi:k."
(Me see'*um* come quick.)
(I saw *it* come quickly.)

"mEE dOHn hi:UHm hAHlAH."
(Me don't hear '*um* holler.)
(I don't hear *it* holler.)

An intrusive "UH" (a) is commonly heard, not only before a verb, as is common in some regional American speech, but also before nouns, as in:

"mEE UHgOH UHhOHm."
(Me *a*-go *a*-home.)
(I'm going home.)

"hEE shUd UHmEHk rAHm."
(He should *a*-make rum.)
(He should make rum.)

The use of "a-we" for "our" is prevalent, as in:
"yOO kAHm AH wEE hAHs?"
(You come *a-we* house?)
(Will you come to *our* house?)

The pronoun "them" is often used instead of "they" or "their," as in:

"dEHm OHpin dEHm AWi."
(*Dem* open dem eye.)
(*They* opened their eyes.)

"mEE nOH wAH dEHm gOH dEHm."
(Me know where *them* go, them.)
(I know where *they* went.)

As observed in the above example, "them" is often repeated at the end of a sentence.

The phrase "it have" is often used instead of "there is" as in:

"i: hAHbv mAW tAWim nAH."
(*It have* more time now.)
(*There is* more time now.)

For "him" many Virgin Islanders use "he-self" as in:

"dOHn yOO hrAHs hEEsEHf."
(Don't you harass *he-self*.)
(Don't you bother *him*.)

When "he" is not used for "her," the pronoun "she" is often substituted, as in:

"mEE drAWibv shEE bAHk."
(Me drive *she* back.)
(I'll drive *her* back.)

For "myself" there is frequently the substitution of "me-self," as in:

"mEE gOH mEEsEHf."
(Me go *me-self*.)
(I'll go *myself*.)

An important substitution in Virgin Island speech is the use of "for" (pronounced as "fUH") instead of "to," as in:

"mEE trAWi fUH shEHt UHm."
(Me try *for* shut 'um.)
(I tried *to* shut it.)

"mEE hAHbv fUH gOH fAWin mEE hAHt."
(Me have *for* go find me hat.)
(I must go *to* look for my hat.)

The phrase "am-be" is often used for "are," as in:

"wEE AHm bEE AHl wi:kid."
(We *am-be* all wicked.)
(We *are* all wicked.)

CHAPTER VII

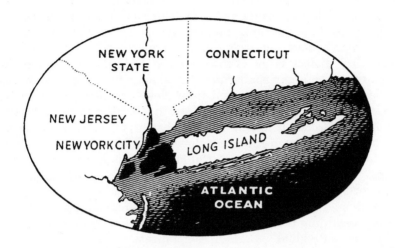

THE NEW YORK CITY DIALECT

MORE THAN SEVEN million people live within the five boroughs that constitute greater New York City. They speak, in some form or other, practically every dialect on earth. About a million speak with varying degrees of Yiddish infiltrations. Thousands upon thousands speak with varying degrees of Irish, Italian, German, French, Russian, and other foreign dialects. A great many inhabitants use some form of regional American dialect. And, finally, hundreds of thousands of native-born New Yorkers use, what has become known as the New York City dialect.

Every dialect receives slight variations from the individual speaker, but greater variations are noticeable between two speakers, both native, who have different educational and cultural backgrounds. Thus the well-educated New Yorker who has a good cultural background is generally careful of his speech and for the most part uses the General-American pronunciation. However, he still uses the intrusive "r" as in "AHidiUHr" (idea), the dropped "r" as in "pAYpUH" (paper), and he frequently uses the "uhEE" substitute for "OI" and "ER" as in "puhEEzn" (poison) and "shuhEEt" (shirt).

But there are certain large groups of native-born New Yorkers who use practically all the variants suggested in this chapter. These are the multitudes who were brought up in the Bronx, in Brooklyn, in New Jersey (bordering the New York boundary), on the lower

East side, and in most of Manhattan's other districts. Although many of these people are well educated, they have remained within their own dialect speaking group and for this reason have found no incentive to drop their own pronunciations in favor of another's.

Research does not bear out the popular belief that the New York City dialect is an offshoot of the Yiddish-American dialect. True, there are many similarities, but similarities may also be noted between the speech of a person from New York and one from New England, or even Louisiana. Since speech is subject to the individuality of the speaker, it is only natural that a person who speaks with a combination foreign-American dialect and New York City dialect will impart a foreign flavor to the latter. This is true, not only of people with different racial backgrounds, but also of people with different social backgrounds.

It would be impossible to lay down hard and fast pronunciamentos regarding the character traits of the New Yorker. They vary with the individual. Certain generalizations, however, may be offered. There is a hurried, seemingly unfriendly quality found in many New Yorkers. The average hinterland newcomer to New York is struck by the aloofness that engulfs him the moment he arrives. On the other hand, many New Yorkers are generous, friendly, and considerate — if one only knows where to look for them in the teeming maelstrom of the city.

The average New Yorker, like many of his fellow-Americans, is insular. He may know little of the country west of the Hudson River. He is often fiercely proud of his city, particularly the borough in which he lives. He is sensitive to ridicule, but at the same time he is not averse to the "rib" — the joshing wisecrack against someone else. He is frequently opinionated. He is sentimental and often phrases his remarks with excessive gentility. He is, for the most part, loyal. He has an independent spirit and a ready wit.

LILT AND STRESS

The typical New York City delivery has a modified singsong lilt marked by a recurring syllabic beat. The syllables are bitten off sharply and cleanly much as though each were a separate word. Although there seems to be an attempt at precise pronunciation, the effect is rather of overemphasis particularly on the stressed words. There is frequently a "mouthed" quality to the sounds. This results from deliberate lip, tongue, and jaw movements which tend to accentuate the sounds. Naturally, this delivery is not common to all New Yorkers. It should be used particularly for a character who speaks with the full New York City dialect.

The simple query "wEH: yUH gU-OOn?" (Where you going?) may be spoken with the following lilts:

It will be noticed that the stressed vowel in the final word of a sentence is usually drawled with a rising-falling inflection. This usually produces a sort of nasal whine. It is this sentence-ending whine which, if exaggerated, may be used in portraying the Broadway gangster or the Brooklyn bum.

This lilt pattern should not be used for the native New Yorker whose speech includes only one or two dialect elements. New Yorkers who speak with a General-American dialect except for the final dropping of "r" and the addition of the intrusive "r" generally use the General-American lilt pattern.

In practicing the material on the vowel changes, the actor should produce the sounds from a forward position in the mouth, unless there is a suggestion to the contrary. The consonant sounds should be produced forcefully and deliberately, especially in an initial or stressed position. Stressed vowels are generally elongated on a single note, while diphthongs usually take their accent on the first element and the second element is used as a glide. The first element of the diphthong generally takes the higher note and the second element, the lower note.

The actor must guard against exaggerating the vowel sounds that seem new to him. He must study and practice these changes until he can produce them in an easy and familiar manner. In the sections on "Grammar Changes," "Common Expressions," and "Interjections" the sentences have been written phonetically using the strong and weak forms that result from stressed and unstressed syllables and words. Naturally, only one interpretation has been allowed for each sentence. If another interpretation were used, the strong and weak forms might vary.

VOWEL CHANGES

"AY" .... as in "take," "made," "break," etc.

Although "AY" may be used, the variant "UEE" is more typical of the dialect speech of many New Yorkers. Both elements of the vowel sound must blend together smoothly. When it is stressed or drawled, the first element "U" receives the accent or elongation, as in "rU:EEt" (rate). This variant pronunciation should be used particularly for a character who speaks with a broad dialect.

The complete vowel sound frequently has a nasal quality and is produced from a forward position in the mouth. An important aspect of "UEE" is the tense or close quality that usually accompanies it.

DRILL WORDS

tUEEk	(take)	krUEEzEE	(crazy)
mUEEd	(made)	stUEEshin	(station)
brUEEk	(break)	pUEEpUH	(paper)

vikUEEshin	(vacation)
brUEEnEE	(brainy)
UHfrUEEd	(afraid)

VARIATION: The variant "AY" may be used, preferably with a tense, nasal quality.

EXCEPTIONS: When "day" is the final unstressed syllable of a word, it is usually pronounced as "dEE" as in "sA:dEE" (Saturday).

The words "radio" and "radiator" are frequently pronounced as "rA:dEE-UOO" and "rA:dEEUEEdUH."

"UH" .... as in "about," "final," "sofa," etc.

Initially, this sound remains the same as in General-American.

For the treatment of unstressed syllables or vowels in a medial position see "Unstressed Syllables."

In a final position "UH" remains the same except that it is followed by an intrusive "r" if the next word begins with a vowel, as in "sEH-OOdUHr UHn wAW:dUH" (soda and water), but "sEH:OOdUH wAW:dUH" (soda water). This intrusive "r" is also used after final unstressed "UH" if the word is final in a sentence, as in "yEH:UH hEH-EEz gEH-OOnUH kyiOObUHr" (Yeh! He's going to Cuba.)

DRILL WORDS

sEH-OOfUHr	(sofa)	binA:nUHr	(banana)
AHidUHr	(Ida)	kimEH-OOnUHr	(kimono)
AHidiUHr	(idea)	kAH:mUHr	(comma)

kEH-OOmUHr	(coma)
UHmEHrikUHr	(America)
kA:nidUHr	(Canada)

"AH" .... as in "father," "park," "calm," etc.

This vowel sound is generally pronounced as "AW:" as in "fAW:THuh" (father). The (:) indicates elongation to make up for the dropped "r." This "AW" sound is produced from a forward position in the mouth. The lips should be in a pursed position but not necessarily tensed. (See Figures 25 and 26.)

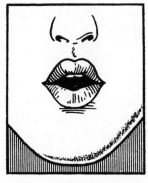

Fig. 25

Fig. 26

DRILL WORDS

pAW:k	(park)	hAW:d	(hard)
kAW:m	(calm)	lAW:d	(lard)
stAW:	(star)	pAW:m	(palm)

AW:thUH	(Arthur)
fAW:mUH	(farmer)
pAW:dEE	(party)

VARIATION: The variant "AH:" may also be used, particularly for a light dialect, as in "kAH:d" (card) and "pAH:t" (part).

EXCEPTION: The word "almonds" has been heard as "AH:mUHnz," "A:minz," "AW:minz," and sometimes as "AlmUHnz."

"A:" .... as in "ask," "dance," "laugh," etc.

This sound generally remains the same as in General-American except that it is flatter, broader, and has a noticeable nasal quality. In our phonetics, this "A:" indicates the "A" of "bAd" (bad) with elongation.

DRILL WORDS

A:st	(ask)	drA:f	(draft)
dA:ns	(dance)	grA:s	(grass)
lA:f	(laugh)	tchA:ns	(chance)

fA:stUH	(faster)
sA:mpuhl	(sample)
pA:thwUEE	(pathway)

VARIATIONS: The variants "AH" or "AA" (see page 30) may also be used, as in "lAHf" or "lAAf" (laugh).

"A" .... as in "bad," "narrow," "crash," etc.

This vowel sound generally remains the same except that it has a flatter, broader, and more nasal quality than the General-American sound. When stressed or drawled, this sound is elongated to "A:" as in "THuh krAsh wUHz bA:d" (The crash was bad).

DRILL WORDS

bA:d	(bad)	mA:dUH	(matter)
nA:rUH	(narrow)	imA:jin	(imagine)
lA:dUH	(ladder)	hA:ruhld	(Harold)

mA:rij	(marrage)
fA:ktrEE	(factory)
bA:j	(badge)

VARIATION: The variant "EH:" may be used before "r" or "rr" plus a vowel, or "sh" as in "pEH:rUHt" (parrot), and "fEH:shn" (fashion). Thus, a character may say "THuh kEH:rUHts wUH bA:d" (The carrots were bad).

"AW" .... as in "ball," "off," "caught," etc.

Although basically this sound remains the same as in General-American, speakers of the New York City dialect endow it with a distinctive quality. This richer "AW" is produced from a more forward position in the mouth; the lips are pursed and moderately tensed; there is a noticeable nasal quality. When stressed or drawled, this sound is elongated to "AW:" as in "hEH:EEz AWfuhl tAW:l" (He's awful tall).

DRILL WORDS

bAW:l	(ball)	sAW:ng	(song)
AW:f	(off)	hAW:nt	(haunt)
kAW:t	(caught)	lAW:st	(lost)

tAW:k	(talk)
sAW:ft	(soft)
kAW:fEE	(coffee)

VARIATIONS: Although this richer "AW" sound may be used for most of the General-American "AW" words, the variant "AH" (or "AH:" when stressed) may also be used when "a" is: (1) preceded by "w"; (2) followed by "g," "ng," "th," "tch," "sh"; or (3) followed by "un" plus a consonant.

Thus this "AH" variant will be found in such words as "wAHsh" (wash), "lAHg" (log), "klAHth" (cloth), "swAHluh" (swallow), "rAHng" (wrong), and "lAHndrEE" (laundry).

EXCEPTIONS: The word "dog" is commonly pronounced as "dAW:g" even by many who use the "AH" variant before "g," as in "mAW:t bAWt THuh rAH:ng dAW:g" (Mort bought the wrong dog.)

"AW" .... as in "more," "forest," "short," etc.

This "AW" sound is produced from a forward position in the mouth, with the lips pursed and moderately tensed. When stressed to "AW:", it is of slightly longer duration than in General-American.

WHEN "AW" IS FOLLOWED BY FINAL "r" OR "r" PLUS A CONSONANT, IT IS USUALLY PRONOUNCED AS "AW:" AND THE "r" IS DROPPED.

The dropped "r" is particularly noticeable when followed by a consonant, as in "shAW:t" (short). When "r" is final in a word, it is generally dropped if the next word begins with a consonant, as in "yUH wAHn mAW kAW:fEE" (You want more coffee?). Final "r" is also dropped before a pause or at the end of a sentence, as in "sAW: hOOz sAW:" (Sore? Who's sore?). However, when final "r" is followed by an initial vowel word, it may be pronounced, as in "mAWrUHn mAW:" (more and more). (See **"R"** under **"Consonant Changes."**)

DRILL WORDS

skAW:	(score)	UHsAW:did	(assorted)
flAW:	(floor)	mAW:dimUH	(Mortimer)
pAW:	(pour)	skAW:tchUH	(scorcher)

kAW:n	(corn)
kAW:t	(court)
fAW:k	(fork)

WHEN "AW" IS FOLLOWED BY "r" PLUS A VOWEL OR BY "rr" PLUS A VOWEL, IT IS GENERALLY PRONOUNCED AS "AH" AND THE "r" SOUND IS RETAINED.

DRILL WORDS

fAHrist	(forest)	AHrinj	(orange)
mAHris	(Morris)	fAHrin	(foreign)
dAHris	(Doris)	kAHruhl	(coral)

lAHruhl	(laurel)
bAHrik	(boric)
sAHrEE	(sorry)

"EE" . . . . as in **"me," "treat," "people,"** etc.

Ordinarily, this long "e" (EE) sound is pronounced as in General-American. When spelled with "y" in a final, unstressed position, it is also sounded as "EE" as in "EE:zEE" (easy).

DRILL WORDS

mEE	(me)	skrEEm	(scream)
trEEt	(treat)	tchEEp	(cheap)
pEEpuhl	(people)	frEE	(free)

wEEk	(week)
dEEl	(deal)
UHgrEE	(agree)

VARIATION: When stressed, a variant pronunciation for this sound is "EH-EE" as in "wEE AW:l UHgrEH-EE" (We all agree) or "gEHd AWf THuh strEH-EEt" (Get off the street!). The

"EH" of the sound "EH-EE" should not receive its full sound, as in "bEHd" (bed). This "EH" is used as a sort of introductory glide to "EE," and it should be very short. In pronouncing this first element, the tongue should be in position for "EE"; that is, the blade of the tongue is against the roof of the mouth and remains there until the complete diphthong has been sounded.

"EH" .... as in "bet," "said," "friend," etc.

This sound may remain the same as it is in General-American. When stressed or drawled, however, it is frequently of slightly longer duration.

DRILL WORDS

bEHt	(bet)	EHmUHr	(Emma)
sEHd	(said)	EHlmUH	(Elmer)
frEHnd	(friend)	brEHd	(bread)

hEHd	(head)
EHgnAHg	(eggnog)
nEHslEE	(nestle)

"I" .... as in "ice," "aisle," "guile," etc.

Although this vowel sound may remain the same as in General-American, many New Yorkers use "AHi" as in "AHis" (ice). When stressed, the first element receives the accent and elongation, as in "AH:iz" (eyes).

The personal pronoun is generally pronounced as "AH" (I).

DRILL WORDS

AHil	(aisle)	tchAHinUHr	(China)
gAHil	(guile)	frAHidEE	(Friday)
trAHi	(try)	sAHidwAWk	(sidewalk)

dAHim	(dime)
snAHipUH	(sniper)
AHilin	(island)

VARIATION: The variant "AWi-EE" may also be used, as in "rAW-EEd" (ride), "plAW-EEt" (polite), and "sAW-EEdUH" (cider). The first element takes the elongation and stress, while the second element is frequently tensed to "i:."

"i" .... as in "it," "women," "busy," etc.

This vowel sound may remain the same, as in "it" (it) and "wimin" (women). When followed by final "r" it is slightly elongated, and with a pinched quality as in "hi:" (here) and "bi:" (beer). This elongation usually occurs if the word is final in a sentence, as in "hiz sUHm bi:" (Here's some beer). The elongation is also present when the word is stressed, as in "its ni: bi:" (It's near-beer). In this final example the two last words receive elongation—the word "near" because it is stressed and the word "beer" because it is final.

The elongation should be kept very slight since the pronunciation of short "i" before "r" is an important feature of the New York City dialect. Although other dialects that drop final "r" usually add an "UH" glide to the vowel sound, this speech habit is not typical of the dialect speech of New York City.

DRILL WORDS

piluh	(pillow)	kwi:	(queer)
bizEE	(busy)	mint	(mint)
lisn	(listen)	jim	(gym)

mistUEEk	(mistake)
thingkUH	(thinker)
UHkAHmplish	(accomplish)

"O" .... as in "on," "bond," "John," etc.

New Yorkers generally broaden this vowel sound into "AH" as in "AHn" (on) and "bAHnd" (bond). This vowel sound is frequently richer and broader than the General-American version.

DRILL WORDS

jAHn	(John)	prAHmplEE	(promptly)
lAHj	(lodge)	dAHktUH	(doctor)
jAHb	(job)	lAHbstUH	(lobster)

sAHk	(sock)
flAHp	(flop)
drAHp	(drop)

"OH" .... as in "bone," "sew," "dough," etc.

Although the General-American "OH" (OH-OO) sound may be used, particularly in lightening the dialect, the typical pronunciation of this vowel sound is "U-OO" as in "bAHb gUHdiz nU-OOdis" (Bob got his notice). The first element is like the "U" in "Up" (up), and the second is like "OO" of "fOOd" (food). The first sound should blend into the second with no break between. The hyphen (-) is used only as an aid to the reader.

This vowel sound must be practiced until it can be produced smoothly and naturally.

DRILL WORDS

bU-OOn	(bone)	klU-OOz	(clothes)
sU-OO	(sew)	bU-OOld	(bold)
dU-OO	(dough)	jU-OOk	(joke)

spU-OOz	(suppose)
hU-OOp	(hope)
grU-OOn	(grown)

EXCEPTION: When used as an interjection, the word "no" may be pronounced as "nAH:."

"OO" .... as in "food," "do," "blue," "etc.

This vowel sound may remain the same as in General-American. It may also be retained for such words as "nOO" (new), "dOO" (due), and "tOOn" (tune). (See also "yOO" as in "use.")

DRILL WORDS

fOOd	(food)	mOOvEE	(movie)
dOO	(do)	dOOdEE	(duty)
blOO	(blue)	sOOvni:	(souvenir)

stOOpid	(stupid)
sOOt	(suit)
kinOO	(canoe)

VARIATIONS: The variant "uhOO" should be used for a character who speaks with the typical heavy stress. Many New Yorkers produce their consonants forcefully, and this results in the natural glide before a vowel sound, as in "juhOOn" (June), "tuhOO" (too), "truhOO" (true) and "suhOOd" (sued).

Some New Yorkers, particularly those who do not speak with the broad dialect, use the variant "yOO" for long "u" when it is preceded by "d," "l," "n," "s," or "t" as in "dyOO" (due), "lyOOrid" (lurid), "nyOOd" (nude), "syOOt" (suit) or "tyOOn" (tune).

"oo" .... as in "good," "wolf," "full," etc.

In the dialect speech of many people this sound is pronounced as "UH" as in "its UH gUHd thi:ng" (It's a good thing). It will be noticed that this suggested variant is the same as the unstressed "a" (UH) in the above sentence. It should never be broadened to a full "U" sound. When stressed, it is slightly longer.

DRILL WORDS

wuhlf	(wolf)		wUHd	(would)
fuhl	(full)		fUHt	(foot)
stUHd	(stood)		lUHk	(look)

hUHk	(hook)
bUHk	(book)
pUHt	(put)

When "oo" is followed by "r," the vowel sound remains the same except for slight elongation, as in "poo:" (poor) and "shoo:" (sure).

VARIATION: Many people pronounce this sound as "oo" or "oo:" when stressed as in "shoo:k" (shook), "shoo:gUH" (sugar), and "koo:d" (could).

"yOO" . . . . as in "use," "cube," "beauty," etc.

This sound generally remains the same, as in "yOOz" (use) and "kyOOb" (cube). When unstressed, it is usually pronounced as "yUH" as in "A:kyUHrit" (accurate).

DRILL WORDS

byOOdEE	(beauty)	pAHpyuhluh	(popular)
myOOzik	(music)	yOOsfuhl	(useful)
hyOOmid	(humid)	yUHnAHidid	(united)

fyOO	(few)
kyOO	(cue)
vyOO	(view)

VARIATION: The variant "yiOO" is frequently heard by people who use heavy stress when speaking, as in "kyiOOt" (cute), "pyiOOpil" (pupil), and "yiOOnyUHn" (union).

"U" . . . . as in "up," "love," "does," etc.

This vowel sound is usually pronounced as in General-American. When stressed or drawled, it is elongated to "U:" as in "hEE dU:z" (he does?). The elongation is frequently slightly longer than in Middle Western speech. This feature is particularly noticeable in the speech of people who use a broad dialect and heavy stress.

DRILL WORDS

U:p	(up)	kUvUH	(cover)	frUnt	(front)
lU:v	(love)	brUsh	(brush)	hUnEE	(honey)
dU:z	(Duz)	hUntch	(hunch)	UndUH	(under)

VARIATION: When short "u" (U) is used in a prefix, the variant "AW" is sometimes heard, as in "AWnyOOzhuhl" (unusual) and "AWnUHstA:n" (understand). This "AW" is usually treated as a short, tense sound.

"ER" .... as in "curb," "earn," "fir," etc.

The New York dialect is supposed to feature an over all substitution of "OI" for the "ER" sound. Actually, there are two prominent pronunciations for this vowel sound, both of which should be used by a character speaking with the New York dialect.

WHEN THE GENERAL-AMERICAN "ER" SOUND IS FOL-LOWED BY A CONSONANT, IT SHOULD BE CHANGED TO "uhEE" AS IN "guhEEl" (GIRL).

The initial element "uh" receives the stress and blends smoothly into the second element "EE." The "uh" glide may be produced either from the back of the mouth or from the front.

WHEN THE GENERAL-AMERICAN "ER" SOUND IS FINAL IN A WORD, BUT IS NOT A SUFFIX, IT SHOULD BE PRO-NOUNCED AS "U:" AS IN "fU:" (FIR).

This "U:" sound is generally produced from a forward position in the mouth.

WHEN THE GENERAL-AMERICAN "ER" SOUND IS USED IN A SUFFIX, IT SHOULD BE PRONOUNCED AS "UH" AS IN "dizuhEEdUH" (DESERTER).

DRILL WORDS

uhEEn	(earn)	nuhEEsrEE	(nursery)
puhEEs	(purse)	duhEEdEE	(dirty)
wuhEEd	(word)	puhEEtchis	(purchase)

kluhEEk	(clerk)
hU:	(her)
wU:	(were)

VARIATION: The variant "ER" may also be used, as in "bERn" (burn), "flERt" (flirt), "fER" (fur), and "mERdUH" (murder). This sound is used particularly by people who speak with a light dialect. But it must be mentioned that many people who speak with an otherwise light dialect retain the "uhEE" and "U:" variants mentioned above.

"OW" . . . . as in "out," "cow," "house," etc.

Many New Yorkers replace this "OW" sound with "Aoo" which is frequently nasalized. The first element "A" receives the stress and blends into the second element "oo" which is used as a glide.

DRILL WORDS

Aoot	(out)	AooUH	(hour)
kAoo	(cow)	pAooUH	(power)
hAoos	(house)	krAood	(crowd)

lAood	(loud)
prAood	(proud)
frAoon	(frown)

VARIATIONS: The variant "A-OO" may also be used, particularly for a character who speaks with heavy stress, as in "A-OOt" (out) and "pA-OOnd" (pound).

Some New Yorkers use the variant "AH" as in "bAHns" (bounce) and "pAHl" (Powell).

"OI" . . . . as in "oil," "boy," "noise," etc.

Many New Yorkers treat this diphthong in two different ways.

WHEN THE "OI" SOUND IS FINAL OR SPELLED WITH "oy," IT SHOULD BE PRONOUNCED AS "AWi" AS IN "bAWi" (BOY).

This pronunciation is common with most New Yorkers whether they use a thick or light dialect. However, if the character is one who uses a broad dialect, the "AW" sound should be produced in the typical New York manner. The lips should be rounded and moderately tensed, and the vowel should be produced from the forward part of the mouth.

WHEN THE "OI" SOUND IS MEDIAL AND SPELLED WITH "oi," IT MAY BE PRONOUNCED AS "uhEE" AS IN "puhEEnt" (POINT).

This "uhEE" diphthong is usually given a tense, forward production.

DRILL WORDS

uhEEl	(oil)	juhEEnUH	(joiner)
nuhEEz	(noise)	spuhEEl	(spoil)
tAWi	(toy)	lAWiyuhl	(loyal)

vuhEEs	(voice)
puhEEzn	(poison)
distrAWi	(destroy)

VARIATION: The variant "ER-EE" may also be used, as in "tchER-EEs" (choice), "kER-EEld" (coiled), and "bER-EEl" (boil). The first element "ER" receives the stress and "EE" is used as a glide. The "ER" is like the General-American "er" in "hER" (her) except that the "r" is silent. This pronunciation should not be used for words spelled with "oy" as these retain the "AWi" sound.

NOTE: In portraying a character who speaks with the New York dialect, many actors have been heard to use "ER" so that they say "ERl" (oil) and "spERl" (spoil). There seems to be no authentic foundation for this change, and it is not recommended. The "r" is seldom sounded before a consonant in the New York dialect, and it should not be inserted arbitrarily in this instance.

UNSTRESSED SYLLABLES

The treatment of unstressed vowels and syllables is an important factor in retaining the authenticity of New York dialect speech.

Initial unstressed "a" may remain the same as in General-American, as in "UHgU-OO" (ago), "uhlU-OOn" (alone), and "UHmAoont" (amount).

Medial unstressed "a" is usually pronounced as "i" as in "stU:mik" (stomach), "brEHkfis" (breakfast), "prAHivit" (private), "pA:kitch" (package), and "kU:mftibl" (comfortable).

Medial unstressed "a" may also be dropped particularly when followed by "r" plus a vowel, as in "sEHprit" (separate), or when followed by final "lly" as in "jEHnlEE" (generally) and "fAHinlEE" (finally).

Final unstressed "a" remains the same, as in "A:nUH" (Anna) or "drA:mUH" (drama). An intrusive "r" is added to final "UH," when it is final in a sentence, before a pause or followed by an initial vowel word, as in "A:nUH lU:vz drA:mUHr" (Anna loves drama), or "A:nUHr UHn AW:thUH hAv sUHm tUHbA:kUHr" (Anna and Arthur have some tobacco).

Medial unstressed "e" is usually pronounced as "i" as in "pAHkit" (pocket), "intrist" (interest), "uhEEnis" (Ernest), "difrint" (different), and "hU:ndrit" (hundred).

When unstressed "e" is preceded by "r," the two letters may be reversed making an "er" combination, and the pronunciation would be "UH" as in "difUHnt" (different), "tchildUHn" (children), and "A:lfUHd" (Alfred).

Medial unstressed "e" is often dropped when followed by "r" plus a vowel as in "intrist" (interest) and "difrint" (different).

Unstressed "e" in a prefix is usually changed to "i" as in "risEEv" (receive), "rituhEEn" (return), "rigAW:d" (regard), "dipEHnd" (depend), "simEHnt" (cement), and "bifAW:" (before). The "e" is frequently dropped in the word "blEEv" (believe).

Medial unstressed "i" is often pronounced as "i" as in "AW:fis" (office), "nUOOdis" (notice), and "mA:lis" (malice).

Medial unstressed "i" is sometimes dropped, as in "A:sprin" (aspirin), "doo:ng" (during), "puhEEspikA:stEE" (perspicacity), and "AHrijnil" (original).

Medial unstressed "o" is usually treated as "UH" as in "fEHluh" (fellow), "pUHtUEEdUHz" (potatoes), "pUHdOOs" (produce), and "inUHdOOs" (introduce).

Medial unstressed "o" is frequently dropped, as in "pAW:n" (pardon), "mEHmrEE" (memory), "plAHit" (polite), "plEEsmin" (policeman), and "tmAHrUH" (tomorrow).

Medial unstressed "u" is usually treated as "UH" as in "rEHguhluh" (regular), "suhEEkUHs" (circus), "sA:dUHdEE" (Saturday), and "dEHpUHdEE" (deputy).

Medial unstressed "u" is frequently dropped, as in "sA:dEE" (Saturday), "rEHgluh" (regular), and "nA:tchril" (natural).

Final unstressed "ar," "er," "ir," "or," "ur," or "yr" is usually pronounced as "UH" as in "AW:ltUH" (altar), "wAW:dUH" (water), "tUEEpUH" (tapir), "tUEEluh" (tailor), "muhEEmUH" (murmur), and "mAW:dUH" (martyr).

The unstressed participial ending "ing" is usually pronounced as "UHn" as in "fA:nUHn" (fanning), "fAW:luhn" (falling), ((A:ktUHn" (acting), and "sAHbUHn" (sobbing). However, when "s" or "z" precedes this final "ing," it is blended into the final "n" as in "misn" (missing) and "sEEzn" (seizing).

When "d" precedes the "ing" participial ending the tongue is placed in position for "d," but before "d" can be pronounced a slight glottal stop forces the sound of "n" as in "bid/n" (bidding) or "hAHid/n" (hiding). This sound is frequently heard in informal Middle Western speech and should offer no difficulty to the actor.

When a vowel sound precedes "ing," only the "n" is pronounced as in "sEEn" (seeing), "trAHin" (trying), and "dOOn" (doing). The last example should not be confused with "doo:ng" (during) where the "ng" is sounded because it is not part of a participial ending.

Many New Yorkers reverse "r" in an unaccented syllable, as in "jOOluhrEE" (jewelry), "mAHdrUHn" (modern), "sU:THrUHn" (southern), and "dA:strik" (drastic).

CONTRACTIONS

The habit of eliding unstressed syllables makes for a great many contractions, particularly in informal speech. The word "for" is almost always blended into the succeeding word. If that word begins with a vowel only the "f" is used as in "finstins" (for instance) or "fUHgzA:mpl" (for example). If the following word begins with a consonant, "for" is pronounced as "fUH" as in "fUH mEE" (for me).

The following telescoped words and phrases are typical of colloquial New York speech:

"mEEnUH"	(mean to)
"di:ntchUH"	(didn't you)
"wUHntchUH"	(wouldn't you)
"AWluh"	(all the)
"wUHjUH"	(what did you)
"dijUH"	(did you)
"fyUHdUH"	(for you to)
"wUHdUH"	(would have)
"kUHdUH"	(could have)
"shUHdUH"	(should have)
"smA:dUH"	(What's the matter?)
"wAHintchUH"	(why don't you)
"jUHhimEE"	(Do you hear me?)

CONSONANT CHANGES

Many New Yorkers are lax in the pronunciation of consonant sounds. There is a tendency to drop a great number, although seldom where the meaning of the word is impaired. Also, in dropping medial "k" or "t" a glottal stop (/) is substituted. However, the consonant sounds they do pronounce are usually produced with excessive stress. This frequently results in a slight aspirate "UH" as in "sUHmUOOk" (smoke), "tUHrAHi" (try), or "buhlAHin" (blind). The aspirate sound must not be overdone, and if used, it should be reserved for stressed syllables.

D — Initially, this consonant sound may remain the same as in General-American. However, many New Yorkers thicken it by dentalization. Instead of producing it with the tongue tip against the upper teeth ridge, about a quarter of an inch behind the upper front teeth, they place the tongue tip against the backs of the upper front teeth. Thus, "d" is thickened and becomes "dTH" as in "dTHrAHi" (dry).

Medial "d" is frequently dropped after "n" as in "wU:nUH" (wonder), "U:nUH" (under), and "lAHnrEE" (laundry). It may also be dropped from final "ddle" as in "fiuhl" (fiddle), "miuhl" (middle), or "sA:uhl" (saddle). When "d" is medial and followed by two consonants, it may be dropped, as in "mist" (midst), "with" (width), "brEHth" (breadth), or "kUHn" (couldn't).

Final "d" may be dropped after "l" or "n" as in "wuhEEl" (world), "kUOOl" (cold),· "lA:n" (land), or "fAHin" (find).

When final "d" is pronounced, it is sometimes sounded so energetically that it takes on a "t" quality, as in "hU:nUHt" (hundred) or "rEHvrint" (reverend).

G — A slight "g" sound is sometimes added after "ng" as in "sing-g" (sing), "strAW:ng-g" (strong), or "bring-g" (bring). This extra "g" sound is particularly noticeable when the next word begins with a vowel, as in "lAW:ng-gAHilin" (Long Island).

H — This consonant is usually sounded as in General-American, except that when initial and followed by the sound of "yOO," it is usually dropped, as in "yOOmin" (human) and "yOOmUH" (humor).

J — The final "j" sound is sometimes pronounced as "tch" as in "kAHlitch" (college) and "kA:bitch" (cabbage).

K — Initial "k" is frequently sounded so energetically that a slight roughening or palatal rasp follows its production.

When medial "k" is followed by an unstressed vowel plus "n" it may be glottalized and the "n" pronounced as the nasal "ng" sound, as in "bEE/ng" (beacon) or "tAW:/ng" (talking). (See **"The Glottal Stop"** page 24.)

L — New Yorkers generally use the darker "l" of "pull" rather than the clear "l" of "lily." In addition, many of them produce "l" with the tongue tip placed against the back of the upper front teeth, instead of at the teeth ridge in the roof of the mouth, as in General-American. This makes for a peculiar discoloration of certain vowel sounds as, for example, the "i" sound in "silky" which takes on an "U" quality "sUlkEE" with the production of the dentalized "l."

Final "l" frequently is preceded by an "uh" glide, as in "fOOuhl" (fool), "huhEEuhl" (hurl), or "bAW:uhl" (ball).

Medial "l" is frequently dropped in such words as "AWwUHz" (always), "suhEE/nEE" (certainly), and "fAHinEE" (finally).

When medial "l" is followed by another consonant, it may be dropped in favor of an "oo" glide, as in "himsEHoof" (himself), "miookmin" (milkman), or "AWoo" (all).

M — This consonant is usually pronounced as in General-American. Some New Yorkers drop it medially and nasalize the preceding vowel sound, as in "sAmpl" (sample) or "A:mbUH" (amber).

N — When medial "n" is followed by another consonant, the "n" may be dropped and the preceding vowel nasalized, as in "kUHnfEHs" (confess), "sA:nwij" (sandwich), or "kAHnvikt" (convict).

Medial "n" may be replaced by the sound of "ng" particularly if it is followed by the sound of "k" as in "UngkAHmin" (uncommon), "kAHng-kwEHs" (conquest), or "ing-kwEHs" (inquest).

Final "n" is frequently of slightly longer duration than in General-American. This is particularly noticeable before an initial vowel word, as in "UHnnA:sprin" (an aspirin), "fAoonnAoot" (found out), or "innEH" (in there). In the last example it will be noticed that the "th" was dropped from "there." Thus it became an initial vowel word.

NG — This nasalized "ng" is sometimes pronounced as "n" in the words "lEHnth" (length) and "strEHnth" (strength).

For the treatment of the participial ending "ing," see **"Unstressed Syllables."**

P — The word "bump" in all its variations is frequently pronounced as "bUngk."

R — One of the most distinguishing features of New York speech is its almost singular treatment of the consonant "r."

Although initial "r" may remain the same as in General-American, many New Yorkers use the "r" *grasseyé*. The lips are spread more widely than in General-American although the tongue may remain in its usual position. This widening of the lips will aid in producing this "r" *grasseyé* which frequently has a slight "w" coloring, but a full "w" substitute must not be used.

Medially, "r" may remain the same, but again many New Yorkers use the "r" *grasseyé*, so that "dreary" sounds almost like "dwiwEE." Some New Yorkers use the widened-lip production for "r," but the lower lip slightly touches the bottom of the upper front teeth so that "r" resembles "v" as in "vEHvEE" (very) or "pvEEvyUHs" (previous). A full "v" sound should not be used.

Ordinarily, New Yorkers pronounce some form of "r" when this consonant is preceded by a consonant and followed by a vowel, as in "lAHibrEHrEE" (library), or "prUHfEHsUH" (professor). However, a great many of them drop this "r" in an unstressed syllable, as in "EHvEE" (every), "sEHkUHtEHrEE" (secretary), and "stUHnAHgUHfUH" (stenographer).

Final "r" is almost never sounded by New Yorkers. This loss of final "r" is noticed even when the next word begins with a vowel, as in "fAW: UHn wAHid" (far and wide) or "sistUH A:n" (sister Ann). Although the dropped "r" is frequently replaced by "UH" in other regional dialects, this substitution is not typical of the broad New York dialect. Vowels preceding a final dropped "r" usually have a pinched quality in the speech of the average New Yorker. This accounts for such pronunciations as "hi" (here), "bi" (beer), "ni" (near), "THEH" (there), "wEH" (where), "tchEH" (chair), "dAW" (door), "kAW" (car), or "stEH" (stare).

An excrescent "r" is frequently sounded after final "AW" and final unstressed "UH" as in "lAW:r" (law), "sAW:r" (saw), "drAW:r" (draw), "kyOObUHr" (Cuba), "sA:gUHr" (saga), and "flAHridUHr" (Florida). This "r" should be sounded if the vowel sound is final in a sentence or preceded by an initial vowel word, as in "THA:ts THUH lAW:r" (That's the law) or "drAW:r it" (draw it).

Final "ar," "er," "ir," "or," "ur," and "yr" are generally pronounced as "UH" as in "AW:lUH" (altar), "mistUH" (mister), and "sA:dUH" (satyr).

S — The New Yorker dialect uses the General-American "s" sound. Many speakers use a very sibiliant "s," while others produce this consonant with the tongue humped against the roof of the mouth so that a lisping quality results. Some speakers change "s" to "z" particularly when it is final in a word or syllable and is followed by the consonant sound of "b," "d," "g," "j," "v," or "z" as in "bUEEzbAW:l" (baseball), "gA:z buhEEnUH" (gas burner), "tchEHz bAW:d" (chess board), "bEHz guhEEl" (best girl), "THiz jAHb" (this job), and "miz vAHin" (Miss Vine).

T — Although "t" may be pronounced as in General-American, it is frequently produced with considerable force so that it is followed by a slight aspirate "UH."

When "t" is preceded by "n" and followed by a vowel, it is frequently dropped, as in "inUHrU:p" (interrupt), "inUHvl" (interval), "inUHdOOs" (introduce), "twEHnEE" (twenty), or "sEHnimint" (sentiment).

When "t" occurs between vowels, it is often sounded as "d" as in "pAW:dEE" (party), "mA:dUH" (matter), "wAW:dUH" (water), or "pUHtUEEdUHz" (potatoes). As illustrated in the last example, this substituted "d" should be used only if "t" is in an unstressed syllable. The "d" should not be given the full consonant sound.

When the sound of "t" is preceded by a vowel and followed by unstressed "le," "on," "en," "ing," or "ain," it is frequently replaced by the glottal stop (/) as in "bA:/l" (battle), "kAH/n" (cotton), "mi/n" (mitten), "si/n" (sitting), or "suhEE/n" (certain). (See **"The Glottal Stop,"** page 24.)

Final "t" is often dropped when it is preceded by "f," "k," "n," or "s" as in "sAW:f" (soft), "fA:k" (fact), "rEHs" (rest), and "frUn/" (front). This last example illustrates another tendency to glottalize "t." When final "t" is preceded by "n" in a word which is final in a sentence or followed by an initial consonant word, the following procedure is typical: the vowel sound preceding "n" is nasalized; the "n" is dropped, and a glottal stop replaces "t" as in "frU:n/ dAW:" (front door), or "Up frU:n/" (up front). But when final "t" is preceded by "n" and followed by an initial vowel word, the "n" sound is retained and the "t" dropped with no glottal substitution, as in "frUnUH THuh hAoos" (front of the house) or "sEHn UH lEHdUH" (sent a letter).

Some New Yorkers drop medial "t" when it is preceded by "l" and followed by an unstressed vowel sound plus any consonant except "n," as in "AW:luh" (altar) or "bAW:luhmAW:" (Baltimore).

TH — This sound may remain the same as in General-American except that when stressed, it is frequently produced with more force.

The variant "d" may be used as in "dEEz" (these), "dEHm" (them), and "dUH UdUH" (the other). This change, however, should be reserved for "dead end kids" or adults with little formal education and a poor cultural background. It typifies the old-time Bowery character and the gangster, but is not characteristic of the New York dialect.

Initial "TH" is frequently dropped in rapid colloquial speech, as in "A:dUHguhEEl" (that-a-girl), "A:ts AWrAHit" (that's all right), "AWluhtAHim" (all the time), or "AWlUOOz" (all those).

th — The character who uses "d" for "TH" should also use "t" for "th" as in "brEHt" (breath), "tin" (thin), "nAW:t" (north), or "tuhEEd" (third).

TCH — Initially and finally, this sound is pronounced as in General-American. But medially, after the sound of "k" it is usually pronounced as "sh" as in "pikshUH" (picture), "frA:kshUH" (fracture), and "A:kshuhl" (actual).

V — Although this consonant sound may remain the same as in General-American, many New Yorkers drop the sound of "v" when it is followed by "z" as in "liz" (lives), "giz" (gives), or "mOOz" (moves). This is particularly noticeable in rapid, colloquial speech.

Some New Yorkers change "v" to "m" when followed by an unstressed vowel plus "n" as in "sEHmnEE" (seventy), "lEHm" (eleven), or "lim" (living).

WH — This double consonant sound is generally pronounced as "w" in such words as "wEHn" (when), "wAHi" (why), and "witch" (which).

X — Although this consonant sound and its several variations may remain the same, some people prefer the single "gs" as in "EHgsrUH" (extra). "EHgsA:min" (examine), and "EHgspEHl" (expel).

Y — A linking "y" glide may be used between a final vowel sound and an initial vowel word, as in "AHiyA:m" (I am).

Z — Those people who produce their consonant sounds forcefully change "z" to "s" because of their energetic production of this consonant, as in "sEErUH" (zero), "lUEEsEE" (lazy), and "rUOOsis" (roses). Many dentalize this "z" sound and also the "s" substitute so that there seems always present a slight suggestion of a lisp.

GRAMMAR CHANGES

The frequency and quality of grammatical errors depend on the age of the individual and his educational and cultural background. Many of the following changes are typical of the average person who speaks with a New York dialect. It is a general rule that as the dialect speech of a character lightens, so also should his gross errors in grammar be lightened.

Errors listed in **"The Common Speech"** (page 7) may be used if they conform with the type of character portrayed. Other locutions common to the speech of many New Yorkers are listed below.

One of the most frequent errors is the substitution of "being" for "because" as in:

"bEEn THuh dAHim sik AHi kAn gUOO."
((*Being* that I'm sick, I can't go.)
(I can't go *because* I'm sick.)

"bEEn THuh dUHts lUEEt wEEl hU:rEE."
(*Being* that it's late, we'll hurry.)
(We'll hurry *because* it's late.)

Another common error is the use of "should" rather than "to" in an infinitive, as in:

"AHi wUHn yUH shUHd sEH-EE UHt."
(I want you *should* see it.)
(I want you *to* see it.)

"wEH yUH wUHn AHi shUHd pUHdit?"
(Where you want I *should* put it?)
(Where do you want me *to* put it?)

"ThA:s nUOO rEH-EEzn yUH shUHd krAHi."
(That's no reason you *should* cry.)
(That's no reason for you *to* cry.)

The personal pronoun "their" is frequently used in place of the correct "his" or "her," as in:

"THuh tAHip puhEEsn THA/ nEH-EEdz THEH slEH-EEp."
(The type person that needs *their* sleep.)
(The kind of person who needs *his* sleep.)

"EHvEEwUHn AW:dUH dOO THEH pAW:t."
(Everyone ought to do *their* part.)
(Everyone ought to *her* part.)

The substitution of "that" for "who" is also common, as in:

"hEEz UH mA:n THAdEEz AWwUHz hA:pEE."
(He's a man *that* he's always happy.)
(He's a man *who's* always happy.)

"shEEz THuh guhEEl THuh/ tUOOld."
(She's the girl *that* told.)
(She's the girl *who* told.)

The use of "leave" for "let" is a well-known error, as in:

"lEEv mEE uhlUOOn."
(*Leave* me alone.)
(*Let* me alone.)

"wiyUH lEH-EEv im dOO yUH duhEEt?"
(Will you *leave* him do you dirt?)
(Will you *let* him trick you?)

An over-use of the word "like" is frequently heard, as in:

"it kUEEm in UH bAHks lAHik."
(It came in a box, *like*.)
(It came in a sort of box.)

"hEEz fU:nEE lAHik."
(He's funny *like*.)
(He's rather strange.)

A repetition of the personal pronoun is also evident, as in:

"THuh guhEElz THUEE gUH tAHiUHd."
(The girls, *they* got tired.)
(The girls got tired.)

"THuh mA:n THuhdEE liz hi."
(The man that *he* lives here.)
(The man who lives here.)

The word "there" is often dropped from the phrase "where there is," as in:

"yUH nUOO wEHz UH tAHl?"
(You know where's a towel?)
(Do you know where *there's* a towel?)

Many speakers are almost addicted to the use of "on account" rather than "because," as in:

"AHnUHkAoon AH did."
(*On account* I did.)
(*Because* I did.)

"mAW:t gUOOz AHn UHkAoon UH A:lis."
(Mort goes *on account* of Alice.)
(Mort goes *because* of Alice.)

The substitution of "should be" rather than "is" or "are" has also been observed, as in:

"mUEEk shoo: hEE shUHd bEE AHnis."
(Make sure he *should be* honest.)
(Make certain he *is* honest.)

"sEE yUH shUHd bEH-EE uhEElEE."
(See you *should be* early.)
(See to it that you *are* early.)

The omission of "if" is noticeable in a dependent clause after a verb of query, as in:

"AH yA:st im wUHd EE gUOO."
(I asked him would he go.)
(I asked him *if* he would go.)

"wEE wAHnidUH nUOO kUHd shuhEElEE kUm."
(We wanted to know could Shirley come.)
(We wanted to know *if* Shirley could come.)

Two independent sentences are sometimes erroneously connected by "that," as in:

"hEE hAz UH siknis THA/ wEE kAndOO EHnEEthing wiTHim."
(He has a sickness *that* we can't do anything with him.)
(He is ill. We can't do anything with him.)

Another popular change is the substitution of "without" for "unless," as in:

"THEH nAHt gUOOn wiTHAoot yOO gUOO tOO."
(They're not going *without* you go too.)
(They're not going *unless* you go too.)

The word "ever" is often inserted before an adverb to indicate positiveness, as in:

"A:m AW-EE yEHvUH mA:d!"
(Am I *ever* mad!)
(Am I angry!)

A pronoun is frequently used in the objective case when it should be in the possessive, as in:

"AH dUOOn lAHik im bEEn hi."
((I don't like *him* being here.)
(I don't like *his* being here.)

A dependent clause describing an action is frequently introduced with "how," as in:

"shEE dUOOn lAHik hAH AWluh tAHim EE kU:mz."
(She don't like *how* all the time he comes.)
(She doesn't like his coming all the time.)

"AH dUOOn lAHik hAoo EE tAW:ks."
(I don't like *how* he talks.)
(I don't like the way he speaks.)

An excrescent "z" sound is often added to "how about," as in:

"hAHz UHbAH/ dOOn UH dA:ns?"
(*Hows* about doing a dance?)
(*How* about doing a dance?)

The word "make" is frequently used in place of a more descriptive verb, as in:

"hEE mUEEks lAHik UH dAW:g."
(He *makes* like a dog.)
(He *barks* like a dog.)

The phrase "how's for" is frequently used in place of "how about," as in:

"hAHz fUH sU/m tEEt?"
(*How's for* something to eat?)
(*How about* something to eat?)

IDIOMATIC EXPRESSIONS

The following idiomatic words and phrases are frequently used by people who speak with the New York City dialect.

The word "party" is commonly used in place of "person," "man," or "woman" as in:

"UH suhEE/n pAWdEE A:st im."
(A certain *party* asked him.)
(A certain *girl* asked him.)

"AW yOO THuh pAWdEE THA/ kAWld?"
(Are you the *party* that called?)
(Are you the *person* who called?)

The word "type" is frequently used in place of "kind of," as in:

"hEEzUH tAHip puhEEsn hOO lAHiz."
(He's the *type* person who lies.)
(He's the *kind of* person who lies.)

"AHm UH tAHip guhEEl hOO wAW:ks."
(I'm the *type* girl who walks.)
(I'm the *kind of* girl who walks.)

The interjection "Believe me!" is used as a sort of clincher for any statement regardless of its importance, as in:

"AHm gUOOn blEEv mEE!"
(I'm going! *believe me!*)
(I'm going!)

"blEEv mEE its hAHt!"
(*Believe me*, it's hot!)
(It's hot!)

Another common interjection that serves no semantic purpose is "already," as in:

"sUOO trAHi UHt AWrEHdEE."
(So try it *already*.)
(Try it.)

"wEH iz EE AWrEHdEE?"
(Where is he *already?*)
(Where is he?)

The word "so" is frequently heard initially in a sentence, as in:

"sUOO AWrAHit! sUH wEEl gUOO."
(*So* all right! *so* we'll go.)
(All right! We'll go.)

"sAH didn lAHik it."
(*S*'I didn't like it.)
(I didn't like it.)

The word "positively" is frequently inserted for emphasis, as in:

"yOO pAHzUHtivlEE gAHt nUOO AHidiUHr!"
(You *positively* got no idea!)
(You have no idea!)

"AH pAHzUHtivlEE AHbzuhEEvd im!"
(I *positively* observed him!)
(I saw him!)

The phrase "still and all" is frequently used when doubt is expressed, as in:

"stil UHn AWl UHt kUHd bEE wuhEEs."
(*Still and all*, it could be worse.)
(It could be worse.)

Many speakers use an excrescent "here" or "there" as in:

"THis hi mA:p prAHlEE shUOOz UHt."
(This *here* map probably shows it.)
(This map probably shows it.)

"THAt THEH hAd iz kAHnEEz."
(That *there* hat is Connie's.)
(That hat is Connie's.)

A statement of fact is frequently modified with an almost apologetic "personally" as in:

"puhEEsnlEE AH dUOOn thingk sUOO."
(*Personally*, I don't think so.)
(I don't think so.)

"puhEEsnlEE AHid sUEE its AWrAHit."
(*Personally*, I'd say it's all right.)
(I think it's all right.)

The hypersensitivity found in many people who speak with a New York City dialect evidences itself in other ways. Any remark that may be interpreted as being indelicate or prying is usually prefixed with an apologetic:

"if yuhl pAH:n EE EHksprEHshn."
(If you'll pardon the expression)

Literary phrases are frequently used, and there is a tendency to overemphasize the social amenities, as in:

"tchAH:lEEz mAHintEHndid."
(Charlie's my intended.)
(Charlie's my fiance.)

"bAHi EHnEE tchA:ns mAHid AH Ast wEHi?"
(By any chance might I ask where?)
(Where?)

"AH AWrEHdEE hAd THuh plEHzhUH UHv hiz UHkwUEE ntship."

(I already had the pleasure of his acquaintanship.)
(I've already met him.)

The word "dassent" is often used to supplant the phrase "not suppose to," as in:

"nAH AW-EE dA:sUHn gUOO!"
(Nah! I *dassent* go!)
(No! I'm *not supposed to* go!)

INTERJECTIONS

The following interjections are frequently used by people who speak with the New York dialect.
"sUEE wUHtsUH big AHidiUHr!"
(*Say! What's the big idea!*)
"sUH gUOO fEHvinsUEEks!"
(So go! *For heaven's sakes!*)
"yoo pAHzUHtivlEE rAW:ng-g AH mUs sUEE!"
(You're positively wrong, *I must say!*)
"jEH-EE wiz AH din rEHkUHnAHiz yUH!"
(*Gee whiz!* I didn't recognize you!)
"yUH nUOO sUmthin AHm gUOOn!"
(*You know something?* I'm going!)
"hEE tUOOld U: hAHdUHyuhlAHik THAt!"
(He told her — *how do you like that!*)
"dijUH EHvUH luhk hOOz hi!"
(*Did you ever!* Look who's here!)

MONOLOG

I'm A Type*

He was givin' me the one-two look with his eyes. "Look —"
I say to the casting director. "I'm a type person that's a type,
believe me! You want a college type? So I'm a college type! Look
what I can do with my Adams. See? A squeeze and it's a collegiate
hat. I got talent. How do you want I should convince you — show
you where I was initiated? You want I should show you where they
tattooed the fraternity pin on my chest? Want my report card,
maybe? I didn't save it. So how should I know I'd want to become
an actor." Now he's smiling. Look how the jerk is smiling. If I
had his set of teeth I'd sew up my lips. What are you smiling at,
Jerk, if you'll pardon the expression? What's funny? What do
you see — a guy with two heads? Personally, on him it wouldn't
look bad. "Look—" I say to the guy. "So, you put out a call for

---

* With permission of the author, Harry J. Essex.

a collegiate type. All right — that's me. Ask me questions. Go
on! Anything. What do you want I should tell you about college?
City College is on 23rd Street. You know something! I can love
better than a certain party that his name is Gable. Gimmie a football
and I'll make like Frank Merriwell. How's about trying me out on
dancing? Charleston-Charleston — That a bad voice? Waltzes,
foxtrots, anything. I got tempo. Timing! Wait a minute fella—
I'll make like I'm cheerleader— Gimmie a break will you? Ricky-
Coax, Ricky-Coax—, Look — For Christ's sakes, look — I'm doing
a sommersalt!"

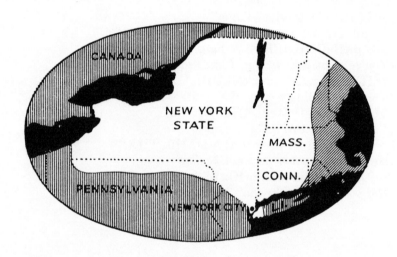

THE UPPER NEW YORK STATE DIALECT

Although many people in upper New York State speak with a
General-American dialect, or a slight modification of it, others use
some or all of the variants listed below. Consonant changes vary
more with the individual than with the section as a whole, except
for an historical or modern rural character. It is suggested that
the actor study "The New England Dialect" to acquaint himself
with the proper production of certain sounds and variant pronunciations. For a modern rural or historical character, in particular, the
sections on "Unstressed Syllables" and "Consonant Changes" in
"The New England Dialect" may be used.

VOWEL CHANGES

Sound	as in	Pronounced		as in
AY	"take"	AY		tAYk
UH	"sofa"	UH		sOHfUH
	"sofa"	i	Variant, particularly for older modern rural or historical characters.	sOHfi
AH	"dark"	AH		dAHrk
	"partridge"	AA	Variant, particularly for older modern rural or historical characters; to be used particularly for certain words like "parcel."	pAAtrij
	"calm"	AA	Variant before "lm" particularly for older modern rural or historical characters.	kAAm
A:	"dance"	A:		dA:ns
A	"bad"	A		bAd
	"catch"	EH	Variant, particularly for older modern rural or historical characters to be used especially for certain common words.	kEHtch
	"narrow"	EH	Variant before the sound of "r" plus a vowel to be used particularly for modern urban characters, although "A" may also be used, as in "kArij" (carriage).	nEHrOH
	"narrow"	AH	Variant, particularly for older modern rural or historical characters, to be used before the sound of "r" plus a vowel.	nAHrUH
AW	"thought"	AW		thAWt
	"wash"	AH	Variant, particularly when preceded by the sound of "w" as in "skwAHt" (squat).	wAHsh

Sound	as in	Pronounced		as in
AW	"sorry"	AH	Variant, particularly when followed by the sound of "r" plus a vowel as in "fAHrist" (forest).	sAHri
	"more"	OH	Variant when followed by "r" final or plus a consonant.	mOHr
EE	"tree"	EE		trEE
	"easy"	i	Variant for final unstressed "y."	EEzi
EH	"fellow"	EH	Particularly for modern urban character.	fEHlOH
	"measure"	AY	Variant, particularly for older modern rural or historical characters to be used for certain words like "AYg" (egg).	mAYzhUHr
	"there"	A	Variant, particularly for older modern rural or historical characters to be used before the sound of "r."	THAuhr
I	"hide"	AHi		hAHid
	"wire"	AH	Variant before "r."	wAHr
	"is"	i		iz
	"been"	EH	Variant, particularly for older modern rural or historical characters, to be used in certain common words before "n" as in "rEHnts" (rinse).	bEHn
O	"doll"	AH		dAHl
OH	"tone"	OH		tOHn
	"whole"	Uuh	Variant, particularly for older modern rural or historical characters, to be used in certain words like "hUuhm" (home). (See page 36.)	hUuhl
OO	"food"	OO		fOOd
	"new"	OO		nOO
oo	"good"	oo		good
yOO	"use"	yOO		yOOz

Sound	as in	Pronounced		as in
U	"club"	U		klUb
	"just"	EH	Variant, particularly for older modern rural or historical characters to be used particularly for certain words like "jEHj" (judge). (See page 39.)	jEHs
ER	"work"	ER		wERk
	"work"	U	Variant, particularly for older modern rural or historical characters.	wUk
	"gather"	Uhr	When final.	gATHUhr
OW	"out"	AHoo		AHoot
	"out"	AAoo	Variant. (See page 30) for the production of "AA.")	AAoot
	"out"	Aoo	Variant, particularly for older modern rural or historical characters.	Aoot
OI	"spoil"	AWi		spAWil
	"spoil"	AAi	Variant, particularly for older modern rural or historical characters. (See page 30 for the production of "AA.")	spAAil

CONSONANT CHANGES

Although many of the vowel and consonant sounds are similar to those found in New England, the consonant "r" is usually sounded in all positions by people in upper New York State, as in "rATHuhr" (rather) and "hAHrd" (hard). The intrusive "r" as in "fEHluhr" (fellow) may be used for an older modern rural or historical character.

CHAPTER VIII

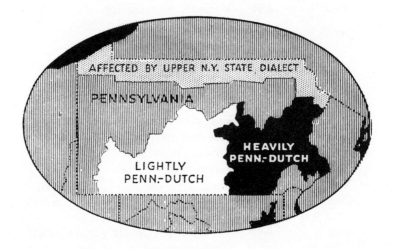

THE PENNSYLVANIA-DUTCH DIALECT

ALMOST THE ENTIRE southern half of the state of Pennsylvania is occupied by people who use what has been called the Pennsylvania-Dutch dialect. These Americans, most of whom are farmers, are the descendants of the Palatinate Germans who answered William Penn's call for settlers in the early part of the eighteenth century. Mostly refugees from religious persecution, they became expert farmers, clannish in their personal and communal affairs, extremely pious, and linguistically insular in that they forswore the use of English and retained the old Low-German speech.

Actually, these people spoke, and still speak, two dialects: a German language dialect and an American-German dialect, both of which are known as Pennsylvania-Dutch. It is with the American-German dialect, of course, that this section will treat. The older people use a broader dialect speech, as is to be expected, while the younger generation is slowly sloughing off the dialect pronunciation. The speech of this region retains, however, many characteristic grammar variants together with much of the lilt.

LILT AND STRESS

The tonal patterns to be found in the dialect are quite unique because many German inflections have been retained. These have been so widespread that they have even infiltrated into the talk of non-Pennsylvania-Dutch speakers. The typical lilt can easily be detected and has been called by Pennsylvanians the "Berks County Accent." It is to be found not only in the lilt and stress of syllables in a word but also in words of a sentence.

In stressed words, the tendency is to use a rising inflection on the accented syllable and then to follow it immediately with a falling inflection, especially ·if the accented syllable contains a "long" vowel. Thus the sentence "OW:dt vfi:dt dtUH lI:dt" (out with the light) would be spoken with the following tonal pattern:

```
                                    .I:
                           lI:        .
            vfi:dt
  "OW:dt          dtUH           .
                                   I:dt"
```

VOWEL CHANGES

The dialect features an excessive elongation, almost a dipththongization, of heavily stressed vowels, especially those of the so-called "long" variety. There are actually few radical vowel changes, although there is a tendency to *umlaut* some of them. The dialect is affected more by its consonant variants.

Sound	as in	Pronounced		as in
AY	"rain"	AY:		rAY:n
	"rain"	EH:	(occasionally)	rEH:n
UH	"sofa"	UH		sOH:vfUH
	"alone"	AY	(occasionally when initial)	AYlOH:n
AH	"art"	AH:		AH:rdt
A:	"dance"	AH:		dtAH:ns
	"dance"	A:	(variant)	dtA:ns
A	"bad"	AH		bpAHdt
	"bad"	A		bpAdt
AW	"all"	AH		AHl
	"more"	OHuh (before "r")		mOHuhr
EE	"he"	EE:		hEE:
EH	"men"	EH		mEHn
I	"ride"	I:		rI:dt
i	"him"	i:		hi:m

Sound	as in	Pronounced		as in
O	"shot"	AH		shAHt
	"on"	AW	(variant, particularly in this word)	Awn
OH	"go"	OH:		gkOH:
	"window"	UH		vfi:ndtUH
OO	"June"	OO		tchOO:n
oo	"book"	oo		bpoogk
yOO	"cube"	OO		gkOObp
U	"up"	AH:		AH:bp
ER	"her"	EHr		hEHr
	"her"	ER	(variant sound which is usually spoken with pursed lips and results in an *umlaut* sound)	hER
	"her"	AWr	(occasionally)	hAWr
OW	"now"	OW:		nOW:
	"now"	AHoo	(variant)	nAHoo
OI	"boil"	OI:		bpOI:l
	"boil"	I:	(used particularly by older people)	bpI:l

CONSONANT CHANGES

(Only the important consonant changes have been listed.)

B — This consonant sound is heavily pronounced so that it receives the coloring of a weakly aspirated "p" as in "bpI:dt" (bite) and "gkri:bp" (crib).

D — This consonant sound is also produced heavily so that it takes a weakly aspirated "t" coloring, as in "dtI:m" (dime) and "bpAWdtEE" (body).

It is generally dropped after "l" and "n" as in "gkOH:l" (cold) and "lAH:n" (land).

F — This consonant sound generally takes a "v" coloring, as in "vfI:vf" (five) and "sAY:vf" (safe).

G — A weakly sounded "k" flavor is given to this consonant sound, as in "gkrOH:" (grow) and "hAWgk" (hog).

J — This sound is frequently pronounced as "tch" as in "tchAH:tch" (judge) and "tchOHuhrtch" (George).

K — This consonant sound has a light "g" coloring, as in "bpi:gk" (pick) and "gki:l" (kill).

Final "k" is often pronounced like a roughened "h" sound (as in the Scottish word "loch" and the German word "ich") and is written in our phonetics as "kh" as in "si:kh" (sick). (See Figure 27.)

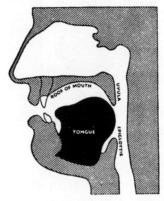

Fig. 27

NG — The "ing" participial ending is generally pronounced as "UHn" as in "vfAW:gkUHn" (walking) and "gkOH:UHn" (going).

NG-G — When the nasalized "ng" is followed by the sound of hard "g," as in the General-American word "fing-gER" (finger), the Pennsylvania-Dutch speakers frequently drop the hard "g" sound and retain only the nasal "ng" as in "vfi:ngEHr" (finger) and "mi:ngl" (mingle).

P — This consonant sound is generally given a light "b" coloring, as in "bpI:bp" (pipe) and "gkAH:bp" (cap).

Q — Because of the changes that occur in "k" and "w," the components of this consonant sound, the actual sound of "q" is a combination "gkvf" sound, as in "gkvfi:gk" (quick). This sound is simply a "g" flavored "k" combined with a "vf" substitution for "w." This may appear to be complicated, but a little practice can make the sound reproducible.

R — Most of the older speakers use the German guttural "r" exclusively (see Figure 28). This "r" is produced simply by "gargling" the uvula against the back of the tongue. Younger people, however, are acquiring the American Middle Western "r" which is usually sounded in all positions, as in General-American.

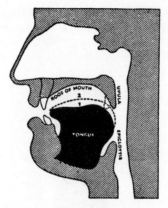

Fig. 28

S — Initial "s" often changed to "sh" before "t" and particularly before "p" as in "shdti:l" (still) and "shbpOH:gk" (spoke). Before a vowel, it frequently has a "z" coloring, as in "zOH:" (so).

T — This consonant sound is usually given a light "d" flavor as in "dtI:m" (time) and "sAH:dt" (sat).

Final "t" is often dropped after "k," "l," "n," "p," and "s," as in "AH:gk" (act), "gkOH:l" (gold), "sEHn" (sent), "AH:bp" (apt), and "vfAH:s" (fast).

TH — Many older speakers, in particular, change this sound to "d" (pronounced as "dt") as in "dtOH:s" (those) and "bpAY:dt" (bathe).

th — This sound is frequently changed to "t" (pronounced as "dt") as in "dti:ngk" (think) and "dti:n" (thin).

V — This consonant sound is often given an "f" flavor, as in "vfI:n" (vine) and "li:vf" (live).

Many other speakers sound it as "w" particularly when initial as in "wEE:l" (veal) and "wi:si:dt" (visit).

W — This consonant sound is generally pronounced as "vf" as in "UHvfAY:" (away) and "vfi:l" (will).

The American word "with" is generally dropped in favor of the German word "midt" (mit).

Z — This consonant sound is generally pronounced as "s" as in "lAY:sEE" (lazy) and "hi:s" (his).

TYPICAL EXPRESSIONS

Actually, this dialect is a combination of rural pioneer pronunciation and German. The Pennsylvania-Dutch have lived in the United States, and especially in southeastern Pennsylvania, since before the Revolutionary War. They retained their German language dialect because they were close-knit and clannish. At the same time, and for the same reason, they have retained certain American pioneer, backwoods words that infiltrated into their German language dialect as American loan words. These loan words and their colonial pronunciations are still to be found in their speech. They include such words as "sich" (such), "kiver" (cover), "purty" (pretty), "nuther" (neither), "tother" (the other), "yonder" (over there), "mebbe" (maybe), "younguns" (young folk), "body" (person), "mind" (remember), "flitch" (bacon), "plumb" (very), "datter" (daughter), "buss" (kiss), "snide" (pretentious), and "sad" (heavy), most of which can be traced back to Middle English sources.

There are also a number of locutions which typify the Pennsylvania-Dutch dialect speech. These add much to the authenticity of the dialect and should be used whenever possible.

The word "ain't" is commonly used in the same way as the German *"nicht wahr"* or the French *"n'est-ce pas."* It may take the place of "isn't it so," "aren't you," "don't you think so," and so forth, as in:

"yoor gkAH:mUHn AYndt?"
(You're coming, *ain't?*)
(You're coming, *aren't* you?)

"AYn shEE vfi:l?"
(*Ain't* she will?)
(*Won't* she?)

Other common expressions are:

"OH dtAHdts vfEHlgkUHm!"
(Oh! *that's* welcome!)
(Oh! *you're* welcome!)

"mAY:gk dtUH vfi:ndtUH shAH:dt."
(Make the window shut.)
(Close the window.)

"mAY:gk dtOW:n dtUH hi:l."
(*Make* down the hill.)
(*Go* down the hill.)

"i:dt mAY:gk dtOW:n sOOn."
(It *make down* soon.)
(It *will rain* soon.)

"mAY:gk dtUH vfI:r OW:dt."
(*Make* the fire out.)
(*Put* the fire out.)

"I vfAWn OW:dt."
(I *want out.*)
(I want to go out.)

'I mEHbpEE bpEHdtUH gkOH:."
(I *maybe better* go.)
(I better go.)

"AY:n yUH mEHbpEE vfEE:luhn gkoodt?"
(Ain't you *maybe* feeling good?)
(Aren't you feeling well?)

"I'm vfEE:luhn tchAH:s sOH mi:dtluhn."
(I'm feeling *just so* middling.)
(I'm feeling *fairly* well.)

"I mI:n UHvf dtUH dtI:m."
(I *mind of* the time.)
(I *remember* the time.)

"gkAH:m hi:r vfAHnsdt."
(Come here, *oncet.*)
(Come here!)

"i:dt vfAH:ndtUHrs mEE vfEHr hEE vfEHn."
(*It wonders me* where he went.)
(*I wonder* where he went.)

"vfAH:dt vfi:l yOO dtOO yEHdt?"
(What will you do, *yet?*)
(What will you do?)

"dtAH:s hEE si:ng yEHdt?"
(Does he sing *yet?*)
(Does he *still* sing?)

"nI:s gkrAHbp UH vfEE:dt sAY nAH:dt?"
(Nice crop of wheat, *say not?*)
(It's a nice crop of wheat, *isn't it?*)

"nI:s dtAY AY:n?"
(Nice day, *ain't?*)
(It's a nice day, *isn't it?*)

"nI:s dtAY dtUHdtAY: AYn UHdt i:s?"
(Nice day today, *ain't it is?*)
(It's a nice day today, *isn't it?*)

"I dtOH:n bpEElEE:vf AWn dtEHm dti:ngs."
(I don't believe *on* them things.)
(I don't believe those things.)

"dtUH dti:nUHr i:s AWl."
(The dinner is *all.*)
(The dinner's all *gone.*)

"bpAHbpAH i:s AWl."
(Papa is *all.*)
(Papa is *dead.*)

"hEE mAY:dt OW:dt dtUH gkAH:m."
(He *made out* to come.)
(He *planned* to come.)

"shEE dtOH:n vfAH:n vfOH dtUH gkOH:."
(She don't want *for* to go.)
(She doesn't want to go.)

"i:dts gkAWnUH gki:vf UH shdtOHuhrm."
(It's a going to *give a* storm.)
(There's going to *be a* storm.)

GRAMMAR CHANGES

Because of his insularity and because of his objection to having his children attend school, the typical Pennsylvania German made, and still makes, frequent grammatical errors. Such errors as "I seen her," "we can't never," "I done it," "if youse could go," and "I fetched the book" are to be found in the speech together with many of the other errors of grammar listed in the section under **"The Common Speech"** on page 7. But some errors are particularly prevalent in the speech.

For example, there is a noticeable preference for "leave" when "let" is indicated, as in:

"lEE:vf hi:m hAH:vf i:dt."
(*Leave* him have it.)
(*Let* him have it.)

Typical of the speech is the ambiguous arrangement of words in a sentence, reminiscent of the German language word order, as in:

"dtrOH: dtUH gkOW OH:vfUHrdtUH vfEHns sUHm hAY:."
(Throw the cow over the fence some hay.)
(Throw some hay over the fence for the cow.)

"hEE loogkdt OH:vfUHr dtUH dtAH:bp OW:dt."
(He looked over the top out.)
(He looked over the top.)

Another typical error favors the use of "would" for any conditional clause, as in:

"i:vf shEE vfoodt bpEE hi:r I:dt EE:dt."
(If she *would* be here I'd eat.)
(If she *were* here I'd eat.)

"i:vf vfEE vfoodt bpEE gkOH:UHn."
(If we *would* be going.)
(If we *were* going.)

The verb "ain't" is also used occasionally in a conditional clause, as in:

"vfAH:dt vfoodt vfEE sEE i:vf i:dt AYn vfAWgk."
(What would we see if it *ain't* fog.)
(What we wouldn't see, if it *weren't* foggy.)

The use of "stay" for "remain" is common, especially when a present-tense verb follows, as in:

"lEEvf i:dt sdtAY: lAY:."
(Leave it *stay* lay.)
(Let it *remain* lying.)

"nOW yOO sdtAY: si:dt."
(Now you *stay* sit.)
(Now you *remain* seated.)

The word "for" is used in a number of unorthodox ways, as in:

"hEE gkAH:n hEHlbp vfOHuhr dtAH:dt."
(He can't help *for* that.)
(He can't help that.)

"vfAH:dt vfOHuhr gkrAH:bp yOO gki:dt."
(What *for* crop you get?)
(What kind of crop did you get?)

"hEE dtUHnOH: vfAH: dt vfOHuhr."
(He don't know what *for*.)
(He doesn't know what it's all about.)

"I dtOH:n vfAH:n vfUH dtUH sEE hi:m."
(I don't want *for* to see him.)
(I don't want to see him.)

The preposition "of" is frequently used in place of "with," "to," and "about" as in:

"vfAH:dts dtUH mAdtUHr UHvf yOO?"
(What's the matter *of* you?)
(What's the matter *with* you?)

"AHlvfAY:s sAH:mdtUHn hAHbpUHns UHvf hi:m."
(Always something happens *of* him.)
(Something always happens *to* him.)

"I mI:n UHvf UHdt lA:s vfEE:gk."
(I mind *of* it last week.)
(I remembered *about* it last week.)

An adjective is often used instead of an adverb, and it is frequently placed before the verb, as in:

"hEE gkvfi:gk OH:bpUHndtUH bpAH:gks."
(He *quick* opened the box.)
(He opened the box *quickly*.)

The word "so" is often dropped from the phrase "so that" as in:

"I:l dtrEHs dtAH:dt I:l bpEE rEHdtEE AHrEHdtEE."
(I'll dress that I'll be ready, already.)
(I'll dress *so* that I'll be ready.)

In the above example, the word "already" was used as an intensifier. The word "yet" may also be used, particularly in a negative sentence, as in:

"AY:n yUH rEHdtEE mEHbpEE yEHdt?"
(Ain't you ready maybe, *yet?*)
(Aren't you ready?)

GERMAN LANGUAGE CARRY-OVERS

In addition to carrying over numerous old-English locutions in their speech, the Pennsylvania-Dutch also use a great many German words pronounced in Low German. Following are some of the words that may be used occasionally:

"gkAH:m shnEHl."
(Come *schnell.*)
(Come *quickly.*)

"dtOH:n AH:gk zOH: lAW:bpish."
(Don't act so *lobbisch.*)
(Don't act so *silly.*)

"yAH: i:dts vfAH:ndtEHrvfool shmEHgkli:kh!"
(Yah! it's wonderful *schmechlich!*)
(Yes! it's very *tasty!*)

"dtOH:n bpEE zOH: shdtroobplEE."
(Don't be so *strubbly.*)
(Don't be so *unkempt.*)

"yoor sitch UH dtoomgkAWbp."
(You're such a *dumkopf.*)
(You're such a *fool.*)

"I gkAH:dt gkUHnoong-gk."
(I got *genoonk.*)
(I have *enough.*)

"hAH:vf UH zi:dts."
(Have a *sitz.*)
(Have a *seat.*)

"AH:r yOO gkrI:sli:kh?"
(Are you *greisslich?*)
(Are you *sick?*)

"shdtAHbp gkrEHgksi:ng-gk!"
(Stop *grexing!*)
(Stop *complaining!*)

"yUH lookg lIgk UH dtAHtchEE."
(You look like a *dutchie.*)
(You look like a *tramp.*)

"zAWbpUHrloodt gkUHn hEE vfrEHs!"
(*Sopperlut!* can he *fress!*)
(*Geeminy!* can he *eat!*)

"i:dt vfUHs shEHndtli:kh hOW: hEE A:gkdtUHdt!"
(It was *shendlich* how he acted!)
(It was *disgraceful,* the way he acted!)

"yOO dti:ngk mEHbpEE i:dts shbpAWsi:kh!"
(You think maybe it's *spossich!*)
(You think it's *funny!*)

MONOLOG

(From *The Betrothal of Elypholite** by Helen R. Martin.)

"I want you — you know how bad I want you -- but you're in the world, Ellie, and I can't marry you! If it breaks my heart and yours, I've got to leave you and cleave unto Christ! It was goin' with you to town done it — and buying them things for your 'Furnishing' and then seein' the dime matynee. I seen, Ellie, how pleasing to the eye it was, but not for the glory of Gawd. And I can't never no more give my countenance to fashionable things. I'm turning plain as soon as I can get to town to get my plain clo'es once. Servin' the Lord ain't easy, it ain't easy. You mind where the Bible says, 'If a man smite thee, turn him the other cheek.' That's pretty hard, and it wouldn't suit me so well to do it. Indeed, I say that. But I must do all them things if I'm a child of Gawd!"

THE PENNSYLVANIA DIALECT

With the exception of the people in Erie, Warren, McKean, Potter, Tioga, Bradford, Susquehanna, and Pike counties, who speak a dialect modified by upstate New York, the non-German inhabitants of Pennsylvania use an American dialect that varies somewhat from General-American. It is distinguished by a peculiar drawl heightened by Pennsylvania-Dutch influences. Certain vowel changes are directly attributable to Irish influences, as the use of

* Reprinted with permission of D. Appleton-Century Company.

"AW:i" for "I" as in "dAW:iv" (dive). The elongation of the so-called "long" vowels stems from Germanic influence. At the same time these elongated vowels, when stressed, receive a rising or falling intonation, as in Pennsylvania-Dutch. It must be mentioned, however, that a great many people in this section speak with a General-American dialect.

VOWEL CHANGES

Sound	as in	Pronounced		as in
AY	"say"	AY		sAY
	"say"	AHi	(variant)	sAHi
	"player"	EH:	(before "r")	plEH:r
UH	"sofa"	UH		sUoofUH
AH	"father"	AW:		fAWTHuhr
	"part"	AW:	(also before "lm")	pAW:rt
A:	"ask"	A	(flat "A")	Ask
A	"bad"	A	(flat "A")	bAd
AW	"ball"	AW:	(generally)	bAW:l
	"four'	OH:	(frequently before "r")	fOH:r
	"watch"	AH:	(after "w" and before the sounds "sh" or "tch")	wAH:tch
	"horrid"	AH:	(when followed by "rr" plus a vowel)	hAH:rUHd
EE	"steam"	AY	(frequently)	stAYm
	"steam"	i:yi	(particularly when stressed)	sti:yim
	"meal"	i:	(before "l")	mi:l
EH	"well"	EH:		wEH:l
I	"ride"	AW:i	(before voiced consonants such as "b," "d," "g," "j," and so on)	rAW:id
	"nice"	AW:	(before voiceless consonants such as "f," "k," "p," "s," and so on)	nAW:s
	"mile"	AH:	(before "l" or "r")	mAH:l
i	"it"	i		it
	"beer"	i:	(before "r")	bi:r
O	"bond"	AH:		bAH:nd
	"on"	AW:	(exception)	AW:n
OH	"home"	U:oo		hU:oom
	"home"	A:oo	(variant)	hA:oom
	"home"	EH:oo	(variant)	hEH:oom
OO	"food"	iOO		fiOOd

Sound	as in	Pronounced		as is
oo	"put"	oo		poot
yOO	"cube"	yiOO		kyiOOb
U	"fun"	U:		fU:n
ER	"curl"	uhEE		kuhEEl
	"sister"	UHr		sistUHr
OW	"brown"	A:oo		brA:oon
	"tower"	A:	(before "r" and "l")	tA:r
OI	"noise"	OH:i		nOH:iz
	"toil"	AW:	(before "l")	tAW:l

In practicing the above vowel changes, the student should guard against caricaturing sounds that vary from his own. Thus, in the sentence "jUH mAHik yUH kAW:l" (Did you make your call?) the word "mAHik" (make) should not be treated too broadly, or it will sound like the General-American word "mIk" (Mike).

The "AW" sounds are generally produced with the lips fairly tensed and they should be elongated to "AW:" as in "hAW:l" (hall). This elongation is particularly noticeable before "l."

Many speakers use a great deal of lip movement when talking. This feature is advised if it is not overdone.

CONSONANT CHANGES

R — This consonant sound, generally believed to be dropped throughout the East, is usually sounded by Pennsylvanians except the inhabitants of sections bordering the New York City area. The "r," however, should not be as strong as the Middle Western sound.

Many Philadelphians, particularly those in the "upper class," disdainfully ignore "r" and prefer the eastern habit of dropping it.

WH — This sound is generally pronounced as "w" as in "wEHn" (when) and "witch" (which).

GRAMMAR CHANGES

Few grammatical changes can be called "typical" of the Pennsylvanian. For the most part, his grammatical constructions follow those of the Middle Westerner who has the same educational background.

Two important usages do occur, however, particularly in Philadelphia. One is the word "skwEH:r" (square) in place of "block," as in:

"its tiOO skwEH:rz dA:oon."
(It's two *squares* down.)
(It's two *blocks* down.)

The other word is "anymore" which is frequently used to indicate a positive continuing action or emotion, as in:

"jim dU:z id AW:l THuh tAW:im EHnAYmOH:r."
(Jim does it all the time *anymore*.)
(Jim does it all the time.)

"Alis lU:vz id EHnAYmOH:r."
(Alice loves it *anymore*.)
(Alice loves it.)

CHAPTER IX

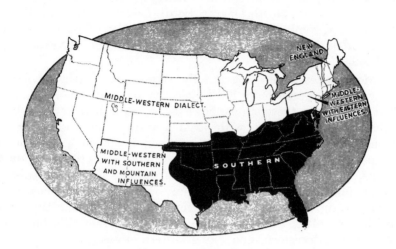

THE MIDDLE WESTERN DIALECT

Mᴏʀᴇ ᴀᴍᴇʀɪᴄᴀɴs ᴜsᴇ the Middle Western dialect speech, or a modification of it, than any other speech in America. Furthermore, it is the only form of American speech that is not undergoing any radical changes other than those that ordinarily affect every language. It is the only form of American speech spreading across regional boundaries and modifying the dialectal speech of those areas. It is the speech to which Britishers refer when they deprecate the American manner of pronunciation. Finally, and most important, it holds the promise of becoming, at some distant date, a fair example of Standard-American speech, which is *not* to be confused with *good* American speech. At present, it comes as close to being General-American speech as any of the other dialects spoken in the United States.

It is spoken, in some slightly modified form, from as far east as certain sections in Maine, New Hampshire, Rhode Island, Connecticut, upper New York State, New York City, and even Boston, that stronghold of New England speech. Altogether it is spoken by more than ninety million people in the following sections: eastern New Hampshire, Vermont, eastern Massachusetts, New York State (north of the environs of New York City), parts of Rhode Island, most of New Jersey west of the counties adjacent to the environs of New York City, most of Ohio with the exception of those counties bordering the Ohio River, Indiana with the exception of those counties bordering the Ohio River, Illinois with the exception of those counties bordering the Ohio River, Michigan, Wisconsin, Minnesota, northern Missouri, North Dakota, South Dakota, Nebraska, Kansas, Montana, Wyoming, Colorado, northern New Mexico, western Texas, Idaho, Utah, Arizona, Washington, Oregon, Nevada, and California.

Most states comprising the Far West and Northwest are too young to have permitted a local dialect to have become crystallized. Most speakers in these states, however, speak a distinct form of the Middle Western dialect with local variations depending on the original regional background of the person. California, for example, became the mecca of a great many Middle Westerners, especially Iowans, during the great land boom of the late nineteenth century. But the influx of Oklahomans, Texans, and other Southerners introduced certain Southern variants into the speech of many of its inhabitants. The same situation exists in other Western, Far Western, Southwestern, and Northwestern states.

But these dialect modifications are few and do not affect the speech sufficiently to make for separate and distinct dialects. There are, however, certain speech islands in this huge territory that do vary considerably from General-American. The speech of many Milwaukee, St. Louis, and Cincinnati people of German ancestry, for example, is colored with the German dialect. Many residents of Holland, Michigan, and the surrounding territory, speak with Dutch dialect variations. The speech of the people of Wyoming has been influenced by the pioneer speech of Indian scouts, trappers, miners, cowboys and cattlemen. Many inhabitants of the mining districts of this state speak Middle Western, but with traces of the Italian and Slav dialects. And certain farming sections show definite Scandinavian speech influences.

But, on the whole, the speech of most native-born Americans is the Middle Western speech of Iowa, Kansas, and Nebraska, with infiltrations from Missouri, Oklahoma, and Texas in the border sections.

The personality traits of the millions who live in this vast territory vary so much it would be futile to attempt a thumbnail sketch of them and expect to characterize more than a few of the people. But certain broad generalizations may be made, as they have been attempted in other sections. It can be said, for example, that Middle Western folk tend to fall between the hurried excitability of New Yorkers and the unworried calmness of Southerners. Urban Middle Westerners, of course, would move at a more accelerated tempo than those who live on the farms. Middle Westerners are generally more friendly than Easterners. The open-hearted, open-handed generosity of the people of far western states is almost legendary. There is something about the "Howdy, stranger!" welcome of a Westerner that exudes good fellowship and unstinted pleasure at being a host to a newcomer.

THE WESTERN DRAWL

One of the most characteristic variants to be found in the General-American speech of the Far Western, Southwestern, and Northwestern states is the use of what has been called, the "Western drawl." The Middle West dialect features the addition of "uh" before "l" and "r" in a stressed syllable, as in "fAYuhl" (fail), "fAWuhrs" (force), "sEHuhl" (sell), "fIuhr" (fire), "tIuhl" (tile), "fiUHr" (fear), "fEEuhl" (feel), "shooUHr" (sure), "tOWuhr" (tower), and "sOIuhl" (soil).

Although the slight "uh" glide is generally reserved for the above-mentioned vowel sounds before the above-mentioned consonants in Middle Western speech, the "Western drawl" extends the use of "UH" to many more sounds. One of the most typical additions comes in the pronunciation of the word "skOOwuhl" (school) which the Middle Westerner would generally pronounce as "skOOl" (school). Western speech frequently adds the "uh" drawl to "OO" when followed by "l". It is also used after "A," "EH," "i," and "OW" before "l" as in "AuhlbERt" (Albert), "EHuhlmER" (Elmer), "fiuhltER" (filter) and "fOWuhl" (fowl). The "OW" sound is also often drawled to "OWwUH" as in "hOWwuhl" (howl).

These drawled vowels make for a speech that is paced quite slowly, often hesitantly and thoughtfully. It is a calm unhurried speech that takes cognizance of the fact that time is not as fleeting as some may think it to be; that cogitation is a prime virtue; that "shooting off at the mouth" is the sign of a fool. If there is a distinguishing feature between the "Western drawl" and the "Southern drawl" it is that, where the "Southern" variety gives the impression of relaxed laziness, the "Western" suggests cogitation rather than mere indolence. This is not meant to infer that Westerners are great thinkers and Southerners ne'er-do-wells.

The Western drawl is not as musical as the Southern drawl. When the Southerner drawls a word, he uses a greater variation of notes than the Westerner who generally elongates the word on but two notes. It may be said that the Southerner uses a gliding drawl while the Westerner uses a more restrained drawl.

LILT AND STRESS

The two basic tonal patterns of the General-American lilt are to be found in the speech of most of the inhabitants of the Middle

West, Far West, and Southwest. The simple declarative sentence "its rAY:ning" (It's raining) is spoken with a rising and falling inflection, as in:

rAY:
"its
ning"

The simple question form uses the rising inflection, so that "iz UHt rAY:ning" (Is it raining?) would be spoken as:

ning"
rAY
"iz UHt

Stressed words are not forcefully emphasized unless the speaker is emotionally disturbed. The average General-American speaker usually has a rather monotonous delivery which is only occasionally relieved by a moderately high or low note.

The tendency to stress initial syllables is not as prevalent in the Middle and Far West as it is in Southern and Mountain regions. The words "hOHtEHl" (hotel), "rUHgAHrd" (regard), "puhlEEs" (police), and "sUHmEHnt" (cement) are usually accented on the last syllable. Some people in the Far West, however, who have a Southern or Mountain background, do retain initial syllable stress in such words as the above-mentioned. But this is not typical of general Middle Western speech with the exception of some rural areas, particularly along the Southern border.

VOWEL SOUNDS

"AY" . . . . as in "take," "grade," "say," etc.

This "AY" sound is generally elongated to "AY:" when final or before voiced consonants, as in "grAY:d" (grade), "AY:j" (age), and "sAY:m" (same). This elongation carries with it the sound of "EE," so that "AY:" is actually "AY-EE" as in "wAY-EEv" (wave). For simplicity this elongated sound will be represented as "AY:" while the shorter sound, found before unvoiced consonants, will be "AY" as in "tAYk" (take).

Before final "l" this vowel sound generally takes an "uh" glide, as in "pAYuhl" (pale). However, this vowel sound is usually a pure "AY" when followed by medial "l" plus a vowel, as in "mAYling" (mailing) and "jAYluhr" (jailer).

DRILL WORDS

sAY:m	(same)	pAY:j	(page)	AYth	(eighth)
fAYuhl	(fail)	dAY:	(day)	nAYuhl	(nail)
lAYt	(late)	hAY:g	(Hague)	tAYp	(tape)

VARIATIONS: When this vowel sound is unstressed in the suffix "day," it is generally sounded as "dAY" as in "mUndAY" (Monday). Some speakers pronounce it as "di:" as in "tOOzdi:" (Tuesday).

Some people, particularly those with social aspirations, say "tUHmAHtOH" (tomato), but this word is generally pronounced as "tUHmAYdUH" or "tUHmAYdOH."

"UH" .... as in "alone," "sofa," "final," etc.

This unstressed vowel sound is generally pronounced as "UH" in all positions. In a medial position it is frequently dropped. See also **"Unstressed Syllables,"** page 311, and **"Weak and Strong,"** page 16.

DRILL WORDS

uhlOH:n	(alone)	EEkwuhl	(equal)
sOHfUH	(sofa)	mAHrthUH	(Martha)
fI:nl	(final)	pUHtrOH:l	(patrol)

muhlI:n	(malign)
UHgEHn	(again)
UHpiUHr	(appear)

VARIATION: Some older, rural speakers substitute "i:" for final "UH" as in "sOH:di:" (soda) and "mAHrthi:" (Martha). These same people generally drop final "UH" when it is preceded by "i" as in "I:di:" (idea) and "nOOmOHni:" (pneumonia).

"AH" .... as in "father," "arm," "park," etc.

This vowel sound generally retains its "AH" pronunciation throughout the Middle West.

DRILL WORDS

fAHTHuhr	(father)	pAHrk	(park)
AHrmEE	(army)	stAHrt	(start)
kAHm	(calm)	hAHrt	(heart)

fAHr	(far)
kAHrbUHn	(carbon)
bAHmEE	(balmy)

"A:" .... as in "ask," "calf," "aunt," etc.

When this "a" is followed by "f" or "s" plus a consonant, "nce," "nt," "th," or the sound of "f," it is generally pronounced as an elongated "A:" as in "A:sk" (ask), "kA:f" (calf), and "A:nt" (aunt). The average Middle Westerner keeps this vowel sound flat and does not attempt to shade it toward "AH."

Although many Britishers complain of the nasality of American speech and particularly refer to this "A:" as a case in point, this sound is usually pronounced without an obvious nasal quality.

DRILL WORDS

bA:th	(bath)	EHgzA:mpl	(example)
klA:sp	(clasp)	A:nsUHr	(answer)
lA:ftUHr	(laughter)	kUHmA:nd	(command)

bA:skUHt	(basket)
dA:nsing	(dancing)
grA:ntUHd	(granted)

VARIATIONS: The "AH" variant may be used when portraying a character with social ambitions. This sound, as in "AHsk" (ask) or "dAHns" (dance) is generally frowned upon by the average Middle Westerner who considers it affected.

Far Western speakers frequently drawl this elongated "A:" to "A:uh" as in "fA:uhst" (fast) and "hA:uhf" (half).

"A" .... as in "bad," "hat," "salve," etc.

This sound, particularly when stressed, is elongated to "A:" before voiced consonants, as in "bA:d" (bad), "sA:v" (salve), and "hA:z" (has).

Before unvoiced consonants, it retains its short form "A" as in "hAt" (hat) and "snAp" (snap).

DRILL WORDS

sA:d	(sad)	nAshnuhl	(national)
tAps	(taps)	frA:juhl	(fragile)
lA:g	(lag)	rA:guhd	(ragged)

Apuhlz	(apples)
krA:bEE	(crabby)
lA:nlAWrd	(landlord)

VARIATION: Older, rural folk frequently use the variant "EH" in short, common words like "hEHv" (have) and "THEHt" (that).

' When followed by the sound of "r" plus a vowel, this "A" may remain the same "nArOH" (narrow) or change to "EH" (nEHrOH).

"AW" .... as in "all," "horse," "horrid," etc.

This vowel sound generally remains the same, except that it is elongated before voiced consonants, as in "AW:l" (all), "hAW:rs" (horse), and "hAW:rUHd" (horrid). Although many other regional dialects change "AW" to "AH" before "r" plus a vowel, the average Middle Westerner retains the "AW" sound in these words, as in "fAW:rUHst" (forest) and "AW:rUHnj" (orange).

DRILL WORDS

wAWsh	(wash)	dAW:g	(dog)
krAWs	(cross)	hAW:g	(hog)
fAW:r	(four)	fAW:g	(fog)

bAW:rdwAWk	(boardwalk)
AWspishUHs	(auspicious)
fAWrwAW:rnd	(forewarned)

It will be noticed that in the last word, "forewarned," the first "AW" sound was not elongated even though it was followed by "r." The reason is that in this example the word has been used with the primary accent on the second syllable. Therefore, the first vowel sound receives no elongation.

VARIATIONS: Some speakers, particularly in Indiana, Iowa, and Michigan use the "AH" variant after "w" as in "wAHsh" (wash) and "wAHtch" (watch).

CAUTION: The Middle Western "AW" sound is relaxed and the lips are only slightly pursed. This sound should not be as tense and prolonged, for example, as the New York City variation.

"EE" .... as in "he," "repeat," "city," etc.

When in a stressed position, this sound remains the same except that it is elongated before voiced consonants, as in "nEE:d" (need) and "EE:z" (ease).

When followed by "l," the vowel sound generally carries with it an "uh" glide, as in "hEEuhl" (heel) and "rEEuhl" (real).

When final and spelled with "y," this sound is pronounced as "EE" as in "sitEE" (city) and "pitEE" (pity).

See also **"Unstressed Syllables."**

DRILL WORDS

rUHpEEt	(repeat)	EE:jipt	(Egypt)
UHgrEE:d	(agreed)	krEE:OHl	(Creole)
rEE:zn	(reason)	sAW:rEE	(sorry)

frEE:dUHm	(freedom)
yOOnEEk	(unique)
krEEAYt	(create)

In the above drill words, it will be noticed that the "EE" of "Creole" was elongated although the "EE" of "create" was not, despite the fact that both sounds were followed by another vowel. This distinction is made because the word "Creole" is accented on the first syllable, while "create" is accented on the second.

"EH" .... as in "leg," "sent," "pair," etc.

Basically, this vowel sound remains the same, except that it is elongated before voiced consonants as in "lEH:g" (leg) and "sEH:d" (said). The "i" or "AY" variant before a nasal should not be used, although it is common in other regional dialects.

When "EH" is followed by final "l" or "r" in a stressed syllable, it generally takes an "uh" glide, as in "pEHuhr" (pair), and "sEHuhl" (sell).

When "EH" is followed by a medial single "l" or "r" it may take the "uh" glide or be elongated to "EH:" as in "bEH:lt" (belt).

DRILL WORDS

wEHuhr	(where)	mEHrEE	(merry)
THEHuhr	(there)	brEH:d	(bread)
mEH:rEE	(Mary)	sEH:nt	(sent)

jEHlEE	(jelly)
hEH:ld	(held)
wEHuhl	(well)

VARIATIONS: The "Western drawl" may be achieved by using both the ":" and the "uh" glide as in "wEH:uhl" (well), "EH:uhlmUHr" (Elmer), "hEH:uhrEE" (hairy), and "sEH:uhd" (said).

Although "EH" is preferred, some speakers use the "A" variant when the vowel sound is spelled with "a" and followed by "rr" plus a vowel. Thus, these people would say "mArEE" (marry), and "mEHrEE" (merry).

Some speakers pronounce "e" before "r" as "ER" as in the words "UHmERuhkUHn" (American) and "vEREE" (very). Generally, however, these words retain their "EH" sound, as in "UHmEH:rUHkUHn" (American) and "vEH:rEE" (very).

"I" . . . . as in "my," "ice," "fire," etc.

This sound is almost universally pronounced as "AH-EE" in the entire Middle Western region. When followed by a voiced consonant, this sound is elongated to "AH:EE" as in "rAH:EEd" (ride) and "AH:EEz" (eyes). It is also elongated when final as in "mAH:EE" (my) and "trAH:EE" (try). For easier reading this sound will be represented as "I:," as in "prI:d" (pride).

When followed by an unvoiced consonant, this long "i" (I) is generally pronounced as "AH-EE" as in "rAH-EEt" (right) and "AH-EEs" (ice)· The hyphen (-) is used to separate the two elements of the diphthong for easier reading, but it does not indicate a pause between the two sounds. This shorter sound will be represented as "I" as in "prIs" (price). Even when stressed, this sound is seldom as long as before a voiced consonant.

Medially, when followed by "l" or "r," the "I" sound takes an "uh" glide, as in "fIuhr" (fire) and "tIuhl" (tile).

DRILL WORDS

fI:v	(five)	sI:zUHbuhl	(sizable)
lIf	(life)	wIuhldfIuhr	(wildfire)
wIuhr	(wire)	tI:mlEE	(timely)

wIflEE	(wifely)
stIuhlish	(stylish)
hIuhr	(higher)

VARIATIONS: Many speakers use "AH:EE" (I:) before voiced consonants but "U-EE" before unvoiced consonants, as in "tAH:EEd" (tide), "tU-EEt" (tight), "jAH:EEb" (jibe), "grU-EEp" (gripe), "lAH:EEv" (live), and "lU-EEf" (life).

If the variant "U-EE" is used, both elements should blend together, and there should be no break between them. The complete sound should be relaxed. Otherwise it will resemble the sound "UH-EE" used in the Scottish dialect.

Although words spelled with final "ile" or "ine" are frequently pronounced with "I" in other regional dialects, Middle Western speakers generally treat this unstressed vowel sound as "UH" as in "jEH:nyUHwUHn" (genuine) and "rEHptuhl" (reptile).

Certain southern sections of the Middle Western region use "AH" as in "tAHm" (time).

EXCEPTIONS: The following words are generally pronounced as "IrUHsh" (Irish), "Iluhnd" (island), and "I-ERn" (iron).

"i" .... as in "it," "women," "busy," etc.

Basically, this short "i" remains the same except that in one-syllable words it is generally elongated to "i:" when followed by a voiced consonant, as in "i:z" (is), "li:v" (live), and "di:g" (dig). In other regional dialects in this book the symbol "i:" is frequently used to indicate a tensed short "i" which approaches "EE". In this section, "i:" indicates an elongated "i" which should receive a relaxed production. This "i:" may also be represented as "iUH" since it frequently takes the "UH" glide before voiced consonants, as in "piUHn" (pin) and "kriUHb" (crib).

The "iUH" sound, however, is most frequently heard before "l" and "r" as in "fiuhl" (fill) and "fiUHr" (fear). The use of this glide is, also, generally limited to one-syllable words.

DRILL WORDS

iuhl	(ill)	iluhnOI:	(Illinois)
thi:n	(thin)	nirlEE	(nearly)
slip	(slip)	tchiUHr	(cheer)

hiUHr	(hear)
kwiUHr	(queer)
wimUHn	(women)

VARIATIONS: Although the participial ending "ing" is generally pronounced as "ing" as in "swimming" (swimming), many Middle Westerners say "EEn" as in "swimEEn" (swimming), and the variant "UHn" is frequently heard in careless speech, as in "swimUHn" (swimming).

Most Middle Westerners retain the short "i" sound before "r" plus a vowel, but others, particularly those in rural areas, use the variant "ER" for such words as "sERuhp" (syrup), "stERuhp" (stirrup) and "skwERuhl" (squirrel).

"O" . . . . as in "on," "bond," "John," etc.

Although similar in production to "AH," this "O" sound is produced from a slightly more forward position in the mouth. It is also slightly shorter in duration as can be seen in the words "fO:dUHr" (fodder) and "fAH:THUHr" (father).

The word "fO:dUHr" (fodder) employed the ":" because the vowel sound was followed by the voiced consonant "d." It is generally elongated before other voiced consonants as well, as in "kO:g" (cog) as compared with "lOk" (lock) and "sO:b" as compared with "sOp" (sop). This elongation is usually limited to monosyllables.

Before final "l" an "uh" glide is usually added, as in "dOuhl" (doll) and "pOuhl" (poll).

DRILL WORDS

bO:b	(Bob)	dOjUHrz	(Dodgers)
krOp	(crop)	hOlOH	(hollow)
lO:j	(lodge)	OpUHrAYt	(operate)

OlivUHr	(Oliver)
pOsUHbuhl	(possible)
OnUHstEE	(honesty)

VARIATIONS: Although generally pronounced as "O:n" (on), this word is frequently sounded as "AW:n" (on) by rural speakers along the southern border of the Middle Western area.

EXCEPTIONS: When short "o" is followed by the sounds "ng" or "th," or by "f" or "s" plus a consonant, the average Middle Westerner pronounces the vowel sound as "AW" as in "sAWng" (song), "mAWth" (moth), "lAWft" (loft), or "krAWs" (cross). This general rule, which applies particularly to monosyllables and their derivatives, should be observed in delineating a character from the Middle or Far West.

The following words should also be pronounced with "AW:" "dAW:g" (dog), "fAW:g" (fog), "lAW:g" (log), and "hAW:g" (hog). The actor should guard against making this "AW" tense. It should be a relaxed sound, but it should not have the characteristics of a diphthong.

The pronunciation "nOluhj" (knowledge) is general, although "nOWluhj" has also been heard.

"OH" . . . . as in "bone," "sew," "home," etc.

When stressed, this vowel sound is generally pronounced as though it were "OH-OO" as in "sOH-OO" (sew). For the sake of simplicity it will be written as "sOH:" (sew). The first element "OH" receives the stress while the second element, "OO," is used as a glide.

The diphthongal quality is more noticeable when final or followed by a voiced consonant, as in "rOH:d" (road) and "lOH:b" (lobe) than when followed by an unvoiced consonant, as in "rOHt" (wrote) and "lOHp" (lope).

DRILL WORDS

gOH:	(go)	spOHk	(spoke)
OH:ld	(old)	stOH:n	(stone)
kOHt	(coat)	uhlOH:n	(alone)

sOHlOH	(solo)
grOHp	(grope)
jOH:b	(Job)

VARIATIONS: Although final unstressed "ow" is generally pronounced as "OH," many rural folk, particularly along the southern area of the Middle West and in Colorado and the Far West, use the variant "uh" as in "fEHluh" (fellow). Some add an excrescent "r" as in "fEHluhr" (fellow).

EXCEPTIONS: The following words are generally pronounced as "flAWr" (floor), "stAWr" (store), and "rAWr" (roar).

"OO" .... as in "food," "new," "due," etc.

In the speech of most Middle Westerners, this "OO" sound is never diphthongized to "iOO." It is retained even when spelled with "u," "ue," or "ew" and preceded by "d," "n," or "t," as in "dOO:" (due), "nOO:" (new), and "tOO:n" (tune), although under such conditions it is pronounced as "yOO" in other sections of the United States. (See "yOO" as in "use.")

This vowel sound usually has slightly more elongation before voiced consonants than before unvoiced consonants.

DRILL WORDS

stOOpUHd	(stupid)	grOOp	(group)
nOO:z	(news)	fOO:d	(food)
nOOspAYpUHr	(newspaper)	shOOt	(shoot)

glOO:m	(gloom)
trOOp	(troop)
tchOO:	(chew)

VARIATION: Although the addition of the "uh" glide before "l" is not a feature of the Middle Western dialect, it is noticeable in the Far Western, as in "fOOuhl" (fool).

EXCEPTIONS: The following words, variously pronounced over the country, are generally pronounced in the Middle West as "brOO:m" (broom), "sOO:n" (soon), "hOOp" (hoop), "kOOp" (coop), "spOO:n" (spoon), "rOO:m" (room), "hOO:vz" (hooves), "hoof" (hoof), and "roof" (roof).

"oo" . . . . as in "good," "wolf," "full," etc.

When stressed, particularly in a single-syllable word, this vowel sound is generally elongated to "oo:" if it is followed by a voiced consonant or the sound of final "l" as in "goo:d" (good) and "foo:l" (full).

Before final "r" it generally adds an "UH" glide, as in "shooUHr" (sure). This glide must be very slight.

DRILL WORDS

soot	(soot)	woo:d	(would)
root	(root)	woomUHn	(woman)
woolf	(wolf)	shoogUHr	(sugar)

UHshooUHr	(assure)
foolfiuhl	(fulfill)
roofing	(roofing)

"yOO" . . . . as in "use," "cube," "few," etc.*

This "yOO" sound is used when initial long "u" is spelled "u," "eu," "you," "yu," or "ewe" as in "yOO:z" (use), "yOOnyUHn" (union), "yOOstUHs" (Eustace) or "yOO:l" (Yule).

It is also used when spelled with "u," "ew," "iew," "eu," "ue." "eau," or "ieu" and preceded by "b," "f," "h," "k," "m," "p," or "v" as in "fyOO:d" (feud), "byOOdEE" (beauty), "kyOO:" (cue), and "hyOOmUHn" (human).

DRILL WORDS

yOOs	(use)	kyOOpUHd	(cupid)
fyOO:	(few)	myOOzUHk	(music)
vyOO:	(view)	yOOnUHt	(unit)

byOOgl	(bugle)
myOOt	(mute)
hyOOmUHr	(humor)

When medial "l" is followed by "u," this vowel sound is sometimes pronounced as "yOO" as in "vOlyOOm" (volume) and "vAlyOO" (value). But the word "voluminous" is generally pronounced as "vuhlOOmUHnUHs" (voluminous).

"U" .... as in "up," "young," "lunch," etc.

Basically, this "U" sound remains the same, except that it is slightly elongated before voiced consonants, as in "rU:b" (rub) and "jU:g" (jug).

DRILL WORDS

Up	(up)	mU:l	(mull)	frU:nt	(front)
yU:ng	(young)	dU:n	(done)	UHnUf	(enough)
lU:ntch	(lunch)	flU:d	(flood)	jU:j	(judge)

"ER" .... as in "curb," "earn," "girl," etc.

This "ER" is one of the characteristic sounds of Middle Western and Far Western speech because it is generally used only by those who pronounce "r" after a vowel. Thus, the person who says "kAHr" (car) would also be apt to say "kERb" (curb) rather than "kERb" or "kuhEEb" (curb).

However, the pronunciation of "r" in this combination "ER" sound should not be as rich and strong an "r" as is heard in Mountain speech. Although the tongue should form an arc in the mouth so that the sides of the center portion of the tongue touch the insides of the teeth, the tongue should not be held rigidly against the teeth.

When this sound is followed by "l" there is a slight "uh" glide, as in "gERuhl" (girl).

When "er" is in a final unstressed position, it is generally pronounced as "UHr" as in "fAHrmUHr" (farmer).

DRILL WORDS

ERn	(earn)	wERuhld	(world)
wER	(were)	pERuhl	(pearl)
tERn	(turn)	kUHnfER	(confer`

lAY:bUHr	(labor)
jERnEE	(journey)
kERfyOO	(curfew)

EXCEPTIONS: The following words are generally pronounced "kERnl" (Colonel) and "mERmER" (murmur).

"OW" .... as in "now," "house," "bough," etc.

This sound generally retains its diphthongal quality and is pronounced as "AH-OO" with the first element receiving the stress. For easier reading the symbol "OW" is used, but the student must remember that basically this sound is "AH-OO" and not "Aoo" or "AHoo" or "AH."

This sound is slightly longer when final or before voiced consonants as can be seen when comparing "krOW:d" (crowd) and "krOWt" (kraut).

A slight "uh" glide is common before "l" and "r" as in "OWuhl" (owl) and "OWuhr" (hour).

DRILL WORDS

nOW:	(now)	dOW:n	(down)
hOWs	(house)	dOWtUHd	(doubted)
bOW:	(bough)	prOWdlEE	(proudly)

sOWuhr	(sour)
prOWuhl	(prowl)
tOWuhl	(towel)

"OI" . . . . as in "oil," "noise," "boy," etc.

This "OI" sound receives its full diphthongal treatment and is usually pronounced as "AW-EE" rather than as "AWi," "AW:," "uhEE," or "AHi" as is evident in other sections.

For easier reading this "AW-EE" sound will be represented as "OI" before unvoiced consonant sounds and as "OI:" before voiced consonant sounds, as in "vOIs" (voice) and "nOI:z" (noise). The ":" indicates slight elongation, and the stress should be placed on the first element "AW."

When followed by final "l," this vowel sound usually takes a slight "yuh" glide, as in "OIyuhl" (oil).

DRILL WORDS

bOI:	(boy)	sOIyuhl	(soil)
pOI:z	(poise)	bOIling	(boiling)
jOI:n	(join)	dUHstrOI:	(destroy)

rOIyuhl	(royal)
kOI:n	(coin)
tOI:z	(toys)

CAUTION: The "y" of the "yuh" glide, as in "bOIyuhl" (boil), must not be stressed so that it takes its full sound. This "y" is a natural result of the second element of the diphthong "OI" (AW-EE) and must be treated as a slight glide and nothing more.

UNSTRESSED SYLLABLES

One of the most characteristic speech habits of the Middle Westerner is his reduction of most of the unstressed vowel sounds to "UH," particularly in informal speech. In almost all cases, no matter what the spelling, if the vowel sound is unstressed it is usually pronounced as "UH" as in "mOHmUHnt" (moment). In the word "dikshUHnEHrEE" (dictionary), however, the third syllable receives secondary stress and thus retains the "EH" sound.

Inhabitants of border regions, as for example, people living near the Ohio River, in Texas, or in the Middle Western states may use the unstressed vowel treatment typical of the adjacent section. But in the main "UH" is used to supplant most of the unstressed vowel sounds, particularly in informal speech.

Initial "a" becomes "UH" when unstressed, as in "UHbU:v" (above), "UHgOH:" (ago), "UHmOW:nt" (amount) and "uhlOH:n" (alone). But, when initial unstressed "a" is followed by "l," "m," or "n" plus a consonant, it is generally pronounced as "A" as in "AlgOnkwin" (Algonquin), "AmbishUHs" (ambitious) and "Ang-gAWrUH" (Angora).

Medial "a" usually becomes "UH" when unstressed, as in "sEHprUHt" (separate, adjective), "sEHpUHrAYt" (separate, verb), "mEHnUHs" (menace), "mAWruhl" (moral), and "dIuhlEHkt" (dialect). However, when medial "a" is followed by two different consonant sounds, it usually retains its "A" sound, as in "kOntrAst" (contrast), "bOmbAst" (bombast), and "rEElAps" (relapse).

Final unstressed "a" also is pronounced as "UH" as in "lImUH" (lima), "sOHfUH" (sofa), and "hAnUH" (Hannah).

Initial unstressed "e" has at least four different treatments in active use. When initial "e" is followed by a consonant plus a vowel, it is generally pronounced as "UH" in careless or informal speech, as in "uhlOHp" (elope), "UHmERj" (emerge), and "UHmOHshn" (emotion). Careful speakers usually prefer "i" as in "inUf" (enough) and "inAkt" (enact); while some use "EE" as in "EElOHp" (elope).

When initial unstressed "e" is followed by two consonant sounds, it is generally pronounced as "i" in informal speech, as in "inslAY:v" (enslave) and "ikstAdik" (ecstatic). Careful speakers usually pronounce this sound as "EH" as in "EHnjOI:" (enjoy) and "EHkstrEEm" (extreme).

Medial unstressed "e" is usually pronounced as "UH" in words of three or more syllables, as in "EHluhmUHnt" (element), "AluhgAWrEE" (allegory), "minUHsOHtUH" (Minnesota) and "EHluhgUHns" (elegance). The "UH" is also used for the past tense "ed" ending when it is preceded by "d" or "t" as in "prEEsEEdUHd'" (preceded), "rAYtUHd" (rated), and "grAYdUHd" (graded). It is also common when a final syllable contains "e" followed by a single consonant, as in "fljUHt" (fidget) and "dribluht" (driblet).

Medial unstressed "e" is usually pronounced as "EH," in careful speech, when it is in the second and final syllable of a word and is followed by two consonants, as in "AdvEHnt" (advent), "ObjEHkt" (object), "prOsEHs" (process), and "kOnsEHpt" (concept). Informal speech treats with it as "UH" as in "AdrUHs" (address).

When "e" is used in the prefix "pre" or "re," it is generally pronounced as "UH" in careless or informal speech, as in "prUHvEHnt" (prevent) or "rUHpAWrt" (report). However, many speakers, particularly those who are careful in their pronunciation, use "EE" as in "prEEtEHkst" (pretext) or "rEEzOOm" (resume).

Initial unstressed "i" is generally pronounced as "i" when followed by two consonants as in "imprEHs" (impress), "infAWrm" (inform), and "ilEEguhl" (illegal). When followed by a consonant plus a vowel, initial "i" may be "i" or "UH" as in "imAjUHn" or "UHmAjUHn" (imagine). The word "idea" and its compounds, is pronounced with an initial "I" sound: "IdEEuh."

Medial unstressed "i" is generally pronounced as "UH" as in "UHbiluhtEE" (ability), "yOOtiluhtEE" (utility), "rApUHd" (rapid), and "mAksUHmUHm" (maximum).

When medial unstressed "i" is followed by a vowel sound, it is, generally pronounced as "y" as in "milyUHn" (million) and "jEEnyUHs" (genius).

When medial unstressed "i" is in the second syllable of a two-syllable word, and is followed by two different consonants, it is generally pronounced as "i" as in "kOnvikt" (convict), "trAnskript" (transcript), and "EEjipt" (Egypt).

Initial unstressed "o" is generally pronounced as "UH" in informal speech, as in "UHfishuhl" (official), "UHbAY:" (obey), "UHbskyoor" (obscure), and "UHfEHnd" (offend). However, in careful speech, initial "o" is pronounced as "OH" when it is followed by a consonant plus a vowel, as in "OHhIOH" (Ohio) and "OHbAY" (obey), and it is pronounced as "O" when followed by two different consonant sounds, as in "Obskyoo" (obscure) and "OktOHbUHr" (October).

Medial unstressed "o" is generally pronounced as "UH" as in "pUHtEHnshuhl" (potential), "mUHnO/UHnUHs" (monotonous), "impUHzishn" (imposition), "kUHmpAkt" (compact, adjective), "prUHpOHz" (propose) and "prUHvOHk" (provoke).

Initial unstressed "u" when followed by two different consonant sounds is generally pronounced as "U" as in "UpbrAYd" (upbraid),

"UnlEHs" (unless), "UmbrEHluh" (umbrella), and "Until" (until). When followed by a consonant plus a vowel, it is pronounced as "yOO," as in "yOOnIt" (unite).

Medial unstressed "u" is generally pronounced as "yUH" as in "rEHpyUHtAYshn" (reputation), "rEHgyuhluhr" (regular)) and "AkyUHrUHt" (accurate). However, when medial "u" is followed by a vowel, it is usually pronounced as "OO" as in "pUHrpEHtchOOuhl" (perpetual), "hAbitchOOuhl" (habitual), and "kUHntinyOOuhns" (continuance).

The vowel sound in the final unstressed endings "ine," "ile," "age," and "ate" is generally "UH" as in "jEHnyUHwUHn" (genuine), "rEHptuhl" (reptile), "mEHrUHj" (marriage) and "pIrUHt" (pirate).

The following list of words will illustrate how a change in syllabic stress, resulting from a change in grammar, causes a change in unstressed syllabic pronunciation:

AnEHks	(annex)	and	UHnEHks	(annex)
ObjEHkt	(object)	and	UHbjEHkt	(object)
kOndUkt	(conduct)	and	kUHndUkt	(conduct)
AdrEHs	(address)	and	UHdrEHs	(address)
sERvAY	(survey)	and	sUHrvAY	(survey)
AdEHpt	(adept)	and	UHdEHpt	(adept)
rEHbuhl	(rebel)	and	rEEbEHl	(rebel)
tEHrUHfi	(terrify)	and	tUHrifik	(terrific)
pEHrUHnt	(parent)	and	pUHrEHntuhl	(parental)
hAbit	(habit)	and	hUHbitchOOuhl	(habitual)
dEHfUHnUHt	(definite)	and	dUHfIn	(define)

In addition to changing the vowel sound in an unstressed syllable, many people in the Middle and Far West have the tendency to drop the vowel sound. However, this habit is not as prevalent as in other regions. Some typical examples of the dropped vowel sound are: "rEHvrUHnt" (reverent), "intrUHst" (interest), "histrEE" (history), "AWflEE" (awfully), "sEHprUHt" (separate) "jEHnruhl" (general), "UHmERkUHn" (American), and "mEHmrEE" (memory).

CONSONANT CHANGES

B — Although this consonant sound is frequently dropped after "m" in other sections of the country, Middle Westerners usually pronounce it, as in "thimbuhl" (thimble), "skrAmbuhl" (scramble), and "nUmbUHr" (number).

D — Final "d" is frequently dropped after "l" and "n" when the following word begins with a consonant, as in "lAn wUHz" (land was) and "wERl wUHd" (world would).

When medial "d" is unstressed and follows "n" or precedes "s," it is sometimes dropped in careless speech, as in "kOnUkt" (conduct) and "mist" (midst).

When medial "d" is followed by the "y" glide, and this is particularly noticeable in the endings "eur," "ure," and "ier," it is pronounced as "j" as in "grAnjUHr" (grandeur), "vERjUHr" (verdure), and "sOHljUHr" (soldier).

H — Middle Westerners generally pronounce "h" in "hyOOmUHr" (humor), "hyOOmUHd" (humid), and "hUmbuhl" (humble) but not in "OnUHst" (honest) or its compounds.

K — In careless speech when "k" is followed by the participial ending "ing," it is frequently dropped in favor of the glottal stop (/) as in "ki/ng" (kicking). (See "The Glottal Stop, page 24.) Many speakers, however, retain this "k," and say "kikUHn" (kicking) or "kiking."

L — Although some Middle Westerners use an initial clear "l," the majority of speakers prefer a modified dark "l" initially, as in "lIk" (like), and a dark "l" medially and finally, as in "sAluhd" (salad) and "fool" (full).

When in a stressed position this consonant contributes much to the Western drawl and moderately to the Middle Western drawl. (See "The Western Drawl," page 299.)

When "l" is followed by a voiced consonant, its preceding vowel sound is slightly elongated, as in "fOH:ldUHr" (folder); but when followed by an unvoiced consonant, the preceding vowel sound is short, as in "kiltUHr" (kilter). However, in a stressed word of one syllable, the vowel sound is generally elongated before "l" although it is still noticeably longer when "l" is followed by a voiced consonant. This can be readily seen by comparing the words "bAW::ld" (bald) and "sAW:lt" (salt).

N — This consonant sound frequently imparts a nasal quality to the preceding vowel sound, but this nasality is not as prominent in the average Middle Westerner as it is in the average Southerner or Highlander. However, it is a common habit, particularly in rapid informal speech to substitute a glottal stop for the final "nt" of a single syllable word, as in "An/mEHrEE" (aunt Mary) and "sAYn/pAW:l" (Saint Paul). The "n" indicates that the consonant sound is dropped and the preceding vowel is nasalized. (See also "The Glottal Stop," page 24.)

R — This consonant sound is one of the most identifying in Middle Western or Far Western speech (see Figure 29). It is pronounced

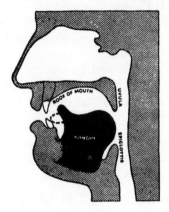

Fig. 29

in all positions and is never rolled or trilled. In an initial position it is produced with the tongue tip pointing upward toward, but not touching, the roof of the mouth. The tongue tip should not be curled backward, or the sound will be too strong. Both sides of the center portion of the tongue touch the inside surfaces of the upper side teeth. The lips are slightly parted. Medially after a vowel, or finally, the tongue tip does not necessarily point toward the roof of the mouth. It is guided to its position by the following sound.

In all but meticulous speech "r" is dropped when preceded by a vowel and followed by the "UHr" ending, as in "EHuhr" (error), "niUHr" (nearer), and "tEHuhr" (terror).

In other medial positions it is always pronounced, as in "ritchUHrd" (Richard), "kArEE" (carry), and "stAWrUHj" (storage). When "r" is in a medial stressed position and is followed by another consonant, it usually takes an "UH" glide as in "stAWuhrk" (stork), "kAWuhrt" (court), and "pAHuhrk" (park). The "UH" glide should be very light and short, and it is generally restricted to final words in a sentence. Thus, in "THuh kAW:rs wUHz hAH:uhrd" (The course was hard) only the last word would receive the "UH" glide. This consonant is one of the two ("l" is the other) that contributes to the Western drawl and, in a limited way to the Middle Western drawl.

Final, unstressed "er," "ar," "ir," "or," "yr," or "ur" is commonly pronounced as "UHr" as in "rOHluhr" (roller), "kUluhr" (color), "mAH:rtUHr" (martyr), "mAW:rtUHr" (mortar), or "sEHluhr" (cellar).

Although an intrusive "r" is not a feature of Middle Western speech, it is occasionally used in the Far West, particularly in Colorado. Its use is limited to the final unstressed "ow" as in "fEHluhr" (fellow) and "widUHr" (widow).

S — Although "s" may retain its normal pronunciation, it is frequently changed to "sh" when the next word begins with "y" as in "THish yUHr book" (This your book?).

T — When "t" is followed by long "u" (OO), it is commonly pronounced as "tch" as in "piktchUHr" (picture), "nAtchruhl" (natural), and "nAYtchUHr" (nature).

This change to "tch" is also frequently used when final "t" is followed by a word beginning with "y," as in "lA:stchiUHr" (last year) and "AtchUHr" (at your).

When medial "t" is preceded by a stressed vowel and followed by an unstressed vowel plus "n," the "t" is generally dropped in favor of a slight glottal stop (/) as in "kO/n" (cotton) and "rO/n" (rotten). (See "The Glottal Stop," page 24.)

However, when medial "t" is preceded by a stressed vowel and followed by an unstressed vowel plus a consonant other than "n," the "t" is produced so weakly that it sounds almost like "d" as in "bAdUHr" (batter), "sidUHr" (sitter), "bOduhl" (bottle), and "UdUHr" (utter).

An intrusive "t" is frequently heard between "ls" and "ns" as in "fAW:lts" (false) and "sEH:nts" (sense).

Final "t" is occasionally dropped after a consonant if the next word begins with a consonant, as in "hApAs fI:v" (half past five) and "UHfEHk mI:" (affect my).

W — When the sounds "OO," "OW," or "OH" are followed by a vowel or "l," the "Western drawl" adds a "w" glide, as in "hOWwuhl" (howl), "gOHwing" (going), and "dOOwing" (doing).

Y — In the "Western drawl" a "y" glide is frequently added after "AY," "I," "OI," and "EE" when followed by a vowel sound as in "sAYying" (saying), "bIying" (buying), "EHnjOIying" (enjoying), and "UHgrEEyUHbuhl" (agreeable).

Z — Although "z" may retain its normal pronunciation, it is frequently changed to "zh" when the next word begins with a "y" as in "hOOzhuhr" (who's your) and "wEHrzhUngmUHn" (where's Youngman).

NG — This nasalized sound is generally replaced by "n" in the participial "ing" ending, as in "hAngUHn" (hanging) and "livUHn" (living). However, when preceded by "k," the "ng" sound may be retained and the "k" glottalized, as in "tAW/ng" (talking).

WH — This sound is usually pronounced as "w" as in the words "witch" (which), "wI:" (why), "wEH:n" (when), and "wEHuhr" (where). However, many people do retain the "h" sound, as in "hwip" (whip), "hwitch" (which), "hwEEuhl" (wheel), and "hwIt" (white).

GRAMMAR CHANGES

All errors discussed in "The Common Speech" are frequently made by some, but not all, the people of the Middle and Far West. The number of errors naturally depends on the cultural and educational background of the individual. Many people who use good grammatical construction when speaking formally lapse into grammatical errors when speaking informally.

It is impossible to state with finality that a person with little or no formal education will make one type of error while someone with more education will make a different type. However, the greatest number of errors in verb tense is generally found in the speech of people with little education who have no desire to improve their speech. Thus, two people of the same age with the same cultural background and the same amount of formal education need not speak alike if one has the initiative to improve his speech.

The following errors are common to most people of the Middle and Far West.

In informal speech, the verb or auxiliary verb is frequently dropped in such interrogative sentences as:

"THishyUHr mAYuhl?"
(This your mail?)
(*Is* this your mail?)

"wAHnUH gOH:?"
(Wanna go?)
(*Do you* want to go?)

The pronoun "who" is generally preferred in place of "whom" as in:

"hOOjUH gOH wiTH?"
(*Who*'d you go with?)
(With *whom* did you go?)

Many speakers use a plural pronoun with a singular noun as in:

"EHvrEEwUHn shUHd dOO THEHr dOOdEE."
(Everyone should do *their* duty.)
(Everyone should do *his* duty.)

An adjective is frequently preferred to an adverb, as in:

"hEE rAn kwik."
(He ran *quick*.)
(He ran *quickly*.)

MONOLOGS

(From *Friendship Village** by Zona Gale.)

"John, do you know what Aunt Nita told me before I was was married? 'You must always look the prettiest you know how,' Aunt Nita says, 'for your husband. Because you must always be prettier for him than anybody else is. An', oh, dearest, you know I'd 'a' looked my best for you if I could — but I never had — an' it wasn't your fault! but things didn't go right. It wasn't anybody's fault. Only — I *wanted* to look nice for you. An' since I've been sick, it's made me wretched, wretched to think I didn't hev nothin' to put on but this black waist — this homely old black waist. You never liked me to wear black, an' it killed me to think — if anything should happen — you'd be rememberin' me like this. You'd think you'd remember me the way I was when I was well — but you wouldn't — people never, never do. You'd remember me here like I look now. Oh — an' so I thought — if there was ever so little money we could spare — won't you get me somethin' — somethin' so's you could remember me better? Somethin' to wear these few days."

MONOLOG

(From *Friendship Village** by Zona Gale.)

"My land! think of it! A party like that, an' not a low-necked waist in town, nor a swallow-tail! An' only two weeks to do anything in, an' only Liddy Ember for dressmaker, an' it takes her two weeks to make a dress. I guess Mis' Postmaster Sykes has got her. They say she read her invite in the post-office with one hand an' snapped up that tobacco-brown net in the post-office store window with the other, an' out an' up to Liddy's an' hired her before she was up from the breakfast table. So she gets the town new dress. Mis' Sykes is terrible quick-moved."

* Reprinted with permission of the Macmillan Company

BIBLIOGRAPHY

Acadians of Louisiana, The, by Alcee Fortier.
American Dialect Dictionary, by Harold Wentworth.
American English, by W. M. Mathews.
American English Grammar, by Charles C. Fries.
American Language, The, by H. L. Mencken.
American Local Color Stories, ed. by H. R. Warfel.
American Pronunciation, by John S. Kenyon.
American Regionalism, by H. W. Odum and H. E. Moore.
American Scenes, ed. by William Kozlenko.
American Speech Monographs, No. 1, ed. by Jane D. Zimmerman.
Babbitt, by Sinclair Lewis.
Back Home, by Irvin S. Cobb.
Back Where I Came From, by A. J. Liebling.
Backwoods America, by C. M. Wilson.
Balcony Stories, by Grace King.
Banjo Talks, by Anne Virginia Culbertson.
Bases of Speech, by G. W. Gray and C. M. Wise.
Bayous of Louisiana, The, by Hartnett T. Kane.
Betrothal of Elypholate, by H. R. Martin.
Beyond Dark Hills, by Jesse Stuart.
Bigelow Papers, by James Russell Lowell.
Birthright, by T. S. Stribling.
Black April, by Julia Peterkin.
Black Border, The, by A. E. Gonzales.
Black Cameos, by R. E. Kennedy.
Bonaventure, by W. H. Cable.
Bright Skin, by Julia Peterkin.
Cabins in the Laurel, by M. E. Sheppard.
Cape Cod Yesterdays, by Joseph C. Lincoln and Harold Brett.
Cap'n Bailey and the Widder Brown, by Charles W. Burton.
Captain, The, by Ambrose E. Gonzales.
Carolina Mountains, The, by Margaret Morley.
Collected Poems, by Paul Lawrence Dunbar.
Colonel's Story, The, by Mrs. Roger A. Pryor.
Congaree Sketches, by E. C. L. Adams.
Conjure Woman, The, by C. W. Chestnutt.
Cowboy Lingo, by Ramon F. Adams.
Creoles of Louisiana, The, by George W. Cable.
Cross-Roads of the Buccaneers, by Henryk de Leeuw.
Cross-Roads of the Carribbean Sea, by Henryk de Leeuw.
Cross Creek, by Marjorie K. Rawlings.
Cy Whittaker's Place, by Joseph C. Lincoln.
Deep Delta Country, The, by Hartnett T. Kane.
Dead End, by Sidney Kingsley.
Defects of Speech, by Ida C. Ward.
Delilah, by Morris Goodrich.

De Ole Plantation, by G. G. Williams.
Dictionary of Americanism, by J. R. Bartlett, 2nd edition.
Dictionary of Modern American Usage, by H. W. Horwill.
Dobe Walls, by Stanley Vestal.
East Side, West Side, by Felix Reisenberg.
Elements of Phonetics, by Walter Ripman.
Elsie Venner, by Oliver W. Holmes.
En Booch fur Instruchta, by E. H. Rauch.
English Language in America, The, by George Krapp.
English Pronouncing Dictionary, An, by Daniel Jones.
English Pronunciation in Virginia, by E. F. Shewmake.
Escape to the Tropics, by Desmond Holdridge.
Ethan Frome, by E. S. Wharton.
Euphon-English, by M. E. De Witt.
Family Style, by K. W. Baker.
Figures In a Landscape, by Paul Horgan.
Florida Cracker Dialect, by W. J. McGuire, Thesis, University of Florida.
Flowering Judas and Other Stories, by K. A. Porter.
Folk Culture on St. Helena Island, S. C., by Guy B. Johnson.
Folks in Dixie, Paul L. Dunbar.
Foundations of Speech, by Wise, McBurney, Mallory et al.
General Classbook, The, by Samuel Willard.
Gentleman of Bayou Teche, A, by Kate Chopin.
Georgia Scenes, by A. B. Longstreet.
Gift of Tongues, The, by Margaret Schlauch.
Glass Window, The, by Lucy Furman.
Golden Cocoon, by Ruth Cross.
Golden Tales of the Southwest, ed. by May L. Becker.
Gombo: The Creole Dialect of Louisiana, by E. L. Tinker.
Good American Speech, by Margaret P. McLean.
Good Speech, by Walter Ripman.
Grandissimes, The, by G. W. Cable.
Grapes of Wrath, The, by John Steinbeck.
Great Big Doorstep, The, by E. P. O'Donnell.
Great Smokeys and the Blue Ridge, The, ed. by Roderick Peattie.
Great Smokey Mountains, The, by L. Thornborough.
Green Thursday, by Julia Peterkin.
Gullah, by Mason Krum.
Gullah Dialect, The, by Reed Smith.
Gumbo Ya-Ya, by Saxon, Dreyer, and Tallant.
Guys and Dolls, by Damon Runyon.
Happy Mountain, The, by M. Chapman.
Hearts Haven, by Sara W. Bassett.
Highland Annals, by O. T. Dargan.
History of Language, The, by Henry Sweet.
History of Rome Hanks, by J. S. Pennell.
Hold Autumn In Your Hand, by G. S. Perry.
Hollow Folk, by M. Sherman and T. R. Henry.

Horse That Whistled Dixie, The, by Jerome Weidman.
How To Write Short Stories, by Ring Lardner.
Human Geography of the South, by Rupert Vance.
In My Father's House, by James Street.
In Shakespeare's America, by W. A. Bradley.
In The Tennessee Mountains, by C. E. Craddock.
In Those Days, by Harvey Fergusson.
John March, Southerner, by George W. Cable.
Languages For War and Peace, by Mario A. Pei.
Laughing Boy, by Oliver La Farge.
Letters From the Allegheny Mountains, by Charles Lanman.
Letters to His Mother, by Thomas Wolfe.
Linguistic Atlas of New England, ed. by Hans Kurath.
Listen for a Lonesome Drum, by Carl Carmer.
Little Orphant Annie, by James Whitcomb Riley.
Lone Star Preacher, by John W. Thomasen.
Look Homeward Angel, by Thomas Wolfe.
Loom of Language, by Frederick Bodmer, ed. by Lancelot Hogben.
Lost Lover, A, by Sarah Orne Jewett.
Louisiana Creole Dialect, ed. by James F. Boussard.
Louisiana, French, by William A. Read.
Louisiana Studies, by Alcee Fortier.
Lure of the Great Smokies, The, by R. L. Mason.
Knowledge of English, by G. P. Krapp.
Madame Delphine, by G. W. Cable.
Mamba's Daughters, by Duboise Heyward.
Manual of Foreign Dialects, by Lewis and M. S. Herman.
Mark Twain Lexicon, A, by P. L. Ramsey and F. G. Emberson.
Men of the Mountains, by Jesse Stuart.
Men Working, by John Faulkner.
Minister's Housekeeper, The, by Harriet Beecher Stowe.
Miss Debby's Neighbors, by Sarah Orne Jewett.
Mis' Wadleigh's Guest, by Alice Brown.
Modern English Grammar, A, by Otto Jesperson.
Mountain Europa, A, by John Fox, Jr.
Mountain Homespun, by Frances Goodrich.
Mountain People of Kentucky, by W. G. Haney.
Mrs. George's Joint, by E. L. Wheaton.
My Dear Bella, by Arthur Kober.
Native Son, by Richard Wright.
Neg Creol, by Kate Chopin.
New Adventures of Huckleberry Finn, The, by Lewis Helmar Herman.
New International Dictionary, Webster, 1926.
New Introduction to the English Grammer, by Jonathan Ware.
New Orleans and Louisiana Negroes, by R. E. Kennedy.
New York Panorama, by Federal Writers Project.
Nigger, by Clement Wood.
Nigger Heaven, by Carl van Vechten.

Nigger to Nigger, by E. C. L. Adams.
North America, by J. Russel Smith.
Oh! Promised Land, by James Street.
Oklahoma Town, by George Milburn.
Old and New, by C. H. Grandgent.
Old Creole Days, by G. W. Cable.
Old Types Pass, The, by Marcellus S. Whaley.
Old Virginia Gentleman, The, by G. W. Bagby.
Our Southern Highlanders, by Horace Kephart.
Ozark Country, by O. E. Rayburn.
Pale Horse, Pale Rider, by Katherine Anne Porter.
Pennsylvania Germans, The, ed. by Ralph Wood.
Pennsylvania German Folk Lore Society, vol. 1-5, 1936-1940.
Pennsylvania German Manual, by T. H. Harter.
Point Noire, by C. B. Huggins.
Porgy, by Dubose Heyward.
Practice Phonetics for Students of the African Language, by D. Westermann
     and Ida C. Ward.
Pronunciation of the English Language, by James Adams.
Pronunciation of Standard English in America, The, by G. P. Krapp.
Pronouncing Dictionary of American English, A, by J. S. Kenyon and
     T. A. Knott.
Pronouncing Spelling Book, by J. A. Cummins.
Prophet of the Great Smoky Mountains, by M. N. Murfree.
Psychology of English, by M. M. Bryant and J. R. Aiken.
Quincey Bolliver, by Mary King.
Relation of the Alabama-Georgia Dialect to English, The, by B. Cleanth.
Rural Dialect of Grant City, Ind., by W. L. McAttee.
Saphira and the Slave Girl, by Willa Cather.
Scarlet Sister Mary, by Julia Peterkin.
Sea of Grass, The, by Conrad Richter.
Shepherd of the Hills, The, by Harold Bell Wright.
Short Turns, by Barry Benefield.
Sis Becky's Pickaninny, by C. W. Chestnutt.
Somebody in Boots, by Nelson Algren.
Some Peculiarities of Speech in Mississippi, by H. A. Shands.
Sounds of Spoken English, by Walter Ripman.
South Moon Under, by Marjorie K. Rawlings.
Southerner Discovers the South, A, by Jonathan Daniels.
"Southern Speech" in *Culture in the South,* by Cabell Greet.
Speech Training and Public Speaking, ed. by A. M. Drummond.
Spell of the Yukon, The, by Robert W. Service.
Star of the Wilderness, by K. W. Baker.
Starry Adventure, by Mary Austin.
Stars Fell on Alabama, by Carl Carmer.
Stories of the South, ed. by Addison Hibbard.
Strange True Stories of Louisiana, by G. W. Cable.
Strange Fruit, by Lillian Smith.

Study of Dialects As They Are Used In American Plays, A, by Mary Alice Edwards, Thesis, University of Southern California.
Study of Negro Influences, by J. Trevor.
Sundown, by John J. Mathews.
Swing Your Mountain Gal, by Rebecca Cushman.
Take It Easy, by Damon Runyon.
Take To The Hills, by Marguerite Lyon.
Talk American, by Lewis and Marguerite S. Herman.
Talk United States, by Robert Whitcomb.
Tall Grow the Pines, by Sigman Byrd.
Taproots, by James Street.
Tar Heels: A portrait of North Carolina, by Jonathan Daniels.
These Are Our Lives, by Federal Writers Project.
These Are The Virgin Islands, by Hamilton Cochran.
Thunder Over The Bronx, by Arthur Kober.
Tilly on "R", by William Tilly.
Toucoutou, by E. L. Tinker.
Trees of Heaven, by Jesse Stuart.
Triumph of Shed, The, by V. F. Boyle.
Uncle Gabe Tucker, by J. A. Macon.
Uncle Josh, by Rose T. Cooke.
Vulgarisms and Other Errors of Speech, by P. M. Bache.
Walls Rise Up, by G. S. Perry.
Way Our People Lived, The, by W. E. Woodward.
Weep No More My Lady, by James Street.
Welcum Hinges, by Bernard Robb.
When The Whipperwill, by Marjorie K. Rawlings.
Wind, The, by Dorothy Scarborough.
Wind Blew West, The, by Edwin Lanham.
Winds of Fear, The, by Hodding Carter.
Word Book of Virginia Folk Speech, by B. W. Green.
Yankee In England, The, by David Humphreys.
Yearling, The, by Marjorie K. Rawlings.
Young Lonigan, by James T. Farrell.

MAGAZINE ARTICLES

"American Dialect," R. L. Dawson, *The Writer,* Feb., 1890.
"American Speech as Practiced in the Southern Highlands," *The Century,* March, 1929.
"Backwoods Scholar," *Illinois Scholar,* Vol. 26.
"Beefsteak When I'm Hungry," *Virginia Quarterly Review,* Vol. 6.
"Can Dialects Survive," *Contemporary Review,* Sept., 1926.
"Causes of Dialects," Mary A. Davis, *Out West,* 1905.
"Dialects," R. H. Bretherton, *The Gentleman's Magazine,* Dec., 1900.
"Dialect in Literature," *The Nation,* Dec., 1913.
"Dialect Lingo in Literature," *Lippincott's Magazine,* Feb., 1895.

"Dialect Studies in West Virginia," PHLA, 1891.

"Elizabethan America," *Atlantic Monthly*, Vol. 144.

"English Language in American English," *The Gentleman's Magazine*, Aug., 1881.

"English of the Mountaineer," *Atlantic Monthly*, Vol. 105.

"English of the Negro," *American Mercury*, June, 1924.

"Errors of Midwestern English," *Correct English*, 1939.

"Folk Speech in America," E. Eggleston, *The Century*, Vol. XLVIII.

"Glossary of Common Speech in Montana," *Frontier and Midland*, 1938.

"Gullah: A Negro Patois," *South Atlantic Quarterly*, Oct., 1908 and Jan., 1909.

"In Shakespeare's America," *Harper's*, Vol. 131.

"Iowa Speech," *Philology Quarterly*, 1922.

"Irish English in America," G. P. Krapp, *The Catholic Word*, Feb., 1926.

"Language of the Southern Highlander," *P. L. M. A.* (Publication of Modern Language Association), 1931.

"Levelling Dialects," J. R. Aiken, *The Bookman*, Jan. 1930.

"Mountaineers of Middle Tennessee, "*American Folk Lore*, Vol. 4.

"Negro American Dialects, A. W. Whitney, *The Independent*, 1929.

"Negro Dialect," W. F. Allen, *The Nation*, 1881.

"Negro Folk Lore and Dialect," *Arena*, Vol. XVII.

"New England Dialect, The," *Billboard*, March, 1928.

"New England Short 'o', The," *Modern Language Notes*, Vol. 22.

"OI in New England," *Modern Language Notes*, Vol. 15.

"Permanent Quality of a Dialect," R. Matthews, *Yale Review*, Jan., 1921.

"Pitch Patterns in English, "*Journal of Philology*, July, 1926.

"Pronunciation of English in America," *Atlantic Monthly*, March, 1915.

"Psychology of Dialect Writing, The," George Krapp, *The Bookman*, Dec., 1926.

"Psychological Study of Individual Differences in Speaking Ability, A," *Archives of Speech*, Jan., 1929.

"Question of Dialect, The," *The Literary World*, June, 1889.

"Report on Language Geography of Pennsylvania," *Yearbook* of American Philological Society, 1940.

"Rights of Dialects, The," *The Nation*, May, 1903.

"Southern Dialect," Trans. of American Philological Association, 1883.

"Studies in Nasality," *Archives of Speech*, Jan., 1934.

"Use and Abuse of Dialects, The," *Dial*, 1895.

"Value of Dialect, The," *North American*, July, 1894.

"Vays, Vayz, Or Vahz," *North American Review*, Dec., 1929.

"Vowels of Chicago English," *Language*, June, 1935.

"Vowel System of the Southern U. S.," *Englische Studien*, 1909.

BASIC EXERCISES FOR
SPEECH CLARITY

Clarity of speech sounds is a responsibility of the actor. All sounds should be, and can be, spoken with ease and distinctness no matter what dialect is used, nor what the educational background of the character may be. To aid the actor in tuning up his instruments of speech, the following basic exercises are included. They should be practiced consistently, and preferably with enjoyment to avoid tenseness.

BREATH CONTROL

1. Inhale deeply. Then exhale, as slowly as you can, through your nose. Inhale deeply. Exhale, again as slowly as you can, through pursed lips. Inhale deeply. Exhale, as slowly as you can, while you read, or count aloud.

NECK AND THROAT RELAXATION

2. Yawn fully. Allow your head to loll forward as the yawn ends. With your head now in a downward position allow it to roll to the right and continue around in a circle, permitting gravity to pull it backward; then, let it continue up past your left shoulder until it lolls forward once again. Repeat this several times, to the right and to the left.

JAW RELAXATION

3. Build up a mouthful of air, so that your lips and cheeks bulge. Blurt it out with a quick "BLAH" sound, letting your jaw relax instantly. Repeat several times.

4. Cup your chin or jaw firmly with one hand. Try to relax your jaw so that your hand can pull down, up, and sideways.

TONGUE FLEXIBILITY

5. Extend your tongue in its relaxed, flattened shape. Tense it in an attempt to form a point at the tongue tip. Relax your tongue, and repeat.

6. Let your tongue lie in its relaxed, flattened position within your mouth. Roll your tongue blade over on its right side, with the left side touching your right, upper teeth. Return it to its original

flattened position. Repeat this flip-flop to the left and to the right several times.

7. Tap the cutting edge of each of your teeth, one by one, with your tongue tip.

8. Try to touch your nose, your chin, and each ear with your tongue tip.

9. Let the front part of your tongue cling to your upper gum ridge. Suck it backward, so that it leaves the upper gum ridge, slides momentarily along your hard palate and then breaks the contact with a clear tongue click. Repeat several times with increased tempo.

10. Pronounce the sound of "t" (tEE) several times, being sure that your tongue tip breaks sharply away from your upper gum ridge without touching your teeth. Combine this consonant sound with various vowel sounds, as in "tAY," "tOO," "tAH," and so on. Repeat with the consonant sounds of "d," "l," and "n," increasing speed while maintaining clarity.

11. Trill the tip of your tongue against your upper gum ridge as you exhale.

UVULA FLEXIBILITY

12. Trill your uvula, as in gargling. Use a few drops of water if necessary. Then practice the vowel sounds, as in "rrrrrrrAYrrrrrrr," "rrrrrrrOOrrrrrrr," "rrrrrrrAWrrrrrrr," and so on.

THROAT FLEXIBILITY

13. Place the fingers of one hand lightly against your throat, over your larynx. Feel the movement which results as you crowd your tongue down toward the throat. Then return it upward to its natural position. Repeat several times.

MOUTH FLEXIBILITY

14. Exaggerate, in silent pantomime, the physical production of each sound in the symbol columns on the phonetics card.

LIP RELAXATION AND FLEXIBILITY

15. Blow a full steady breath of air through your closed lips, forcing them to vibrate like the rolling snort of a horse.

RESONANCE

16. Inhale deeply. Exhale slowly as you hum on one note. Try for a tingling sensation in your lips. Repeat, using a two-note pattern, then three notes and so on. Keep your throat, lips, tongue and jaw relaxed.

NOTES

NOTES

NOTES

NOTES

NOTES

NOTES